TIMELESS KINGDOM:

A STUDY OF SON OF MAN, SCIENCE AND SEFER YETZIRAH

Revised Edition 2024

By
Bettina Morello

Acknowledgment

Without the encouragement and help of close friends and Educators, I might never have had the courage to share some of the treasures that many of us found in our journey to the One. Many critics have voiced their opinions for centuries and I would like to use my voice to reaffirm the value of unbiased research into something that is much more important than anything else in the entire world. There were many people and public institutions that provided their assistance and I would like to thank them and acknowledge their contribution to this work. I thank my family for putting up with me over the years.

For over twenty-four years, I had a very transforming experience with wonderful people at Marygrove College in Detroit, Michigan, where I worked, researched, and completed my degree in Religious Studies. I thank the library staff there, especially Sr. Anna Marie Waickman, the Librarian who supported me and let me take the 'forbidden' books home to read at my leisure, and Ron Stinson, who ensured that the library holdings were up to date and helped to secure reference materials and books from other lending institutions.

I thank the English Department for a superb curriculum and an untiring dedication to students. It was the best time of my life. I thank my Advisor Mary Ellen McClanaghan, for her friendship and guidance over the years and encouraging smiles and great ideas. The professionalism and expertise of Dr. Frank Rashid, and Dr. Loretta Woodard certainly helped many others as well due to their literary skills and talents in the classroom. Dr. George Alcser, my Mentor, friend and Adviser, appointed me his proctor to excite others with the desire to learn in the classroom. He also spent many hours helping me to develop my unusual essays over the years; because I might not have been brave enough to pursue the research that would lead to my degree. I have all of them and others to thank for my love of literature.

I would like to thank Wayne State University Library Facilities, the Detroit Public Library, the University of Detroit Library, the Sacred Heart Seminary of Detroit, and many other rare and out-of-print booksellers such as John B King Books and Dove Booksellers that do an excellent job in securing quality ancient biblical reference books and rare texts. Thank you to John and Jeff at Dove Booksellers for all your dedication to this literature. I am especially indebted to Margaret Barker, who encourages me not to give up when things get rough and to never lose sight of what is really important – restoring as much of the ancient tradition as we can.

It is Professor Barker's publications that have inspired me to continue walking down a very narrow road that very few dare to walk upon. She has been an anchor in a stormy sea for many years, and I will always cherish our friendship and love of Wisdom. I would like to thank Michael John Murphy, Victoria Baker and her family who played such a large role in restoring my determination to share this research with others. His extraordinary research and work into the concepts of the Tree of Life and Quantum Physics gave me the courage to face the critics who always say there is nothing else – stop looking. His work inspired me to trust my own intuition and let me know that others can already see the invisible Kingdom that is there.

I would like to thank Margaret Barker for reading the manuscript in its first stages, and a host of friends and Colleagues that have also offered me their ideas and suggestions. Several chapters in the book were originally essays completed at Marygrove College. A Science and Religion class I attended in my senior year there inspired some of the ideas.

None of this would be possible without the real support and help of an amazing group of talented and creative people.

Most of all, I owe them all my thanks and gratitude for their morale and inspiration, along with their literary support over the last 6 months to help me bring the 2024 Revised Edition of Timeless Kingdom: A Study in Son of Man, Science, and Sefer Yetzirah to life. McGilligan Publishing, and in particular Logan Walsh and his extraordinary team of experts, helped to shape and form the new edition for a larger audience regardless of background. Their dedication and help during a very chaotic and hectic time in my life is the reason I am able to complete this life-long project after years of being asked to republish by many people.

Finally, but most importantly, I thank all those brave men and women of antiquity who gave their lives to ensure we would have these documents today; they are the true heroes.

I would like to dedicate this Revised Edition to Karen Lydiz Currie, a true friend, and scholar who continued to study and reveal great truths over the years with me and others as well. We will all miss her presence, but not her love and longing for the Kingdom. And to my brother, Bryant F Williams, who also loved to read and study, and my mother, Ruby L Sparks, who is the true inspiration and reason for this book.

Scriptural quotations are from the Holy Name Bible, A.B. Traina, 1965 except where otherwise noted.

Contents

Abstract

Humanity is beginning to lose its visionary imagination; this blind spot continues to grow in proportion to the evolution of human materialism. Many of us find it hard to visualize and cannot imagine the formless, immeasurable nature of the Spirit when human nature requires data that the five senses can measure. The Spirit, because it is ineffable, is known through attributes or forces that produce and execute the work of divine creation in several steps of phase transitions.

The process is the key to life on Earth in Time. Very little is left to human imagination in this fast-paced world where everything is explicitly revealed and processed in the media and the Internet. Time moves as fast as our minds can take us. Our brain is forced to continually upgrade its built-in hard drive as our heart hopes to keep the beat of our mechanical lifestyles. We live in the scripts of our daily lives, like words lost in a sentence due to our lack of literary imagination. We are bombarded with megabytes of facts and fiction that are posed as reality. Facts can become extinct, and reality is not always what it appears to be on the surface. Sometimes, what seems like important facts aren't really facts at all. Still, the human need for meaning and a feeling of connectedness is unfulfilled, and our facts don't seem to matter much in the face of adversity and death.

The public opinion of Apocalyptic and Pseudipigraphic texts is a good example of how unchallenged facts can hamper the progression of human and spiritual evolution. This literature carries a symbol that means very different things to different groups. The idea most commonly associated with the term 'apocalypse' involves doomsday cults and military religious sects. Its original connotation implies 'revelation' and a continual revelation of hidden things, to be exact.

Cultural, national, and political symbols are not always factually true, but they have a great influence on public opinion. Can symbols be factual? Yes. Symbols represent realities to the degree that they represent the experience that led to their creation. Have we lost the ability to consciously experience the meaning of spiritual symbols? Many of us do not understand how to apply or understand the mystical symbols of apocalyptic texts; we do understand ordinary symbols needed to survive in the business and scientific world. Our higher spiritual consciousness is not being nurtured if we only rely on cultural, national, and physical symbols.

The destiny of humanity is to restore the higher spiritual consciousness of Primordial Adam. The function of mystical symbols is to allow the mind to transcend its physical limitations, and many ancient mystics documented their experiences of this in the literature that has such a negative image in the public eye today. Should there still be so much antagonism towards the literature that plays such a major role in the development of Christianity?

The three topics, Son of Man, Science, and Sefer Yetzirah, seem to agree upon very little, but they have one very important function in common. All three have the ability to influence the destiny of Humanity and to help it to rise above its lowest nature. They represent three views of the human state and condition of life. Science states that Adam is a unit of chemicals and genes that evolved into Homo Sapiens that strive for perfection through adaptation and natural selection. Traditional religions state that Adam is a fallen, debased creature of flesh consigned to death for transgressing a commandment. The two extremes create a distorted perception of reality. The ancient scientific view is markedly different in the estimation of Adam and the Creator. Ancient scientists complemented spirituality with scientific observations and discoveries. Adam has an entirely different role in apocalyptic literature and is not considered a limited, substandard version of some greater model.

Today, there are so many major conflicts between science and religion that symbols cannot compete with them for public attention. Atomic energy, cloning, and genetic engineering are all very controversial issues, as are military and religious regimes entering the world of high-tech bombs and terrorism. This study does not attempt to deal with those issues directly because there are hundreds of books available on the coming 'apocalypse.' But I am not entirely convinced on how the whole story is being told.

Are world wars, diseases, pain, and suffering the themes these authors really intend to convey to their audience? Have we really only heard the clatter of confused doctrines of religious factions battling with each other over doctrines and laws? The main area of confusion between religion and science surrounds the authenticity of the Genesis narrative and the Semitic concept of time. Science attacks the Genesis narrative based on the assumed conflict between the two creation stories. The Semitic Bereshith deals with the two first chapters in the book very differently.

Non-canonical literature can enrich the canonical gospels in many ways. One very important way is in the field of Hermeneutics because apocalyptic texts are actually known for containing the 'revelations' of previous 'visions' given to the ancient prophets of Israel. The books that have been left out of the canon can dispel the modern misconception of the scriptures and give power to the individual who can read and apply its wisdom in their daily life. The interpretations enable the reader to understand how to apply the imagery of the ancients in today's terms.

Religion, science, and mysticism can work together to bring harmony to an ailing world. We are lacking in symbolic awareness and we continue to rely on empirical, impersonal scientific data for stability. Still, science falls short and the public love affair with traditional science leaves the world empty of meaning. Religion and science need the spiritual energy of mystical symbols to free them from the bondage of structured, lifeless doctrines of despair. This symbolism is found in many texts of the ancient Near East; there is virtually a library of spiritual experiences just waiting to be tapped into with the mind's eye. Emerson says that the true "Poet" will learn how to live with nature through communion with natural symbols such as trees, air, and water. Can we learn how to live in higher dimensions through divine symbols?

Einstein's theories changed the way scientists view the nature of Time and the origin of the Universe. Einstein argues that due to curved space, there is no past, present, or future moving in a linear progression. In the Semitic scientific view, past, present, and future are one. Ancient mystics after Enoch claimed that the Universe was alive and that 'science mystics' recorded their scientific theories in the Sefer Yetzirah [Book of Creation].

Witten's recent breakthrough in the world of Quantum physics resulted in the M-Theory. This theory may actually confirm what ancient mystics discovered through spiritual journeys to the dimensions of higher space. Humanity now inhabits a sphere that is actually in a lower dimension than Heaven's other creatures. M-Theory states that there are 11 dimensions and that the dimension humanity currently inhabits has been separated from the higher dimensions. Science cannot currently reach the higher dimensions or 'branes'; however, it might be within the reach of ancient scientific concepts found in the Sefer Yetzirah. Enoch describes the Son of Man as an intellectual Pleroma or Tree of potent energies that can transform mortals into angelic beings. The tree is guarded by a cherub who draws a great circle around the Garden thereby blocking the entrance into Eden. The Angel of

יהוה or the Unique Cherub has been appointed to lead the way back into the Holy Place or Garden of Eden. The Elect are guided by the Unique Cherub, a magnificent human angel, into the darkness of 'Ayin' to discover the light of 'Ayin SOF Aur,' the radiance of Salvation. But who will still be the roaring voice of accusation that warns readers to beware of the book of Enoch? Deconstructing the taboo of apocalyptic literature is still a very challenging task, and it is the purpose of this study to scratch the surface of possibilities.

Apocalyptic texts mention the fact that 'hidden books' exist that have important information for a particular generation. Perhaps the books were written for the benefit of our generation. The books still remain 'hidden' even after years of biblical scholarship. The 'spirit' of the books is deliberately suppressed for cultural, political, and doctrinal reasons. Many apocalyptic themes are positive and contain constructive, positive commands to care for humanity, nature, and the Universe. However, because the term 'apocalyptic' is automatically associated with disaster and calamity, many readers never attempt to read them, while others try to bring about the 'end days' with bombs, guns, and sheer destruction. Even though this view of the literature is the result of perception and is not a fact, the general populace believes the false perception of war and death, and they often look for these motifs in the literature and disregard the scientific value altogether.

The Aeon is the result of an explosion of light energy that then goes through a process of transformation into a denser substance until it becomes fully embedded in a material substance.

Atoms, stars, and superstrings also exhibit transformative properties that are ignited with heat, energy, or fire. The three states of energy are gaseous, liquid, and solid, and all elements and particles are subject to the law of energy conservation. A common characteristic between ancient science and modern science is the fact that two transitions occur in the exchange of energy or form: 1st order phase transition and 2nd order phase transition; one involves a violent bubbling, and the other a smooth type of evaporation. The two creation stories in Genesis can be further defined through the two phases referred to as 'true vacuum' and 'false vacuum,' which are terms used to explain the time before and after the Big Bang. Words can be used to elevate one's consciousness into different dimensions. The words 'Eternal life' may be more than just a phrase to indicate salvation. Adam Kadmon once contained the primordial light of life until the vessels were shattered. Words were once metaphors for translating the experience of life into concepts. The Divine World consists of spoken revelation that takes place in the Day of Eternity before the act is finally created in time. Discovering the origin of words can give us a glimpse of the origin of the Universe and Eternity.

Is all truth only relative to one's experience of it? Is there no higher Truth that all humanity will one day become a part of? Facts and fiction often become one, and this transforms into real and imaginary concepts that can become either true or false perceptions that distort the nature and reality of how the Supreme Being exists. Spiritual concepts should be re-examined in light of new observations and facts presented in the pseudipigraphic literature. The 'hidden books' remain 'hidden' only to those who refuse to read them.

Preface

BM is pioneering a new way of reading mysterious ancient texts. Many scholars are now engaged in similar studies but from a completely different standpoint. Objectivity and detachment are the virtues of contemporary scholarship, 'often described as 'controlling the source material.' BM has a different approach; she has steeped herself in the ancient texts and allows them to control her. The results are quite amazing.

When Ezra, the Jewish scribe, was inspired to restore to his people their scriptures, which had been lost when Jerusalem was destroyed, he dictated to his scribes far more than the books we know today as the Hebrew Bible. The story, as it was told in the first century CE and recorded in 2 Esdras 14, was that Ezra received from God 94 holy books, of which only 24 were to be made public. The remaining 70 were only for the wise because they contained the spring of understanding, the fountain of wisdom, and the river of knowledge. This is what the first Christians must have believed, too.

We can only guess what these texts were. Since many pre-Christian Jewish texts were only preserved by Christian scribes, their importance for the Church is beyond doubt. The Enoch books were almost certainly among them, and the traditions, which were later set down in the Merkavah texts, recorded the visions of the chariot throne mystics. The strange philosophy that was later to be called Kabbalah had ancient roots, as did many of the traditions that appear in early Christian writings. All describe the world of the angels - a world that has been neglected and almost all but forgotten in the post-enlightenment sophistication of modern theology and biblical scholarship.

BM reconnects us with that world. There are remarkable similarities between the discoveries of modern physicists and cosmologists and the revelations of the ancient seers. Still, the

Enoch literature, for example, does not disclose its real meaning to the methods of modern critical scholarship. Many today can read the words of these ancient books –perhaps far more than ever before - but their meaning is as elusive as ever, and it is this meaning that BM seeks to uncover.

Wisdom, said the ancient sages, was given to those whose eyes had been opened. The Gospel of Thomas attributes a similar saying to Jesus: that the Kingdom is all around us, but people do not see it. The invisible world is not invisible to all, and the timeless world is part of the fabric that is experienced in human history. Or rather, used to be experienced as human history. The world of the angels and the world of human beings are one and the same, but we have sight of this.

To appreciate the significance of the whole creation, the visible and the invisible, we need to read ancient texts with the eyes of those who wrote them.

BM is opening our eyes to this way of reading the texts. Many familiar passages in the New Testament take on a new significance, and we may be reading for the first time what the biblical prophets and seers actually wrote.

Margaret Barker 02/2005

Derbyshire, UK

Introduction

What matters is that those who incorporated the creation lore of Babylonia and other Oriental nations into the sacred books of the Hebrews mixed it with their own conceptions and deductions. What matters is that Darwin changed the whole aspect of our creation myths; that Lyell and his compeers placed the Hebrew story of Creation and of the deluge of Noah among legends; that Copernicus put an end to the standing still of the sun for Joshua; that Halley, in promulgating his law of comets, put an end to the doctrine of 'signs & wonders'; that Pineal, in showing that all insanity is a physical disease, relegated to the realm of mythology the Witch of Endor and all stories of demonical possession; that the anthropologists, by showing how man has risen everywhere from low and brutal beginnings, have destroyed the whole theological theory of 'fallen man'?

(A.D. White History of the Warfare with Christendom 208).

All these things matter if we want to find a string of logic among all the confusing ideas that camouflage the origin of the Universe and humanity with dark, chaotic pools of belief. Science has reduced Adam to little more than a unit of chemicals, genes, and atoms, while mainstream traditional religions of the West see Adam as the progenitor of sin and death. It is hard to find a medium between the two views of material life and spiritual death. We need to support a symbiotic relationship between science and religion in order to provide a platform for metaphysical, spiritual, and scientific facts without infringing on the integrity of either. Mathematics and complex scientific calculations do not alone determine how scientific discoveries are applicable in society; ancient cosmologists, mystics and prophets all claimed to have some

1

kind of scientific understanding of the basic rudiments of the universe.

Even Job, who seems to know very little in comparison with the apocalyptic seers, does know some things about the

Pleiades and Orion.

Job 9:7-9: 7. He speaks to the sun, and it does not shine; he seals off the light of the stars. 8. He alone stretches out the heavens and treads on the waves of the sea. 9. He is the Maker of the Bear and Orion, the Pleiades, and the constellations of the South.

This is one example of ancient biblical scientific knowledge of the ancient sages, which the modern worldview leads us to believe, is a bygone and unnecessary model of reality. How can we allow others to force us to disregard this knowledge now; it will always remain our only foundation for survival. Like us, previous civilizations were subject to censorship, manipulation, and control. Each one of us, no matter what age we are born into, lives in a physical reality that is constantly changing and growing, challenging us both intellectually and biologically. The difference between our age and their age, time alone, cannot be measured, but through spiritual consciousness and experience, we can re-experience the creation of the 'Beginning' (Wisdom). The Wisdom that has been left behind or subsumed by various later religious traditions and communities is why there has always been Revelation and Visionary experiences in every culture and age since time began.

The prophets' most common trademark is experiencing ecstatic trances where they suffered horrifying events in visions, which concerned our past and our future. This was, however, only one by-product of this type of spiritual activity; another product was the ability to transcend time and space. A particular genre of literature purposely censored and maligned for many centuries has left a spiritual deficit that leaves our current generation wanting in common sense and simple, humane mercy and kindness. What good is it if scientists discover everything about the material creation, and lose their own ability to acknowledge those invisible principles all the ancients built their society on? Knowledge and consciousness are two sides of a mirror that eventually become one within the self-actualized person. This holistic approach to spirituality and science seems submerged beneath the rubble of biased controversy that wears the veil of skepticism and debate. Ancient scientists and mystics did not oppose each other; the Universe talked to them daily through the constellations, planets, and stars, and they willingly exchanged ideas for the advancement of understanding and discovery. A house divided cannot stand, for one will always be at war with the other. Is this not the state of affairs globally today? Is there anything that we can do to find strength to endure what is coming?

I will try to demonstrate how many aspects of apocalyptic literature can help to elucidate our understanding of how to interpret scientific facts in order to imagine the profound depths of the Universe. There is a considerable amount of Hebrew literature: Prophecies, Wisdom, Psalms, Apocalyptic, Dead Sea Scrolls, and Kabbalah that make up the rich spiritual heritage destined to help humanity become wise and shine like the stars. Nevertheless, science and religion remains a house divided when it comes to the idea of 'designed' multiverses. In light of the advancement of theories on evolution and genetic research, there is little room left for a spiritual ethos. This has left many new scars on an already damaged society and new unanswered questions among spiritualists and scientists.

We all realize without a doubt that modern science will and does lead the way to discovering more about our origin, but it also wants to prove history. Something binds us to our own intellect, thereby cutting us off from our faculty of imagination. The human personality can only accept what it can physically see; we must perceive the Timeless Kingdom with 'spiritual eyes' that can see invisible realities. However, the way to do this begins when we consider the many changes and alterations that have presented us with half the story before deciding to do away with the problem we now call 'religion.' Very little sacredness remains to soften our imagination in this fast-paced world, where we live in a society that dictates to us that we should think and feel about the Creator through the religious and scientific media the majority adopts.

Now, we must rely on our own insights and search even harder to find credible information. Time moves as fast as our minds can take us. Society forces our brain to upgrade its built-in hard- drive as our heart hopes to keep the beat of our mechanical lifestyles. We live in the scripts of our daily lives as words are lost in a sentence due to our lack of literary imagination. New ideas and concepts bombard us with megabytes of facts and fiction that pose as reality. We must consider that facts can become extinct, and reality is not always what it appears to be on the surface. Sometimes, what seems like important facts are not really facts at all. Still, the human need for meaning and a feeling of connectedness is unfulfilled, and our facts do not seem to matter much in the face of adversity and death. Unchallenged facts can hamper the progress of human and spiritual evolution. For example, one word carries a symbol that means very different things to different groups. The idea most commonly associated with the term 'apocalypse' involves doomsday cults and military religious sects due to the violent reactions of cults and sects on the fringe of religious rebellion. More importantly, is that the original meaning of this term implies 'revelation', actually a continual revealing of a hidden spiritual consciousness, which conveys spiritual realities built into the text.

Our destiny is to remember our lost higher spiritual consciousness, the one we possessed before we fell from Eden or our original spiritual state into our material consciousness.

Gnosis and divine symbols allow our mind to transcend its physical limitation; many ancient mystics document their experiences in this literature, which has such a negative image in the public eye today. Should there still be so much antagonism towards apocalyptic literature? Ancient and modern research both demonstrate that it played a major role in the development of Christianity. I will try to show that what the earliest community may have taught and practiced has little in common with Christianity today. We owe it to the people who gave their lives to learn what they died for and what is at stake. We now stand at the crossroads and will soon find out firsthand what they went through at the end of their age. We will need courage and faith to withstand some of the things this literature reveals through the missing apocalyptic, Pseudepigrapha, mystical, and Kabbalistic texts, which many people have overlooked.

While the concepts of the Son of Man, Science, and the Sefer Yetzirah might appear to have little in common, they share one crucial element. All three have the ability to influence our destiny and can help us rise above our lowest natures that keep us bound within time and darkness. Each represents three views of our human condition and state of mind. Science and

Darwinism, specifically, state that Adam is a unit of chemicals and genes that evolves into Homo sapiens that strive for perfection through adaptation and natural selection. Traditional Abrahamic religions teach that Adam is a fallen, debased creature of flesh consigned to death for transgressing a commandment. Both extremes create a distorted perception of reality. The role of Adam has an entirely different role in apocalyptic literature, not a limited role in a substandard version of some greater model, but the very image and form of divine life.

This study does not attempt to deal with conspiracy theories or 'end of the world' paranoia directly because there is a multitude of books available that warn of the coming 'apocalypse,' albeit there are as many versions as there are authors. The controversial wars between science and religion will continue to grow as materialism seeks to imprison spiritual consciousness.

Still, I am not entirely convinced that we have heard the whole story. Are world wars, diseases, pain, and suffering the only things these apocalyptic mystics really intend to convey to their audience? Have we really heard only the clatter of confused doctrines of religious factions and scientific anarchies battling with each other over doctrines and human laws? Apocalyptic texts contain the 'revelations' of previous 'visions' given to the ancient prophets of Israel and the book of Genesis is actually a vision of Moses. The books deemed 'unworthy' are missing from our Bibles; this is unfortunate because they can dispel the modern misconception of the Scriptures and give authentic spiritual power back to us. The various levels of interpretation left in these mysterious documents enable a reader to understand how to apply the imagery of the ancients in our modern world. If we try to incorporate some of the original concepts of early experiences of 1st-century communities before the rise of Constantine's version of

Christianity, I believe religion, science, and mysticism can work together.

However, each person must decide if these three fields could work together; if given half a chance, we can and will continue to evolve and experience the higher dimensions, which pave the Way for survival through a true gathering of like minds, with one goal and purpose. Lost in our own world of ideas we lack the spiritual awareness and intuition needed to protect ourselves from the onslaught of darkness and negative energy as we continue to rely on empirical, impersonal scientific data for stability. Science falls short and the public love affair with traditional science leaves the world empty of meaning. Religion and science need the spiritual energy of mystical symbols to free them from the bondage of structured, lifeless doctrines of despair. A potent spiritual reality is just waiting to rise in our consciousness with penetration of the mind's eye. Emerson says the true "Poet" will learn how to live with nature through communion with natural symbols such as the trees, air, and water. Is there another more important reason why humanity should learn how to live in higher dimensions through divine symbols?

We may be alone, cut off from the higher dimensions because of our lack of Gnosis. Deconstructing the taboo of apocalyptic literature is still a very challenging task that each of us must face before we can scratch the surface of spiritual realities. Apocalyptic texts all refer to 'hidden books' that contain important information for a future generation. We always think this means some unknown faraway time, but it refers to our own age. These ancient misunderstood texts written for the benefit of our generation remain 'hidden' even after years of biblical scholarship. Ancient laws suppress the 'spirit' of the books deliberately for cultural, political, and doctrinal reasons. Even though this view of the literature is the result of perception and is not a fact, many believe in the false perception of war and death. They often look for these motifs in the literature and disregard the scientific value altogether.

OVERVIEW OF THE KINGDOM

The Timeless Kingdom

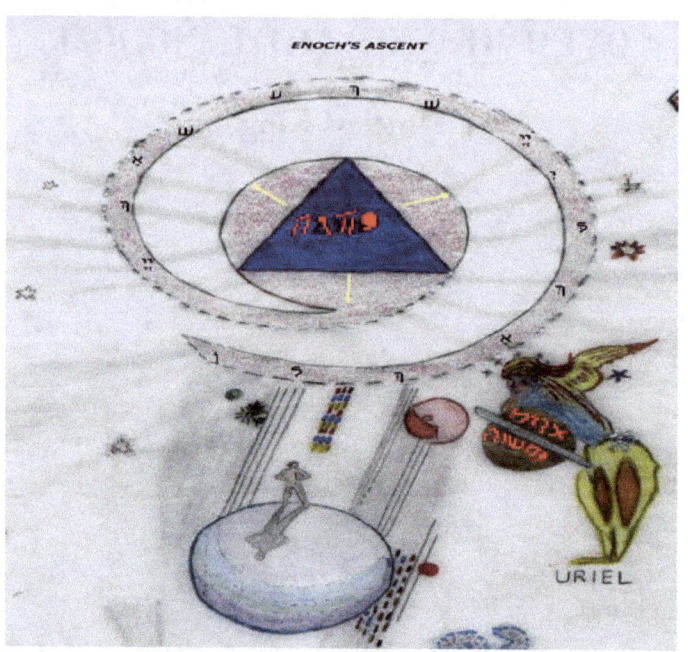

The winds in the vision caused Enoch to fly upward, and as he soared into the first Heaven, angels lifted him up onto the Wings of the Winds of Shekinah; then he traveled to the place of the West and began to lose all sense of time. He then begins to feel as though his whole body and being was soaring through the heavens and he can see the Throne and Merkabah with a mysterious figure sitting next to the Most-High. As he enters the darkness of Ayin, he describes what he witnessed. Enoch said, "There was a wall built of crystals surrounding both figures, but I could hardly see into it because of the wind and darkness. I felt that I would fly away into nothingness unless something pulled me back in time. Then, little flashes of white and gold lights danced in the air all around me. I tried to touch them, but my hand went right through them as if they were not there at all. The crystal wall absorbed them, and then I suddenly became surrounded by tongues of fire that whispered words I could see but not understand. I then saw a second house greater than the first; for it resembled a triple flame of fire that shined so bright I could not bear to look. My eyes felt

10

like they were burning, and tears streamed down my face, and then I knew intuitively that this was the 'Place' (Makom) of the Most-High."

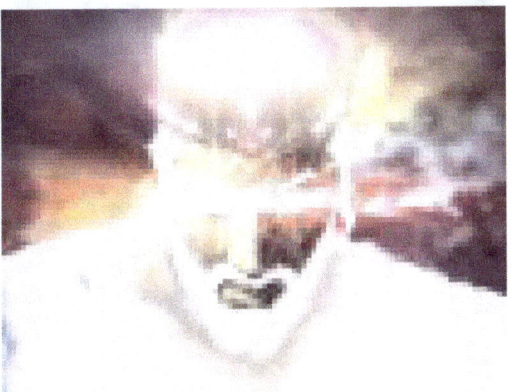

Enoch sees what will happen.

Enoch saw the Seraphim take documents of accusation that Sataniel wrote against the righteous. As they were destroying them by fire, he saw all the secrets of the Heavens and Earth like a collage of pictures or visions fall through the spheres, settling into the thoughts of humanity.

The angels had written their own books of death for humanity, and only certain humans would be able to awaken from the slumber of forgetfulness and Time in order to reach out and eat from the Book of Life and live.

Letters of Accusation

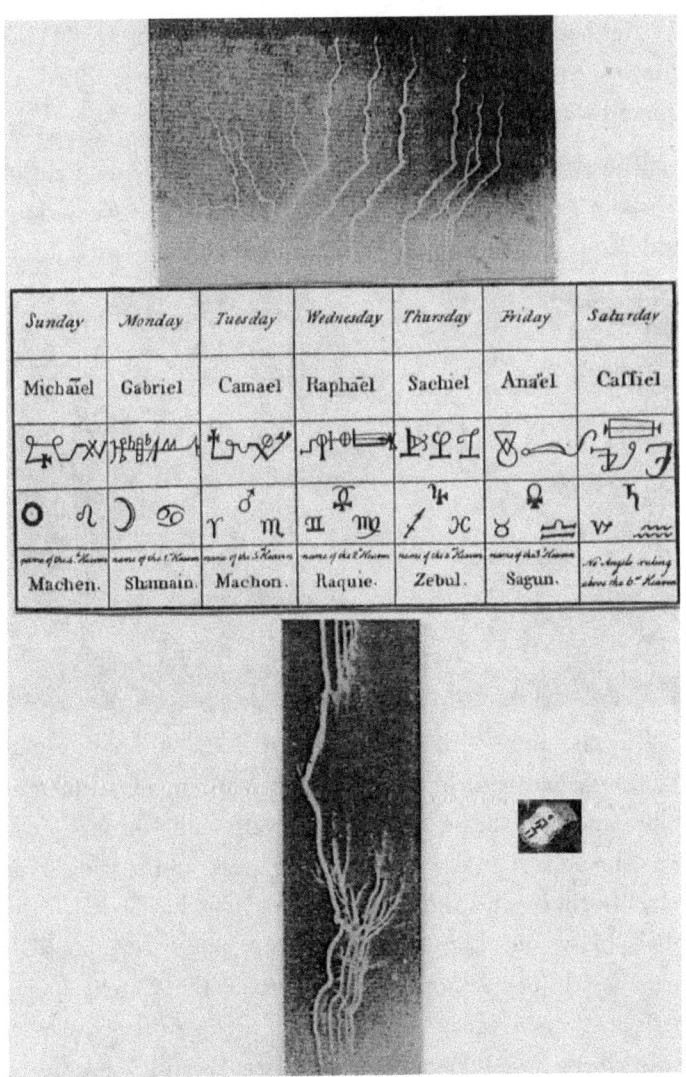

Sunday	Monday	Tuesday	Wednesday	Thursday	Friday	Saturday
Michāel	Gabriel	Camael	Raphāel	Sachiel	Anaël	Caffiel
name of this Heaven	name of the t Heaven	name of the S Heaven	name of the 8 Heaven	name of this Heaven	name of that Heaven	No Angels ruling above the 6.ᵗ Heaven
Machen.	Shamain.	Machon.	Raquie.	Zebul.	Sagun.	

Enoch was frightened none would survive and then remembers he saw how the actions of all will be weighed in a balance, many will be found empty of knowledge and true Wisdom. His heart is saddened and horrified at the display of terrors that will grip the Earth in its final hour as materialism seeks to swallow the light.

He then hears a Voice that shakes the Heavens say, "Don't grieve over these things, Enoch, for I have determined all things by a just and equal measure.

Those who discover my real identity will have the light of Wisdom to guide them. Those who listen to the accusations and lies of the fallen ones will suffer all the things you saw."

The cherubim of the Shekinah were like a path of stars and lightning, between them were fiery cherubim of a different appearance. I heard a Voice reverberate through the atmosphere like an ocean of rolling waters, and it said, "Fear not, Enoch, come nearer to my Throne; why have you left the High Holy and Eternal Heaven, the highest of the high heavens?" Enoch responds to the Voice, "The Watchers have petitioned me to speak on their behalf because they have been exiled from your Presence, but I refused because I am only a man made of dust and the drop of life." A voice of wind blows upon Enoch as the Watchers see the Angel of Yahweh burn the message into Enoch's soul without his awareness. As he feels the hot sensation that starts at the top of his head and then moves down to the bottom of his feet, he immediately feels warm all over and begins to perspire as small vibrations shake him back and forth. Just as he is about to faint, he hears his mouth uttering words to the Watchers, who were standing by, piercing his soul with their eyes. He hears his voice say, "All the mysteries haven't been revealed to you, only worthless earthly (Razim) secrets that you and your clan stole from the heavenly tablets." You only have parts of the Secret, and I am the one sent here to take them back. The Secrets you stole!"

Enoch is reassured when he sees the 7 Spirits surrounding the Throne in the Heaven of Heavens.

These seven Archangel's eyes search the Earth and Heaven in order to report their findings to the Heavenly Tribunal. Mikhael and Gabriel stand to the right and left of the Throne of Glory, the Great Princes or Captains of Hosts (Zebaoth) that send and receive communications from humans to the higher Heavens.

Enoch perceived the structure as a great Tree whose branches extend from the heavens to the earth. He saw how mortal humans could contact their angelic guardians by reciting the Song (prophecies) written in the books of humans.

Those who abused this right have their branch severed from the tree and their root blocked so that no further communication could occur with the spiritual being above. He saw how false messages began to reach the earth as the fallen angels began to teach humankind to write their own songs in their image. Enoch is bewildered at the power of words to distort truth and reality and he wonders how the children of Adam will ever recover. By reading the curtain of revelation, he gradually understands how the Elect will rise in the invisible Kingdom when the Elect Son of Man sits on the Throne of Sapphire, and lightning shines from the east to the west. The Earth and Heavens restore the canopy of Araboth/Heaven, and it will shine in blue as the Chamber of Treasures is open to Adam once again.

Metatron's (Resurrected Son of Man) mouth shall pour forth all the Secrets of Wisdom, and these words begin to wrest the earthly consciousness away from darkness, redeeming those destined to join the angelic hosts of Heaven. Through this secret wisdom unknown to the fallen angels, the Son of Man will overcome the angels of destruction and show humans how to escape the six days of time. The voices of the seven days reverberate in heaven like concentric circles of vibratory motion as angelic voices rise in unison and descend in harmony, expanding and contracting the development of the Universe. In a former visit, Metatron told Enoch that the hoofs of the 'living ones' were surrounded by seven clouds of burning coals and that outside these clouds of burning coals were seven walls of flame. Seven walls of hailstones surround the flames as stones of hail surround the 'Wings of the Tempest.' Enoch did not realize this was an angelic secret only time reveals when humanity learns its true origin.

Enoch then begins to give an account of what he could reveal of the things learned during his journey. He explains how the secrets of lightning, thunder, and the winds are whispered to him, and he understands the contents of the chambers that contain the celestial and elemental forces. He realizes that the Sun, Moon, and Stars all have a conscious existence. He sees the Son of Man battle the fallen angels by the Word of his mouth, and then he hears the Voice of many waves of waters boldly shout, "He will rise up kings and mighty ones from earthly and heavenly Thrones, and he shall erase the face of the strong, wicked ones from the Presence of Holiness!"

He describes a future terrible destruction of the evil one and how all the holy ones will refrain from their usual works as they unite in one Voice to give thanks and to bless the Name of Holiness that will perform this great task. He begins to realize that the pre-existent Son of Man was destined to be a staff to the righteous as they travel through the wilderness of spiritual Sinai in order to undergo the tests and trials of the fallen angels. "Who is this Son of Man? He thinks to himself, "What have I to do with him?"

He heard one of the angels tell him, "Then the water of spiritual consciousness that is above joins, with the water of earthly consciousness below when the male (spiritual) and female (material) waters of Supernal Wisdom awaken from their sleep of forgetfulness. The sound of their movement together will send a wave of vibrations that continually emanate to transform both heaven and earth in One Day. Humans and Angels will become whole.

The Day of Wisdom's Light (Aur/Avir) will brighten the whole Universe and will never end. The mighty quaking of the heavens will make all negative angelic hosts quake and shiver with fear as they begin to understand that time, something the fallen angels were once impervious to, would finally put an end to their existence. Enoch takes time into the fallen angelic realms in order to destroy the seven 'archons' that keep humans bound in a lower consciousness. He has the Keys that open the door to the portal of time, so the realm of angelic hosts becomes subject to the cyclic evolution of time. Before this, seconds or hours did not capture angels. Enoch's journey into the realm of Eternity coupled with his earthly mortal consciousness, actually did introduce time into the hierarchy of angelic existence.

The angels of elemental forces could not keep the secrets of the depths of the earth and the height of the heavens away from Enoch's mind any longer. As he continues, a gradual realization that he, too, performs a work like the Son of Man, destined to be the Judge of a Heavenly household, becomes more apparent to him. In the past, no evil could get power over men until they had learned the Secrets and sorceries of the fallen ones. Since the letters of accusation have fallen into the lowest depths of human hearts, evil has grown rampant and more ferocious. Only the Wisdom light can wrest one's soul from these black holes of annihilation. Who among Adam's children will go before us to take back that original Light?

Enoch sees the fallen angels known as the Grigori and, he sees how they influence human life through the age. This is how humans fall into idolatry and the worship of their own creations for this was the way of fallen angels that worship their own Wisdom.

DARK SPEECHES

They taught man to worship himself instead of the Creator. Only the letters of the Divine name (יהוה) that created Heaven and Earth and the seas and rivers could seal these angelic rebels into a perpetual suspension, so their influences no longer influence people on Earth. Angels escort Enoch back to the seventh heaven while his family and friends watch as the Shekinah carries him above. They saw the four streams of living fire that continually flowed from the four sides of the house, and to this day, they are continually running throughout the Universe, but mere earthly eyes cannot see them. Enoch could see them only after his induction into the angelic army of the Son of Man.

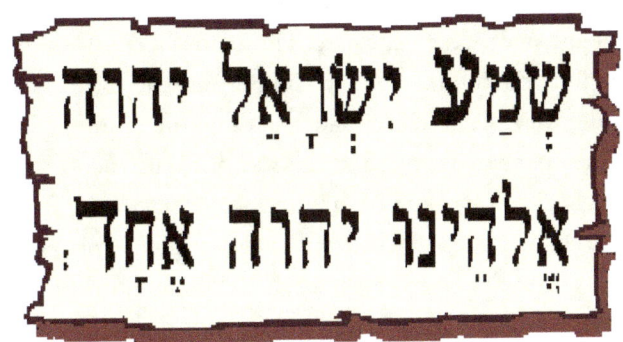

שְׁמַע יִשְׂרָאֵל יְהוָה
אֱלֹהֵינוּ יְהוָה אֶחָד

21

Shema Israel YHVH Elohenu Echad

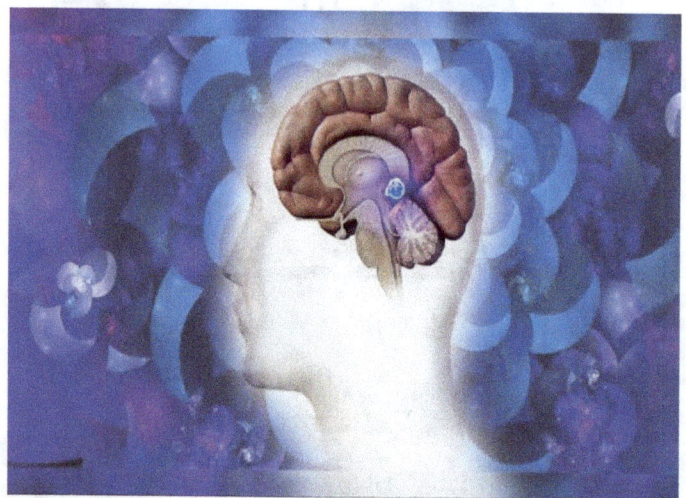

These four streams were the rivers of light and wisdom that issued from the sides of the Garden of Eden on high.

The four streams now live inside the four angelic hosts that guard the Merkavah and surround the Throne. None among humans can see these things, unless they too enter the ancient Wisdom. Enoch's translation into the Heaven of Heavens projects him into the Holy Place of the seventh Heaven, where he looks down upon all human thoughts and dreams to help prepare them for the final hour. Some people will rise to glory, and some people to dishonor. The seventh Hall or Palace contains the Throne of Glory enclosed in a wall of crystals like the Garden of Eden enclosed Ha-Adam like a fence. The Seraphim, Cherubim, and Ophannim were the Court Round About. They sleep not while guarding the Throne. These Merkabah angels appeared as figures with four Faces. One of an Eagle, Lion, Ox, and Man. Together, these formed E-L-O-Him, the Gan Eden in which Adam was originally placed. The Eagle, Lion, Ox, and Man figures that surround the Throne represent the four worlds of Elohim. Enoch now knows that the Son of Man is the restored Garden, Temple, and Merkavah.

However, the Pargod or Curtain (Veil of Revelation) prevents humanity from returning to the invisible reality of the Son of Man. The heavenly tablets contain all the deeds of humanity engraved on a Curtain like a veil between eternity and time that is still open to human inspection. This Curtain or Veil reveals the meaning of the historical events that will occur in our own future. Seventy Princes of Angels govern each Nation, for each has representative archetypes in heaven that set the stage for the earthly kings and rulers that will re-enact the war in the heavens on the earth.

As the guardian angels of the Throne and the warrior angels fight alongside the King of the Universe in the Great Day of Judgment on the fallen angels, all life on Earth will experience the intense struggle of night and darkness fighting to take the place of day and light in the entire Universe. This angelic war takes place on earth as the nations and people rise against each other for the last battle.

Humanity has become the most dangerous tool of the fallen angels out of all the products found on the earth. Man has the potential to become whatever he wills to become because the earth has been flooded with the presence of Shekinah knowledge and its manifold supernatural powers. In the Wings of Shekinah, Mother Wisdom escaped from the bondage of the fallen angels when the Messiah fought and bound Satan at Calvary. Since then, the pneumatics and psychics have bombarded us with advanced knowledge and power of technology and atomic energy; whether humans are conscious of this feminine presence of wisdom or not has no bearing on its impact. All will be flooded with the power of celestial mechanics and physics.

Enoch foresees a time when the oppression of the seventy ruler angels will gradually cause great storms and winds to come and surround the earth, as great portents appear in the sky during a great lightning storm, as the fallen angels and technology will wage the biggest deception of all; a war of ideas.

Human imagination and technological advances will soar beyond the limits of rational reality. Through will and force, principalities and powers will create artificial life forms that thrive on the negative existence of light - Nuclear energy. Fallen angels will continue to teach humanity how to capture celestial atomic fire from the sky and harness its powers; humanity becomes abandoned to a hell of its own making. Bereft of true Wisdom and Understanding, their consciousness is pierced with confusion, and anarchy reigns as the storms grow stronger.

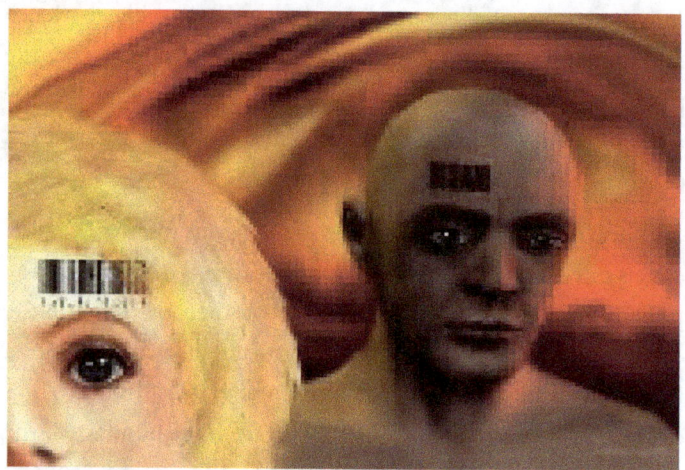

Enoch then saw three bright lights that appeared to be strings and how each was a part of the other, yet each maintained its own shape and form. These celestial lights contain the secrets of how the final translation of Enoch transformed him into a magnificent celestial being that sees the future things and the celestial events of the heavens for the children of the earth. Enoch realizes that the ability to think the 'Thought' of Yahweh results in prophecy, for all things are then clearly seen through the things that are created in the past, present, and future of the physical world. The vision he saw, concerned the realization of an important identity of the Son of Man, and as he heard the Words of holy angels speaking to him, the words began to shape and form his consciousness. Through a renewed spiritual consciousness, the Kingdom restored within humanity initiates the invisible ministry of Messiah in the Heavenly Kingdom of his Father.

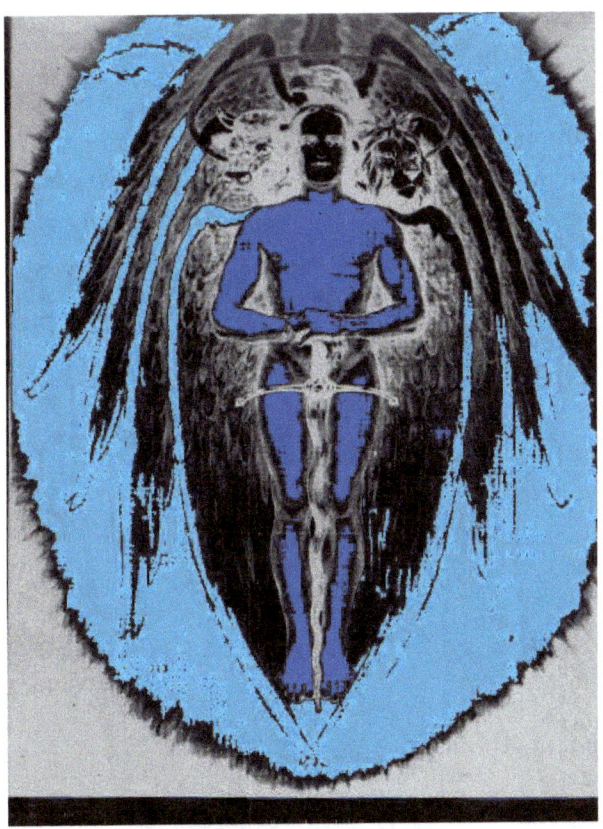

Enoch requested that a special sword be prepared. This two-edged sword allows the elect to transcend their lower consciousness so they may escape the power of many oppressive angel shepherds that use whispering words to seduce them. As the Elect learn how to think the 'good thoughts,' they discover the power that knowledge has in the heavenly realms, and something begins to happen. The accusing dark angels relinquish their place around the Throne as their lies are exposed and become dust in the air of Adam's memory. As the fire of Ruach grew more and more intense, the spiritual atomic energy of the songs vibrated throughout the Universe, sending magnetic sparks and streams of solar flares unto the earth. The wings of Shekinah sound like a symphony of crickets and great waves of the ocean as they travel through the air in oscillations, preparing the vortices and pillars of fire. When the ministering angels utter the threefold Holy, all the pillars of heavens and their sockets tremble and shake as the gates of the halls of Araboth and Raqia are shaken out of their place and foundations of Shechaqim and the Universe (Tebel) are moved, and the orders of Ma'on and Makon's chambers quivered.

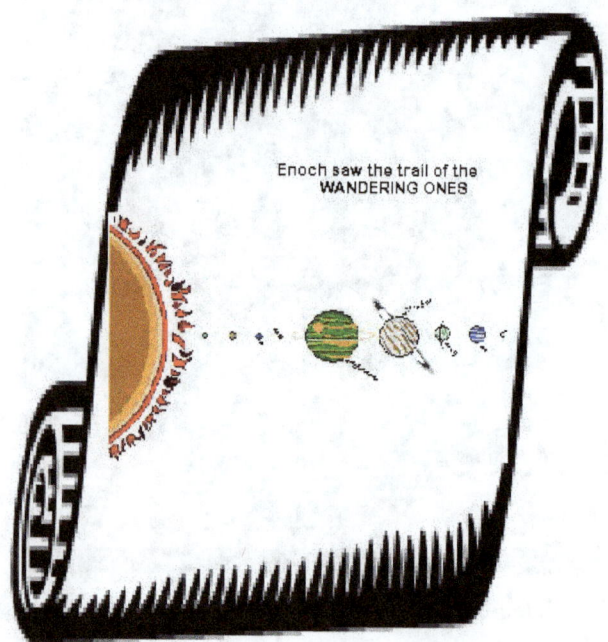

Enoch saw the trail of the
WANDERING ONES

The constellations and the planets become agitated and confused so that they leave their appointed course as they seek to throw themselves down from the heavens. This is a major prophetic sign to the Elect. Uriel explains that during Enoch's initial ascent through the six lower heavens (6 Days of Creation), he was still only a mortal Man. Upon his arrival in the outer regions of the seventh heaven, they summon Enoch before the Presence of the Holy, where he is under the care of the Archangel Mikhael, which means 'He Who Is like El,' who shows Enoch the 'rest' of the seventh day, which opens up the eighth day of freedom and new life upon earth. Enoch's transformation into an angelic being, like one of the archangels, caused his flesh to change into fire as he was clad in the Celestial light garments of Shekinah.

His earthly robe (nature) changes into the spiritual garments of Avir when the Kabod filled with the Holy Oil of the Shem Ha-Mephorash (יהוה) anoints him.

Enoch's new identity emanates throughout the Universe with vibrations and waves of the Wings of the Tempest, freeing all the lost memories of a previous spiritual life in Eden. Some of the angels begin to shout protests at Enoch's elevation, a mortal man born from a worm (sperm drop) and dust of Adamah. The enthronement of Enoch was a trial for the angelic hosts, who could only experience the image and form of earthly realities but not the essence. They feared that mortal man would win their places around the Throne. The newly appointed Son of Man is amazed at the response of the angelic hosts to his appointed position. All of this was new to him, and before he could decide what he thought about a particular event, something else happened. He feels as if he were in a whirlwind of motion, though he was lying prostrate on the ground. As he tries to stand up, sounds whiz in and out of his ears while various colors and static images cross his eyes.

He then began to feel vibrations moving him back and forth from deep inside. Before he could recover, the next phase of this experience caused him to hear the roaring sound of waves rushing through his head. He tried desperately to hold onto something tangible, but there was nothing to support his weight. He felt as if he could just blow away with the strong wind that surrounded his body. He is desperate now to provide a means to leave each generation his scrolls. The Most High promises him that there will be individuals to communicate them to the next generation until the End of Time. Therefore, the Timeless Kingdom continues to grow as people assume the duty of passing on the meanings found in ancient Hebrew texts. For the secret hidden meanings will invisibly be revealed to those worthies of receiving them. He hears his voice shouting: "There have been many books from the beginning of Creation and shall be to the end of the world.

But none shall make things known to you like my writings,"

Timka wakes with a startle and tries to remember what she saw and heard before she forgets. She does not know who is shouting these things yet. She tries to hurry and write down what she vaguely remembers now of her journey beyond time into the Kingdom. As she continues to write, she begins to think aloud, "Enoch realized the mysterious Events of the Yom YHWH (Day of Yahweh) have already dawned, but false interpreters molded an artificial image of the account with pagan clay of religious ideology. Therefore, the real victory of the Messiah does not yet exist for everyone. She now understood a verse in an ancient text, which once escaped her: how a spiritual existence will manifest its message to humanity, but it will occur in ten weeks. She always wanted to understand when the ten-week countdown began. She did not yet know that the countdown began before the earth existed.

Nevertheless, after that night, she somehow knew through a feeling of familiarity that the Son of Man assimilates all ages and dispensations of time back into the world of eternity; the battle continues until the week is completed.

She thinks aloud again, "Our Universe continues to suffer under the oppression of angelic powers that continue to misguide us through religious and scientific doctrines that oppose and contradict the true reality. "Yes, yes, that's it! That is how the fallen angels continue to fool us!"

The Resurrection has taken place, but hardly anyone has entered the Kingdom. She finds herself growing impatient and anxious to know what will happen. Every day, her heart fills with love and joy but also sorrow and anxiety. Timka is not aware that she has been shouting strange things since she woke up. "Timka, what on earth are you rambling on about now?" said Joel her boyfriend. "Go back to sleep or get up, but you know I have to work tomorrow morning." he then turned over and put a pillow over his head. Timka goes on unabated by his lack of interest.

Timka had tried to share her heart with Joel several times and met with indifference or irritation and she now feels very uncertain of their connection with each other. She says to Joel, "The early disciples of the Nazarene were vaguely aware of these things and tried to prepare the community by teaching that the Son of Man would one day return in Glory and Victory as the King. The crucifixion and his role as suffering servant was only the first step of a two-step process that happens in our time, contrary to popular opinion, for some are still waiting for something that has already happened. The truth is the Son of Man never left the earth, and the spirit sleeps in each of us until the gnosis awakens us. Mistranslations and false teachings hide His secret identity. We must leave hatred and fear behind in order to rise in thought; an enhanced consciousness is what allows one to 'receive' the Messiah."

Timka's mind continues to climb ever higher. The Voice she hears brings her thoughts to life; they begin to interact with her soul, and Timka is speechless as she visualizes what she just read. She suddenly stops talking midstream; she hears Joel snoring in the background, and her words fall on the floor of the room without a response. This does not deter her or the Voice that continually impresses images and unknown ancient knowledge upon the waters of her mind. She cannot stop thinking about what she just saw and heard after seeing Enoch's vision. Then she remembers she heard someone say, "The ability to understand this ancient mystery would not really exist until the end of the age."

The Son of Man's existence is only a Name at first. Still, it becomes a reality and distinct phenomenon that will help those who ask for the ability to see and hear it again whenever people understand the words/signs correctly. Timka had waited for this moment for a long time; everything up to now has been a rehearsal for the final day. The Kingdom comes into existence at the end of the age during the most horrible tribulations and death the world will ever see. She grabs her books at the foot of the bed, feverishly searching for the reference she needs to confirm her experience; she finds a passage by Rudolph Otto and reads, "Taken strictly, the meaning is that He Himself would not really exist until at the End. His existence is at first only that of the NAME."

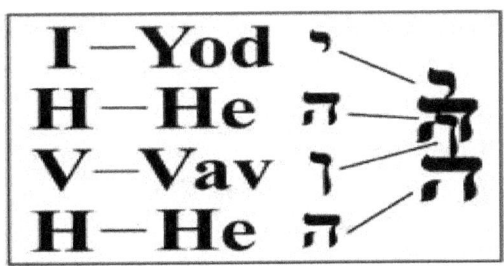

Timka keeps looking for a way to convey this knowledge to others, but she also knows the delusions of the fallen angels flood the Earth with knowledge, which is like a spiritual flood of water that drowns almost everyone, as in the flood of Noah's Day. There will be so many warring waves of contradictions and discrepancies that very few people will be able to maintain true faith; oppression and inhumanity to man and woman take the souls of many.

Some will use science to confuse the facts and issues surrounding the ancient texts, and others will use religion to encourage would-be students to stay clear of the dangerous ideas of apocalyptic doctrines. Many will teach and preach in the name of יהוה, but it will be according to their own vain imagination. As she lays there in the bed, she keeps trying to understand what is happening to her and what she is supposed to do, "I am only one person; what can I do alone? No one can even hear me most of the time. Even though I speak clearly, they cannot hear me." Timka is not aware that she is in the Kingdom. She knows so much about it through her research, but it will take more time and experience before she knows she is actually in the Kingdom of the Son of Man. She hears the Voice in the back of her mind so clearly, and she is not afraid of the unusual things that happen to her like the words on the page growing bigger and sometimes a yellow shadow from her fingers would project light unto the pages.

Once, she was standing up and talking to a friend from school about Elohim, and the whole room became black. She could not see anything, not even the phone in her hand, but she could hear her voice talking on the phone with her friend. She was not afraid; she trusted that this, too, was part of the journey. Her vision returned shortly. Many unusual things she did not share with anyone; somehow, she just knew what to say and what not to say.

Nevertheless, most importantly, she did not want to speak of visions because they are not an important aspect to consider. The prize we must keep our eyes on is the Crown! – Keter is what matters. What Timka does not fully realize is that wicked willfulness pervades human thoughts; this anti-human sentiment will convince humans to think they are truly invincible and capable of even re-duplicating themselves. All humans, as a result will be under attack with wicked thoughts they cannot control. Thoughts that seem to focus only on material things and artificial intelligence, the human mind is under attack because it is the Most Holy Place of the human Tabernacle. The war in heaven takes place in the consciousness of humanity. Only those who learn how to read the hidden 'word/signs' will be able to control their thoughts and behavior.

Timka frets as she pounds her head once again in frustration and murmurs, "But how? How can I and just a few people help ancient saints and angels fight the greatest battle of all time?" She feels intuitively that the great dragon is getting closer to her heels. She can feel its breath now upon her neck, tightening up the muscles in her scalp so that she often feels her head is in a vice-grip of some kind. The feelings of weakness, fear, and doom always chase her, trying to devour her soul and manipulating her loved ones to turn against her. She is, for the moment, truly alone within the Kingdom.

Then she hears a new 'still' Voice inside her. It speaks in her own voice and says, "The ability to discern and choose the Tree of Life remains hidden inside of everyone's heart until each is able to put forth a hand to eat from it and live. Everyone has to take from the Tree and eat to undo the curse of the original Tree of Knowledge." She thinks to herself, "Why do I have such experiences and thoughts from reading a book, I don't understand how it has such an influence on me.

Maybe I am just making it all up in my mind; I am deluding myself like Joel always says." Then, a scripture comes to her mind from deep inside her thoughts; it calms the dreaded weight upon her heart. "Remember the former things of old: for I am EL, and there is none else; I am Elohim, and there is none like Me, declaring the end from the beginning, and from ancient times the things that are not yet done!" She hears a knock at the door that startles her as a book falls off the shelf simultaneously. She picks it up and notices the title contains the word 'Shekinah' and remembers that is what carried Enoch to the seventh Heaven in her dream. She is sleepwalking in the vision she saw earlier; even though her physical body is awake, she is not aware of herself on Earth yet. In a daze, she goes downstairs to see who is at the door.

In bursts Alexa, who says, "If we don't keep a careful watch on what scientists are doing behind closed doors, there may not be another world to escape to! My instructor is now teaching that the reversibility of time also has an effect on the elementary particles that are the foundation of all material life.

I think their continual scientific quests for dark matter and anti-gravity could mean the destruction of the entire sub-atomic level of life. In class yesterday, my physics Professor said: "For example, suppose we apply a 'time reversal' transformation and let time run backward, forming the initial particles out of the final particles; would the reaction then be irreversible in time?" Alexa says, "If the action is irreversible that could mean there would be no way to 'undo' the effect on the Universe. Will scientists find a way to undo the creation itself when they learn to produce more anti-matter and dark matter? Perhaps the Big Bang will once again become an empty void!"

Alexa grows more agitated the longer she has to wait for an immediate answer from Timka, her study partner. Alexa does not see any value in science, only what it has done to destroy the land, atmosphere, and waters. She calls it the destruction of the earth's LAW. She always tries to draw Timka into a battle of words because of her dislike for technology and science. Alexa silently thinks to herself, "Timka will say that science is necessary and that I should try to learn from these discoveries, at least before disregarding any conclusions. I really hate when she tries to be so open- minded. Science has done nothing but given men the ability to destroy the entire Universe." Alexa puffed up with self-righteousness and feeling secure in her own viewpoint crossed her arms over her chest. She is not aware of her body language. She just stands there staring at her with big eyes. Timka says, "The first battle began in heaven, Alexa, and since then, it continues to multiply on Earth. Therefore, evil reigns in high heavenly places, and it perpetrates itself on earth as wars, controversies, and schisms." Alexa grows even more berated; she starts shouting at Timka, "Society tends to view everything through physical eyes. It has no personal imagination left, and the future implications of actions today are not seriously considered. People sit on time like it is a chair or another physical phenomenon to be classified, tested, and manipulated by their intellects!" Alexa is very adamant about Einstein's influence on society; she thinks that scientists have no business meddling with the Universe or treading on the spiritual ground with scientific perspectives that deter young people from learning about spirituality.

Alexa is infuriated that it is against the law to have faith or even try to say there is a Creator. She does not realize how much stress it puts on her mind and heart to harbor these feelings and thoughts. Her family had a great religious influence over her, and this perspective colors her view of life on many different levels. Alexa cannot really understand Timka, but she really likes to study with her. They experience amazing things together, yet both still feel alone. Alexa wants to be able to help others, too, during the end of the age. Her own fear and doubt plague her mind, and she does not always think logically; her emotions always get the best of her. She cannot yet hear the things that Timka describes, but she longs to experience more – she wants to hear more, something compels her to visit Timka even though she often argues with her. Paul the Apostle always said that it is as if one was pulling another out of a fire just to try to share the Wisdom with others – it is a battle at great personal cost.

Timka abruptly interrupts and says, "Many spiritual commandments and prohibitions have been moved out of the way by both scientists and religionists. The use of technology and religious doctrines seems to abrogate true spiritual authority. Where will it stop? Alexa, you do not see the whole picture. You are only using one side of your beautiful brain! Some creationists propose fantastical creation theories based on geological and radioactive dating and astronomical anomalies rather than dealing with the mystical portions of

Genesis. When will more people realize that the hidden key eludes us until each one finds out how to accept responsibility for who we are? Why do so many religious-minded people in universities and seminaries continue to only focus on the six days of creation and entirely neglect the significance of the entire scriptures?"

"Did you know that Enoch and Paul both described spiritual wars that will grow upon the earth in these last days and that many things will seem right to most people but in reality, are full of error and will lead to massive deaths? These modern terrorists are creating a new set of sins and laws for which there is no escape, for these atrocities are committed with an anti-humanistic fervor that is unexplainable. Human self-will poses as human 'rights', and now only those who are capable of selflessness will be able to escape the black hole of personality. The abyss has opened, and the world is going into perdition; violence will increase, and love will continue to leave human hearts until only darkness remains, when the black hole of inhumanness seeks to swallow human consciousness!

Human life now seems meaningless, for greed and selfishness have reared their angry heads. Nations attack other nations, families attack each other, and nature's transformation will attack all. Sickness and man-made plagues reduce the population, and artificial drugs are forced on innocent children who sustain injury with no rights. There will come a time when many of us will be thrown into camps and removed from our homes. Many people will not survive as rulers and warmongers rise in power. The whole world will become transformed through horrible atrocities and death before the Timeless Kingdom is fully operative." Each girl speaks from her particular perspective and understanding; the lines of communication are not yet connected as their words fly through the air back and forth like darts, which do not quite find the bull's eye. Alexa quickly speaks her mind as though she heard nothing. Timka just said, "Their fervent desire to create antimatter and artificial elements and aether is a sign of the end. The world has already changed; it is not the same anymore. People do not believe that evil exists, yet some people manifest evil actions globally, and no country is exempt. People are not safe anymore; more religion will cure the problem! The nations still have a hatred of one race towards another. The rape and murder of innocent children through human trafficking and women selling their babies is still on the rise, and hundreds die every year with no justice. So many heinous crimes are committed daily that the holy angels mourn the death of the Universe. Yet, there are a hundred prisons and rehab programs, but nothing seems to help. The double standard that exists between the ideal of technology as presented to the world and the stark reality of individuals drowning in the mass pool of disposable labor in the workplace is the ultimate form of division and tyranny.

Economic depression and lay-offs continue to destroy people, and evil spirits feed on human fear and become stronger." Timka raises her voice now over Alexa. "We must learn to fight the evil thoughts that come into our minds, Alexa. It is the only way!

We have to learn to love one another also, you and I! We are all one people; stop focusing on what the world is doing. Don't you know the fallen angels taught people to control others through stereotypes, race, and individual artificial distinctions? A divided house will stand no more when liberty's voice is heard from behind the door." She then controls her breathing and continues in a quiet and yet determined tone, "Religious establishments are impotent in teaching us how to expand our moral conscience, for they left the true Name behind, and society doesn't care what we expand unless it includes making money, it encourages acts of aggression to demonstrate power through might. The prophets all agree that our level of intelligence and sense of morality will gradually fade away until evil looks good and even good looks evil. This is the 'darkness' John says we dwell in, and because it is our perception covered in 'darkness' (the unknown), we cannot comprehend the light of truth. Paul explains that people will not want to retain the true Elohim named YHVH in their consciousness, in fact, they deliberately set about to re-create their own version of spiritual reality. There are hundreds of versions found in religions, philosophies, scientific theories, and political parties.

All have their viewpoint and reasons concerning what is important and why we are here and yet one event really happened that almost the entire world rejects. Whenever a new theory is developed, or an idea challenges the credibility of another idea, our re-invented reality prevents a clear view of the true reality. Ignorance of the unknown finally overcomes the human psyche. The real divine power of the Holy Spirit wages the war that will release all of us from the depths of perpetual darkness. The Son of Man spoke about our inability to discern this true reality in the end days. This is what the book of Enoch is all about!"

Then Timka's eyes begin to glaze, and she looks straight ahead and speaks with a different voice that seems to create an echo that fill the room it is so loud: "He answered and said to them, 'When it is evening, you say, it will be fair weather; for the sky is red. In the morning, it will be foul weather today, for the sky is red and lowering. O, you hypocrites, you can discern the face of the sky, but can you not discern the signs of the times? Before this, Enoch said, "I swear unto you, to the wise and the foolish, for you shall have manifold experiences on the earth. In royalty and in grandeur and power, and in silver and gold and purple, and in splendor and food, their souls will pour out as water from broken bags. Therefore, they will not know the ancient teaching that can save them from the fallen angels' deceptions. They are wanting in doctrine and wisdom, and they shall perish thereby together with their possessions and with all their glory!" Timka is so frightened of what will happen to children when concentration camps and migrations begin on a grand scale. Children are separated from their parents and forced to be with strangers as human civilization stagnates without natural affection or love. Strangers will rule over everyone. She often wakes up in fear for her children after one of her dreams. Even though she has different dreams of running and hiding, they all have a common element.

She sees how many children are huddled together and running to a dome-shaped shelter where they are temporarily safe from soldiers and guns. The soldiers speak in a foreign language; it is the same dream she has sometimes of having to be quiet and not move while squatting in the coldness where only their own breath is a source of warmth. Once confronted by a Roman soldier, she felt that she had gone back to the time of the disciples during the time of the persecution. She thought she had, somehow, been transported back to a time long ago; she saw a woman who was all at once a guardian, mother, provider, and protector of a hiding place that she and several children occupied. She often wakes in a panic, not able to breathe, thinking that the time is today; it exasperates her trying to find a way to save her family and her community. As the Cosmos eventually transforms into chaos and destructive patterns of anarchy, imprinting its image of darkness, fear grows greater as natural disasters force people to move into new areas. As if some evil force was maliciously setting the stage for a horrific tragedy that no one else seems to realize. All of it is very overwhelming for Timka. In her heart, she knew that evil intentions and humanistic doctrines of superiority would grow stronger as social mores and values disappeared. She is so grateful for the time of peace she has now. She always knew that one day it would not be peaceful at all, and she prepared for that day every day of her life.

As more innocent children are exposed to adult goals, their young hearts grow darker, and the light of their eyes and the shine of their souls are covered. Eventually, everyone will be deceived, and people everywhere will see each other as an enemy due to distinctions, labels, and rallies. The dragon is always there waiting to devour the child, but |YHVH| prepares a place for the woman. That is Timka's way of dealing with her anxiety; she holds on to those scriptures that are meaningful to her in a way that others cannot seem to do; she thinks that if only they could see the Kingdom, it would help them to survive mentally and emotionally. She explains to Alexa that all races will be against each other, males and females will become natural enemies, children will continue to kill others, authority figures will market humans as resources in the struggle to live on earth, and people are bound to human transport containers upon the seas. "Then will the 'end' of humane people come, and only those who find the way to escape from their own spiritual ignorance will find and put on the true Son of the Father's name.

Those who find the Father's Name and prevail to put it on become the servants of the Timeless Kingdom; they are not specially set apart, nor do they inherit physical power to fight their oppressors. That is the way of the material world; instead, they inherit that Mystery from the foundation of the world destined to activate the signal. Their strength lies solely in their ability to hear, see, and obey the message of the Kingdom. Alexa, you have to realize that science and religion are brother and sister. We have to learn from the best of each." Alexa looks at her very strangely now, and her eyes are not as large. Her voice is also changed she seems almost calm now as she says, "You've been up studying all night again; you haven't listened to one thing I've said since I came in the door. Look at the state of the environment and all the sicknesses and deaths that science and technology created in the aftermath of its advance on humanity. The ancient ice of the North Pole has begun to melt at an alarming rate, the atmosphere has changed, and the oceans are heating up. Maybe people do not realize the fallen angels are using them to destroy the creation." She almost began to cry, but she was much too angry and stubborn for that.

Timka used this moment of silence to continue where she left off, "Again, the prophet Isaiah knew about this time of tribulation. He wrote about the day when the whole world shall tremble, and all the children of the world shall try to hide themselves in holes and caves because they cannot imagine salvation anymore.

They shall go into the holes of the rocks and into the caves of the earth for fear of the impending destruction of the heavens and earth as the 'day of judgment' terrifies the earth." Joel, now awake and irritated with their discussion, stomps down the stairs and shouts over both of them. "Members of the Israelites were told to go to Mt Sinai to receive the law from the Creator, and they cowered in fear and begged Moses to go on their behalf because they didn't want to hear the Voice. Supposedly, they heard the Voice again as the precious Messiah baptized by John came up out of the water. People did not want to hear it then and still don't want to hear the Voice today; why can't you just accept that?" Joel did not care much for their study sessions. Something inside him rebelled that he did not understand. He is not able to prevent what comes out of his mouth, even when he tries to suppress it; something rises up in him and takes over his mind. He then begins to speak more arrogantly against the two girls, "People today still refuse to hear the Voice and plug their ears in defiance against any sound doctrine that contradicts their personal biases or prejudices.

Scientists have to continue their work and research for the advancement of humanity; they will find another world humans can live in; just give them a chance; this world is messed up now anyway. War is inevitable; it helps reduce the population, and it will boost the economy in the end. So, just get over it, Alexa! I am so tired of hearing you go on and on about religion and how lousy science is. You do not know what you are even talking about." Timka steps up to the plate and says, "Yes, but now we will not escape the Voice of Yahweh, for nature itself is the appointed messenger that will bring the storms of judgment and cleansing.

Luke the Physician wrote: "There shall be signs in the sun, moon, and stars; and upon The earth distress of nations, in perplexity for the roaring of the sea and the billows, men fainting for fear, and for the expectation of the things which are coming on the world; for the powers of the heavens shall be shaken..

Then shall they see the Son of Man coming in a cloud with power and great glory." Joel laughs aloud, "Ha ha ha!" and says, "What exactly is this cloud you are always talking about, and how does the Son of Man come with it? Do you hear how ridiculous you sound? This is just another one of those strange ideas you find in some useless scrolls of apocalyptic mystic stuff. The things you talk about do not seem real or true to everyone, you know what I mean? You sound nuts, Timka; you should listen to yourself sometime. People are not interested in 'hidden' books or the outcome of their future, and you two should not keep reading this stuff if this is what it does to you. You both need to get a 'life' or get over it." No one spoke for about five minutes. His words were like torpedos that hit their targets and fulfilled their mission. He felt very sure and confident of himself that he shut them up this time for good. Alexa listens quietly as Timka continues, "When he arrives to terrify the earth means a great human war shall arise and surround Galilee because Galilee was the first place where the disciples were attacked, then later provinces of the Holy Land were destroyed, it will therefore first appear in Galilee and then upon the rest of the world. The events are still unfolding from within a central location of this ancient city that will ultimately change the whole world. The battle of the fallen angels that will confuse humanity will last for years.

The Son of Man resurrects as the story is re-enacted on earth, and the Kingdom to come will arrive through the fulfillment of the prophecies written thousands of years ago by Hebrew prophets and other anonymous authors regarding this generation and the geographical place doomed from long ago. Since the fallen angels still influence this region, there has never been peace. Even if it seems that there is peace, the violence re-awakens again at the end of the age to bring about the most horrific war ever waged. Nation will be against nation as the angelic battle in heaven also takes place on earth, for the reflection of the war in the heavens is brought into our world because so many have abandoned the search. The angels appointed to guard our earth begin to battle the fallen angels to regain their seats around the Throne; our earth and body are the places where heaven and hell meet. They will be the breeding ground for the worst global catastrophe of all ages."

Timka's heart was racing as fast as she tried to explain what she was told. She began to cry. Joel laughs so loud it infuriates even Alexa, and as he grows more sarcastic, he seems to enjoy taunting the girls. "Where do you two come up with these ideas? You are both absolutely nuts; I told you not to study this stuff so much! That is all you do is waste your time and money on these stupid books that bring you nothing but worries." He quickly runs around the room pointing at the bookcases as he begins to attack Timka. "How much did this book cost and this one too? How about all of these on this shelf? They are all worthless; we could have used the money for household things or going on a trip! He aggressively knocks books off the shelf, and Timka finds herself feeling faint. In a daze of mixed emotions, "What is happening to me?" she thinks right before she feels herself sinking down, down into nothingness, and the room around her seems to evaporate into specks of grey before she sees the blue circle open its eye.

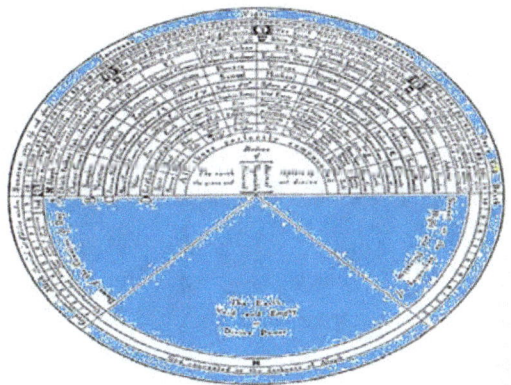

The buzzing in her ears almost numbs Joel's voice; she can hardly hear him anymore. She tries to look into the blue circle, but it still does not permit her entrance. Once again, she tries to relax her thoughts, but it is too late. Joel sees her about to fall to the floor. As he grabs her head in his arms, he looks down into her beautiful glaring eyes and says, "Why can't we just be the way we used to be, Timka, when you didn't act like this and we just enjoyed life together?" You, me, the kids, you know, the way we used to be, before the deaths. You have to let go of the past, baby. Live here now with me while we can. He waves his hands in the air frantically as if to get her attention in order to pull her back from some unseen force that had taken hold of her mind. His heartaches get the best of him, and he is devastated again. He misses the life they once had together, so it is easy to blame it all on her books and that crazy world she talks about all the time.

He has seen this look before; it takes over her face right before she faints and falls to the floor. Joel has come home sometimes to find her walking in her sleep and talking out of the window because she heard something banging outside; she might see a fire burning or a great light shining in the room with her. She refuses to take medication; he just does not know what to do for her anymore. He attributes it to the grief that has ruled in her heart since the deaths. They did not discuss the deaths much, but it was always hanging over both of them as they faced their loss in silence.

Death seems so final; death affects some people less than others, but everyone death touches responds in different ways. He tells himself she is just grieving and then decides to try a different tactic. He speaks very gently and says, "Timka, can any of these things help you pay your bills, or can it change the fact that your mother has passed away? Your nephew is gone, and two study partners; we all have loved ones who will pass away. You have to deal with death. You have to get a grip on reality, sweetheart. I love you, and I am very worried about you right now." He walks her over to the couch and lays her on it as he continues his speech. "When was the last time you really had a good time or fun – why must you be so serious all the time?" Timka looks up at him through tear filled eyes and tries to find that ole familiar smile to make him feel better, but she cannot manage to locate its place just yet. It is hard for her to find the words to express all the deep feelings she has inside; sometimes, she is bubbling with great love that sends waves of happiness throughout her whole body. Then, there are times when there is such sadness that her eyes cry on their own without her awareness.

She very calmly says, "Joel, why must you always fight so hard against what is happening to me? Why can't you try to understand why it is so important to me? I have a responsibility to pass on to others what I see. Enoch and the other characters are symbols of real human abilities and spiritual energy, the Logos will use anyone that hears to communicate with humanity. This is why some books I love so much are important; the Spirit of YHVH inspired them, and people wrote these things to help us. It is just that simple and yet so hard to explain.

I don't know why it was shown to me, sweetheart, but it was, and if I am wrong, then I will be wrong and hope for mercy from Yahweh, but if I am right, then it is my duty to at least try to share this information with those who want to hear it." Alexa grows irritated now and blurts out defiantly, "Your duty is to the Kingdom, Timka; you shouldn't keep worrying about what is happening in the world and how to fix it; you have to concentrate and learn from what has been shown to us. You do not need scientific theories to help explain mystical concepts; they can stand on their own. Leave the world to the world. Just keep opening up your eye – your eye, Timka, keep it open! Science corrupts everything it is holding you back. People do not care about what we are trying to do; why do you care about them so much? The more you expand your spiritual consciousness, the more humanity's consciousness will awaken, until the time of the 'beginning' opens up once again and the harvest starts."

You see Alexa, like many other people, believes in a judgment of the wicked and punishment for their evil deeds for the destruction of the LAW. Now, the two of them begin to berate each other. Joel glares at Alexa, and his brow wrinkles as his nose tightens, and he snorts, "Who asked for your stupid

47

religious opinions? Don't egg her on Alexa; she is already in a bad state; she wakes up sometimes screaming in fear, and I don't know how to help her. I feel so impotent and useless in her world. These supernatural beliefs and prophecies are for monks and mystics; you're just a couple of frightened girls; what do you know about the mysteries of the Universe and science?" At this very moment, something swells up in Alexa that she cannot control; she is under its power. She hears her voice change, and she feels the echo of water in her ears and wind blowing upon her face.

She begins to shout because she cannot hear anything but the sounds of water ringing in her ears and the dim sound of crickets that seem to grow louder and merge, creating a symphony of roaring waters. Then, she hears her mouth uttering these words, "For the days shall come upon you, when your enemies shall cast a trench about you, and keep you in on every side, and shall lay you even with the ground, and your children within you. Men of war shall not leave in you one stone upon another because you knew not the Time of your visitation. The great angelic march will accompany his arrival in Galilee it is from there that he stirs up war against the whole world. After 40 days, a pillar of fire and cloud will reveal a visible star from the east shining in all colors of the spectrum, and seven other stars will surround it."

Alexa explains how the seven sides or attributes represent things like: (Light, Energy, History, Concepts, Etymology, and Wisdom) and how all will play a role in discovering the Kingdom; because artificial facts are not always accurate, some facts are altered. For instance, there are various views regarding the Son of Man motif, regarding function and roles assigned to the Son of Man. Mistranslations of ancient texts and the original names in the Bible do not appear in our English versions. The original name of Moses is really Yehoachim, which means 'Who Yahweh establishes,' and Moses is his Egyptian name." She continues speaking: "All of these sides will be attacked three times a day for seventy days. The entire world will see these things take place. But the Star (in the East) will fight against the others with beaming sparks of fire, flaming and sparkling. It will force itself against them so violently upon all sides that it will swallow them every night but eject them again every morning so as to renew the war before the eyes of the entire world.

We will be lost in a perpetual virtual reality war that will affect human consciousness!" Joel cuts her off and quickly interjects, "We are all familiar with the portents, signs, and prophecies of many psychics and prophets who have continued to warn humanity about World War III and the mark of the beast, and blah blah blah! Most people disregard these things as the ramblings of crazy people who just cannot seem to fit into society. Others are taking up positions in the hills and mountains with enough artillery to start their own personal war, and this, indeed, is what the prophets saw for this age - one huge war. Nostradamus predicted terrible things, and he saw numerous race wars, nations at war, mental confusion among the people, and nuclear explosions as the signs of the times approached. I have heard all about this stuff, too, you know; I am just not obsessed with it that I forget how to live in the real world. I don't think you know what you are dealing with because it is changing you, Timka. We are all going to die from something anyway. Why are you so worried? Live for today, no one can change anything; you will die just like everyone else. There is no proof of some special Kingdom that has saved anyone. If you two are not careful, they will label you as the next doomsday cult, and then you will really see what it is like when the world persecutes you! What makes what you are saying any different from any other religious group? They all seem to know about the special divine names you hold so dear, and they aren't behaving the way you do. What's up with that?"

Timka begins to withdraw within herself more rapidly now and thinks she failed once again to explain it well enough so that Joel could see. She knew deep in her heart that he really was not ready or able to listen.

As usual, she could not bring herself to give up trying to get him to realize just one little thing without later denying it. This is what usually happens; people can see for a moment, but later, the idea flies away with the winds of a new thought. The power of the Kingdom is the ability to think a particular thought and then to hold this thought above all others. Timka knew the difficulty involved, and her previous attempts to share the message with others acquainted her with the grief and heartache of trying to battle with the confusing doctrines of religions and the nihilistic theories of scientific research. Higher education frowns on anything that is beyond the status quo; the separation between the soul and heart has begun, there is no turning back, the damage is done nothing can avert what must happen. These two armies were very daunting in disarming the faith of many unsuspecting people.

She starts to speak again, but very slowly this time: "As hatred continues to descend upon the earth, those who base their faith and knowledge on anything less than true spiritual knowledge will perish mentally, physically, and spiritually. The darkness is at hand all the prophecies are unfolding. If people do not emerge from the darkness within, each will become a black hole after death, stuck in the event horizon of their ego. I fear this might be that 'second death' the Bible says to beware of, for only a few will escape the 'second death." The human soul will disconnect from the mystic thread, and all the divine attributes such as love, beauty, faith and understanding will fade away to be replaced with their opposites on a global scale. The only thing we can do to help anyone or ourselves is to rediscover the true meaning of world events, which remain hidden in the historical background of ancient Judaism and early Christianity. You have to understand what happened to the meaning of certain texts through editing and misinterpretations of later generations. Various editors, for different reasons, cut out many ideas that are crucial to understanding what is happening on the earth right now. As you read these ancient texts, you are not going back in actual time, but you are now involved in a divine vision that transcends time and space. We are not looking at what Moses looked like in the flesh anymore, or Yahshua's physical face, but Yahweh is creating an inner vision through a pattern of the invisible principles so we can understand the invisible realities of who we really are. Do you think this war is going to end any time soon? No baby, it is only the beginning of a war that will renew itself for 70 Days, for according to Enoch, these 70 Days are also weeks.

The countdown began in the seventh week when the Elect received the sevenfold teaching about the Timeless Kingdom. The Messiah and disciples of Nazareth received that true doctrine, but since then, it has been lost on purpose. The Apocalypse of Weeks in the book of Enoch outlines the complete details of each week; it is possible to locate which week we are now currently passing through. I have a source that explains how the disciples of the school of Elijah, the ancient Merkavah mystic, taught that the world is to exist for 6000 years. The thing is in Hebrew interpretation, the number 'thousands' denotes things that happen in the future or the 'world to come'. It does not mean a number of physical years, even though literary history has recorded six thousand years of events. Genesis is about 6000 eternal years: 2000 years of darkness, 2000 years of Torah, and 2000 years of Messianic Grace." Joel sarcastically remarks, why do you always have to start quoting from books I don't even see, why can't you just say what it is yourself?" Alexa rolls her eyes at him and begins to fidget in her purse. She begins to realize that she, too, antagonized Timka like Joel; it is so hard to believe her ramblings about the past, her dreams, and the children she must protect. She thinks to herself, "I keep assuring her the kids will be fine and that we will survive whatever we must endure to see it to the end.

Secretly, I antagonize her, because I cannot bear to imagine the advancing devastating terrors happening on the earth now, nor how to protect those I love. How can I try to talk her out of her fears when they are valid? Will some people escape death and walk into the Kingdom of Light? This is a time in the world when we have to learn to stand our ground and get ready for anything that might happen. No time for stress or debate --- I like the flow of this easy creative energy that is beginning to lift me up and out of the confusion and chaos of academics and artificial science pretending to be truth. Skepticism leads to certainty if one can follow it to the end of the material egos and false illusion of power structures, which seek to control everything and everyone." This was a new perspective starting to emerge within Alexa; Timka felt encouraged and smiled.

She explains to Alexa some of the reasons why many calendars contradict the chronology of the ancients and many of the concepts found in apocalyptic texts. "One Day is as a thousand years, and according to Genesis, the Kosmos continues to unfold through a number of dispensations or seven days. The seven days come into focus when we consider the fact that the Son of Man was born into the world in the 4000th year, according to the most ancient sources of Bishop Usher. Our calendar has nothing to do with the true and accurate measurement of time. It keeps track of secular and religious moveable feast days such as Easter and the Passover. Moses and Enoch have the true key to the calendar and the actual time we are in, according to the orbit of the Sun and the constellations.

To establish the approximate date of the ending of the 1st 2/3 of the 6000 years, you have to understand there were 172 years to go before the completion of the 4000 years when they destroyed the Temple. It was at this point that the calendar was restarted with 0 A.D., and the first century really only exists in modern calendars. We are actually living in a period of grace; the seventh day of the Messianic Kingdom is here but unseen to many. Mercy endures until the very last hour, but our lack of understanding and an inability to decipher spiritual symbolism has caused the Messiah not to appear to those who are still asleep at the end of the 4000 years. You see, Alexa, we must add the missing years previous to the Julian and Gregorian calendar to see that our year aligns with the Hebrew calendar."

Alexa intuitively picks up where Timka leaves off and says, "People that schedule their life around man-made concepts are prevented from knowing how to 'receive' the Messiah in their consciousness and daily lives. The real Wisdom is not the same as the world's wisdom. Humanity is an inanimate creation until the Ruach–Breath fills its clay bodies. Then, the soul can discern between truth and error regarding the sacred history of יהוה. Our calendar is not in alignment with the movement of our Solar system. Historic events and the appointment of Pharaohs and Caesars are markers that civilizations use as benchmarks in Time's domain. Alexa, A group of people we never met, decided which ideas and books are unimportant, which ones to ban, and discard or hide under names like 'Apocrypha.' Why did the early Church leaders start the calendar over with 1 A.D.? Why is there such controversy over whether the Messiah was born four years before or after this event? It must be a very important part of the whole puzzle if these individuals went to so much trouble to revise these dates. The destruction of the second Temple occurred in 70 A.D. This was 37 years after the crucifixion of the Messiah of Nazareth. Could the hidden 70 years be the key to unraveling the true date of the calendar?" Alexa was almost out of breath before she finished the last sentence, and Joel and Timka both looked at her in amazement as she finally settled down on the couch in silence.

Alexa was more in tune with Timka now, and how she managed to put all these ideas together was a mystery to her. She did not really understand many of the things Timka said either at first, until that very moment. Neither girl realized the effect the knowledge had on their lives or in the world around them. They both thought they were in control of what they learned and understood. They do not realize that knowledge is transforming them, and as it does, it transforms the world. Timka finishes the conversation Alexa began and says, "The length of the year is itself changing because of gravitational disturbances the earth goes through from the other planets around it, especially the moon. The magnetic field is also changing due to the core in the center of the earth, and time is moving faster. There will always be a difference between the calendar and the time of the solar system." Joel just stands there looking at them with an odd look on his face; he is not sure what to do now with the two of them, going to this otherworldly reality. He wants no part of this stuff; he silently thinks, "I can't reach them. They are so lost in this maze of myth and fantasy. I have to find a way to reach them through their books, and then they will listen to me and give up this ridiculous mission." "No!" He hears a different voice, strong and fierce, and listens to a different thought, "I have to find a way to get rid of those books once and for all! This is why people should not read these books, it makes them think strange things and have weird experiences. This must be harmful, and she refuses to admit this; she foolishly believes it is a good thing."

Timka slowly begins to understand more of the experiences she had earlier that morning when she dreamed of Enoch's journey to the divine world. She heard herself muttering words she remembered hearing, "Time changes as the new order of the ages begins. Paul said, "That knowing the time is near, we must awake out of this land of Nod, for now, is our salvation nearer than we believed. The night is far spent, the day is at hand: let us therefore cast off the works of darkness, and let us put on the armor of light." Timka cries, "Yes! The armor of light is in the eight garments that once clothed Adam and Eve. The eighth day releases us from the spiritual curses and catastrophes, preventing us from realizing the angelic dimensions that really exist inside our minds and hearts. Until now, none look for Spiritual reality willingly, but the Son of Man. However, after the eighth day begins, many people will want to know the true Creator! We have yet to experience the full impact of this event; each of us has to escape the darkness and realize time has us trapped inside the reality of six days of creation, where life fluctuates back and forth between good things and evil things. Now, there is a portal of time that will allow us to go back to the Garden of Eden, but how can anyone enter something they can't see?"

Joel restlessly paces the floor and smirks at Timka; he shouts at her as if she were a defendant and he a prosecutor, "According to things you allegedly discovered in the books of Enoch, you think you know everything about when the seven days will be complete. Science says our earth is much older than the biblical account; research and geological exploration tell me they have rock-solid evidence to support their beliefs. What do you have, Timka, huh? - How do you know that what you say you know for sure is even real? You can't prove any of it!" Timka knew this was the next stage of Joel's strategy to break her down and make her doubt her own heart; only he had this power over her because of her love for him. It takes everything she has not to cry and give in to the sharp pains that pierce her heart and travel down her arm, ending in a dull ache. She can feel her neck aching and her heart pounding. She lived with pain for many years because of arthritis in her spine, and having to go on disability really struck a blow. "Breathe, Timka, breathe through your nose and exhale with your mouth." and has to be careful not to get upset, for she suffers panic attacks. She is oblivious to the fact that Joel triggers them with his attacks.

She swallows hard, takes a deep breath to push the pain back down, and says, "What will be will be, Joel; I cannot change the winds of time; it is written in the wind; we will see what we will see. All of us will have a change of consciousness, some for the better and some for the worse.

We all will be slowly and gradually changed in accordance with our thoughts, so beware what you think Joel, beware!" Joel continues the prosecution, "Timka, all you do is repeat what you read. You do not try to help the churches, you do not donate to charities, and you frown on many things that other people find normal. No one can know the Creator without going to a Temple, Church, or Mosque of some kind. Who do you think you are, the Son of Man? You really need to get a grip on reality, woman!" Alexa comes to her defense and says, "You cannot see it, Joel, because you don't understand the words/signs all around you and inside you. The mystery hides itself, and we see it through the symbolic universe of the ancient mystics. You just do not know how to navigate in an unseen land. I do not have to prove it to you, Joel, and neither does Timka. The fact that we know anything of this ancient teaching they tried to hide from the world is proof enough to us that it is real and not our imagination. I didn't always understand what Timka was going through, but now I, too, have heard and seen the words/signs happening, just read the news or turn on the television to see and hear how the 'archons' continue to influence the world." There is something very sinister going on, and I feel like a sitting duck, just waiting to become entangled in their traps."

There is a knock at the door; they are all startled, and they each slowly prepare to answer the door. A stranger apologizes for knocking and asks for directions to a bookstore they frequent now and then. They all think it is a bit strange, but they look at the clock and realize they all must begin their day in the material world.

Each goes about their daily lives as if nothing had happened earlier. The reality of daily life snapped them out of the journey. Timka looks forward to coming home after work to continue her journey in more detail. Alexa wonders at her ability to learn things spontaneously and Joel begins to wonder if maybe he should do a bit more research. The Timeless Kingdom waits within each of them until the next moment it comes from within their hearts to change their daily lives. They must learn to navigate through the scientific facts and spiritual experiences that confront them in order to help bridge the gap and heal the breach between angelic pre-history and human history.

We all too quickly forget that the life of our inner soul feels the sense of understanding, urgency, and desire to accompany the Divine Presence, but we wear the masks of human nature. Joel decides to search these things out for himself. Either he convinces Timka she is wrong, or he might have to leave her; all this tension and confusion leaves him uncertain of their relationship sometimes. His journey begins with research into the power of symbols. Timka and Alexa are always talking about symbols, he has no idea how anything so stupid could be this important to them. "I read a book or two," he thinks to himself, "I really do not understand why they take all this stuff so seriously; what am I missing?"

MYSTICISM OF SYMBOLS

Joel starts by looking through her thousands of books that fill the house from top to bottom. "Look at all these books; I cannot even imagine how much money she spent on them.

Now, where is a book that will help me convince her she is wrong," he thinks that if he just reads a little of this stupid stuff, perhaps he can win her back. The first one that he finds is Payne's Encyclopedia of Biblical Prophecy. Aha! A good place to start finding a way to shake her faith in these crazy prophecies, I need to understand what they are about first before I can help her. After a few hours of studying, he determines the world of the Bible contains symbolic imagery and visions that are very different from his way of thinking. Most of the imagery seems so bizarre that he finds its symbols bereft of logical reasoning and very boring. Nevertheless, he is determined to understand how symbols transform ancient knowledge into modern reality and why they seem so important to them. He realizes this is a vague area of investigation. He likes things he can touch, feel, and see; he does not appreciate having to read such nonsense. He begins to compare similar themes he finds in Hebraic-apocalyptic literature with ideas of Native American traditions. He does know that both cultures have managed to survive and maintain some semblance of their ancient traditions. Symbols play a large role in these cultures, and both share a great loss and determination to survive in spite of the historical and current obstacles to advancement and success. Humanity is very indebted to these two spiritual traditions. He picks up a different book and decides to start with the Wisdom of Redtail. Redtail, a very wise elder, says, "Of all existing symbols, the most universally occurring in nature is the circle. It is the approximate shape of Earth Mother, Grandmother Moon, Father Sun, and other planets. Redtail

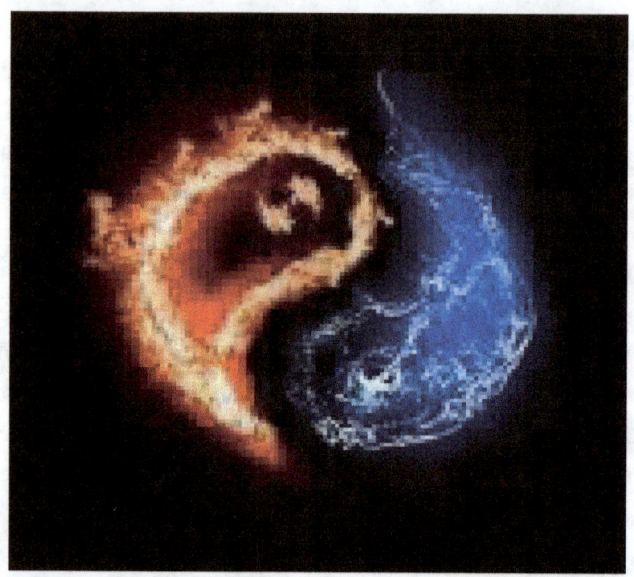

"What – the circle is an important symbol? I never thought about a circle as a symbol. He begins to think the power of symbols is in the meaning we assign them according to our cultural, religious, and political background, for we perceive life through these blinders. Some interpretations are more in accord with the true reality of life, and some are not even close.

Reality only responds to that which is in accord with its true nature. The only way to live the reality is to be in accord with what a symbol actually means to convey. He wonders what any of this has to do with the reality that Timka experiences. She claims that she has tasted a true or genuine experience of life that generates the power of biblical spiritual symbolism. She thinks we can overcome death and ignorance as we realize a symbol's intended meaning. He begins to understand that not all symbols are life-giving potencies. Some are merely manmade forms of instruction, such as traffic sign symbols and the universal symbols for driving and restrooms. He eventually will see that powerful symbols come from different places and enter our world when we experience the reality they represent. Native American spirituality is very complex and rich in symbolism and this makes it very difficult for others to grasp or conceive. Symbols have many functions in Native American culture: they provide the spiritual needs of the individual, clan, and tribe. It is also a mechanism for social recognition. Symbolism is a type of visual prayer used for protection from the various elements in nature. The animal symbols help neutralize something that is feared. Symbols also teach correct behavior and discourage incorrect behavior according to the specific clan or tribe. Finally, he learns how symbols show the rank or status of people within the tribe; for instance, feathers are a sign of distinction. This leads Joel to analyze the Medicine Wheel, a type of matrix, for the whole of its parts known in apocalyptic texts as the attributes.

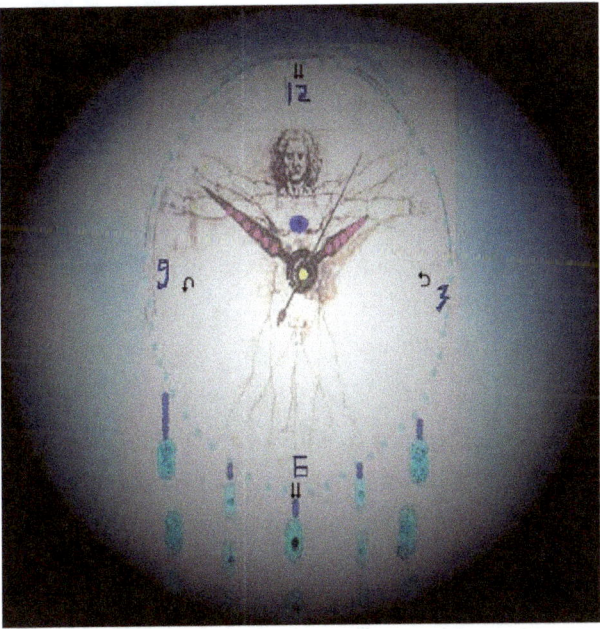

Figure 1 Medicine Wheel Clock

The oldest Medicine Wheel in the United States is in Wyoming, in the Big Horn National Forest; it is 10,000 ft. off the ground level. He finds it interesting that the Wheel of Life, something Timka mentions all the time, is the universal symbol respected by most Native American cultures who respect nature and the environment. It represents the wholeness and unity of all things rather than a mere hierarchical power structure that grows through division. He still does not really understand how the 'Wheel of Life' in Sefer Yetzirah, symbolized as a great circle of Sephirot is made of four worlds and ten levels that unfolds within us after its reality initiates us into its powerful meaning. Timka has many charts and books regarding the word 'Sefira'; he sees now that it means three things [measurement, book, and weight]. These three concepts explain how we relate to the spiritual Body of the Creator.

What Joel does not realize is that certain Christian doctrines and mainstream Orthodox Judaic teachings frown on the strange ideas of a Creator with a Body. He finds this fact intriguing and yet confusing; it does not occur to him that many religious factions still forbid people from reading the contents of certain ancient Hebrew texts. Joel feels his heart beating like a drum; his breath seems to slow down as he listens to the words again. "The Creator does not have a body." He never really thought about this before, he did not realize any of these things. "Wow!" Joel thinks, "What have people seen if they have seen not the body? Right at that moment, there is a knock at the door.

He puts the books down and walks toward the door to look outside. Alexa is standing there looking at her watch and banging on the door. Joel opens the door. "Joel, what took you so long? Why didn't you open the door? I am going to be late for my class! I have to talk to Timka, where is she? Joel is trying to ground himself and be attentive to Alexa; he is surprised to find that he is enjoying her company. She had a doctor's appointment today she will be back soon. What can I do for you?" Alexa is shocked that he spoke to her and offered his help. She looks at him up and down and walks around him, just looking at him very intently. She feels that something has

62

happened, but she is not sure what it is exactly. "Joel, what have you been up to lately, I have not seen you around much, and now you are being nice to me – you are scaring me? What's going on?" Joel replied, "Alexa, wow! I did not know I had that effect on you. I am sorry." She did not believe him, she said come on out with it, what is wrong with you? Is that a book in your hand? That is one of Timka's books; what are you doing with it? Are you trying to get rid of her books? 'No, no!' Joel replied, I am reading them." Alexa said, "You are reading her books, yeh right." Now I know something is wrong with you; really, what is going on here? Where is Timka, and who are you? Joel begins to hear his voice speaking to him in his own thoughts, "Symbols are a source of communication that is older than words and yet more effective than speech. Now, I am getting somewhere, he thinks to himself, "The term 'Kingdom' is itself a symbol for a hidden reality we cannot see. It must be experienced first in order to become visible." Joel continues standing there listening to the words, and Alexa grows more anxious with his behavior, and she starts to back up towards the door to leave. Joel looks at her and says, "I am sorry, Alexa, I have been a jerk. Wait, wait, do not go yet; I have been reading her books, I admit it. I found out that these books are helping me to discover many things. For example, I found out how the symbol of the circle is a very powerful medicine. Many Native American interpretations of reality involve the use of a circle, as do Hebrew mystics who practice this weird esoteric science Timka studies all the time. Ok, I am sorry; I did not mean to say it is weird." "Joel, are you serious? You read some of her books, and does she know?" No, Joel said, and please do not tell her yet; I want to find a way to help her, so I thought if I read some of them, I can talk to her." In the back of his mind, he still intended to prevent Timka from falling further into this invisible world. Even though Joel could not see that many spiritual, metaphysical, psychological, and theosophical doctrines use the image of a circle and four

63

directions in their practices and meditations, Joel does not understand how various doctrines converge to lead one to the true experience of spiritual reality.

He grows frustrated, with Alexa reminding him of his behavior and outbursts lately; little does he know, but his studying something new was already beginning to form concepts in his mind that will provide springboards for his future insights to take root. Joel explains to Alexa how Native American spirituality is dedicated to the experience of reality and seeks to teach its community how to live in every way, in accord with the 44 paths of the Medicine Wheel. Joel tells Alexa, "The Kitchi Manitou or the 'Great Mystery of Existence' pervades the very being of all native spirituality. This great Wheel of Wisdom ultimately represents the whole Earth and the place of every living thing within it. Living in harmony and peace with other living beings, systems, and ecology is being in accord with reality. The drumbeat symbolizes the rhythmic beat of the earth's heartbeat pounding within itself." As he hears himself thinking, without speaking, he wonders if the Holy Spirit could feel like this in each of us.

If we let the pounding rhythm of the shofar that brought down the walls of Jericho ring in our ears, perhaps we, too, can overcome what is about to happen. He does not share any of these thoughts with Alexa yet; he is not sure what to think of it all either, yet he hears something speaking from within that gives him a sensation of urgency and excitement.

He continues talking to Alexa without really revealing his true thoughts. "Some people use flags, cars, jobs, titles, degrees, and even guns as symbols. However, not all tokens lead to living in accord with reality. The symbol we respect reveals our heart's desire, and this is how symbols can become 'idols' if we are blind to them.

Some symbols are life-affirming, and some symbols can be destructive. The circle is a very fundamental symbol in mystical texts, and so are the four cardinal directions. They are spiritual messengers known as Malakim that rest at the points of the circle's perimeter. Early Hebrew mystics believe that a messenger angel lives in all living things as commanders, which incites them to act. Philo even considers language an Angel of the highest degree and explains how language is like a mirror to show us the invisible nature of the Creator.

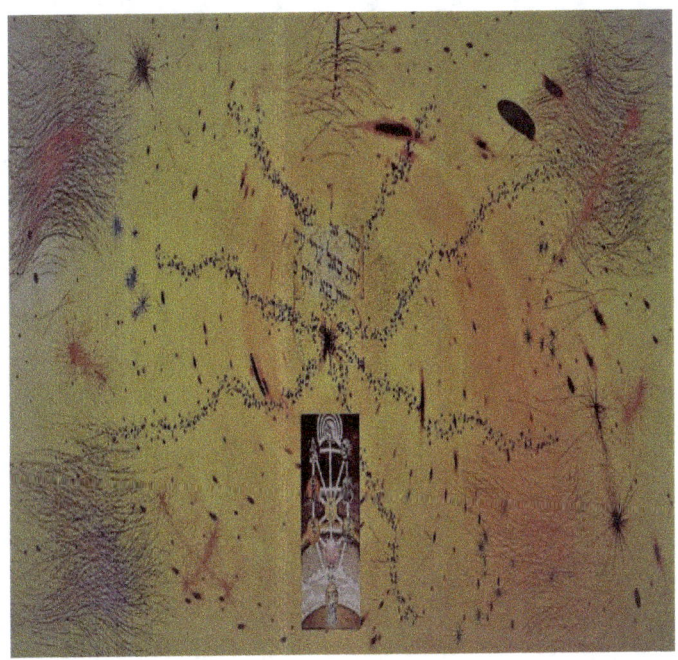

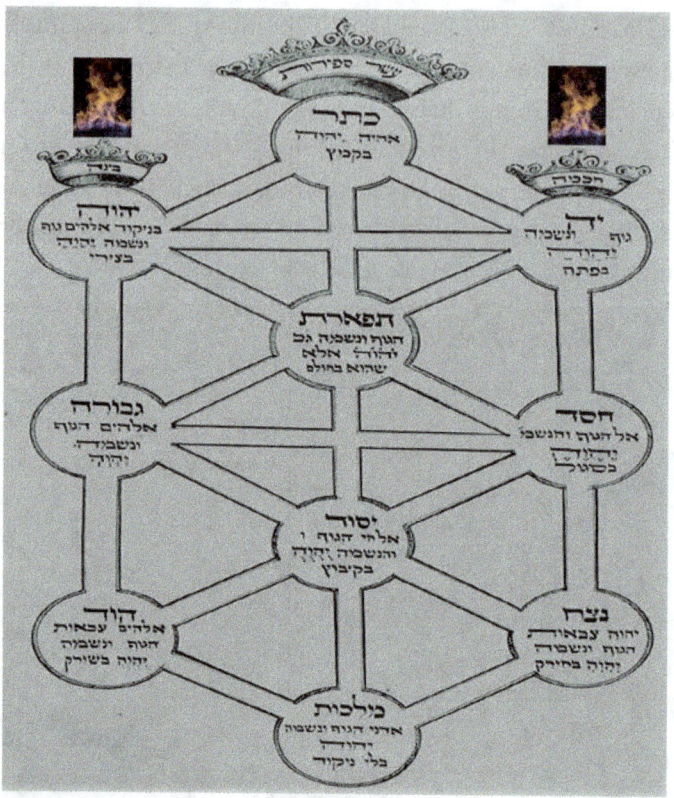

The ten levels of the angelic hierarchy give definition and form to the function of the ten dimensions of the Universe. The Supreme Being is at the apex, and levels of messenger angels live between the Great Spirit and humans. Alexa, did you know that most religions do not believe the Creator had a body? You know, I never really thought about it before like that." Alexa just stands there staring at him; she is mute and almost shaking from this 180-degree change in his behavior and words. She is not sure what to think. Finally, she says, "Joel, umm listen, let Timka know that I stopped by, and I will check in on her again later. Okay, can you do that for me, please?" Joel nods his head and walks her to the door. He begins to wonder why Alexa was so upset in his presence; most people do not realize how much they hurt others and that when one is hurt, it is not very easy to trust again. As Alexa walked away from the house, she thought, "I hope Timka is well; what is going on now? Oh my goodness, I don't think I can take much more of all this drama; the world is not what it used to be. We are all changing. Timka is changing, and so am I, now Joel, this is too weird – I do not trust him at all."

Joel continues to hear his voice speaking these thoughts. "Mysticism and shamanism share similar elements; the main difference between the two is the direction or focus of prayers. Mystics seek to rise above the earth to gain heavenly knowledge hidden from humanity. It is through their mystical ascents and meditation on circles of names and numbers that they can soar to other dimensions.

They also seek to learn about the future and past of their ancestors. Our spiritual ancestors are the characters described in biblical texts. Native American shamans seek to gain earthly knowledge of future events, healing remedies, and food gathering techniques, curative properties of sacred stones and grasses, and the significance and history of ancient sacred places. Most important is the Vision Quest that, if performed successfully, endows the practitioner with characteristics of their personal Nuwalli or animal guide. Mystics have guides; four always attend the Chariot or Merkavah, and each has the face of an Eagle, Lion, Ox, and a Human that symbolizes the four worlds.

The four symbolic images comprise ELOHIM, a Hebrew term that means "Powers". Joel speaks aloud to himself, "It is strange that the term Elohim is translated as "God" and "Gods" according to our English language." This prompts him to find one of Timka's many dictionaries; he decides to research this mysterious phenomenon again. "Hmm…it says here in Webster's Dictionary that the word 'God' is of Germanic origin (Gott). After going through several other dictionaries, he realized that many dictionaries indicate a 'god' is a 'molten image' that is worshipped.

This word actually did not exist at the time Moses was inspired to write Genesis; in other words, Moses and the Israelites were not in the wilderness pronouncing 'Gott' to appeal to the mysterious force that dwelled upon Mt. Sinai that religions teach, does not have a body. Joel slowly begins to realize there is a Medicine Wheel inside of everyone, and we each have 'attributes' that must be experienced in our hearts and minds before we learn how to reflect them in our outer world. "Maybe this is why I could not tell Alexa what is happening to me; I am hearing things that I read, talk back to me somehow." How can this be real?

Etz Hayyim – Tree of Lives

He remembers how the divine limbs of the Tree of Lives connect to form paths and all paths have a negative and positive side that must be in balance. When he read the Sefer Yetzirah, his thoughts seemed to absorb details of various paths as his consciousness actually transformed at each level of growth. He understands that these traditions teach us that humans must learn how to walk on the middle path by a continual effort to balance the attributes within heaven, earth, and oneself. "Maybe I am changing; what if I do not like the change? What if I become obsessed like Timka and I will not be able to help her? This is so confusing; why is it so hard? What is happening to all of us?

Joel does not yet know that a mystic cannot know the true essence of the Great Spirit; one can only begin to relate to the aspects or attributes in a symbolic way. Mercy, Wisdom, Intuition, Strength, and Beauty are just a few of the attributes that will establish a connection between heaven and earth. There has to be a 'grounding' of some kind performed in one's heart in order to satisfy the nature of reality. If we fail to take symbolism seriously or place any value in it, the invisible 'world to come' becomes impossible to experience without the true power of reality. No one will deny that there are four directions of the earth, yet these four corners actually fit into a circle. Some think this idea is better off left to the realm of mysticism and the occult. This biased point of view continues to berate the true spiritual experience of mystics. Joel goes back to Sefer Yetzirah for answers.

In Sefer Yetzirah, four principal powers are assigned to each of the directions and to each letter of the Tetragrammaton יהוה, a Name that denotes 'the cause of existence' or 'being' in mystical traditions. The Zohar explains how this 'Existence' is the point and center of the circle; its circumference and extension form six paths: North, South, East, and West, including an above and a below. Joel remembers that Timka always talked about how six of the dimensions surround us, and the other four are in us. She would say, "We experience the world in three dimensions, and time is the fourth. Ancient mystics had a similar system of communing with the Creator who inhabits the very center of the circle of the Universe." Joel suddenly opens the Bible, and his finger falls on something the prophet Isaiah wrote in chapter 40:21-22.

"Has it not been told you from the beginning? Have you not understood the foundations of the earth? It is He who sits above the circle of the earth, and its inhabitants are like grasshoppers; who stretches out the heavens like a curtain."

Joel is startled, for he hears the meaning of the text shouting at him from some distant place. He begins to hear a voice whispering to him about how the circle contains the past, present, and future as one continuous cycle of time. "Nevertheless, time also travels in a linear direction that moves forward towards a goal. He does not yet realize this is the underlying idea behind apocalyptic history itself, that the creation did have a beginning and will have an end or final realization.

An end that ultimately leads to the 'world to come' that we can only imagine exists right now. Apocalyptic traditions are full of symbolic imagery that depicts the 'alpha' and 'omega' idea of time. Cycles demonstrate unity and the line demonstrates distance and measurement used by scientists to manipulate and control the environment in different ways." "Who is speaking to me?" Joel wonders, in amazement, that he can definitely hear someone or something explaining things to him. This is the first time he admits to himself that someone is actually speaking to him through his thoughts. "Am I going to lose myself now like Timka and Alexa?"

The voice from within continues to speak as if it could hear Joel's thoughts and would respond in return. The voice said: "Ancient sages taught the true spiritual experience of reality is how humanity must find its place within the circle; they must not try to change the circle.

Our carnal nature cannot conceive of the unity of connectedness of living organisms and the earth. We live in a world of separation in the six days of the creation, and unity is a distant idea many only dream about." Joel feels an urge to consult the book he read about the Hopi view of time and space. This book seemed to offer more insight into a reality he knows nothing about. He finds the book by Ernesto De Martino very interesting. He begins to study the magical aspects of visions and reality and he explains how things are real even if scientists have no empirical evidence that satisfies their disbelief. Joel is surprised that visionary reality is just as fundamental as any other branch of knowledge:

What is 'real' for us is not necessarily real for other civilizations, whether they are ancient, primitive, or contemporary with our own. It is Western man's conviction that his own worldview is finally the only valid one that leads him to make presumptuous judgments upon phenomena that play no part in his own set of culturally conditioned concepts. (Martino, Primitive Magic 1990).

Joel picks up where he stopped reading, about how Martino describes the Shamanic experience known as the "gaumanek," which means "luminosity or illumination." He finds out that Native American teaching will cause an awakening to the power of a different consciousness that gives one vision and power. Some of the traits associated with the true spiritual experience of a Shaman are:

A mysterious light which the Shaman suddenly feels in his body, inside his head, with the brain, an inexplicable searchlight, a luminous fire, which enables him to see in the dark, both literally and metaphorically speaking, for he can now, even with closed eyes, see through the darkness and perceive things and coming events which are hidden from others; thus, they look into the future and into the secrets of others. (46-47)

Joel thinks to himself, "The otherness or 'primitive religious belief' endows its recipient with the power of symbolic

71

imagery. The loss of this knowledge among so many in the world today results in spiritual blindness, complacency, and apathy towards the earth and its people." Joel feels the urge to get up. He seems hungry, and has the urge to go the restroom as his heart beats harder in his chest. Something is happening to me when I read this book. He stumbles across the floor and notices another book by Carl Starkloff, which examines the concept of the Center and its significance for humanity today. He opens it up, and his finger directs him to read, "As Carl G. Jung maintained a society that has lost its capacity for myth is like a man who has lost his soul" (Starkloff, The People of the Center 22). He continues to read the following:

When we speak of 'the primitive,' we ought literally to take off our shoes. If we lightly dismiss all elements of the supernatural with such a term, intending it to mean any quality that belongs to a benighted, bygone age or a backward society, we sadly misconceive our own world and ourselves. (22)

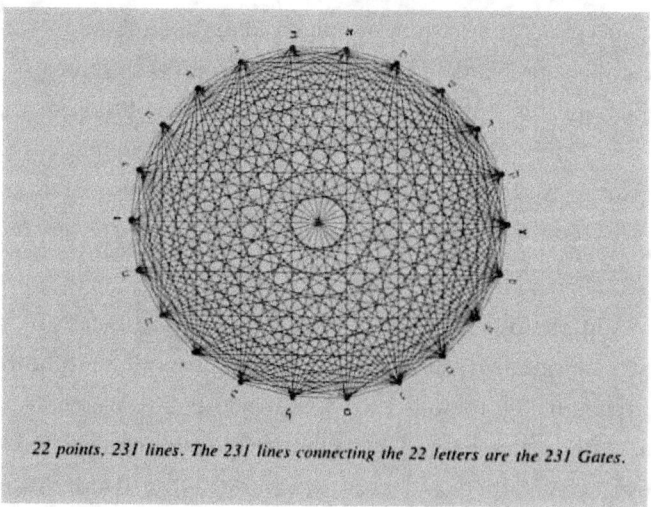

22 points, 231 lines. The 231 lines connecting the 22 letters are the 231 Gates.

Joel slowly begins to see that he has lost something; he has never felt anything like this before. The power of symbols and the meanings behind symbols are very powerful things. He still does not yet know the true dilemma of how this applies to today's society and an inability to view the reality of symbolism that prevents many from experiencing the hidden Kingdom. He heard a song come on the radio: "Heaven is a place on earth." It was very surreal. It seemed as if everything was coming together around him to show him something. Unfortunately, it is true that few people can realize just how trapped they are by the manmade symbolism that surrounds them on every side. Stereotypes and racial slurs are all symbols used by others to keep things and people in their own perceived hierarchy; it is a form of control. Each person has a value system of some kind that determines their ethos or worldview; the problem is that everyone thinks they have a right to judge others by their own standards. Joel heard a voice say:

"When tyrannical powers rule, the loss of freedom is always evidence that the 'archons' control negative energy and this affects our lives through principalities and powers in high places. Doctrines, theories, plans of conquest, eugenics, and mass depopulation all have a symbolic expression first that becomes ingrained within society at an unconscious level that keeps them blind to these outside intruders.

Many critics perceive apocalyptic as pathetic literature of those who have been conquered or dominated by a stronger malevolent power or government. Yet, Apocalyptic texts are the result of strong spiritual communication needed during a great time of conflict and human crisis that provides a source of sustenance and strength for this world and the next. Its true power is in the realization of symbolic images that project the invisible universe to us. Joel sinks down to the floor in amazement. The realization seems to hit him like a freight train, "This world is stranger than I thought." These were his last words before he fell into a sleeplike state. As Joel is sleeping, he hears people talking among themselves as to whether they should pull him out of the water or not. Some said no, and some said yes. They could hear his thoughts, and one voice told him to relax do not be afraid. They pull him out of the water, and he begins to see an old Pueblo community surrounding him. He sees many straw buildings that flank the two sides of a river.

After following them up a beautiful mountain, where the air is so bright and the sky so blue, he thought this did not feel real.

The mountains he walks upon are so vibrant and beautiful, and the air seems to reach out and touch him, sending shivers down his body. He hears people talking among themselves, wondering who this stranger is. They show him an abacus, and he attempts to use it but realizes he does not know anything about it, yet he seems to please them when he moves a stone into place. They exchanged many things, but he could not remember much when he woke up. Again, he picks up Starkloff's book, except now he feels more aware of something in himself he never felt before. He opened up to this passage:

"The notion of the primitive is not chronological or geographical, but existential: it explains those hidden forces in individuals and collectivities that call for expression and interpretation" (22).

Suddenly, Joel knows that the concept of a center is known by primitive people as comprising the central foundation of

Creation within the creation. Still, this idea seems to be absent from Christian environments that place Adam on Earth as the center of the Universe. Oriental Semitic traditions consider the "Center" the dwelling of יהוה. He is still unable to deal with this new reality, but he tries because he loves Timka so much, but he is afraid he is losing himself.

Meanwhile, Alexa is wondering what is happening to Timka and Joel. They were both very close before the deaths and debates. She would like to think they could work out their problems, but she knows that relationships can and do change, some people seem to be able to stay together, and some cannot manage to even have a relationship. "Why is life so complicated?" she thinks. Alexa decides to try reading a book Timka suggested to her. Alexa is surprised to find that the Pistis Sophia, a Gnostic document of the early communities of the second century, contains an account of how the Messiah and the twelve disciples perform a ceremony with a center and four directions.

She reads about the three disciples who stand at each of the four directions and perform the appropriate prayer for each quarter of the circle. She thinks, "The editors of our Bible censored this and many other books, but why?" She continues to read; maybe I can help Timka if I read the book that is so interesting to her.

Alexa learns that there are different levels of Wisdom and that each person has to overcome the lion within; once each one overcomes the devouring lion (false ego), one becomes a conquering lion in the Kingdom.

Alexa thinks aloud. I want to give Timka more support, but she does read some strange books; my church does not allow us to read this kind of material. Timka does seem to say very crazy things sometimes. Am I going to become like her if I read this book? I do not want to lose control over my life either; I do not know what to do! Why is life so hard?" Meanwhile, Joel grows more interested in learning about Native American spiritual traditions. He wants to find balance and harmony in his quest for truth by maintaining the wisdom of the Elders. "Perhaps I can encourage Timka to become more interested in this, too! This sounds much more reasonable and safer than what she is studying now. I understand now what I must do."

Figure 2 Ezekiel's Vision from Bear Bible

England 17th cent., excerpt from Ha-Levi Tradition of Hidden Knowledge 37

He remembers a picture that is very important to Timka; it is above her bed, and suddenly, Joel sees that there is a relationship between this figure and an ancient Native American doctrine he just learned about becomes apparent to him.

Joel noticed that the name of the Great Spirit used by the Arapaho is "Chebenia-tha or Ichebeniatha" and "it means literally, 'Man-Above' or 'White- [i.e., shining] Man-Above" (30). He finds this interesting because of the fact that mysticism, too, speaks of a 'Shining Man' above, known as 'Adam Qadmon' in some groups and the Son of Man in others. The figure that sits high above the Earth on a Throne known as the 'Kabod' is a celestial figure glowing with Light to signify its spiritual nature and origin. This figure, also known as יהוה, whose name was too sacred for speech, could appear in visions and dreams and appear as a human. He understands why Alexa always says that modern Christians have very little left to defend their belief system, except creation stories that conflict with the scientific hypotheses of Darwinism and the theory of evolution. Joel takes note that, according to Starkloff, there is only one remedy to this plight of Christianity:

If Christians are no longer able to feel secure with "proofs" of God's existence from scientific arguments, they will be rewarded richly by observing these less clear-cut but still powerful signs in primitive human nature pointing to the One who must sustain man lest he cease to be. (33).

Science has failed to satisfy the spiritual urge and yearning that is in every heart regardless of what belief system one supports. We must not forget that powerful symbols in nature have the ability to transform the physical world and humanity's perception of life. After Paul's ascent to the Third Heaven and his spiritual transformation, he began to speak of the unity of the 'Body' of Messiah; Native American belief, too, honors the idea of a corporate reality that includes not only an individual but the family, community, tribe, and nation at large. Starkloff sums it up very well:

If an individual performed well, the whole community would benefit, and if he was selfish, not only would the tribe suffer, but he, too, as virtually an organic part of the body, would suffer. As should be evident, the Pauline notion of the Body of Messiah is very close to such a doctrine of solidarity. (83)

Circles of Infinity

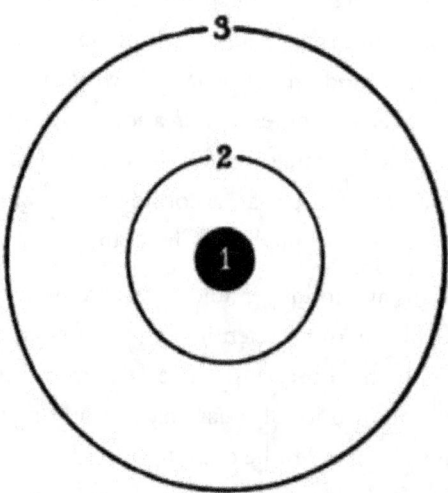

Fig. 3 Three Circles of Light

The first light of the Universe permeates all substances, all space, and time. In Figure 3, all material life is limited by circle three and ruled by the second light. Circle three represents the dividing point between divine existence and human reality or heaven and earth. The point in the center is where the two are balanced. The Temple of the Universe rests in the motionless harmony of zero-point energy. The idea of a hierarchy of circles that emanate and extend from a single localized point or center is demonstrating the design of the divine world, not the physical earth. This, too, demonstrates the basic family unit. From there, it branches out into tribes and nations, like ripples in a body of water.

Fig. 4 Native Circle Vision

The symbol of the circle, as Joel perceives now, is a very ancient concept. The line indicates a point extended in time and space.

It was from these extensions or measurements that physical creation came to exist. All things dwell in solidarity within the circle of the One. Joel reads,

It is not surprising that when native elders and sages tell us that their revelations and visions revealed the Creator source,

God the Great Spirit, as a circle, a circle of white light (Free Soul, John Redtail Breath of the Invisible 47).

He begins to take an interest in Native symbolism; he has some Native American blood, but he knows very little about it. Joel thinks to himself, "This is a good way to learn about my background, and it will give me ammunition to deal with Timka." The main idea that lends authenticity and credibility to Native American religions is that Native Americans have a spirituality that also acknowledges how the circle, as the universal sum of symbols, also represents the Presence of the Creator in all things at all times.

The circle is a sacred container for powerful and protective healing characteristics. Ancient mystics seek to maintain ritual magical practices to gain power over the environment. Knowing the name of a thing gave them the power to know its existence or phenomenon. Symbols play a large part in how mystics ascend through the seven halls or heavens. Joel is now getting very excited about his new ideas that seem to take on a life of their own. He is even more intrigued with learning all he can about his heritage. Joel decides to remain focused on this for a while longer. He started keeping a journal now. He never felt the need to journal before, but he wants to keep a record of what he has experienced. He writes down the following for his first entry:

One has to know the correct name of the angelic gatekeeper to gain entrance into the heavenly palace shaped in circles within circles. These circles are the dimensions inside us, and sometimes we catch little glimpses of a higher consciousness. Redtail explains the functions of the Medicine Wheel:

1. Learn to focus on finding a balance or direction that will promote the expansion of consciousness.

2. One learns how to realize the present moment of the Now known as self-realization.

3. It helps a person to center the self.

4. It is a communication device to the world of spirit.

Figure 5 Four Angelic Servants

The four angelic presences, Michael, Gabriel, Raphael, and Uriel, are similar to the "Servants of Matteo", the divine messengers that guide human beings. Each guardian angel was appointed for each cardinal point and served as a spirit that was summoned. "Each of these four spirits is a spirit keeper of one of the four directions (and winds) of the circle of life, the Medicine Wheel" (50). Some of these spirits are benevolent, and some are malevolent, as in most traditions. Redtail provides us with more details of the Medicine Wheel:

The center of the Medicine Wheel is motionless, the eye of God. We, Cheyenne, call this center 'the blue sky' where the Creator resides, where all direction, medicine, power, quality, and perspectives are compacted and concentrated, from which existence flows, to which existence returns. (54)

Joel begins to see more of a connection between the book of Ezekiel and other mystics. They all seem to describe the same phenomenon called the Throne Chariot. Each one explains how they envisioned a blue sapphire platform that the Chariot rests upon. Mystics find balance by living in the middle of two attributes, such as Mercy and Judgment or Wisdom and Knowledge. The middle path between Mercy and Judgment, known as "Beauty" or Tiphereth, is the line of extension that permeates through each world. On the Medicine Wheel, a person's totem or nature is determined by the season in which birth occurred, but his or her place is not stationary; a person can progress along the circle by performing the forty-four attributes. In apocalyptic mystical literature, though, one finds lore of those who traveled the Tree of Life or Jacob's ladder to the Heavens in an up-and-down movement through forty-nine gates. All of these things are symbolic, visionary phenomena that can actually touch and awaken our soul or Nuwalli, and this is the aim or goal of the practice. Joel wants to experience his Nuwalli for the first time in his life. He dives right into the Hopi doctrine of Becoming.

Hope Time

The Hopi concept of time is very different from mainstream society because it centers on duality and balance and not on a continuous progression of Past-Present-Future as in the Western worldview. The Hopi concept states:

We may call MANIFESTED and MANIFESTING (or UNMANIFEST) or, again, OBJECTIVE and SUBJECTIVE. The objective or manifested comprises all that is or has been accessible to the senses, the historical physical universe, in fact, with no attempt to distinguish between present and past, but excluding everything that we call future. (Whorf- An American Indian Model of the Universe 124)

It is thought that all things are stored or contained that ever will exist or does exist, and religious rituals and knowledgeable Shamans can learn and experience it directly from the Source now. It is always 'Becoming' and is in us now, but it must be experienced through symbolic images that represent the invisible realities themselves. It is moving and yet still; it is not coming to meet us but already lives in us; it does not need a cycle of motion to manifest itself within us or to us. We are part of its very center of being.

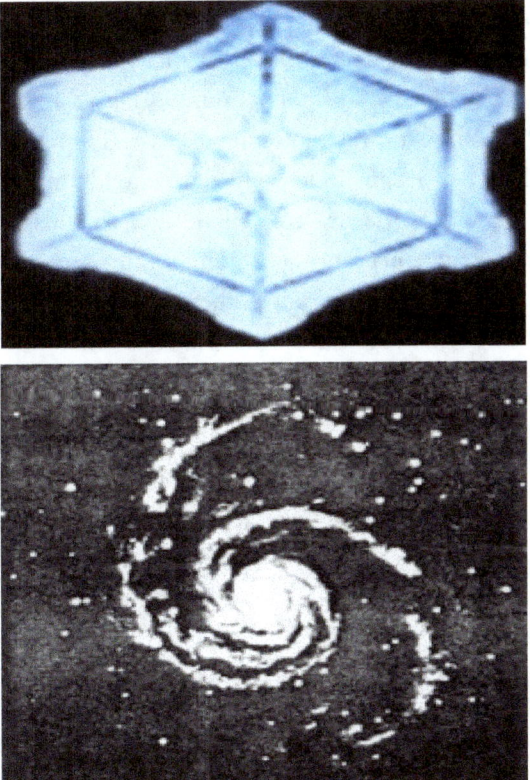

Joel discovers the foundation of this Hopi concept involves a subjective reality.

"Hope or Hoping," words like "reality, substance," space, and time are unknown in Hopi thought: "Such a term in Hopi is the word most often translated "hope" – tuna'tya – 'it is in the action of hoping, it hopes, it is hoped for, it thinks or is thought of with hope" (126).

This is the most fundamental and important foundation of Hopi philosophy. Hoping is indicative of becoming or manifesting on the physical plane. It is thought that the very idea 'comes true' with the hoping: "The inceptive form of (tuna'tya), which is (tuna'tyava), does not mean 'begins to hope,' but rather 'comes true, being hoped for'" (126). Joel now hopes that he can reach Timka from his heart. Hope and faith are substances in ancient Near Eastern traditions. Thus, hope can have a measurement and weight that produce changes in the physical objective world. For example, faith can endow one with the ability to 'move mountains.' The Hopi concept of hierarchy involves an 'inner axis' that extends into the four directions and is the heart of all things. This axis links all phenomena together and the origin of the created world: "Corresponding to each point in the objective world is such a vertical and vitally INNER axis which is what we call the wellspring of the future" (127).

Joel wonders, "How can ordinary people, not mystics or shamans, have a taste of this spiritual reality?"

Traveling Scrolls

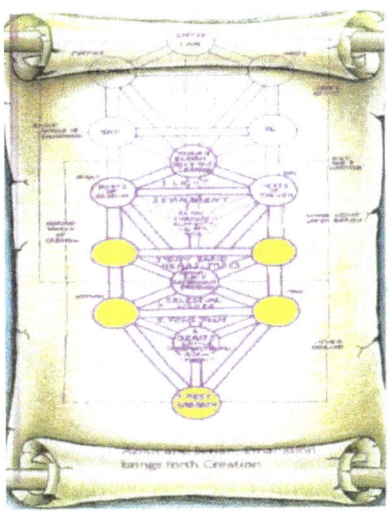

Joel has discovered how to travel through spiritual time as he begins to comprehend the pattern and logic of apocalyptic thought. "The wisdom light that translates us into the invisible world of celestial physics and heavenly astronomy hidden from the foundation of the world is now descending upon us all. The Apocalyptic mystics conceive of a realm that exists now, then, and always have visited there and documented it. We now refer to it as a genre, 'apocalypse,' a story filled with esoteric knowledge of what exists in hidden realms known only to shamans or mystics." Joel is amazed and wonders at his ability to instantly know and understand things he never knew before. These experiences really do take place in another world they are real and central to the salvation of humanity.

The ability to decode complicated symbolism is the key to experiencing and receiving the power to travel to other realms of existence and reality not perceived by physical eyes alone.

Joel is still fighting with the ideas because he is frantically searching for something to shake Timka's foundations. This will slow down his progress, but he has to walk the road many of us travel as we try to change the people we love. Even though he hates to admit it, he learns that symbols seem complicated because they are foreign to us; if we learn what they mean to the early Christian assemblies, we can restore their power. The inner spiritual eye is active when we experience the power of symbolic expressions. When the meaning and richness of the biblical symbols shape and form our waking reality with inner promptings of intuition, myth becomes reality. Myth is a collection of symbolic realities designed to evoke memories of that distant world called the 'blue sky.' Blue is the symbolic color of the 'world to come.' According to these myths, the only way to find reality is to experience what the symbols originally represent within their own context and cultural background. The three worlds are not located on Earth per se but are hidden states of consciousness or being, another idea prevalent in Jewish mysticism.

In Hebrew mysticism, these three worlds of Atziluth (Emanation), Beriyah (Creation) and Yetzirah (Formation) all reside within the Earth. The mystics were capable of going to other dimensions and dispensations of time within these worlds and bringing back hidden knowledge to help their communities survive attacks and conflicts. Joel has a faint glimmer of the chain of links that bind the spiritual reality and physical reality together. All things were possible to those people who were able to interpret all universal symbols, and when seen in this context, it explains the point of this Shaman's wisdom:

The Shaman does not really fly up or down, but inside to the meanings of things. Shamanism is a magical flight into a hidden, internal, experiential dimension in which time, space, and distance as we know them, as well as the distinction between subject and object, merge into a Unity"(192).

The Oglala view is very similar and illustrates how the symbol of the circle contains everything within itself: "The circle is the symbol of time, for the day time, the night time, and the moon time are circles above the world, and year time is a circle around the border of the world. (Sword-Invocation 218)

Joel thinks, "Aha! I've got her now; humanity learned to calculate time by the cycles of the Sun and Moon, just like modern scientists use meteorology to predict the weather. Of course, they all think each of their ideas is right, and very few listen to one another. Nevertheless, she is right that people perceive these powers all over the earth in a different way, but all agree it was from a Great Spirit or Source outside them. Only modern society, in its arrogance, foolishly believes only in humanity. Joel says aloud, "Humanity is blindsided by its own reflection." Then Joel re-reads what the Shaman said regarding the process. He said a person does not fly up and down as if it appears in movies or books of fiction. Instead, they go inside the meaning of a thing or fact. Wow! Now that is deep," Joel sits back, and a big smile appears on his face as he thinks about his discovery. Black Elk, a very wise medicine man, gives testimony to the oneness and unity of the Great Spirit. These symbols activate hidden forces within other dimensions of our consciousness, and this is what fueled the ancient world before the rise of materialism and capitalism.

Symbolism plays a very crucial part in the spiritual transformation of the Nuwalli or Ruach Ha-Qadosh, the [Holy Spirit] of wisdom that acts upon the believer. Humans have the seeds of all life hidden within their own Medicine Wheel, but the seeds need the water of true spiritual reflection of a person's thoughts before the seeds flourish in this prepared soil. Joel is eager to learn more about these things and he does not realize how much time has gone by. "Our will has to influence our inner soul before it can find the right path. Perhaps the 'Red Path' Black Elk travels is the 'Way' of the Essenes and Nazarenes.

These maskillim and other scribes gave their lives to bury scrolls that contain the most cherished visions of our origins and destiny. The vision of life and a path of the 'Way' are just terms we repeat mechanically until we experience them personally." Joel crossed over from a lower plane of thought. Now, he begins to move within. Modern Christianity censors and eradicates any trace of mantic or shamanistic spirituality from the consciousness of its members. Mantic spirituality, a relic of the powerful spiritual experiences of Moses, remains misunderstood due to cultural barriers between the ancient Near Eastern and the modern Western world. The current translations of Hebrew concepts into Greek scriptures contain so many fabrications that very little resemblance to the original ideas is left. Secular Theology based on modern interpretations leaves many people at a great disadvantage because many cannot read the original languages.

There was no letter 'J' in the Hebrew texts or in Greek Bibles because it did not develop in the English alphabet until much later in history when King James used it in the 'Authorized Version' of the Bible. The Hebrew name Yahoshua became Iesous, then Jesus, from a Greek hybrid of dubious origins. Joel cannot even imagine what has really happened yet; he has only experienced a small taste of reality, but it is enough to sustain his journey for now. Timka returns home to find Joel sleeping on the floor of her library. She sees her books sprawled all over the room in disarray and wonders if Joel is going to be in a bad mood. She gently nudged him to wake him up. Joel wakes up and sees Timka standing over him, and he is excited to share what he realized. "Timka, I saw something today; I know what I have to do now! I did not understand what you were trying to tell me, but I do now. Let me tell you what you need to do to survive what is going to happen!" Timka is not used to this side of Joel, and she is not sure what to make of what he just shouted at her. "Joel, I do not need you to tell me anything about survival. You are the one who needs to learn how to survive. The only way to escape the labyrinth of religious warfare and misinformation is to research the significance of the alphabets and symbols used by previous cultures and put them to the test; those that fail to add to the harmony and balance of all life must be suspect. There are many symbols in all traditions of the world, but they do not mean the same thing at all. Each of the twenty-two letters in the Hebrew alphabet has a symbolic representation. Symbolism, when taken seriously and practiced with sincerity, becomes an alphabet of divine language. When people learn to speak this divine language, we will begin to find the point of Oneness that exists in the center of all things. Black Elk explains the same thing in his own words right here in this book:

"Peace comes with the souls of men when they realize their relationship, their oneness, with the universe and all its powers, and when they realize that at the center of the Universe dwells Wakan-Tanka and that this center is really everywhere, it is within each of us" (39).

Mainstream society exploits the concept of personal power coupled with capitalism and prosperity at the expense of the many for the grandeur of the rich. This allows individuals and nations to rationalize the oppression and domination of others perceived as inferior in their hierarchical system. Wakan-Tanka will only accept humble and meek people who care for others; those who dominate and interfere with others move further away from the true center of being. Brown states it very precisely: "In the past, humans had to protect themselves from the forces of nature, whereas today it is nature that must be protected from humans" (40). The destruction of Land-Air-Water the Mighty LAW is a great tragedy that has yet to find vindication, but victory is destined in its own time. Alexa is right about the destruction of nature and maybe even our planet. You are only excited because you made a connection with a book, but there is way more to it than that." After years of abusive criticism and arrogance from Joel, Timka reacts based on her emotional state of mind; this is what happens when she re-enters the material world. She cannot help but focus on mental paradoxes and ecological problems that have no solution that will fit all. She is so used to being a victim of the environment in some way that even if someone does have a glimmer of light in his or her eyes, she sometimes cannot see it. She is not ready to face the 'new Joel' yet. She does not trust him with her heart anymore.

"Joel shamans and mystics have seen and experienced the great destiny that hides in the center of our natures, and it is not all peaches and cream. There are hard realities to face and overcome if one wants to enter the Kingdom.

Yes, mystics and shamans sound like fascinating video game material to people now, but life is not a video game, Joel. There is a very real sense of timelessness. Still, the very real presence of past and future events actually occurs in our daily lives when we have an increased understanding of our true situation. The Tikkun is about personal practice and the correct application of mystical symbols to develop energy to live and grow during these events. Numbers have a symbol, too, but modern mathematicians have lost this knowledge. Pythagoras wrote about how the Monad and Decad are as Beginning and Ending of the reality of life and nature. Energy and Nature exhibit a logic and series of steps, according to ancient philosophers. Each number is a sequence in the creation process, just like the Hebrew letters of Sefer Yetzirah." Timka thinks to herself as she hears her voice speaking to Joel, "What is going on with Joel? This is awesome. It almost feels like old times when we were happy together and life was carefree. I like this 'new Joel,' but I am not sure where he is headed or why he was in my library sleeping on the floor. This is not like him at all." My mother always told me that there is something missing, something is wrong with the King James Version of the Bible. I wish I had been more aware and awake then, I would have asked her more questions, and now it is too late. Everything changes, and opportunities have a window; once it is closed, there is no way to reopen the same window twice.

We cannot step into the same water twice or experience life in the same way again. My mother was and still is my heroine; I remember when she helped to save a First Nation reservation that entrepreneurs wanted to transform into a golf course. I was so proud of her! She told me many times that "Everyone has some type of religious belief, but very few really obey or practice living the terms behind the convictions of their beliefs. However, due to the extreme persecution of Native Americans over the years, it is a form of survival for them to preserve and practice their ancient beliefs. Many were lost in the battle for the 'new land', but not many survived horrendous atrocities during the 19th century. During the revolution, there was a time of great change because of not only industry, railroads, and Colonialism but also because of the rise of international inhumanity of man-to-man. Through methodical, spiritually destructive corruption of biblical principles and the intrusion of unlearned, unfaithful men, it brought about the onset of mechanical enslavement of cultures and people with the application of science, intellectual prowess, and technological power. Native Americans and life on the reservations was but another form of slavery; other leaders of the new land were still in the process of exploring what to do with the existing slave trade in the South, and others were deciding how to do away with the political foundation established by the founding Fathers of this country. Freemasons divided among themselves, some stayed in America, and others went to France. The rest of the known world was already conquered, and this land, our country now, stolen from one of the last ancient civilizations descended from the tribes of Israel, was the last frontier. This unsullied paradise was like a sleeping land that many countries were compelled to awaken from its pristine innocence. |The First Nation maintained a country that seemed like a Garden of Eden, and they maintained a balance between horticulture and the land. They had a great respect for wildlife, trees, and the water. These were all mainstays of any civilization, and only a crazy man would destroy this balance. Native Americans learned to adapt to the major changes in their political, social, and economic lifestyles and actually found a way to excel in the spirit world where others have failed. Many Semitic people continue to outlive the various pogroms, death camps, and social ostracism so characteristic of the twentieth century. As we go further away from the 'beginning,' we fall further into our own dark natures. Names and symbols are imperative for identifying things in one's environment and in one's spiritual journey.

Everything has a meaning in some way, but not all will seek to find a harmonious vision. Not everyone will understand the various rituals enacted by various cultures, and yet, we all have the ability to be a bridge that provides a platform to receive universal truths experienced by the ancients. Timka could envision how the rocks and trees would cry out, if they could, to tell of all the awful deaths and tribulations that occurred in the name of civilization and the advancement of an artificial future world. She cannot trust Joel yet, and Alexa is only beginning to experience what it is to hear the voice. She feels so alone, even though she has them in her life. She longs for a sense of community and security, but it is so hard to attain. The pain in her heart heals moment by moment when she soars into the higher heavens and tries to remember the things she sees and hears in order to bring down a flicker of firelight that burns in her soul.

ORIGINS OF ADAM

Joel gets up and grows confused by Timka's response to finding him in her library. "Doesn't she realize that I am trying to help her? All I was trying to do was show her that I learned how Native Americans revere holiness and power, and they practice right action and thoughts tempered with effective behavior. I cannot help it if the world is out of balance. She did not even listen to me; she was so lost in her other world that I was afraid I might lose her forever. She needs a taste of reality and guidance. One without the other is out of balance and, therefore, considered evil. It is this sense of balance and harmony that pervades our very existence and yet escapes our grasp. How can we reach out and hold onto the reality of an invisible world? This is why many Christians thrown into the lion's den in Rome, were murdered for believing they had entered an invisible world. I do not know what to do. I am trying to learn how to help her the best way I can, and nothing seems to work; she cannot hear me anymore.

What is happening to Joel is what happens to many people today. It is a very hard thing to break free and take back your individuality in order to think for yourself. Society is the modern voice; the status quo speaks the loudest and has a big influence over everyone. What is important to learn here is that many aspects of apocalyptic mysticism can help interpret scientific facts in order to elucidate the profound existence and validity of the Supreme Being. With both science and spiritual teaching working as one, it becomes more solid and tangible.

Joel hears a thought arise in his mind- he knows that he did not think this thought, "Today, science and religion is a divided house when it comes to the idea of cosmology and the pattern that Moses saw when he was given the knowledge to design and create a version in the wilderness. The Supreme Being is obscure to people now, in the aftermath of different theories and hypotheses, not only evolution and recent developments in genetic research leave little use for a Creator. Scientists can now clone the life they examine. Can they clone our souls or help us find out who we are before it is too late?" Joel seems more serious now; he was so excited earlier, and Timka did not respond in the way he expected. "I just do not understand her at all sometimes," he thought, "I do not know what to do. If I say something is good, she will say it is bad; if I am happy, she seems to be sad – I do not understand why we cannot meet in the middle.

Alexa feels that something is going on with Joel; she wonders why he seems interested in Timka's books all of a sudden. Her heart grows heavy; life is very hard – why is it so hard – she hears her own thoughts talking to her heart, trying to console her. One of her thoughts said, "The 'Origin' of man may seem a very confusing idea when only viewed through the eyes of 'religion versus science' when there is such a 'controversial issue' between them. When we want to conduct a polite discussion of wars, we call them 'controversial issues' and even the oldest historical documents say the first war began in Heaven. This is not something readily taught today in most religious groups, but there are documents recording an event that very few individuals believe. It is possible that the validation of scientific study would only serve to solidify the foundation of spiritual thought if given the chance.

Actually, science and spirituality should support each other, if it were not for the archaic practices of modern religion and the dynamics of scientific imperialism. Cooperative ideology does not have a chance to share the spotlight, and competition cannot afford to compromise power for the sake of life. One discipline, be it science or religion, or science and spirituality, cannot dominate or destroy the other. Science is a productive and necessary tool that goes back to the beginning of civilization and it has now found the means to go back beyond time. Science without conscience is like a wild animal in the jungle of intellectual sophistry, battling with young minds, seeking to find out who they are before they begin to enter the arena of life and survive. Everyone wants to know when the end will come, and if there will be an end to all this oppression and inequality; no matter what people do, nothing seems to matter or change the situation that people are trapped in. No matter how many groups stand up for their particular rights or special interests, all will still suffer because, without understanding and wisdom, the people perish from within.

Alexa grows very self-conscious now. She feels some kind of negative energy in her thoughts that seems to give her an increase of anxiety, even though she can feel a sense of peace in her heart. She hears herself thinking about things she never knew before. "The importance of finding the correct calculation and interpretation of 'time' is imperative to understand how prophecy and history run parallel to eternity. There are many ways of calculating time and not all methods agree. The calendar can never accurately reflect the solar movement of the earth and planets, because time is always losing time. Leap year is evidence of this phenomenon. There are different ways to interpret the years. In some Kabbalah circles, the 'thousands' designate life in the 'world to come'; other mystics discuss the seven thousand years of apocalyptic literature as stages in a process, and some believe there are seven thousand years of time before the end of the creation. The Hebrew Mosaic calendar apparently began 4004 years before the birth of Christianity; does that mean these first historians were interested in only recording a measurement of time in space? Maybe they penned the prophecies they knew would one day explain the purpose and meaning of human history." She stands there, moving back and forth like something is moving her from within; a pendulum swings her forward and backward, her thoughts begin to expand with a new sense of wonder, and she actually feels a tingle of light flicker in her eyes.

The voice continues to speak to her, and she is not afraid anymore. She wants to listen. She asked a question, "Is Genesis a story of how creation takes place in six days?" The voice answered, "It all depends on what you understand about the 'six days.' Some say it is about how six directions of space converge at a single point in time. Others teach that the entire creation took place in six thousand years. Christianity refers to the center point as the Sabbath or seventh day. After what scribes, editors, and apologists have done, the book of Genesis has very little in common with Sefer Bereshit besides words. Science will and does lead the way to discovering more about our origin, but it also wants to describe history. Scientists use history to explain evolution; in apocalyptic literature, prophecy creates history. The word religion comes from the word 'Religare,' which translated means 'to be bound together,' and religion certainly has become a binding, not to mention a restrictive force in the world today. Spiritual concepts should walk side by side with science." Alexa, is amazed that she could really hear something or someone speaking to her. "Who is this person?"

Something strange also begins to happen when Joel begins to reason within himself, and he hears a different type of voice say: "Stop battling against Timka. Try to focus on overcoming the force that enchants Timka. He starts to wonder, "Have I explored all possibilities?" "Timka is missing something important; I just know that something is taking her away from me," Joel remembers things that Timka used to say years ago about etymology and history; he found it all so boring. What he is studying now seems so much more interesting to him, but he finds it hard to stop now, yet he hears her voice clearly in his thoughts talking to him. Am I going insane? What is happening to me? I knew this literature would lead to something bad. No wonder people used to burn books; I understand why some books should be burned." Timka would always say to me, "Joel, the origin and history of words teach us about our history. Religious creationism sees a limitation of six thousand years, and evolutionists see an infinite number of years; both systems are near-sighted when it comes to holistic idealism. Should we allow a number of years to stand in the way of understanding the nature of the Universe and the Supreme Being? Time and creation only seem to oppose each other when science goes up against spirituality." She always explains the books of Moses, but she seems to have forgotten about all the other teachings in the world," thought Joel.

"The attempt to dismiss the Genesis myth because science cannot reconcile its calculation of time to biblical time is redundant. Scientists seek to find the truth; spiritualists seek to accept the truth. It is the same truth. We need to know this and end the war between these two systems." Joel agrees with the facts of science, but he also disagrees with some of the interpretations of scientists, just as he disagrees with some interpretations of spiritualists. Webster's Dictionary says the word "origin" comes from the Latin 'origo' from 'orior,' which means to "rise or become visible" and implies the idea of something coming into being. Origin literally means something evolves in order to come to life. Evolutionists did not discover this fact first because it had already developed in ancient Near Eastern sources. He wants to know what it is that comes into existence; it seems to Joel that life itself exists now; what else is there besides this?"

Beginning of the Origin

Joel begins to wander in his mind; he feels sure that he is able to get his relationship back on track, yet he feels the weight of what will happen if he doesn't help Timka before something worse happens. Something is rising up in Joel; he does not know that there is a particular Voice, which many people can no longer hear. There are many voices calling out to innocent bystanders like those that the Greek sirens positioned in strategic places in lower waters. He decides to follow another line of thought; he looks on the shelf this time and finds Sefer Bereshith, which contains a different analysis that describes how Adam was born in the Garden of Eden. Adam emerges from within the Adamah, a particular type of land. There were other types of Earth seven in all, with names such as Tebel and Eretz. Joel reads for a while but manages not to fall asleep; for the first time, he is able to understand that some Hebraic doctrines explain Adam's origin in purely mystical obscure terms meant to convey esoteric gnosis to initiated students of the Torah. To others in orthodox doctrines, Adam is a generic figure who is part of the creation, not the Creation. However, the teaching regarding 'The Way' has an entirely different view of Adam. Paul spoke about a Second Adam, why would there need to be a Second Adam? Joel thought to himself. If these 'origin' theories and stories seek to give meaning and substance to our life and existence in some way, why is it so confusing to understand? Nevertheless, when science rears its head and says to cut off all the other heads, we should all become very concerned. Whenever one lowers its head and accepts the other head, we should all marvel at the miraculous evolution of thought. Acceptance and true inclusion is what allows life to become."

The fact that man may have derived from a primitive species neither proves nor disproves the role of a Creator. There is a scientific evolution of man and an eschatological evolution of man. Both are systems of growth and development; when humans stop seeking to learn and control their environment, their brains will die. Brains must have this energy to survive. In the same way, the earth thrives on the energy of the four forces that surround it, like the four rivers around the Garden of Eden. Our brain's design is to be on a quest. All children ask questions and expect answers. We all want adventure and miracles in our lives, but often, we neglect the necessary prerequisites for obtaining the prize! Scientists and spiritualists are like children asking hard questions and sometimes not liking the answers. Joel graduated with 'life experience' and has now entered the first level of the Kingdom.

His victory overcomes his blindness, but he remains torn by indecision and must face his own voices (negative thoughts, fears, doubts, and worries) that seek to overcome Timka before he can really hear the Son of Man and clearly perceive His Voice. Like, homo erectus, the species that began to walk upright, if we can't learn to raise our head up to another level of understanding and acceptance, we will never evolve or be able to 'rise' above a previous level of growth. Ultimately, humanity will have to stoop or slump to fit into a version of scientific reality and artificial intelligence designed to enslave and indoctrinate the innocents. Instead of stooping to see the reality of the Universe, we must look up and aspire to enter the higher space dimensions. Our Universe may only be one membrane or dimension within 26. Joel begins to wonder what any of this has to do with the average person, who is not equipped with the spiritual tools to comprehend the first four basic dimensions. How can reading the Book of Enoch help anyone now that we live in an age of an Information Superhighway with an electronic platform that has taken the place of the Greek Academy, which admits global voices where debate is expected, not answers - this is a travesty." The mystics and scientists of the past were far more intelligent than I thought. Alexa keeps talking about how Witten's M-Theory predicts that our Universe may be lower than the other ten and that we really live in the eleventh dimension. Human consciousness seems to have devolved instead of evolved, and how low will it go before it exists no more? Will human consciousness be stolen from people without their knowledge?"

He remembers Alexa coming in one day all excited and big eyed over something she learned. She said, "Scientists currently cannot reach outside the current membrane to experience these higher levels of reality, but there may be another way to experience these dimensions. It might be within the reach of ancient scientific concepts found in the Sefer Yetsirah, a text that explains how to connect the ancient temple of the cosmos with the invisible and visible Torahs and the ten dimensions modern quantum physicists are beginning to understand as a set of membranes. There are very similar patterns and requirements found between these things that warrant further attention in order to explore the nature of the mysterious energy that brought the Universe into existence. Michio Kaku, author of Hyperspace, says that,

Most people who have not been trained in physics probably think of what physicists do as a question of incredibly complicated calculations, but that is not really the essence of it. The essence of it is that physics is about concepts, wanting to understand the concepts and the principles by which the world works. (152)

Alexa was talking about concepts of physics; what does physics have to do with Enoch? Joel can now understand

100

Timka's infatuation with Gnosis. He thinks to himself, "Both she and Alexa see something else behind these texts because when I read them; I do not draw the same conclusions. There is a way to make sense of really hard concepts if we understand what symbols represent in different systems. On the other hand, many others think the complicated mystical words are beyond their reach or desire. Yet, these very 'words' or Logos hold the answers to the origin and construction of the Universe and human souls. Joel, like many others in the modern world, did not see any value in Gnostic texts; he seemed to focus on accepted or canonical texts. He finds it ironic those scientists have a four-fold description of M-Theory, because it reminds him of the Tetragrammaton.

M-Theory stands for Mother, Mystery, Matrix, and even Magic, according to Witten in a PBS broadcast of the revolutionary subject of the century, the Elegant Universe. Scientists are divided over the implications of string theory; many have a hard time accepting mystical concepts intrinsic to the theory, and others choose to call it a philosophy rather than science. Joel sees that even within science, there are various opinions and theories on the nature of reality. Regardless of how M- Theory is taught, it is valuable at a time like now to open up new vistas and avenues to explore the ten divine realms ancient mystics described as heavens hundreds of centuries ago. Each heaven has a firmament or brane. Joel has a strange thought…" Do the prayers of ancient prophets continue to influence the development of the Universe?

He hears or rather feels an impression that announces: "Yes, whenever we realize the promises and hopes they cherished, these prayers can continue to guide and protect us as we enter the infinite depths of the mysterious Kingdom inside us. Negative connotations associated with the terms Kabbalah, Cabala, and Qabalah have had a disastrous influence on this literature. Unfortunately, as a result, very little serious scholarship or public attention is given to these texts.

Terms can be misleading and deceptive. The term 'qibbel' originally meant 'to receive' it was later disguised under the word 'tradition'. The mysterious angelic teachers give us the insight to understand biblical events through the unfolding of human history. History is the mystery destined to unfold at the end of the age. Many texts found at Qumran outline the details of the war between the 'Sons of Light' and the 'Sons of Darkness.' What is not always readily apparent is how the war is fought.

The Sons of Light fight an almost unseen war through a constant vigil to discover and expose the deceptive teachings that rise like thorns and thistles scratching and tearing at our minds and hearts, turning us against one another." Joel stops breathing for a moment; he feels himself lifted up from the earth, and he cannot see anything; he is full of wonder. "Can you hear me? He said to the air around him. That is amazing you can hear my thoughts! – Who are you? Joel realized that many teachers and prophets rise up in various ways, but they minister falsehoods, propaganda, and fear disguised as misinformation that leads to conspiratorial paranoia in people. They use the television, radio, or building to teach things that generate more paranoia and fear of others until the only real enemy left becomes themselves. He knew that even the term 'conspiracy' means different things to different groups, yet all members, regardless of affiliation, would say it is 'others' who are the true enemies.

This gives people the sense of having to live in fear of many imagined evils from a variety of authoritative speakers that may or may not really be credible. Joel thought, "Even Paul said we fight not against flesh and blood. Wow!" Joel's experience of realized eschatology begins to transform his soul; he can see now what has happened. As his thoughts begin to show him pictures and images of things within seconds he never saw or knew before concerning the mystery of the Son of Man, Joel sees the Throne in the picture over Timka's bed. He sees the Man of Light sitting there, his eyes of fire looking in all directions all at once. Joel drops the book, and he seems to be caught in suspended animation; he stops breathing and is free now of any thoughts.......

During his journey, he learns that Enoch prepares a small group of people by sending them a seven-fold teaching that shows them how to 'receive' knowledge concerning the secret mystery of existence and how to avoid the great lie taught at the end of the age. Spiritual guidance transmits from the medium of 'Chockmah-Wisdom', which angelic beings deliver to those people able to discover the hidden Kingdom. The Son of Man [Ben Adam] is the one who 'receives' and 'gives' salvation to everyone; as John says, the light shines in the world, but it is not comprehended by our dark conscience. According to Joseph Dan,

"Kabbalah is an abbreviation of 'secret tradition concerning the divine world" (Dan, The Heart and the Fountain 8).

In Apocalyptic literature, the need for a human mediator is not necessary once the 'revelation' of the prophecy is apparent to the reader. Many ancient and modern mystics refuse to teach about this or explain it; one has to live it to experience it, and this is how it became a hidden teaching. However, its destiny remains to be revealed.

APOCALYPTIC TEXTS: DECONSTRUCTING THE TABOO

Now I know this mystery: For they (the sinners) shall alter the just verdict (the word of truth), and many sinners will take it to heart, they will speak evil words and lie, and they will invent fictitious stories and write out my scriptures on the basis of their own speech (1 Enoch 104.10-11).

Timka opened up to a passage in 1 Enoch; it is an important passage to her. She knows that this is exactly what happened already, and it is up to her to 'receive' through the Words of Messiah the lost meaning of Enoch's books. Timka discovered many things by reading the forbidden texts. At first, it was hard to find them; only certain libraries made them accessible, and they did not circulate for public use. She remembers going to a religious bookstore with Alexa, and she asked the clerk if they had the Book of Enoch; the man started yelling at them. "No! We do not have that kind of book here; we will never have that book here! That book is evil …." His face grew red, and his eyes were bulging. I said, "Ok, thank you, and then we both started laughing and ran out of the store. We have had some very strange experiences just trying to find the so-called forbidden books. It is so hard to reach the public with this information that is so important; m-theory predicts there are ten dimensions of hyperspace; even so, scientists cannot reach or touch them. There are things out of reach.

The ladder of angelic communication is what Enoch, Esdras, and Baruch used to travel to higher dimensions, but now they are part of the angels that continue to climb into the 'heights' beyond the fourth dimension. Apocalyptic texts are the result of reflection and understanding on the part of responsible individuals who sought to restore material edited by earlier scribes. The censorship of these ancient sacred words and ideas is something that the prophets of Israel had to contend with, and even John spoke out against it vehemently,

I warn everyone who hears the words of the prophecy of this book: if anyone adds to them, God will add to that person the plagues described in this book; if anyone takes away from the words of this book of this prophecy, God will take away that person's share in the tree of life and in the holy city (Harper and Row (Revelation 22:18-19).

"Very few individuals heed this message," thought Timka. Many apocalyptic books used during the early Christian era were 'taken away' and literally cut out of the modern Bible. As a result, this crucial knowledge barely reaches people seeking to find some meaning and help in the dark days that lie ahead. Timka reads a passage from II Esdras; he re-wrote a set of ninety-four books to replace the Torah burned previously during a war:

I will light in your heart the lamp of understanding, which shall not be put out until what you are about to write is finished. And when you have finished, some things you shall make public, and some you shall deliver in secret to the wise. (Metzger, Oxford Annotated Apocrypha 2 Esdras 14:26-27)

Twenty-four books of the ninety-four survived the scissors of censorship, but the remaining 'suspect' seventy books remain locked away until the seventh day. Biblical scholars and academics seem to sequester them. Most of the books Timka was able to find were only available to seminary students, scholars, and 'mystics.' Apparently, the [70] original books comprised the [66] books of the Old and New Testament along with Enoch, II Esdras, Barnabas, and the Shepherd of Hermas.

The '70' hidden books was a secret phrase to refer to this literature applied by some unknown group now. They want us to know how the books share a common story of the suffering righteous ones guided by a Unique Cherub in human form that shows them about a figure named Enoch who becomes Metatron. He helps people before the flood and he is destined to redeem those of us after the flood. Who will still the roaring voices of accusation that continue to warn everyone to beware of Enoch? Remember the two sets of water that Timka describes; the waters are not what they appear to be. Deconstructing the taboo of apocalyptic literature is a very hard task. Timka clearly heard a voice reminding her of all these things she already knew. Timka speaks to the Voice, "Time does have a way of redirecting our memory of experiences and events; they seem to lose their form and morph into emotions and thoughts that change our life repeatedly. We forget what was once important, and we remember what we should already know."

Journey into Angelic Mysteries

Joel decides to research a new topic. He is not sure why, but following his intuition, he is led to an idea he had once before. Timka always talks about some kind of 'mystery' she seems obsessed with about something that is 'secret and mysterious' and must remain hidden away. Joel does not realize yet that the apocalyptic genre of 'Apocrypha' is a field devoted to visions that humans receive from an angelic messenger. The prophet Esdras receives a historical record of the events before Adam right down to the 'end of days' that he writes down in his book. The authors of the text use this as a literary device to encode the texts with information otherwise considered 'secret'; the human prophet or seer writes down information transmitted by angelic figures to be transmitted to those able to read and decipher the texts.

He decides to go to the library, something he rarely does, Timka's library that is, the one where he fell asleep on the floor. He finds D.S. Russell's The Method and Message of Jewish Apocalyptic. As he flips through the pages, his eyes begin to widen, "Wow," he thought, "This is complicated but interesting. The seers take the name of an ancient figure such as Adam or Enoch, these names serve as a code word to future readers. However, detractors insist this is where the term 'Pseudepigrapha' or 'false letters' originate. Others say there is no secret chain of tradition that handed down any books from Adam to Enoch. Mere ignorance is, unfortunately, not the only reason why a group of authorities removed these texts. In fact, according to the content of the books, their removal is a sign to the Elect. 1Enoch 104:10-11 describes the neglect expected by the authors of these books; some also expected individuals to find light and hope in them:

"Again know another mystery! The righteous and the wise shall be given the Scriptures of joy, for truth and great wisdom" (Charlesworth 1Enoch 104:12-13).

Joel is beginning to see there is an amazing mystery.

The major texts, such as Enoch I-II-III, II Esdras, II Baruch, and the Apocalypse of Abraham, mention the fact that 'hidden books' exist. Joel thinks, "We must listen to the books written for the benefit of this generation if we are to understand our place in Christianity." He experiences many different feelings in his head and body, and his thoughts and emotions seem alive. A light shined in the room and lit the whole room up with a vivid yellow light that began to grow brighter and brighter. Joel falls to the floor in suspended animation. His soul enters the Kingdom, but flesh and blood cannot ever enter.

The religious experience attributed to the pseudonymous seer reflects the actual religious experience that the author underwent or of which he knew intimately. This may be true of many of the other Jewish apocalypses of the Second Temple period. (Stone, On Reading an Apocalypse 73)

Timka seems to have had an effect on Alexa and Joel. Authorities in the field explain how each seer undergoes a

107

psychological experience, and traces of it remain in the text; this experience is only complete when the reader has a mystical experience of some kind. Adela Yarbro Collins, at McCormick Theological Seminary, offers an explanation, 'Apocalypse' is a genre of revelatory literature with a narrative framework in which a revelation is mediated by an otherworldly being to a human recipient" (Collins 62). Collins explains that the content of the disclosure relates to eschatological concepts and journeys to another world. We journey to a hidden land called the 'world to come' here on earth through knowledge. Apocalyptic literature is 'revelatory' in order to inform and educate readers to understand history and take action for social justice. Once the reader has entered the world of these ancient prophets and can hear their message and decode the hidden meaning, they have actually entered the Timeless Kingdom.

The prophets were able to see the prophetic fulfillment of things they saw and heard in the divine world. People do not really believe that any of this is true; that is the main reason it remains hidden. However, something extraordinary happens when readers realize the things the Hebrew prophets foresaw; ancient prophets are able to see into our own age, which is their future. In Figure 6, the 'ladder' of angelic communication is made of a Host of angels that send a message to this prophet that enables him to travel to other dimensions.

Figure 6 Jacob's Ladder- Dictionary of Angels
Gustaff

Not all revelations come in dreams; some revelations come through human comprehension of divine mysteries. Some dreams contain the ingredients of the 'end.' Eschatology is a term that refers to a branch of biblical knowledge regarding both 'things of the end' and of the 'world to come.' The biblical theme that this world is passing away and the new world is coming is a very familiar idea in canonical New Testament books. However, this idea originated before most of the Christian texts were written in the late 70's and 80's A.D. Some apocalyptic texts contain a framework of historical events that parallel biblical prophecies, such as those in the books of Daniel, Jeremiah, and Isaiah. Daniel is one of the only apocalyptic texts that remain in the Bible. In the New Testament, the book of Revelation or 'Apocalypse' is extant. The literature came to be associated with 'things of the end' when originally the word 'Apocalypse' referred to an unveiling or a continual revealing of some unknown divine phenomena.

When a person continues to witness the unveiling of mysteries embedded in these 'hidden books,' he or she has had an experience of the 'new world.' The supposed mythic images come to life and begin to manifest as historical events in the world of time when we read and understand the texts in their own cultural context.

Revealing the Hidden Things

Timka does not understand why she is so interested, and other people seem to have very little interest. Alexa always tells her to stop worrying about them. She can hear Alexa now, "Girl, you need to slow down; you have to focus on what is being shown to you; stop trying to teach anybody else. The world is full of confusion; if someone is going to learn, it will be because that person wants to learn. It is impossible to show this invisible reality to others; they will try to lock you up, as Joel said. Even Alexa does not encourage Timka to share the information, but she cannot help it if she receives it and does not give it, this interrupts the flow. Alexa does not concern herself with the lives of others; she thinks everyone has their own manifest destiny. She still has some confusing thoughts surrounding the words "apocalyptic" and "apocalypse," according to Klaus Koch in the article "What Is Apocalyptic"? "Apocalypse" is an adjective that has nothing to do with the current connotations associated with the idea of "apocalypse" as a noun. Many doomsday cults misappropriated the word, and this has resulted in an unfounded prejudice by many today.

She is amazed that the original Greek "apokalypsis," which means 'revelation' is now associated with "The book of Revelation, i.e., secret divine disclosures about the end of the world and the heavenly state" (Hanson Visionaries and Their Apocalypses 16 1972). Books that contain prophecies about the 'end' have been lumped together under one term, 'apocalyptic,' even though not all apocalypses were apocalyptic in nature. Modern research has revealed a variety of texts with different functions. Christopher Rowland explains the central feature of an 'apocalypse':

One of the features which characterize eschatological passages in the apocalyptic literature is the way in which a period of distress is said to precede the coming of the Messiah and the New Age. (Rowland, The Open Heaven 33). Alexa is at odds with many modern teachings and the way they seem to corrupt the message. Alexa allows her thoughts to speak, something she will never tell Timka. "Timka continues to read all these different things about Theosophy, Kabbalah, Alchemy, and Quantum Mechanics; I do not understand how she is so open to all these concepts. Surrounding the words "apocalyptic" and "apocalypse," according to Klaus Koch in the article "What Is Apocalyptic"? "Apocalypse" is an adjective that has nothing to do with the current connotations associated with the idea of "apocalypse" as a noun.

Many doomsday cults misappropriated the word, and this has resulted in an unfounded prejudice by many today. She is amazed that the original Greek "apokalypsis," which means 'revelation' is now associated with "The book of Revelation, i.e., secret divine disclosures about the end of the world and the heavenly state" (Hanson Visionaries and Their Apocalypses 16 1972). Books that contain prophecies about the 'end' have been lumped together under one term, 'apocalyptic,' even though not all apocalypses were apocalyptic in nature. Modern research has revealed a variety of texts with different functions. Christopher Rowland explains the central feature of an 'apocalypse':

"One of the features which characterizes eschatological passages in the apocalyptic literature is the way in which a period of distress is said to precede the coming of the Messiah and the New Age" (Rowland the Open Heaven 33). Alexa is at odds with many modern teachings and the way they seem to corrupt the message. Alexa allows her thoughts to speak, something she will never tell Timka. "Timka continues to read all these different things about Theosophy, Kabbalah, Alchemy, and Quantum Mechanics; I do not understand how she is so open to all these concepts. It is as if something drives her, some unseen force, to find something, but she does not know what it is yet. No matter how much she learns, she must have more. She seems to be ever-learning and never coming to see the truth. Why does she feel the need to tell?

She picks up one of her favorite books by Mircea. "Timka cannot see that the essential message of the various texts has been ignored and the call for wisdom and mercy forgotten. Eliade Mircea, a respected biblical scholar, states, "Apocalypticism is almost by definition preoccupied with the revelation of secret knowledge" (Mircea Apocalypse 341 1987). Mircea categorizes this 'secret knowledge' from another world into two main types: historical apocalyptic, which gives order and meaning to events on earth about a hidden secret plan of the Creator, and the otherworldly apocalyptic type outlines details of the seer's journey to heaven. There are ten heavens or realms, and the third heaven contains Paradise. Apocalyptic concepts express themselves as social phenomena when readers are encouraged to take action in the community in a positive way. Nevertheless, there are not many readers of this literature; Timka is isolated in an invisible world, which others may never experience until the end of their world.

John Collins makes a very significant point in the article 'Apocalypse':

The kind of knowledge displayed in Apocalypticism is a total reversal of the kind of knowledge known from scripture" (Collins Encyclopedia of Religion 340).

Collins' contrasts of the limited knowledge of Job with the super knowledge of Enoch are a great example of the different intent of each text:

We find that almost everything that in Job's eyes appears to be an insurmountable intellectual challenge opens up like a book in the case of the 'Enoch' visionaries. (341)

Alexa begins to hear or rather feels a new sensation due to this line of thought. She remembers a conversation she and Timka had a few years ago regarding the canonical text of Job; the figure asks the Creator many questions but receives very few answers, whereas Enoch receives an encyclopedic array of knowledge. In my opinion, Collins warns readers of the need to be aware of different points of view. Apocalyptic texts contrast canonical scriptures such as Isaiah or Jeremiah. He considers this problematic in terms of how mainstream society will view the texts and the fate they will ultimately suffer if not accepted by mainstream society. Alexa agrees.

Alexa thinks to herself, "Timka would say that people who would benefit from this literature are those who are interested in biblical traditions of the ancient Near East, such as Judaism, Christianity, and Islam. People who want to know more about their inner spiritual tradition. This literature is not for violent social movements that fight for political change." At that moment, Alexa stops thinking mid-stream, and she hears a voice, "Daniel says the Maskillim will teach others to be passive and resist all forms of war and violence. This is a sign of the Kingdom in them. The authors intend for the texts to be universal in scope: "The members of the non-Israelite nations will also partake of the coming salvation" (Koch 26). Unfortunately, many groups use biblical ideas to condemn one another when they do not see eye to eye on religious doctrines and or customs. Koch has found that: "Every apocalypse expresses anxiety for the whole of mankind."(26) this is an idea that modern society can definitely benefit from.

Enoch, the protagonist, Master of Astronomy and Meteorology, records pertinent information in books, for he sees and learns of the future conflicts and terrors that will take place on Earth. This is why Collins warns readers of the two parallel sets of ideas running throughout the canonical and non-canonical texts in order to avoid misinterpreting the author's intent.

One set informs an audience that is capable of understanding the secrets. The other set is the official version for public use; this set is known as the Bible. One set lays down a particular tradition to follow, and the other set contains a spiritual message of great urgency regarding carefully buried scrolls written to preserve the continuity of hidden secrets shown to those capable of ascending to heaven. The authors of the texts use many literary devices to encode readers with 'gnosis,' specialized information; the prophet or seer writes down this information that is pertinent to each community. This otherworldly knowledge is the basis of the ascent experience, and it was a common practice among ancient Hebrew mystics." Alexa closed the book and said see what I mean; here we go again. "Not everyone can experience these voices, words, and colors flashing across their eyes. My eyes feel like they are burning, and I saw my own eye sockets as I looked out of them!" What is happening to us? What do my eyes have to do with these texts? How can books have this kind of effect on me?"

Mystic Eyes

There is a tradition of 'handing down' knowledge that continues as each modern reader begins to 'receive' a new worldview or ethos, one that more readily reflects the concerns of the ancient prophet Enoch. This is the purpose of apocalyptic literature, and angelic mediators reveal it to those who are willing and able to hear the story. How does Timka know this? The Son of Man appeared to her thoughts in the twinkle of an eye. Our eyes are made to reflect and refract light; without Light, our eyes would see only shadows. Once the story of Messiah is learned, a new set of 'spiritual eyes' begin to envision the same events that occurred in the angelic realm before time began. In terms of its historical development, apocalyptic developed derived from a central branch of Wisdom literature that had its inception in Israel, but has now grown into a very complex system of conflicting categories. There are many traditional cultural ways and processes involved when interpreting Hebrew literature. It all depends on what the reader is looking for and what methods may be employed, but the texts speak of a different meaning that still eludes those with sophisticated gematrias and number codes and notarikon to distill inner secrets from the Hebrew letters. Many are still consulting angelic names and days of the week, but not in the way taught by Henoch, the 7th from Adam. The biblical personalities, starting with Adam to Enoch, represent a set of events (experiences) (1-7) that take place in all of us. When it does take place, the Chamber of Treasuries guarded by Metatron, the Angel of the Covenant, will open, and the Spirit of Reality is free once again. Everyone is looking for a key to some treasure on earth, but this unique key finds you. No one finds the key.

Alexa was not sleeping, but she was lying down after her eyes started burning and tearing from something she realized caused her thoughts to stop in motion; she had to lie down and rest because it felt like the room was spinning. She noticed that this experience affected her whole body. Lately, she does not know she falls asleep when she studies sometimes. Another time, she had a dream of a hand and fingers pointing to pages in a book written in a foreign language she could not read. She heard herself saying to them, "I can't read it." "That was years ago, she thought, why did I think of that now? Alexa entered the Kingdom not too long after Timka, but only this moment became receptive to it in her heart; you see, the mind can tell you about faith, but it is the heart that will experience that faith. Like Alexa, at first, does not understand, most people who think of the term 'apocalypse' associate it with the 'end days', and they envision religious zealots fighting against the secular world. They, too, do not understand.

Timka knows that Apocalyptic seems to have developed as a result of political and religious persecution of local Jewish and Christian peasants during the rise of Alexander and his conquest of the empire, but it may have already existed in oral forms of Torah handed down in the near east, before the time of Moses. She remembers telling Alexa about the invisible Torah that existed before the creation of the world. She was so excited to share this with someone, and Alexa seemed sincerely interested to hear about the Name and the Torah, even though her family is Christian and she could not read Hebrew, nor desired to read it. Timka told Alexa, "Apocalyptic texts recount historical events in terms of a prophetic clock, "The author of the earliest real apocalypses, the book of Daniel, was composed during the climax of the Maccabean struggle for freedom in 164 B.C., before the death of Antiochus IV" (Martin, Hengel Judaism and Hellenism 176) most critics associate it with times of oppression. This period, characterized by revolution, religious zealotry, political intrigue, and the desire for world conquest, is typical of how the prophets describe civilization. This is the foundation of the modern world." She remembers how Alexa just kept asking her, "How do you remember all these things?"

Timka would just keep talking; she also learned new things when she talked; she loved to share Wisdom, and whenever she had a chance to share, she was happy to help complete the circle. Timka continued sharing the history of apocalyptic with Alexa, "The historical period of Christian apocalyptic developed over the course of three centuries: 'Early Christian' is understood as belonging to the first three centuries of the Common Era" (Collins Early Christian Apocalypse 61). There has been very little "systematic" research done on apocalyptic books (61). The majority of apocalyptic texts were composed between 300 B.C. and 300 A.D.; Klaus Koch has a more modest estimate:

During the period between 200 B.C. and A.D. 100 – that is to say, the late Israelite period- in which the mass of the apocalyptic writings came into being, Israel had an appearance of anything but unity, whether in Palestine or in the Diaspora (Koch What is Apocalyptic? 19).

Timka was quick to point out that Koch is expressing his own opinion based on theological criticism and archaeology; Timka told Alexa that many biblical critics see something completely different than the message of the texts. "Alexa, for example, a standard dogma was not the main thing that concerned the very earliest communities; it was later, when the fear of free thought began to rear its ugly head that the canon became a tool of censorship. Koch explains that the extent of the church's absorption into Hellenism throughout its formative years determined the decline of apocalyptic writings in the church. Hebrew concepts changed places with Greek philosophy. However, this did not only happen in the church; "The same process of elimination took place in the early Judaism organized by the Rabbis after A.D. 70" (18). The Second Temple fell in 70 A.D., and the early Christian communities were suspected of heresy and treason. Many banned the misunderstood 'hidden books' considered dangerous enemies of the Empire; eventually, many were burned in the pogroms and lost forever. The crucifixion of the Messiah occurred in 33 A.D., and within 40 years, many of the original disciples were no more, and that world of the Temple did come to an end. By 325 A.D., when European Christianity became the dominant religion, many of the original ideas of these books were censored through discrimination of anything Semitic or Hebrew. The closing of the canon was destined to shut the door to future revelations." Alexa looked at Timka for a long time before she said anything – Timka could tell she was

117

having a hard time listening to some of the things she told her. It seems that when people are very religious, they are always afraid of something they should not read or learn based on their particular denomination; Timka was used to this; it happens all the time and gives rise to many debates rather than completed circles. She is sensitive to some things that affect others, and she tried to change the topic since it was making Alexa uncomfortable.

Timka changed her tone and said, "You know what? Language is also a barrier; most people living in the first century spoke two or three languages, although not all could read. The texts were originally written in Hebrew and Aramaic; the temple Priests used Hebrew, and Aramaic was the language of peasants. The Messiah spoke in Aramaic, and most of his speeches were in Aramaic. Most people today cannot read Hebrew or Aramaic and, therefore, have to rely on others for translation of these ancient texts. So much has been lost in the mistranslation of several ideas and words that what we have left is little more than a fairytale. Besides that, apocalyptic literature is permeated with very complex symbolic systems: "The language takes on a concealed meaning by means of mythical images rich in symbolism" (Koch 23) due to the fantastic descriptions of angels, heavens, hells, trees, and animals the underlying meaning of the texts seem to be a paradox of riddles. The ones destined for initiation are able to detect how divine prophecies give insight into current world events taking place during their lifetimes. Only trained minds capable of reading, listening, and interpreting in accordance with revealed 'secrets' given to them by the angelic messengers could correctly understand the message and its urgency. Koch says a special training was involved:

The picture language of the apocalypses is so noticeable and so curious that it stands out clearly from the normal framework of the literature of the time and suggests a particular linguistic training, perhaps even a particular mentality. (24)

"We all use language to convey our ideas and thoughts to others, and we take for granted that what we say others will understand. Unfortunately, biblical metaphors and symbolical imagery are not as clear and tangible. The metaphorical language of apocalyptic conveys information about a topic so foreign to our mortal nature that it is impossible to know except from an analogy. This literature has symbolic imagery that speaks to us in a foreign dialect and thought. There is little reason for people to be attracted to this literature when it seems so complicated. The ancient bans on esoteric concepts have added to the confusion of readers and students caught in the debate over language and the meaning of symbolic images. Mainly because previous church authorities have dominated scriptural interpretation and so thoroughly neglected native Semitic biblical interpretations, most students have not been equipped with the tools needed to study these texts for themselves." Alexa could not take much more at this point; she stood up and said, "Well, what if I do not agree with you? What then? "How dare you try to tell me, someone who actually goes to church, anything about the Bible – I was raised by the Bible!" Alexa grew red in the face, and her self-righteous indignation took over the conversation. I happen to have learned in Bible class that there are many reasons why we should not read those books, and besides, they are not necessary, everything we need to know is in the Bible, Timka."

"Do you know why 'Apocalypse' has many different meanings for different people? Because people have rights to their opinions just like you do!

This is a free country. In this country, we speak English, and the English version matters more. People do not have to read Hebrew anymore; we have Jesus now to save us. So, what? If other people read it according to their own particular view, why shouldn't they be able to interpret it, too? Hebrew literature does not determine the meaning given to words in the Bible, what nonsense Timka." Even though many church fathers such as Irenaeus, Tertullian, and Clement believed in the authenticity of the 'hidden books'; the legitimacy regarding their canonical status was often debated: "At the close of the fourth century, Jerome spoke out decidedly for the Hebrew canon, declaring unreservedly that books which were outside that canon should be classed apocryphal" (Oxford Apocrypha XV). The term 'Apocrypha' describes a multitude of documents that were not included in the Hebrew canon. The word 'Apocrypha' loosely means "things that are hidden" (XI). "You see," said Alexa these books are better off hidden from public view; even if people were able to read them, should they read them – what if something terrible happens!" The paradox we face today, things that can help us are hidden away, and the things that do not help us are in broad daylight but still are not seen or received. We can learn about personal identity through the encounters we have with others; this should not make us enemies; everyone is in a battle for survival under various situations called the accidents of life.

The ambiguity of terms, in many instances outside of religious or scientific jargon, is also subject to confusion and misunderstanding; the nature of miscommunication results when the circle is not complete. Timka and Alexa experience their spirituality in two separate strands of faith, which results in the emergence of two different connotations; Alexa smiles when she sarcastically remarks, "Some have suggested that the books were "hidden" or withdrawn from common use because they contain mysterious or esoteric lore, too profound to be communicated to any except the initiated." This view, upheld by the rabbinical attitude towards esoteric mysticism in general and apocalyptic eschatology specifically, still prevails. The information is very powerful, and charismatic gifts such as visions, auditions, and prophecy are typical by-products.

Therefore, this kind of information withheld from public use became the sole possession of Priests and scribes. The other view, Timka, let me tell you, was less positive; some thought the same term "Apocrypha" meant the literature is evil; the exact idea was, "Such books deserve to be 'hidden' because they were spurious or heretical" (XI). Ironically, the meaning of 'Apocrypha' all depends on the point of view of the definer. Eventually, all the books considered 'apocryphal' and classified as 'non-canonical' were available exclusively to biblical scholars. You see, Timka I know a few things too about these books you think are so important. There is another reason for the censorship of this literature; it has to do with the esoteric nature of the texts themselves. Christopher Rowland, a renowned scholar in apocalyptic literature, has found that many of the ideas found in apocalyptic books were familiar to religious leaders and that; actually the response of the reader is what really troubled them the most:

The enthusiasm of apocalyptic religion and its fervent expectation were features, which led the rabbis to distance themselves from this type of religion, according to: (Rowland, The Open Heaven 31)

Authorities always contend these texts incite rebellion and promote controversial issues that encourage us to stand firm for social justice in the face of religious and political oppression. Nevertheless, the texts are actually apolitical in terms of social change; they encourage self-empowerment and encourage students to continue striving for the wisdom of the Kingdom and revelation of the 'Mystery.' Timka, the evidence has been weighed, and scales are not balanced; the negative effect on society outweighs anything positive." Timka remembers, thinking, "Wow! Well, I told you it was too soon," to herself. Out of hundreds of people that I might have mentioned these books to, only a handful even took the time to open one up. Actually, I take that back; there were some who did read them but did not hear the message; there must be a reason for everything. The books are not for everyone, but all called to the Last Supper have a chance to find the Kingdom while there is time. At the beginning of the point, it must extend into a line before the curve of the circle can vibrate energy strong enough to break the false light. Timka fights to pull out whoever can see and hear; there is not much time, and those ready will be steady. In spite of the debate, Timka has a feeling that Alexa will make a great study partner. She felt her heart and not her fear. Therefore, she continues to sacrifice her own time and energy to battle with confusing ideas that keep everyone locked inside a box.

Salvation Wisdom

"Alexa, wow, I am impressed; you are learning something in that Bible College. You are right about the reasons certain scholars support those views. Out of the desire for order and unity, they spread the fear of unorthodox contagion of the Torah, and therefore, they eventually "Regarded prophetic apocalyptic conceptions with mistrust" (176). The authorities of the period claimed the authors of apocalyptic texts were heretics, and thus, their emerging literary genre became a type of thorn in the side of Orthodox Judaism; it remains to this day. There are many groups against this teaching, did you ever wonder why? This is one of few books with a pre-history of the Messiah. The Book of Enoch is all about the Hebrew Messiah written in all the books of Moses, the Prophets, and the Psalms. Perhaps the main reason why we should approach not only the book of Enoch and the other so-called 'Apocrypha' is that people of the earliest Jewish Christian communities, including Paul of Tarsus, considered these books a foundation of their most cherished faith tradition. Enoch is the older strand of traditions that helps us to identify the hidden Son of Man. Paul Hanson's solution to the ambiguity is viable and clear:

What is called for is a scholarship that is sensitive both to the contemporary human issues on which the ancient Jewish and Christian writings may have some bearing and to the responsibility of the scholar to present the testimony of the past as faithfully and objectively as possible. (13)

Timka grows more confident now, she is very nervous, and her hands begin to shake; she can feel the dark forces challenging her, whispering in her ear, "Alexa will never listen to you; you will not win here back from me." She just keeps on letting the words fall out, "Hanson points out that the book of Revelation is for spiritual communities dealing with the reality of oppression, conflict, and death in their immediate environment. Terrorism is what we call it now. The terror of the conflicts taking place on earth was meant to be lessened through the message of hope that a future world 'Olam Ha-Ba' is about to dawn. This is a central function of the literature, to offer solace to those living in the 'end days,' Hanson refers to the healing value of this literature right here; Alexa looks:" Reality, intolerable in its present form is transformed through the mythological enactment of an envisioned Ideal future in the present, making the effect of the apocalyptic work a form of therapy. (Hanson 11)

"Alex, apocalyptic books may actually help alleviate the destructive tendencies of religious groups that associate 'apocalypse' with war and death; a serious study of this literature will reveal its power to uplift communities and individuals during times of crisis by giving them a sense of purpose and a vision of destiny. The ultimate purpose of the texts is to impart information to an audience that can and will respond. Timka does not usually call her friend Alex. She will only use this name if she really wants to get her attention: Alex, did you know that "A passage from the Apocrypha encouraged Christopher Columbus in the enterprise that resulted in his discovery of the New World" (Metzger Apocrypha XX); that new world is now known as America. Isn't that cool? Look, it's right here; read this page where my finger is pointing. See how these mysterious authors of the apocalyptic epic try to present a historical pattern to the events that take place on earth, and some humans become privy to hidden details. It is up to each person to seek the Kingdom from within to learn how to understand the strange and seemingly bizarre ideas in this literature. We cannot continually change the ancient ideas behind this literature to whatever suits us at the time, or the Gospel message will no longer be an inspired message. It will have become another man-made speech. Alexa, the Day of Eternity may be closer than you think. It is embedded in the center of our being, yet so many are further away from it than ever before as we plunge into the hole of selfishness. The idea of Unity and purpose is central in the apocalyptic and biblical texts, yet both seek to describe this unique expression of Oneness in its own way.

Apocalyptic literature challenges humans everywhere to live responsibly in deed and thought and to feel accountable for one's actions towards oneself and others. One's destiny lies within the Mystery that continues to give us little glances into our future life. The apocalyptic authors challenge us to enter the Mystery and understand what is possible to know concerning our origin and destiny. Most things in our physical world are contained within other things, and getting to the core of what we are contained in means finding the center of one's soul.

"How does one find the center of the soul, Timka?" See, you had me until you started talking about finding the center of the soul, which sounds like New Age stuff to me. Alexa started squinting her eyes and frowning to show her disgust as she imagined concepts she was not comfortable discussing.

Everyone has a built-in radar system to detect things that are not comfortable or acceptable according to one's personal identity; things are this way for a reason; we must move out of our comfort zone. We automatically have to participate in conditions we are born in. There is no choice. The reality of nature and the world around us is discovered when we go beyond our comfort zone; having an open mind is good for the brain; it needs data, experience, sensations, and our desires to rule, but sometimes our will is stuck in second gear. As victims of innate liabilities, there is something we need to re-establish before we can access our will and redirect our desires.

A Mystery Within Us

Timka looked back on those days, and it warmed her heart to see how far Alexa had come since that day that seemed so long ago.

Figure 7 Universal Soul

She knew in her heart that at the center of our soul dwells a Mystery destined to find its ultimate revelation in all of us if we want it to be. We can bring our ideas to life and see their creation; we do this every day with the use of our imagination and intellect. We exist to reflect the Light; we are to refract the 'image' of Elohim into the Universe. Olam is a Hebrew term

125

that means both 'Universe' and 'Eternity' derived from Elam, a term that means 'concealment'. Thus, the Universe 'conceals' the Creator, so the true image is not seen directly but is reflected in all that has been created. This belief is within the context of Hebrew mystical thought, and Paul explains the very same thing in Romans Chapter 19, where he explains the things created typify invisible realities of Eternity. Eternity is something won, not found. We have to run the race to win the victory. In Colossians 1:26, Paul points out a specific Mystery that has eluded many in previous generations but is now open to 'babes' in the hidden evangel. Paul says,

Even the Mystery, which has been hid from ages and from generations, but now is made manifest to His righteous ones: To whom Yahweh would make known what is the riches of the Glory of this mystery among the Nations; which is the Messiah in you, the hope of Glory.

In ancient mystical doctrines, Adam is androgynous, possessing both male and female sides and genes in a state of unity. Also, know that two natures lie within Adam, known as Michael and Sammael or the 'yetzer ha tov' and 'yetzer ha ra'; it is the origin of the inner war that still inflicts the human heart. A way to overcome this inner struggle, Paul calls a 'war' is to balance the two natures. One side always seeks to overcome the other due to the nature of this constant struggle between two opposite forces, which maintain the circulation and motion of an ongoing expansion and contraction of creation within the matrix of our Universe. How this spirit law pervades the Universe through three transformations is the focus of the Law of Three.

ANCIENT SCIENCE & ORIGINS

Forces of Ancient Science

<Thesis-Antithesis-Synthesis>

"Thesis, Antithesis, and Synthesis represent the development of an idea, an opposing idea, and the reconciliation of the conflict between two polar forces (positive/negative) that pervade the structure of the Universe and humanity. This same dual force of energy swirling through the Universe is like a galaxy in motion that remains unbalanced until we recognize how it is in our daily life." Joel has progressed very much since the last time he talked to Alexa; he realizes that it will not be easy to deal with her, but learning about the synthesis of opposites helps him to see the dynamics of their relationship. He must admit that he feels like a completely different person.

Figure 8 Circles of Sefiroth Hall Secret Teachings of All Ages

$2^3 = 8$

After Joel studies the Circles of Sefiroth, he thinks, "How can we find a connection to something so elusive? It does not know that we, too, are invisible, we speak words that we do not see unless written down. We have thoughts that are words in motion, yet most of us do not notice it at all, we take our invisible self for granted. Our spiritual self does seem elusive in the beginning stage of our ascension. Daniel C. Matt presents a detailed analysis of the intricate relationship between science and mysticism in God & the Big Bang. Joel actually went online and found an Internet article, Intersection between Science and Mysticism, in which Marion Brink highlights the most important points of Daniel Matt's work, the unity of energy and matter in all its manifestations. Joel begins to listen to the voice that guides him through a maze of ideas and concepts that seem to overwhelm him sometimes. "Mystics speak of spirit and flesh, and scientists dialogue through theories of how energy and matter interact. Brinks says that Matt defines mysticism as where the person doesn't focus so much on the effect of the spiritual experience as on the results of what happens afterward. Enraptured by the feeling of spiritual exhilaration, many people tend to neglect the basic tenets of the mystical doctrines. The ultimate experience of reality is to realize that all is one. Humanity is continually being born, and innumerable personalities emerge, yet all remain connected in the cosmic soup of the Universe. "This is very interesting, but I do not recall Timka talking about 'cosmic soup,' he thought to himself. Joel does want to understand more about how Timka feels when she is experiencing the things she describes in such detail, but he also wants to overcome her delusion and help her see the light. This is the nature of human nature, the desire to shape and mold others in a particular idealized image each one perceives, appropriate based on his or her personal sentiments. Joel is at a crossroads and finds an Internet article, Intersection between Science and Mysticism, in which Marion Brink highlights the most important points of Daniel Matt's work, the unity of energy and matter in all its manifestations. Joel begins to listen to the voice that guides him through a maze of ideas and concepts that seem to overwhelm him sometimes. "Mystics speak of spirit and flesh, and scientists dialogue through theories of how energy and matter interact. Brinks says that Matt defines mysticism as where the person doesn't focus so much on the effect of the spiritual experience as on the results of what happens afterward. Enraptured by the feeling of spiritual exhilaration, many people tend to neglect the basic tenets of the mystical doctrines. The ultimate experience of reality is to realize that all is one. Humanity is continually being born, and innumerable personalities emerge, yet all remain connected in the cosmic soup of the Universe. "This is very interesting, but I do not recall Timka talking about 'cosmic soup,' he thought to himself.

Joel does want to understand more about how Timka feels when she is experiencing the things she describes in such detail, but he also wants to overcome her delusion and help her see the light. This is the nature of human nature, the desire to shape and mold others in a particular idealized image each one perceives, appropriate based on his or her personal sentiments. Joel is at a crossroads; either he beats Timka at her game, or he joins her in an invisible reality he does not see. "Science tends to take the mystery out of nature, but some scientists appreciate its unity. Not everyone will agree on everything, but I see that at least one scientist does agree that at the subatomic level all life is connected. I do not understand what temperature has to do with spiritual things, but Timka is always using scientific analogies, because she believes we can learn to see the invisible things through the invisible things that Elohim created. Energy undergoes three chemical transformations. Gas, liquids and solids exchange their form for another, depending on the temperature applied to each, which is the catalyst for transformation. Not all scientists agree on the exact set of conditions that caused the Big Bang. So, why does Timka think that she understands something when scientists have various theories they all disagree on and cannot prove until after years of intricate calculations and analysis? Some physicists explain how the Universe explodes from within a very small dense Point.

Figure 9 Point of Light

"Some scientists explain this Point was very dense, and as chemical combining and recombining took place, and the elements inside grew denser and denser, the temperature began to create great tension. Eventually the tension gives way to a great release of energy and elements that eventually cooled and settled into what we know as our Universe. Other quantum mechanics physicists state that in a scientific context, spirituality involves an experience of intuitive knowing, wherein one actually participates in realizing the Oneness of all things within the evolutionary creative process." Joel thinks it is also important to remember that the Big Bang is not a fact; it is still only a theory, but intuition is a real experience and way of interacting with the Universe. Joel has reached a new plateau. Still, he is no closer to understanding Timka. She seems like a tight, condensed point that refuses to expand and allow the world to examine her. Joel begins to like this new perception he seems to have just acquired; little does he know he is moving further away from what Timka wants him to know. Joel has a feeling of ambivalence, almost as if by studying these other materials; he is in some way being unfaithful to her. The feeling is so strong that he stops reading to call her. He dials the number; her phone rings. His heart is beating so fast that she finally picks up the phone. Joel says, "Timka, how are you? What are you doing right now? Timka replies I was about to take a walk." Joel just blurts out, "What do you think about the Point? You know what I mean when you talk about the Big Bang? You get so excited about some 'point'- what does it mean to you?" Timka replies, "Joel, what are you doing? Why do you want to know about the point all of a sudden? Joel, are you okay?" He replies, "Yes, yes, I am fine; I just want to know, that's all; I am interested in what you are trying to tell me all the time."

Timka does not believe Joel, but she talks to him anyway. "Moses De Leon, a very controversial Kabbalist of the thirteenth century, said, "The beginning of existence is the secret concealed Point." Modern research reveals the entire Universe was energy or light and that nothing else existed until the source and substance of the 'All' shrinks to a very small dense point. The Point is equivalent to the contraction known as the 'Tzimzum' in Kabbalistic doctrines and it is a contraction that allows the material world to come into being. There is a significant similarity between the mystical concept of Ayin 'nothingness' and 'quantum vacuum' that is the supposed foundation of the Big Bang theory. Joel says to himself, "Matt has proven that kabbalists and scientists have doctrines and theories that are becoming more similar than not.

They do seem to be saying the same thing about the creation, but what does this have to do with the 'end days' or soldiers and children running for safety? I do not see any connection between what I have read and what Timka describes. It is almost as if she is in a different place and time, and when she talks about it – it seems so unreal, but she is so certain of her own explanations. She is definitely a paradox. Why does she feel that what she and Alexa are studying is any different from what other people study and practice?"

He thinks to himself silently, in case anyone or something is listening to him, "I do not see what she is really saying; her ramblings on about the invisible world and wars and diseases sound nuts to me; I do not seem to be any closer to curing her at all." Joel decides to listen to her more when she talks about details regarding the 'point,' which seems so important to her.

Wisdom's Place

The Point of Singularity

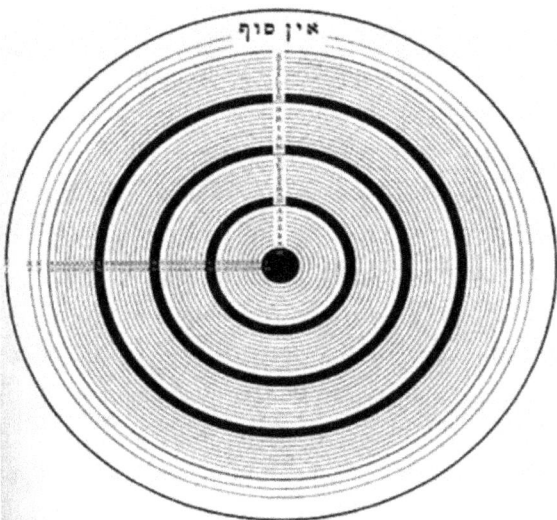

אין סוף

Figure 10 Ayin

Timka explains to Joel that Pythagoras, Plato, and others also knew about this point and line that extends into space. Timka thinks the point is an example of how light enters the void of darkness and creates the four forces that will give shape and form to Adam. As seen above, the line of time intersects the four worlds of concentric circles that represent the different levels of development of the six days. This is one doctrine, which she always goes back to; that she says has to do with Aether and light propagation. She believes that both scientists and mystics agree that the creation emerged from a central point known as a singularity. Timka replies to Joel, "Singularity is a point located in the densest center of all things. Because all life contains atoms and their constituent parts, such as the electron, proton, and quarks, we, too, are made of the same material as the Universe. Do you see how all life connects with us through emanations of energy that flow through the divine attributes of Elohim?

When we become who we are, we are actualizing our own individual identity and this gives us the ability to be unique. The Universe is the world's Soul; it becomes a learning guide for Maskillim to follow in the steps of mystics. People who experience the Divine consciousness are restored to the sacred symbolism of numbers and letters that constructed the Universe. Matt says the Big Bang happened "15 billion years ago. The primordial vacuum was devoid of matter, but not really empty" (Matt 19). He compares this idea with 'Reshit', meaning 'Beginning,' to explain a spiritual transformation of humanity in terms of the relationship between energy and matter in the Universe. However, I do not think it took 15 billion years; it was an instantaneous creation when Elohim spoke "Yehi Aur!" Joel, researchers, and scientists are abiding by each of their own fields; I am not bound to fields, labels, or distinctions; these are the things that prevent us from seeing the unified field of reality. Matt argues it is so important for us to realize that things are really one in reality and that the duty of all humans is to be cognizant of this unity, which is the consciousness we call Mind.

Myth and our own personal identity are intimately connected. Matt believes that myth and humanity, so inseparably entwined, like energy and matter, represent the synthesis of two realities.

He describes the relationship between myth and humans by saying that, "We have lost our myth" (Matt 29). Science, in many instances, has taken its place in society through its everyday application of technology and theories of evolution that seem to contradict the ideas of spiritual concepts. Yes, Joel, our Mind is undermined by false theories and mythological concepts disguised as empirical and theological truth based on human perception and traditions. You cannot just learn things without having a reference place; the Son in the form of the

Word will guide you through the storms so you can clearly see and hear the right thoughts."

Joel questions Timka regarding how and why the Big Bang has an echo.

Apparently, cosmic radiation can actually emit sounds, "wherever they turned the antenna, they picked up a mysterious background hiss. (Matt 21).

This demonstrates the organic harmony of the elements and the forces of creation. Hydrogen and helium are the two most common elements found in the Universe and on Earth. From these two elements, other elements and processes evolved and formed many galaxies. Even stars contain very dense amounts of hydrogen and helium that combine with other elements that become even more dense. Eventually, the rise and crescendo of pressure that builds up from the temperature upon its release is how a star dies just to be one with the hydrogen and helium that produced its life. The energy then emitted from the dying star creates a shock wave; according to Matt,"

The star explodes, in the violent process forging even heavier elements: copper, silver, tin, iodine, gold, mercury, and lead.

These, along with the lighter elements from the exploding star, are spewed into space (23). Timka, "This is a general account of the process that brought about the Universe. From these seven elements, all that is called the material universe we inhabit. You say that Enoch describes them as seven great mountains. Well, I found out a very interesting little-known fact: according to Matt, "The first Big Bang theorist was an obscure Belgian priest and mathematician named Georges Lemaitre. And between 1927 and 1933, he proposed that the eruption of a 'primordial atom' had given birth to the Universe" (26). Ironically, it was a priest and not a scientist who first proposed the theory that shook the religious world for years to come. Matt seems to provide us with a standard model to compare the connection between physics and spirituality. While, mystics explain the birth in terms of a 'breakage', "As a result of the breakage, it seems that we are no longer part of the one, and we act as if we are autonomous, exercising what feels like free will" (85). The 'divine withdrawal' the contraction in combination with the 'breaking' involves the act of making choices and the ability of humanity to make decisions about the events of life." Joel is astonished at how well he was able to articulate what he had just read.

"The 'fall' in Genesis reflects the 'divine withdrawal' and it too is concerned with the choices we make. All of us struggle to find opportunity and advancement it is the nature of human evolution, but many strive to find opportunities for personal freedom. Matt believes assumed free will is evidence that there really was a 'fall' or 'breakage,' and it is humanity's duty to help repair the breach with selflessness. As a result of the big bang, there was a 'shattering of the vessels', and the world lies in a state of confusion and is in need of repair that only humans can make. Balance is the key to solving any equation." Joel listens on the line waiting for Timka's response. He is ready to battle with the other world that seems to take her away from him.

Time before Time

Timka is always interested in hearing what others say, and feel, and she is beginning to let her guard down a little to entertain Joel. Her intuition guides her feet as she treads dangerous waters, she knows when to step forward and when to step back. She replies to his long soliloquy with genuine excitement and inspiration, "Joel, in ancient science, the time before the Big Bang is called an 'Equilibrium Balance', but Atomic science calls it the "Grand Unification Epoch," which is actually a name for a time immediately following the Big Bang. Did you know that recent scientific research indicates the four forces, matter, and energy, were in balance and equilibrium until 8 seconds after the 'Big Bang'? An Internet-based article I found, Expo/Science & Industry/Cosmos, contains an article written by its Board of Directors. It is a controversial essay, "In the Beginning", they discussed the symmetry or Oneness found in the Universe after the contraction and before the expansion had begun:

The period from 10-43 to 10-35 seconds after the Big Bang—that all matter and energy were essentially interchangeable and in equilibrium. What's more, electromagnetism and the two nuclear forces were as one (gravity, the fourth and weakest force, had separated from the other three at the beginning of the Grand Unification Epoch. (McClean In the Beginning: The Big Bang P1 para 3)

"Something happened in the space of 8 seconds that changed the very operation of the Universe. The original symmetry was broken as the "Universe underwent a phase transition" and this resulted in 'the breaking of the vessels' according to Isaac Luria. The 'breaking' is the result of one of the four forces separating from the others. In the beginning, the strong force broke away from the other three according to the article, "Physicists call this process "symmetry breaking," and it released an enormous amount of energy (A Burst of Inflation P2 para 1).

The strong nuclear force keeps neutrons and protons attracted to each other, while gravity holds everything together and down. Distance from other objects and mass is what determines the effect of gravity on things. The earth is constantly spinning on its axis and gravity is what keeps the atoms of matter from slipping off into hyperspace. The strong nuclear force is like the middle pillar of the Tree of Life; it is the mediating center of balance between the opposite pairs of positive and negative pillars. This middle pillar, also known as Metatron, balances itself between every polar opposite causing the two sides of the tree to attract each other. The constant contraction and expansion mimics the breathing of Brahma, giving birth to world souls or Kitchi Manitou, ensouling spiritual heroes everywhere. The sacred Monad, Dyad, and Triad work together beneath the material constructs, as the invisible principles of spiritual creation emanating, polarizing and reconciling all things in a bond or Covenant." The invisible shapes that consist of a point, line, and triangle are the building blocks of creation. This is a natural law of cosmic physiology and Kabbalistic mysticism that numbers represent creative energy in motion. Rest and motion are central factors in both spiritual literature and scientific theories. Science has no means of probing beneath symbolic expressions and can only construct mathematical theories that explain how things function and evolve but not why they are. The true nature of mysticism is to delve into the inner recesses of human experience in order to expand its physical limitations. That is how we enter the invisible Kingdom Joel! Do you see that now, everything is connected from the center, and its connectivity expands outwards toward infinity? Aleph the small is known as (1) but ALEPH the tall is (1000)." Timka feels so happy that she and Joel are relating at this level. She has not felt this close to him for a long time.

Aleph -Palace of the Garden

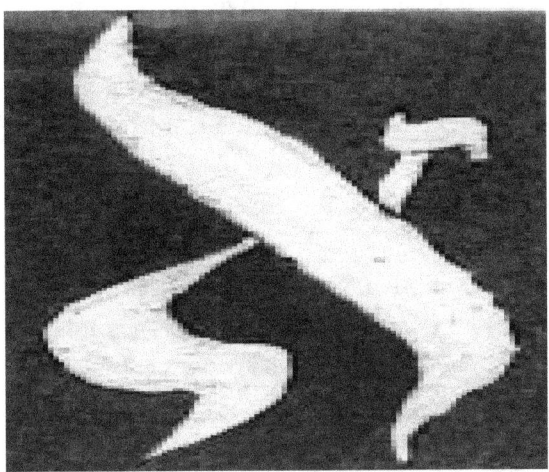

Aleph is the first letter of the Hebrew alphabet it also is a symbol of the Holy Palace and Breath. The origin of Ruach the spirit essence breathed into Adam. Many mystics have contemplated the magic and spiritual experience contained in the beginning letter of the divine alphabet. It is composed of the Hebrew letter (VaV) and two (Yod's). One upper Yod rests upon the VaV and the lower Yod holds up the VaV. The letter VaV is numerically equal to the number six. Thus Y+V+Y = 26. Timka explains to Joel how Aleph, therefore, shares in the properties of יהוה, which also has a numerical value of 26. "Aleph is a force from the world of Emanation (Aziluth) that extends into the letter Yod in the world of Action (Assiyah). Aleph is the invisible spirit energy that can take on shape and form, Yod is the visible physical matter that performs the will of energy. This process takes place as conceptualized by mystics in the 10 components of the sefiroth. When the ten attributes are active in one's life the Holy Spiritual Essence returns to the Gan Eden to dwell in the renewed Temple and sanctuary in the center of one's soul. Originally, this Garden or 'Gan' signified an ordered sequence of events that result in organized constructions such as a garden, body, or world. It can even represent a Universe. The term 'Heden' signifies a time, season, age, and eternity, and it is the origin of the term 'Eden'. The 'Ed' of 'Eden' is an element or piece of time and space; other connotations include pleasure and witness. (Fillmore, Metaphysical Dictionary 181). The Garden of Eden (Time) existed in Eternity 'in the beginning'. This was before the breaking of the vessels or the dispersion of cosmic light. Since the fall of cosmic light into darkness and matter, a new creation has been set in motion. Now the 'Gan Eden' is not a place in our physical experience of time or space. The garden was once a state of consciousness that allows a person to experience knowledge both physical and spiritual. Joel, Eden is our spiritual consciousness!" Timka is so excited now; she can feel the energy of spiritual consciousness surging through her again; it has been so long since he and she felt this close. Joel does not realize that words alone cannot comfort Timka; she needs to feel a connection through the shared receptivity of the central message. Timka can now hear the sound of roaring waters in her ears, and the wings of Shekinah that sound like crickets, but the experience is not as loud this time. Her voice begins to change, as she talks to Joel.

"The essential unity of the Big Bang and society is inherent within the universal laws that govern the universe. Spiritual doctrines must reflect basic scientific truths, while science must learn to refract its theories in the light of mystical thought. As a result of the big bang, there was a 'shattering of the vessels,' and the world lies in a state of confusion and is in need of repair that only humans can make.

Matt points out the problem and how to solve it, "By mending the world- socially, economically, politically – we mend God and mend what is torn within us, between us, around us" (Matt 151). Now, Joel, these ideas based on Lurianic Kabbalah are not what the disciples or Apostles were teaching after the fall of Jerusalem. The fact that this esoteric,

140

mysterious knowledge or 'gnosis' can create change and alter one's perception of reality is why many of the original ideas behind ancient mystical texts are not publicly discussed or taught today. Knowledge undergoes various phases of transition in the human mind before the data is classified, stored in our memory, and remembered, for the human brain is constantly changing and evolving to adapt. The Wisdom interacts with our consciousness because of the Word of YHVH manifested in the Messiah of Nazareth. The Messiah is the Tzaddik who restored the Kosmos so that we can hear the Voice again. Be careful, Joel, which voice you listen to; they are not all teaching the same things." Joel is confused again. "Timka are you saying that the Messiah goes inside our consciousness and somehow can change our mind? And what do you mean there are many voices?" Now you are starting to sound nuts again; just when I thought I was on the same wavelength, you changed the frequency again!" Joel asserts his ideas again as he begins to fight the 'thing' that comes over Timka. Joel thinks he has a better perspective on science than Timka and that he can help her to understand without freaking out on him all the time.

"Sweetheart, I know all about how atoms, stars, and superstrings also have phases of transition that allow them to change from one form into another. The rate and frequency of vibration determine the way waves will transform into electrons or gravitons. It all depends on the structure of the atom and the material form it has. Heat is the agent of change that determines what the form will be. The Hebrew prophets always agreed that Yahweh is like a 'consuming fire'; the universe has systems the same way human beings have nine systems that operate and control their body, and heat is always the source of life in the macrocosm and the microcosm. Life changes us and forces us to adapt to different situations every day, and how we perceive events is what alters our consciousness at any given time. This is more than a design theory; it is a fact that matter will change its form under the right conditions and temperature, and so will human consciousness if it is altered enough. However, science and spirituality are subject to your personal interpretation; we must accept the facts as presented by professionals and academics. You should not try to teach anything you cannot prove. No one will listen."

Timka replies, "These conditions seem to be 'prepared' and have very exact prerequisites. This Being of consciousness can be whatever Being wills to Become. Joseph Dan mentions the role of the "Unique Cherub" in maintaining the operation of the Universe and as the mediator between humanity and the Creator.

This Cherub undergoes a transformation and becomes everything that exists in the material world. It can also enter human consciousness. YHVH יהוה is the name of the amorphous, invisible essence in the form of vapor and light. The Avir/Aether is the substance created through Elohim אלוהים, which is a title that represents plurality. Elohim has form, can be visible and invisible, and appears in visions and dreams. The Son of Man Yahshuah יהושה represents form and substance manifested as solid objects.

The chemical transformation of elements and the thermal law of conservation of energy are the most fundamental scientific and spiritual laws of the entire Universe. These divine names demonstrate the spiritual law of transformation that occurs from the unity of vapor to the multiplicity of matter. This reiterates the earlier premise that cosmic dust brought forth energy, gravity, electromagnetic force, and atoms that contain three invisible realms known as the electron, nucleus, and proton. These three realms or heavens gave birth to the lower seven elements of matter. As ancient sages would say, the Ayin, Ayin Sof, and Ayin SOF Aur, known in Christianity as the Father, Son, and Holy Spirit, created and then formed the seven doubles and the realms of duality. There is a Universal Spirit law that operates on the earth through two basic energies that first emerge from a state of unity. There are two basic elements common to the Big Bang process: hydrogen and helium.

These two energies are contained in water and fire, which results in the creation of 'eshamayyim,' literally fire and water, translated in English as 'Heaven.' Joel, when you put fire and water together, it makes a sound .... Esssshhh, this sound mimics the actual Hebrew words! What the Universe was like before the two energies evolved is what compels both mystics and scientists to continue looking back in time. We need to look forward towards the 'new creation' time is behind us, eternity is in front of us."

Timka is very obsessed with mystic lore that one has to learn to find the 'beginning' in order to know the 'end' of the great mystery. She perceives life as a universal challenge in the great 'race' the Apostle Paul prepares us for; when she used to read the epistles of Paul, she felt she could hear his voice speaking to her at times. When this happened, it jettisoned her soul into the 3rd Heaven state of consciousness. Normally, the things she heard and saw there, she could not explain to anyone else. She is so excited to hear Joel so inquisitive and learning on his own that she does not even mind that he tries to undermine her. "Joel, there is a way to perceive all these things; it will come to you – give it time. Did you know that the term 'false vacuum' is a word physicists use to describe the condition of the Universe as having no space, time, or matter? In such a condition, the universe contained more energy than matter. As we learn to see the invisible forces that brought the Universe out of its point of origin, we peer into the deep recesses of our own natures. It is so exciting, and you can actually feel it increasing your spiritual awareness; to me, that is the reparation of the shattering vessel of Light.

When humans begin to return to Eden, the Garden of spiritual awareness, the Kingdom will come. The Kabbalistic theory is consistent with this first premise also because the concept of 'Tzimtzum' states that all things that come into existence do so because of the contraction of all that "IS" into a 'point' that allows the existence of matter to take place within the void of light." Timka reminds Joel of an illustration she feels represents the ancient view of the Universe, according to the mystic science of the Sages. "Joel, do you remember that picture I showed you, one of the various levels of sephiroth and how the light and darkness are spread over certain areas of the world? The Universe literally exists in the absence of Light in a 'void' place; this is why the lens of our eyes reflects the physical dimension of objects in our physical environment to our brains. Actually, the force of Light enables our brain to reflect our vision of life. Time is actually moving backward as the future creates our past. We need the light to reflect what we see before we can realize anything material around us. Light travels to us through waves and particles into the 'void' of our night, pulling each of us out of the black hole of nothingness.

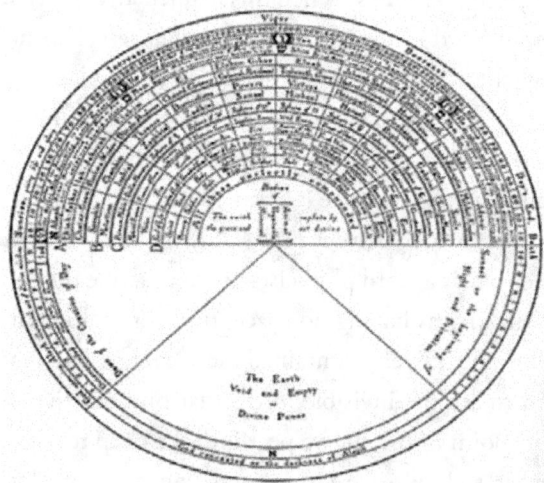

Figure 11 Contraction Hall CXXII from Fludd's Operum

Big Bang Time

Joel, maybe you should consult Isaac Luria's book Etz Hayyim (Tree of Life) for a further explanation of Tzimtzum and the role of humanity in repairing the Universe and reconsider what I shared with you about the Messiah of Nazareth; he said his words are Light and Truth. Tzimtzum or 'contraction' is the second phase of three transitional states. The Tikkun represents the Unification of the separate forces and the gathering of broken vessels. Luria grappled with these ideas over 400 years ago, but it is only recently that scientists have actually found proof that there really was a 'shattering of light.' Adam McLean explains the significance of Isaac Luria's doctrine for modern Physics today in Kabbalistic Cosmology and its Parallels in the 'Big Bang' of Modern Physics. He analyzed the four worlds of cosmology and noted the parallels he had found in various scientific theories. His explanation of how the broken vessels of light parallel the Higgs fields is revolutionary in scope. According to McClean,

The energy that the universe contained was bound up in special fields of force (the Higgs fields named after the physicist who first described them), which were essentially unstable. (Inflationary Universe P6 Para 7)

The author compares the 'fields of force' with the sefiroth or the vessels that were shattered because they could not contain the extreme intensity and power of the original light. In the original symmetry of the Universe, the Higgs fields were in equilibrium due to the temperature of the earlier period. The Higgs fields were in balance, and all forces were evenly distributed. There was no mass or weight until the fields were broken and they released their energy; a change in temperature brought about the transition called "spontaneous symmetry breaking."

Matter was once contained in energy (spirit) and had no mass until released from the intense heat of its symmetrical state. Once the shattering began, the Universe began to expand, and it is still expanding. In reality, the Universe as we know it is the result of the broken symmetry of Eternity. According to McClean's article,

This breaking of the unified symmetry between the four fundamental forces results in the separation of gravity from the other forces and, consequently, the emergence of particles of matter. (P6 para. 2)

Thus, there is scientific evidence of Luria's "Shebirah" or broken vessels motif so prominent in Lurianic Kabbalah. McClean writes:

The matter in the universe arose out of the breaking of the symmetries of the Higgs fields, which Lurianic kabbalah parallels with the Shebirah, or "breaking of the vessels," and the falling down through the worlds of the husks or shells. (P6 para. 4)

"Joel, how these four worlds unfold in the creation of the spiritual Universe and within the consciousness of humanity is the great secret and mystery of apocalyptic literature! Figure 12 is from the Cambridge Cosmology website. It is a diagram of a cross-sectional string that shows four distinct regions within the string's core as it emits radiation. Notice the concentric circles of radiation look very similar to the circles of the Sephiroth.

Figure 12 Cambridge Cosmology String Radiation Quadrupole

The 4 Phases of Tzimtzum	4 Phases of ADAM QADMON
Undifferentiated Light	Universe of Malbush (Garment)
Constriction around a Central Point	Neshamah of Adam the 1st Space
Ray	Ruach of Adam (the hidden Adam)
Center Point	Nefesh of Adam (the body)

"The 'undifferentiated' light is the Garment of the Universe called (Avir) in medieval wisdom, and it came forth from the light (Aur) of Eternity that bathes the Universe. The original light contained all the colors within and appeared as a very bright, blinding white light until each of its waves separated into the Electromagnetic spectrum. Then there was the contracting vortex creating a central point to contain the first undivided light. From this central point, a 'ray' of light shines forth, illuminating the 'hidden Adam' or 'Ruach'. This process reveals the creation of Adam from the 'nothing' (Ayin) and only today's physicists can actually confirm the Genesis creation, even if they do not realize it personally. Three Hebrew terms for the word 'soul' do not appear in our English version, yet they are noted in Hebrew literature. Nephesh, Ruach, and Neshamah all represent three stages of change in a process. Nephesh is the material earthly world of the soul that governs us through our biological drives, senses, and instincts. Whereas emotions and thoughts take place in Ruach or the intellectual world of choice that allows us to choose between darkness and light or good and evil, all three affect our internal world to some extent. Neshamah, the mystical soul, is the 'world to come,' and we strive to taste it while we are still in the world of Nephesh and time.

Many do not believe that it is possible to experience the 'Olam ha-Bah' until you have passed into the Glory. Ruach means breathing and wind and it calls forth the breath that comes from the center point in our soul as our consciousness expands. It encompasses all things and everyone, and yet very few can see it. The Universe does have a center point and heart; its continual breathing in and out is what allows it to expand and contract. It is the zero-point field of energy that Bernard Haisch calls a "background sea of light" that everything swims in, including the Universe." Joel, did you read an article called "Brilliant Disguise: Light, Matter, and the Zero-Point Field?" You should look for it; Astrophysicist Bernard Haisch exonerates the Genesis account of how there was actually a 'first' Light that existed before the light of the Sun was placed in the sky. This has been a sore spot and source of contention among critics for centuries. Since the superstring explosion in quantum mechanics, physicists are beginning to discover how the Genesis account is actually closer to the nature of scientific theory than earlier suspected. Many now know that the 'first light' is the beginning of the Electromagnetic spectrum and that even its waves bathe in the sea of light of low background radiation. Haisch writes,

To put it in somewhat metaphysical terms, there exists a background sea of quantum light filling the universe, and that light generates a force that opposes acceleration when you push on any material object. That is why matter seems to be the solid, stable stuff that we and our world are made of. (Haisch P3)

"Haisch explains the Heisenberg 'uncertainty principle' that basically says that all waves must move in order for motion to exist, but with zero-point energy, there is no wave fluctuation or motion, and this totally contradicts what earlier physicists taught. He explains how media devices such as radios, television, cell phones even microwaves operate by sending and receiving electromagnetic waves of some kind. He thinks that visible light is itself a frequency of the original light. He asserts, "Visible light is the same thing; it is just a higher frequency form of electromagnetic waves." Each wave corresponds to an attribute or spiritual force and has the properties of every other force. We can compare it to a symphony of light sounds that fluctuate and rest in perfect symmetry. According to Haisch, "All are electromagnetic waves which are really just different frequencies of light" that, like superstrings, can transform into different particles such as quarks and gravitons. According to Luria, the electromagnetic waves developed as a result of the Shebirah or the 'breaking of the vessels.'

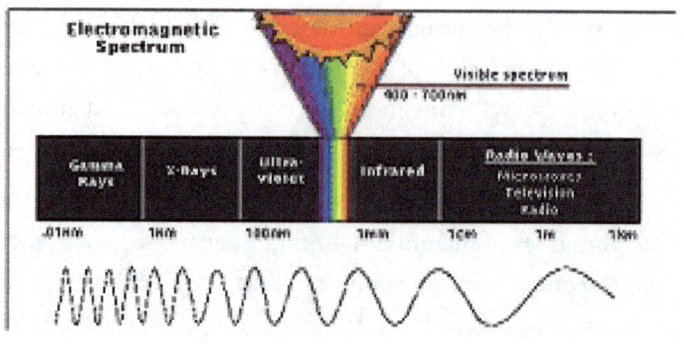

Figure 13 Electromagnetic Spectrum Zero Point
Energy website

Joel, if you consider the term Ayin denotes the zero and infinite space that comes out of its center point, it opens up an entirely new way of interpreting scientific data. The Ayin or the 'nothing' is the darkness or cavity void of light. The creation, as we know it, is born from this 'nothing' (Ayin Aether condensed) as it receives the light. Light is the transforming energy that sustains the earth. Ayin is the boundless, unknowable, ineffable lowest subatomic level of reality that emanates the world of knowledge or form. It is the world of the infinitely small that Quantum physicists seek to discover. Before form everything was 'Ayin' or hidden in the center. At the lowest subatomic level of superstrings, the elements are very chaotic and unordered, and the darkness of the 'nothing' dissolves right and left into today and tomorrow.

When Ayin becomes conscious of itself, the 'tzimzum' or 'contraction' begins as the central dimensionless point suddenly expands into Ayin Sof. This is when the Avir begins to change its dense form and emanate the 26 properties that break into two flows. There is a zero dimension on the edge of the dense point; some call it the Logon; it does not exist anywhere in space. It only really exists in infinity, yet it is the very thoughts of Logos expressed in the Universe. The zero point of dimensions is like the 'point' of potential life contained in an egg that will later undergo division and mitosis before finally developing into an embryo. Human birth is evidence that such a small point can contain a Universe. The nine waves emanate out from the zero point and the electromagnetic spectrum is born. It begins to form further geometric patterns that give life to various forms.

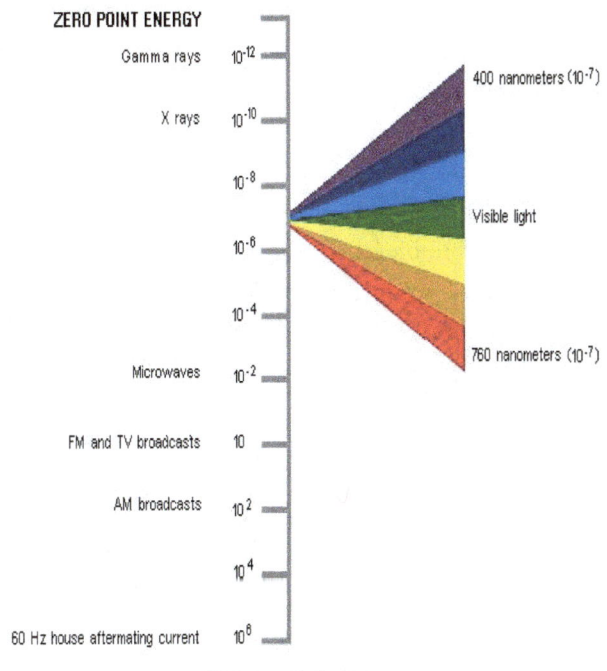

Figure 14 Diagram from Zero Point Energy website

"If these zero 'dimensions' is the 'point' of the center that creates a vacuum, then the next dimension is the line that contains points that move out and away from the center. Energy leaves the Garden of Eden to rest in the matter of Adam and Eve. The whirling forces of the Chariot wheels seen by Enoch, Isaiah, and Ezekiel called the [Reshit Ha-Galgalim] appear to create a vortex that promotes the wave undulation of circles that aid in the contraction that opens the point to create the six days. The primordial point, or 'Yod,' is the first phase that gives life to everything. 'True Vacuum' is a scientific term used to describe a universe of space, time, and matter; it is the 'all that is.' The world of form is what distinguishes between "false vacuum" and "true vacuum" states. In other words, limits and bounds exist to allow the creation of the material universe from the raw, unprocessed primordial substance. Phase transitions influence the formation of 'cosmic strings' and their expansion into 'membranes' that seem very similar to the 'firmament' Moses describes in Genesis. True vacuum and false vacuum are the two phases of a process. First-order and second-order phases both include the process of transformation; one is more active. In the 'first order,' the transitions occur through the formation of bubbles of the new phase in the middle of the old phase; these bubbles then expand and collide until the old phase disappears completely and the phase transition is complete. (Cambridge P2 para. 4)

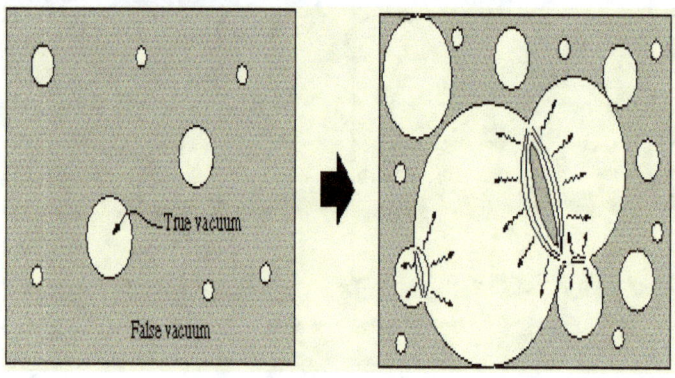

Figure 15 Cambridge Cosmology -Phase Transition Illustration

In the diagram above, "A bubble of the new phase (true vacuum) forms and then expands until the old phase (false vacuum) disappears" (P3 para 1); think of how steam produces bubbles that rise after they expand to picture the process in your mind. The 'second order' is 'smooth' in comparison: "The old phase transforms itself into the new phase in a continuous manner" (P3 para 3). According to the article, trapped matter can only escape by "nucleating bubbles of the new phase, that is, the 'true vacuum' state," so it appears that matter must be able to expand in order to rise. When the pressure builds, the bubbles expand; when the bubbles burst, the energy flees its bondage. This imagery reminds me of the biblical theme in Genesis. As the breath of air is blown into Adam's nostrils, the lungs become extended, and they (material and spiritual) become living being that could rise and walk in the material world. Can we find this phenomenon in scientific terms? Through the logic of science, it is possible to see the hidden creation of the mystical worlds.

The wave of creation is found in Genesis 1:26: "Let us make Adam in our image" because there are 7 'Let there Be commands that undulate like the 8 steps of a wave cycle. Like the Atom, Adam has 7 shells to be filled; the shells are garments that are filled with Aur/Avir. Elohim spoke Adam into existence, and we live through the living word/signs, and if you listen to a higher level of or frequency of consciousness, the Middle Pillar – Metatron receives this communication from Elohim and gives us waters to drink and manna to eat that will never fade. Joel, I bet you did not know that verse 1:26 is evidence of a relationship between the number 26 and the purpose of humanity's creation in the image of Elohim. Now, it is possible to see the invisible things hidden from our view, and it is largely due to a new phenomenon some call M-Theory. Physicists have recently proven how four dimensions (height, width, length, time) continue to expand outward, while six other dimensions remain curled up so tight it seems that nothing can penetrate them except 'motion.' In a recent article, it is stated, "The idea is that degrees of freedom like the electric charge of an electron will then arise simply as motion in the extra compact directions" (Cambridge M-Theory P2 para 3). A particle's ability to rise and expand is exactly what allows it to enter the compacted higher dimensions. Human consciousness must also learn to expand if it is to escape the confines of gravity and 'rise' into the higher dimensions of the garments of Heaven.

The six other dimensions lay dormant inside us until they stir from their 'rest' and jump into 'motion.' Joel, I think this is the restoration of the Kingdom within; this is what all the mystics, prophets, and sages were describing would come one day. Physicists have begun to understand these 'string dimensions' as the harmonic structure of potential energy before it has cooled down to the manifestation of atoms and molecules in matter. The world of quantum mechanics is the arena for explaining all the activity of the first three forces: Electromagnetism, Weak Nuclear force, and Strong nuclear force. It is also an arena for elucidating the scientific aspects of the three forces of the Sephirot Tree of Life. The ten dimensions may have different density and mass according to theorists, and they know that gravity is weaker on other dimensions and yet heavier on ours." Joel is blown away by everything Timka reveals to him; he actually begins to see things he never considered for the first time.

Fire, Ice & Genesis of One

Joel replies to Timka because he cannot hold in his own thoughts any longer. He was trying to hide things from her, but he did not know why he felt that way anymore. "Timka superstring theorists believe that due to the extreme heat of the early Universe, it was in a state of 'unification' or symmetry. When the Universe began to cool, the symmetry began to lose its wholeness until it eventually became disordered, resulting in solid crystalline structures. The solid crystalline structure is what we perceive as material things. According to the Cambridge Cosmology research on cosmic strings,"

The universe becomes hotter and denser until matter actually changes its phase; that is, it changes its form and properties. (P1 para 1)

"Once again, we see that it is a temperature that plays a vital role in how 'phase transitions' occur, and a very common analogy is how ice (solid phase), when melted, becomes liquid (liquid phase), and when heated up, it becomes a gas (gaseous phase). What is most relevant to the discussion is that "steam is 'more symmetric' than water, which is, in turn, more symmetric than ice" (Cambridge Phase Transitions P1 para 2); thus, at the very earliest point in the emergence of the Universe there is symmetry, as things cool down the symmetry is lost." Timka replies, "Mystic apocalyptic seers tell us that Enoch travels to the hottest place in the Universe where he sees a crystalline structure surrounded by fire. The bizarre thing is that the roof of the structure he describes has a ceiling covered in ice. The scriptures assert that the Supreme Being is a consuming fire, and Moses sees how there is a fire inside of fire at the burning bush. Enoch is afraid to approach the great Being surrounded by fire that symbolizes the absolute Unity or symmetry of the Most Holy Place! Did Enoch go far enough back in time to see the origin of the Universe when fire and ice were one? For the sake of the creation, the two forces separated. Now, at the top of the Tree of Life, the Supreme Being symbolized as a consuming fire with no shape and form, takes precedence. Still, at the bottom of the Tree, this amorphous cloud gets heavier as atoms combine and form the crystalline matter of physical life. 'As Above, So Below' is the way the ancients describe it, but according to Sefer Yetzirah, fire and ice were one before the fall of light into matter.

The world of Emanation represents the time before the Big Bang, and each subsequent world describes how the Universe developed in three further stages beyond the Big Bang. As we discussed earlier, before the Big Bang, the forces of the Universe were in a state of equilibrium; it is the 'breaking' of this balance that permits the earth to even exist in the Universe. The earth, as we know it, is the result of an event that shatters the 'symmetry' of a primordial perfect state, a state of innocence in the Universe. Have physicists proven that ancient mystical gnosis is a valid and credible science? Cambridge physicists know that matter, as we experience it, comes from an invisible shapeless state of non-being energy (zero point) and transforms into a solid structure of being.

It begins in a unified or 'symmetric' phase. Then, it passes through a succession of phase transitions until, at lower temperatures, we finally obtain the matter particles with which physicists are familiar today, that is electrons, protons, neutrons, photons, etc. (Cambridge).

The Universe is the point of infinity, whereas the sphere of our Earth is a point of finite circles or cycles that solidify or (contract/'Tzimtzum') until material substances such as the elements are born. Particles and zero-point energy actually emerge out of the contraction.

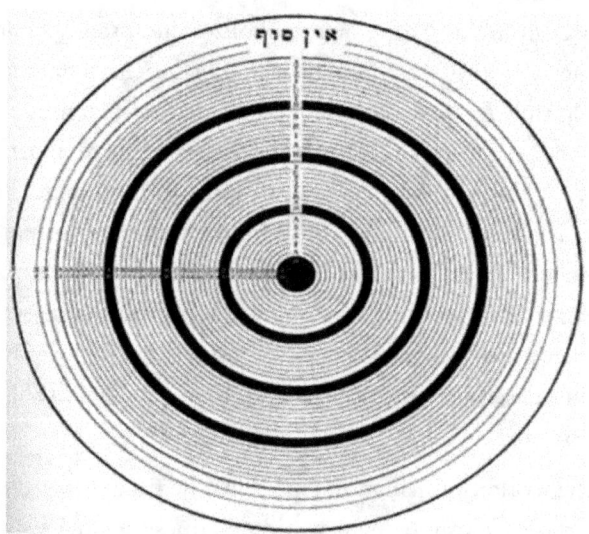

Figure 16 Hall CXXIV Solar Dimensions of the
Universe from Maurice's Indian Antiquities

Earlier, Joel learned how zero-point energy trapped in bubbles is the 1st phase of transition. Many used to think a vacuum contains 'empty space,' but this is not true anymore. According to the new quantum theorists, the zero-point energy is itself bound in a tight magnetic grip in the center of the 'vacuum,' and when the bubble bursts, this energy is released.

Joel hears his thoughts speaking to him again, "Remember that Ayin signifies the 'nothing' and the singularity point. From the Ayin came an explosion of energy that was later divided into four forces: EM, G, WF, and SF. Therefore, Joel thinks that zero-point energy theories illustrate how 'something' can come from 'nothing'; more importantly, it predicts that circles or spheres contain energy. The circle is the most mystical symbol of all, for it ties all the inner esoteric teachings together."

"As the temperature of the bubble rises, the zero-point energy released from the bubble then helps build gravity that influences the EM. Magnets influence gravity. Black holes are a good example of how zero-point energy works. Black holes emit radiation, according to Stephen Hawking, and the energy contains antimatter and matter. This zero-point energy pervades the center of everything and is more intense than any known energy in use today. This is just one other way to illustrate the process of generation referred to in the Garden of Eden in Genesis and an explanation of how something can come from 'nothing.' The Garden itself is central because this is where Adam and Eve are situated and it has a perimeter to show there are limits and bounds." Timka is really starting to like this new 'Joel.' Her distrust is starting to fade more and more.

The Son of Man put a light in her eyes, and she felt hope in her heart; it caused a tiny smile to appear at the corner of her mouth. She then speaks to Joel in her own words, not reading from a book to confirm and prove her knowledge. She actually feels inspired by him, "Joel, in light of this, perhaps the different divine names such as Elohim and Yahweh found in the original Genesis narrative, symbolize different states of energy evolving and changing the structure of our thoughts and consciousness, as the new creation finally materializes in humanity. This is what the books of Moses, Psalms, and

Prophets seek to hand down to anyone who can hear enough to see.

These names are 1 series of processes that take place in 4 worlds through 10 different functions. Did you know the verse Bereshith bara Elohim translated in modern versions as "In the beginning God created" is misleading because it does not take into account any of the ancient Mosaic methods of interpreting the text in regards to the creation process? Modern world religions embraced a later orthodox viewpoint, whether it is Judaic or Christian; in many cases, the original message of Moses is hard to find and buried under commentary criticism and later additions. Actually, the Hebrew denotes 'In the (Ba) Beginning (Reshith) created (bara) Powers (Elohim). The term 'bara' presents an idea of hewing or carving out, such as how a sculptor might cast a figure. The Son of Man is also an Architect who restructures our thoughts so we can perceive the Father. The term Reshith signifies both the terms 'six' and 'Wisdom.' Careful analysis will reveal how the author describes a particular structure built through Wisdom and that the process involves six aspects or sides that extend in six directions. The Zohar contains similar themes of how six phases are subject to scales and measurements before they eventually rest in a central point in the middle pillar of the Tree.

Metatron measures the extension of the Divine Attributes within us; the Kingdom is not outside of us – it is inside our point. Many people of varied backgrounds have speculated on the meaning of this text and decided that it meant days of time, but according to the Sefer Yetzirah commentary on Genesis, that assumption is false. It is the first stage in a two-part process. The first chapter of Genesis is a cosmological account of a spiritual kingdom and the second chapter represents the second phase that results in material existence and its perpetuation as it arose from its shells or organic existence. The angels created before Adam came from an invisible spiritual Kingdom. Professor Elton Hall explains the point of the second chapter:

"Then the creation story is given again in substantially reversed order, beginning with the emergence of earth and moisture, followed by water and eventually breath (Nephesh). This account occupies 21 (3x7) verses" (Iyer In The Beginning: Bereshith 24).

The protagonist is Elohim throughout the chapter and is responsible for building the creation. Hall explains how,

The first account flows into the second chapter, suggesting that these are not two separate stories pasted together but rather one continuous teaching dealing with levels of manifestation. The 'second creation' is a kind of lower-level inversion of the first. (24)

Joel, most modern biblical criticism and interpretation is based on the Documentary Theory, which assumes the Divine Names show there are four different narratives mixed together.

This prevents reading the documents as whole rather than segmented views. However, the two levels of manifestation do seem to parallel the descent and ascent traditions found in many texts that discuss the operation of sefiroth. The divine energy of the Universe can manifest as pure spirit vapor and then back again into the solid crystalline ingredients of matter. The process of precipitation is a prime example of how an element transforms from one state into another. The sefiroth are the vehicles used by Elohim to enter the world of form and the Merkavah is the vehicle that allows a human to travel into the realms of heaven and the formless Ayin from which Avir emerged. When a person learns how to visualize the formless structure of the Universe, he or she is capable of transcending space and time in the Merkavah of knowledge. Professor Iyer explains the process:

The individual is in the world but no longer of it, and humanity is led by imperceptible stages toward that earthly paradise, Pardes, that mirror the archetypal Garden of Eden. Having eaten of the Tree of Knowledge, humanity may rise up to taste the Tree of Life Eternal. (25)

Do you see that there are stages, Joel? It does not happen overnight. This is a vision of Moses, if we are able to correctly identify and name the steps, we too will see the vision! Then the first chapter of Genesis becomes the next stage in the process of our spiritual evolution. During the 13th c. in Spain, there was a small group of Philosopher-Kabbalists during the Medieval period who described the same process as various 'spheres' or 'sefiroth' that unfold or emanate from within the point of Keter to form the light and darkness. Each has a 'firmament' or 'membrane' between them. Again, bear in mind how the Electromagnetic spectrum operates and it will help you to visualize what the ancients may have tried to describe. The wisdom of the Zohar explains:

The Holy One, Blessed be He, found it necessary to create all these things in the world to ensure its permanence, for there must be, as it were, a brain with many membranes encircling it. (Iyer 48)

"Like the 'branes' described in M-Theory, these spiritual membranes also protect an inner core that contains all the seeds of potential existence. Raghavan Iyer, the General Editor of Bereshit, said,"

Although at first a membrane or vesture, each stage becomes a brain to the succeeding stage. The same process takes place here below so that on this paradigm, man, in this world, combines brain and shell, spirit and body, for the harmonious ordering of the world. (48)

Joel, captured by her spell does not notice she began quoting from the books again. Ironically, he does not seem bothered by her habit of pointing at the pages of the book for the first time in his life. He just smiles a little and continues to listen. "According to Superstring theorists, something similar happens in the Universe as the three forces emerge from the point of 'unification' to become distinct forces:

Viewed from the moment of creation forward, the universe will pass through a succession of phase transitions at which the strong nuclear force will become differentiated and then the weak nuclear force and electromagnetism. (Cambridge P2 para 3)

Joel, do you remember why each force proceeds out of the other? According to Wisdom literature, the four forces Einstein describes are not what I am referring to regarding this particular level of interpretation. It is important to remember that Genesis is not a story about when, in Time, the creation took place. It took place in just one day actually and not six, yet this eternal, ongoing, cumulative process has a definite aim. The Day of Eternity (Symmetry) contains all the prophecies (properties of Avir) that become history (materialized Aur) in time. The prophets all received their visions from this earliest Day, which is not equivalent to a number 1, but the One. Physicists receive their scientific data from going back into the earliest stages of the Universe; Philosopher-Kabbalists receive their scientific data from Day One. The physical creation held together by particles, atoms, and fields of force, however, does take place within Eternity in Time.

Eternity contains Time. Quantum physicists have actually begun to realize how the four forces originated from the point of the Universe and how the state of energy changes as the Universe continues to expand. Einstein's General Theory of Relativity only dealt with the really 'big things' in the Universe, such as the planets and space itself; it did not account for the really 'small things' that can only now be discovered with the aid of quantum mechanics. The invisible things of the

Kingdom can be seen through the things are made, is literally, philosophically, and metaphysically true." Timka was set on fire with inspiration, just letting the words fall right out of her mouth effortlessly and with power – she felt an increase of energy as she heard things she did not know before that very moment.

A Garden of Time

The term Gan Eden denotes a defined period of time and amount of space that is embodied or surrounded by an organized sphere of activity or force. The Garden of Eden contains eternal time, but language and censorship seem to make us oblivious to how this world of light, which created us in the beginning, is not included in the story of creation in the world of matter. Science does not accept that spiritual reality bound by physical time and space can interact with man's mind at all, due to Cartesian philosophers. Time exists in the Garden as a revolving sphere of movement and energy. There is more than one method to detect and measure time. Waves move in time and yet are limited by cycles for their movement, whereas particles can be anywhere at any time, in and out of time. Waves continue to move outward, cycles begin to accumulate, and galaxies evolve into superclusters as the Aether continues creating time and space. The next figure is one researcher's early attempt to describe the eight cycles of wave movement. What is significant is that there are eight steps needed in order for a wave to complete a revolution or undulation. There are 8 Garments the High Priest wears to show forth the Glory of YHVH.

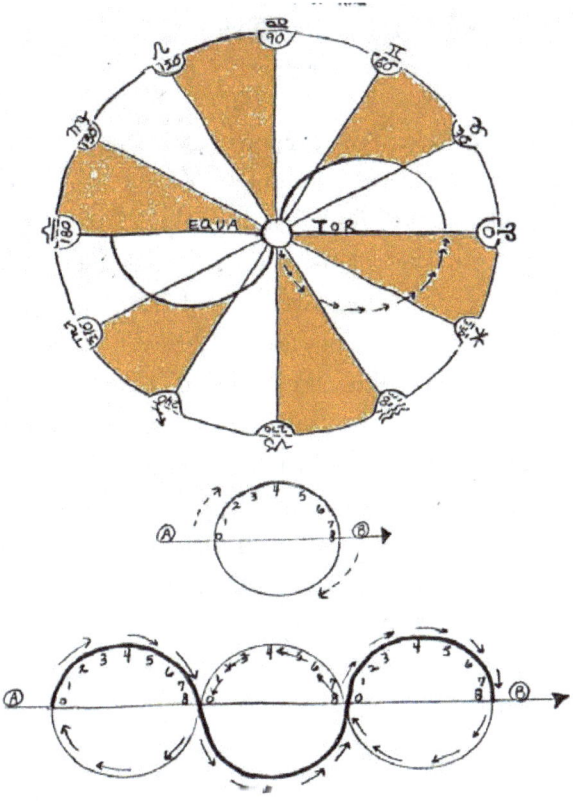

Figure 17 Cycles of a Wave from Spectra-Biology

The Wheels of the Chariot prepare and maintain the Garden that symbolically denotes a living, moving, evolving form of life. The four elements of Pythagoras symbolize the figures (Eagle, Lion, Ox, and Man) around the Chariot.

It is a fact that an atom needs eight shells to be stable and material life, as we know it, bound by this rhythmic eight-cycle movement is limited. Our spiritual life has to be free from the oscillation and fluctuation of time in space in order to experience the divine worlds of Light. The world of light is a continuous rest in the glow of energy. The 7th wave of the cycle of light must end in the 8th movement that completes a wave-front. During the 8th Day, many of the prophecies will manifest in the world through the Light.

Timka tells Joel she has to go for now and that she will be home soon. The truth is Timka did not want to go home before because she was stressed out. Now after she and Joel completed the circle, she feels better. Now that she is alone, she goes to her special place. Her thoughts decide where they want to take Timka, and she finds herself thinking about the author of II Enoch, who describes a figure named Adoil or "Yad-El" (Hand of EL), a figure that Gershom Scholem says shaped and formed everything in the physical universe out of the 'Ayin' or 'nothing'. Slavonic II Enoch contains an account of how the invisible and visible light came out of "Adoil". According to Gershom Scholem, the Primordial "Great Aeon" is a connotation of the name "Adoil": "Ado" also means 'his eternity' or 'his eon.' The "il" is a reference to 'el.' This could be a variant form of 'Ed, Timka says to herself.' If so, 'Adoil' means the "Great Aeon or Age of Elohim." The Great Aeon/Year is 10,000.00 yrs. or the 10 Weeks of Enoch's Apocalypse.

Humanity has literally been born 'out of Time' in accordance with the views of the apocalyptic seers. The Secret Age began in the Garden of Eden, and Enoch's 10 Week Apocalypse vision is an attempt to help readers find historical parallels to the prophet's visions. The amorphous, infinite, limitless source and substance of the Universe was unknown to any mortal being until disclosed to Enoch, the harbinger of the Messiah who takes on the mysterious garment of יהוה. Timka falls into a deep sleep as she hears the Voice begin to awaken her from inside the Kingdom. "Timka, let us dwell upon the idea that there are two principles that arise from the invisible boundless Elohim, and this is the origin of the dualism governing our physical life. Paolo Sacchi, author of Jewish Apocalyptic and Its History, sees an Iranian influence on the concept of "from not being to being, from invisible to visible." in ancient times, Iranians, Jews, and others shared and embraced many common spiritual traditions concerning the sacred science of the Universe. At that time, civilization was not as entrenched in aggression and violence; all seemed to spend more time contemplating the ancient sciences as understood at that time. What the author of Enoch adds to the Iranian concept of creation is unique:

The world is created, but the author thinks that spiritual things and beings were created before physical things and beings. (247)

This is exactly what we see in the two creation stories in Genesis. Chapter 1 deals with the creation of spiritual realities and a spiritual creation called Adam. Chapter 2 refers to the physical creation of Adam and this is where the generations of time began. The 'Toledoth' or generations of Adam show a progression of individuals, families, communities, nations, and finally, empires. Enoch's role is to teach the Elect how to see Elohim this is how one becomes a Son of Man. There are many sons of darkness and sons of light born from the Son of Man as they all begin to participate in the Tikkun. Some see this Tikkun as a Holy War among the angels in heaven and on earth.

However, there will be many sons born from the emerging Kingdom, but the true elect learn the secrets of the Son of Man are for the sake of healing the broken vessels, never war or aggression. The true heirs of the Kingdom perform non-aggressive roles through their 'understanding' and 'wisdom' into the secrets and mysteries hidden from humanity. The act itself becomes their desperate prayer for the restoration of the Universe. The Universe is the tabernacle of the Divine Energy or Plurality of Power (Elohim), and the harmonious order of Kosmos is the tabernacle of humanity.

Adam is a tabernacle of the Holy Spirit. The three components function as one unit. Humanity lives in a three-dimensional world with two polar opposites for each dimension. The six days or edges of the Universe, with good and evil at each of its points, provide us with a method to visualize the geometry of the creation as a way to change our consciousness through geometric sacred principles and forms.

EMERGENCE OF ADAM II

Timka, Joel and Alexa are 'caught up' in the Shekinah that feels like a powerful whirlwind in their lives at first. We all manifest polar opposites as a mingling of invisibility/visibility, flesh/spirit, and life/death, whether one has faith in a Creator or not. Rudolph Otto described the pre-existent Son of Man as a Reality that dwells in a two-fold mystery; aspects of the Reality are revealed to the world as a process known in Christianity as the First and Second visitations. However, in the book of Acts, the original Movement known as 'The Way.', many people are still waiting for the Second Coming and are not aware that the Messiah is here acting as the Paraclete at first until one receives the Kingdom from within. He then becomes King and manifests in our thoughts as in a cloud, enthroned alone in the primordial light. As Ruach begins to pass through our consciousness, it calls forth Adoil from the depths of non-being, and from his stomach is then "born" a 'new being' as if it were different from Adoil. Adoil is the great Aeon of Light that bears all creation. The Hand of YHVH, once held behind his back, now extends to save and deliver as a Mighty warrior. The war of the Heavens has always held humanity captive to delusions. Imagination and Intellect, when not balanced with Wisdom, is a dangerous combination.

This creation parallels the primordial light and background radiation that precedes the rest of creation. This is how the light of the 1st day, or the first light in Genesis 1:3, differs from the light of the 4th day. Scientists now do not believe in the first light, and they consider Medieval Philosophers- Kabbalists, who wrote about it extensively, as frauds. Toledo, Spain, around the time of 1240, was home to the most advanced group of scientists the world will ever see. Without telescopes or anything other than knowledge of Aether and YHVH, I literally knew and realized that the nature of Aether is unlimited and undifferentiated. The doctrine of the Ether was the talk of the town. As the original 'hidden light' descends into the lower world as 'hidden wisdom,' many find its pearls, and they are gradually transformed into human angels in a state of innocence and knowledge, two characteristic traits of the eschaton. The Mystery is that most have forgotten or never heard of the role of Aether and Light during this chaotic period, which eventually ended when the Hebrews had to leave Spain due to pogroms and tribulations. Perhaps this is why they inherited such potent supernatural wisdom. A Wisdom that had to hide itself, to save itself from a great darkness that descended upon the thoughts of all.

Wisdom found not a Place on earth where she could inhabit; her dwelling, therefore, is in Heaven. Wisdom went forth to dwell among the sons of men, but she obtained not a habitation. Wisdom returned to her place and seated herself in the midst of the angels.

When the Elect are born from this immeasurable age of light, a 'thought-filled' light inducts some into the invisible heavenly kingdom set up by the Son of Man that has no day or night, time or error. According to Scholem's analysis of this ancient mystical theory, there are two lights in Ayin Sof:

'Thought-filled' and 'Thought-less'. The 'thought-filled' light contains the thought of creation and form, while the thought-less light is self-absorbed in its negation of form and wants nothing but its own essence. (Scholem On the Mystical Shape of the Godhead 84).

This light-filled with 'thought' is a type of light that deals with 'ideas' and archetypes. The 'golem' is the pre-existent state (Aziluth) of the physical creation (Assiyah) that emerges into a state of contemplative consciousness through the spiritual shape and form of Elohim that mirrors the Universe. The

167

pattern Moses saw he called Elohim. All is dormant in the chaotic formless world of strings until given shape and form through various atomic combinations that result in matter. The other light delights in the darkness of the void and feeds only on itself. Chaos does not reflect the light but only absorbs its potent essence, changing it back into nothingness. He further explains that "The 'thought-filled' light is the medium for the process of 'tzimtzum' (85), but not all of the light participates in the event. He says, "When the thought-filled light penetrated into primordial space, it only penetrated into the upper half of the realm freed for creation" (85). He says the 'golem' or lower half was actually a 'formless matter,' and this 'formless matter' is a good way of visualizing the home and chaotic world of strings. The 'thought-filled' light helps give everything its form, shape, and eventual emergence from the abyss of formlessness and chaos. Something does come from 'nothing', and once again, science has proven this is true. These two different 'lights' are actually two realms that pour into each other perpetually until the end of time. Scholem writes,

Creation could not proceed without this substratum. The further the process of the worlds' coming about proceeds, the deeper the interpenetration of these two lights (86).

Nathan, the prophet of Sabbatai Zevi, composed a doctrine concerning the 'Two Lights' in order to explain the origin of evil. According to Scholem's view of his theory, there will come a time when the formless matter of the chaotic abyss is finally subject to shape and form. Scholem explains that,

At the time of the Redemption, the rays of the thought-filled light will penetrate to the dark 'lower half' of the scene of creation, the abyss whose depths contain the thoughtless principle, lacking in shape (86).

Apparently, all 'shapeless things' will be given a shape and form in the eschaton. In the world of 'little things' (Quantum mechanics), where there is no order or lasting form as each string vibrates and changes in different particles, the 'thought-less light' operates as the power of the abyss. In the world of 'big things' (General Relativity Theory), things have shape and form and are solid objects used in the world. Ultimately, Scholem thinks the primordial space 'tahiru' created by the 'tzimtzum' will be entirely filled with the 'thought-filled light' finally giving shape and form to all shapeless things when it fills the entire abyss of darkness with the life-giving properties of an undivided Divine light. This will have an influence on us also because although the Divine light gives shape and form to all created things, humanity operates and has its being under the power of the 'thought-less light.' This is why Adam (humanity), after being spiritually shaped and formed in the image of Elohim through the divine attributes, contains the only 'Emet AUR' - true light emanated from the foundation of the Olam (Age). The equilibrium of the 'two lights' results in a balanced Universe within our mind, capable of reflecting its inner light into the physical creation of our ego. Scholem concludes that the first worlds that were created were destroyed because this true shape had not yet achieved its perfection so the balance and harmony in which everything exists through the secret of this shape had not yet been established. (45)

Joel, there is a particular organization the Sephiroth will measure us by; all are unbalanced at first until we help by activating our inner organization through the conscious realization of the ancient sacred meaning of each sefirah.

We can only achieve the 'true shape' when we learn how to name and recognize the various structures of our inner world mirrored in the Universe through experiencing them. We all encounter things and certain events that can change our world, from up to down. Ecstasy and Agony are the great transformers of human life; we will all experience a measure of each aspect in various ways during our lifetime. Knowing how to decipher the events and words/signs gives us a clue about what stage we are going through. When you figure it out and 'name' the experience or state of consciousness, you reconnect with each attribute one at a time until you complete the process. Each sefirah provides 'Form' or 'Tzur' through 3 branches (writing, measuring, and numbering). When a person learns how to reflect his or her inner light outward into the creation in a positive and constructive way, all three branches form one tree that grows inside your mind, feeding you from your own desire and intent. At first, we only want to experience the physical things of the earth; only secondly does one desire to pursue the Divine Light or that Wisdom from above consciously; many will not be able to do this. Thus, the 'thoughtless light' syndrome is what controls everything right now. Hardly any people are able to escape in time to receive the Kingdom while they are here and conscious of desiring to attain the Crown." Timka had been talking for a while and did not notice that Joel had fallen asleep. She is not upset about it, though; she just smiled to herself, cleared her throat, and said a little louder, do you understand Joel? A (higher consciousness) has to dwell inside our lower consciousness in order to give it shape and form. The Son of Man is the true Wisdom that awakes in human consciousness. Light-like Wisdom can be obvious or mysterious due to the proportion of its manifestation in matter and form. Chrapowicki, the author of Spectro-Biology, explains that as light sinks into the matter, the less luminous its character will be:

It is a fact of common knowledge that just as a disturbance of matter may give rise to light, so also light may disturb matter. It is impossible to separate light from matter, even though the presence of light is not always evident. As the condensation of matter increases, its luminosity diminishes. (Chrapowicki Spectro- Biology 10)

This indicates that light is contained in everything at first, but as it remains in its container of matter, it begins to lose its luminescent shine but is still always there in a different state of wave states. Though the luminaries did not shine until the fourth day, Moses wrote that Elohim creates light on the first day this is how Eternity (First light) can exist in time even though it appears outside of time. The light of the fourth day literally contains the light of the first day. The light of the first day was such a blinding light that all the Hebrew prophets describe it as a light brighter than the sun itself. The Undifferentiated Avir of the 13th century was considered an infinity of infinities. It is so bright we do not even see it there. According to Haisch:

The zero-point field is such a blinding light. Since it is everywhere, inside and outside of us, permeating every atom in our bodies, we are effectively blind to it. It blinds us to its presence. (Haisch P2)

"Joel, any light we actually are able to see is like a crumb in comparison to the light of zero point energy. At the zero point energy level, there is no movement but only rest as the waves of energy settle into each other in a dense circle of brilliant white light. Perhaps the seventh day of rest has validity that is more scientific if we look through the eyes of physics. Joel managed to say, "Timka, I, too, need to have a moment with no movement; your light is very powerful; we can talk again later, ok? Love you." Timka just smiled and hung up the phone. She was now looking forward to more conversations with Joel when he actually participated.

If you can imagine how energy rests in matter, then you can also imagine how Adam waits in time. Ancient mystic lore says that the original 'man of light' named Adam Qadmon observed the light of the first day. He could see from one end of the Earth to the other, according to rabbis. This light wisdom, withdrawn and reserved for the righteous at the 'end of days, is fully activated in the 'world to come.' The ancient heavenly light older than the light of the fourth day, belongs to Yahweh's essence; the sun and moon receive light from the spark of this heavenly light so infinitely brighter than any light on Earth. It surrounds the Throne Chariot and even the angels cannot look upon it. The elect are destined to receive this light and rejoice during the eighth week when they receive the two-edged sword.

II Enoch 25:1-3 describes a mystical account of the emergence of the heavenly light above Yahweh's Throne. According to the author, on the second day of the creation, the spirit of the firmament, described as an angelic being, will rise from the Great Age of Light. This is not describing the creation of earth and heaven but the creation of a heavenly spiritual structure or Body. John describes it to his community as the Logos and Light of the Kosmos. However, the author of Enoch wants us to know that the pen of false interpreters molded an artificial image of this figure with the pagan clay of religious ideology. Hidden behind various myths and heresies, the real story of the Son of Man buried by the 'thought-less light' is hard to perceive until reflected in the consciousness of Adam Kadmon. When the Son of Man rests in the Father on the seventh day, human consciousness will be one with heavenly awareness.

Rediscovering the Son of Man

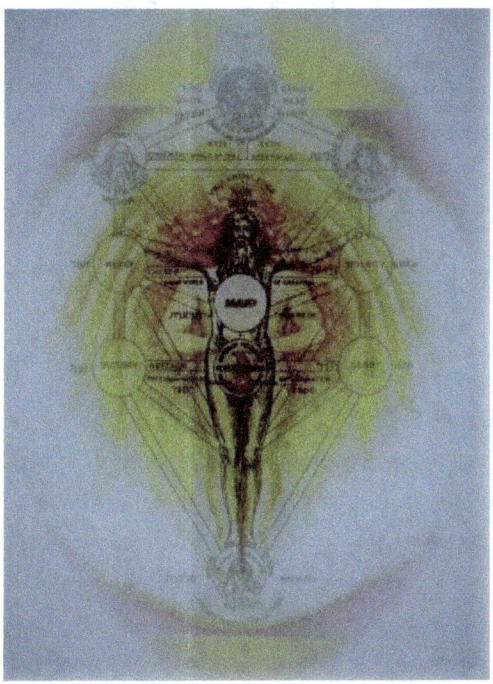

Figure 18 Angelic/Human Tree of Life

Alexa wanted to help Timka, but she did not know what had transpired between her and Joel. Alexa is very concerned about Joel's sudden interest in the books. Four things can happen to the seed once it is placed in the ground: the parables are hidden from those who do not recognize the Messiah. If the seed fell on hard soil, no spiritual discernment can pierce the hard heart; if the seed took root and began to grow, the least troubles that occur can quickly feel like defeat. There was one out of four chances; the seed would reach the prepared ground, take root, and grow within before finally producing fruit, after its own kind. Even though there are many different scenarios presented throughout the Evangels, there is one primary goal in all four. The goals of the Son of Man are to overturn common ideas, reveal signs of the coming Heavenly Son of Man, introduce the 'hidden' Kingdom, and teach people how to see the invisible, formless Father. This is not that apparent by today's standards and interpretations of the biographies of his life that we call the 'Gospels' now. Countless authors and scholars provide a history, analysis, and interpretation of this figure's role in both canonical and non-canonical literature. Alexa, in an effort to help Timka deal with Joel's issues, for lack of a better word, decides to outline a brief summary of general images found in the Bible publicly acknowledged and loved among many denominations and communities.

Her family taught her to use the Bible as a foundation; she is very knowledgeable but still lacked a deeper understanding of the inner dynamics and esoteric nature of spiritual reality. There was also a need to control what others believed, but she was not aware of how much it influenced her behavior and decisions. She and Timka studied for many years, but Alexa clearly remembers how they did not see eye to eye on many things. Somehow, they managed to pull through the rough spots in spite of their differences. Alexa felt the need to contribute to Timka's goal, to let her know she was standing by her side. She went through each of the four Evangels one by one and compared them to each other, and the results were amazing.

Alexa started with Matthew's Servant of Yahweh theme, which relies on the extensive use of Isaiah's apocalyptic imagery, and the importance of lineage is salient. Mark portrays the image of Messiah, who they called Christ, an esoteric theurgist, exorcist, and healer endowed with great power from above. Luke presents a truly human person with emotions, thoughts, and a spiritual consciousness. This image, placed in a historical context with scriptural allusions to prophets of old, such as Isaiah and Jeremiah, creates a truly historical portrait. Finally, John illustrates an image of the Son of Man as the personification of the Word. His personal identity is the central axis of the entire gospel. For John, one's reception of the promised Comforter or Paraclete is a witness to his glorification. The 'Beloved One' motif is not in the other three gospels at all, yet it is evident in the Enochic literature. Clearly, each author has a different purpose and level of knowledge that influenced the contents of their account. Each one seems to add another detail not seen in the others' works, and together, in spite of the apparent contradictions, there is unity and wholeness.

The four Gospels correspond to PARDES-or Paradise. Peshat, Remez, Derush, and Sod are the historical, literal, analogical, and mystical levels of interpretation. In this respect, Matthew corresponds to peshat (historical), Mark corresponds to derush (analogical) meaning, while Luke corresponds to remez (literal), and John, of course, would correspond to sod, which is the mystical esoteric interpretation.

Luke was a physician and historian; Mark uses literary devices and a third-person narrative voice to tell and show the events from outside the immediate circle. Matthew writes an account of the events in accordance with orthodox Jewish traditions. The author of John writes a metaphysical cosmic drama about a Divine Logos that humanity must learn to embrace. John's speaker uses the first-person narrative through most of the gospel and often says 'I AM' or 'I will be' according to the Hebrew meaning. Many different images of this single figure spin around in our minds like bits of images in a kaleidoscope of signs until we put them in place.

Matthew's Evidence

Matthew writes from a historical point of view where genealogical background is the primary importance. Matthew 1:17 gives an account of generations in order to prove the historical validity of the birth. There are also apocalyptic images in chapter 24 that outline specific instructions to those living in the 'end days,' and Matthew 7:1-10 describes discipleship as works done during a harvest; in this way, he also provides a timeframe for the harvest. The importance of the Kingdom is prominent, especially in chapters 5-7 and 13. Matthew explains that it is near and even present, yet still waiting for its full realization.

The Sermon on the Mount motif recalls the revelation of Moses on Mt. Sinai; by comparing this event with the Son of Man going up to the mountaintop to preach, Matthew is saying that the Son of Man is the new Moses. Matthew expects a person to take personal responsibility for choices; he did not want people placating the rabbinic or foreign authorities. We should exceed the righteousness of the religious establishment. Matthew teaches that realization of how our behavior affects our perception of the Kingdom is the thing to strive for in order to escape the woes destined to come. Matthew brings out what is new and what is old by going back to the Hebrew prophets and grafts in his explanation of how particular prophecies relate to the Son of Man.

The transfiguration scene is reminiscent of Moses and Mt Sinai and is Matthew's way of saying that this is the new Moses if you have the mystic's ears to hear and eyes to see. Matthew portrays the new Moses as a teacher, healer, and criticizer of authority. Aaron's appointment as Moses' Voice parallels John the Baptist who is a Voice crying out in the wilderness. Judgment falls on the people through John's apocalyptic message, and many receive a taste of the Kingdom.

Matthew records a very detailed story of the betrayal of the disciples not found in Luke or John's Gospel. The author writes that one of them will betray the Son of Man before the night is over, and all say it is not true. All say they would never betray him, not even for death. Twice more, he admonishes them, even saying at one point: "Stay awake and pray that you may not come into the time of trial." Is it possible that if just one were able to stay awake, the cup could have passed from him that night? We may never know, but what is certain is that no human could save him or herself because of the weakness of the flesh. None could stay awake. This is echoed in the saying that the "Spirit indeed is willing, but the flesh is weak." This is why he had to drink the cup for no human being found on earth could. Many similar things take place after these events in the synoptic gospels, but some of these things are not in John's gospel. The idea that humans cannot save themselves and that they must be redeemed is central to the early Enoch texts, as illustrated in a comment by Paolo Sacchi,

What particularly hurts humans is that they must fight forces superior to them, and for this reason, salvation can only come when they are safe in the Valley of the Just. The destiny of this historical world is to end in the other world.

Sacchi describes a place or container for the souls of people that will gain a habitation outside of time:

God has arranged a place in the other world (or in this one, at some halfway point?) where there are valleys in which the souls of the just are kept safe from the attacks of the demons, close to a spring of water of light. (Sacchi, Jewish Apocalyptic and its History 84).

John describes this place as a 'Being of Light' called the 'Logos'. Is this what the author of Enoch describes as Adoil?

Mark's Evidence

Mark was a good friend of Peter and his gospel was written much earlier than Matthew and Luke, some say around the late 60's A.D. The main image in Mark is of a victorious, suffering servant. This Servant opposes all religious doctrines not in accord with the Prophets. His figure uses familiar ideas in the parables and then deliberately announces that they are now obsolete. We meet a figure who presents revolutionary ideas and who acts contrary to accepted norms. However, Mark wants us to know that his strange behavior only seems inverted because of the darkness of the world itself. The world of the flesh cannot see the truth. Like Matthew, some of the main ideas found in Mark involve suffering and death, true discipleship, sacrifices, and helping to pluck souls from the fire during the harvest.

How followers should try to live during the transition between the beginning of the Kingdom and its consummation at the final age is a central theme. No stories of birth and resurrection, as in Matthew, are in Mark. The Messiah is a mysterious Maskil who reveals and yet conceals simultaneously the true Kingdom. Many expected a political Kingdom, but Mark outlines a hidden mystical heritage. Matthew begins with a genealogical description, but Mark begins with an examination of the role of John the Baptist, who he calls the "Preparer of the Way." Mark starts his gospel at the scene of the baptism, and this provides a link with Elijah, who stood against the Baal worshippers. In Mark, however, the temptation scene is not as developed as Matthew's dialogue between Satan and the Son of Man. The ministry starts after John's arrest, and Yahshua begins casting out evil spirits; in all the gospels, the people ask him to leave when he casts the spirits into the swine, and they run over a cliff. The community believes his work is malevolent, and only Mark provides more details about the exorcisms. The daughter who asks for the head of John the Baptist is Herodias in Mark, and in Matthew's, she is Salome.

Mark's Son of Man gives the disciples power to exorcise demons, but in Matthew's, their lack of faith prevents it from happening. Mark gives the reader a very different perspective: The Son of Man displays powers considered divine, and the chief priests fear his ability to mesmerize the public. Like King Solomon, Yahshua too is a kind of judge and discerns right from wrong; he is a kind of arbitrator, and an example of this is the question about the tax due to Caesar and the things given to Yahweh. In Chapter 13, the figure gives interpretations of apocalyptic ideas that are entirely eschatological in nature. A truly humane image of the Son of Man is of a man who gives women a sense of self-esteem and worth. Not many other male religious leaders allowed women inside their doors nor granted permission to follow them in public. Yahshua's public encounters with women are a common occurrence in Mark's gospel. The betrayal scene is very similar to Matthew's when the young man in a linen cloth runs away. Interestingly, Pilate does not wipe his hands of the blood of the innocent man. The soldiers mock and scourge him with the crown of thorns and a purple cloak. Simon of Cyrene helps carry the cross. Mark records the appearance of darkness upon the land during the crucifixion and adds the duration of suffering and time of death. The darkness upon the land indicates the supernatural nature of the event. There is no mention of a soldier piercing his side with a spear. Mark concludes with a list of signs and the ascension of the Messiah into Heaven; Matthew does not mention ascension.

Luke's Evidence

Luke focuses on the mission of the Son of Man and tells the story through different forms of parables, wisdom sayings, and homilies. Basic to all the forms used by Luke are the historical and theological backgrounds that are so integral to the structure of the entire gospel. Luke explains that the Son of Man's crucifixion was for a bigger purpose and was all a part of a divine plan. Luke, like Matthew, uses many scriptural allusions to explain how the Son of Man has a hidden identity and mission. Luke opens his gospel with the how and why he, too, is indebted to hand down an account of the events himself. Matthew began with a genealogical image and Mark begins with the relationship between the Baptist and the Messiah. Both of them share a conception of supernatural means, for Elizabeth was past the age of childbearing, but Yahweh used her as the fulfillment of Sarah's type, the wife of Abraham who too was past the age of childbearing but is blessed with Isaac. Luke fills in more details of the birth of John the Baptist than the others. This serves to give us a background to the events within a particular framework, the mighty works of Yahweh in the life of John. Neither Matthew nor Mark mentions John's parents in any detail. Luke tells us that John had the Holy Spirit even before his birth. This creates a very different perspective on the role and identity of this hidden figure. He, too, has a role in the Father's divine plan.

Luke also mentions something no other gospel does: the story of the female prophet named Anna, who never leaves the temple day or night, and how she went out teaching and heralding the birth of the Messiah. Luke describes more of his active daily life; he tells the story of the Temple visit when he was twelve and how old he was when he first started preaching. Luke's genealogical account goes back to the son of Adam and the Son of Elohim (God), while Matthew starts with Abraham and descends to the birth of Messiah.

Matthew seems to have selected an idea familiar to Orthodox Judaism, the patriarchy of Abraham and the claim to an inheritance.

The transfiguration in Mark takes place eight days after the feeding of thousands, but in Matthew's, it takes place in just six days. Luke says that the disciples were sleepy during the transfiguration; Matthew and Mark do not mention this at all. Luke clearly defines the relationship between the Son and the Father. None can know the Son except the Father or who the Father is except the Son unless the Son chooses to reveal the Father to others. This is what he said he came to do. The Seventy that are able to cast out demons in the Name do not appear in the other gospels. The image of the Son in Luke includes the ability to explain the life cycle of demons, their practices, and how to avoid them in verses 11:24-27. We see a personality that condemns the rich and the religious institutions that are full of hypocrisy and pretense. Luke's image of a Judge who will punish those who fail to grow in the true righteousness of the Kingdom is prominent throughout chapter 12:49-54.

Luke cites many catastrophes wherein sinners perished in contrast to their own personal responsibility to accept the terms of the Kingdom or perish; these images are missing from Matthew and Mark, such as buildings falling on people and so on. The parable of the cursed fig tree is also more detailed, and the added twist of three years is unique to Luke. Luke presents many more parables of the Messiah than are found in the other gospels: working conditions, fair play, relationships built on trust, and most importantly, love. Luke includes many prophecies and says that many will not be able to perceive the Kingdom, but it will take many by surprise as in the days of Noah. This is a common practice for Luke to continue to bring the prophecies of old in line with the previous predictions and speeches. He gives all the scriptures a sense of continuity and inner unity. His apocalyptic theme includes armies surrounding Jerusalem on every side, wars and earthquakes, families turning against each other, conflict of nations, and the eventual divine intervention by the Son of Man.

Another contrast between Luke and the other synoptic gospels is the record of the figure advising the disciples to obtain a coat and sword for their journey during evil times for the times require them to be prepared see Luke 22: 35-38. At the time of the betrayal in Matthew's account, the Son of Man goes to the disciples three times; in Luke, it's only once, and there is an angel involved not mentioned in Matthew or Mark. Luke's use of the stranger on the road to Emmaus is unique and insightful and lends a sense of credibility to the reaction of those who saw the resurrected Messiah.

John's Beloved Son

John's image is more spiritual and esoteric and is meant for the community of the Beloved ones especially taught by John. The elect and the 'little flock' are paramount subjects throughout the gospel. John records meditations and mystical prayers uttered by the 'Word'. There are long soliloquies that add drama and suspense. There are traces of ideas that seem Apocalyptic and Gnostic in nature, and there is recent evidence to support its connection to the Essenes according to modern scholarship. Mainly it is a personal, emotional expression of the longing and feeling of an angelic human being who knew the Father intimately. John's gospel, written between the 80's and 90's, is abundant in spiritual themes and lessons for the inner soul of humanity. He had developed its ideas for a long time and felt that his assembly was the Elect one. The speaker in the gospel has great feelings and sincerity, like a father talking to his children. It portrays an image of a person who has a divine identity, and this is what gives John its distinctiveness. This gospel is very rich in esoteric and mystical concepts that date back to the authors of Bereshit/Genesis. The divinity of the Messiah from Nazareth is its main concern.

Matthew, Mark, and Luke all begin their gospels in a different way, but for the most part, they all pass through the same places on the road to Golgotha. John, in contrast, breaks completely with the type of framework found in the synoptic gospels. His image is of a divine figure known as the "Word" or Dabar, also known as "Memra," a spirit of Wisdom that descended upon the ancient prophets. This 'Word' entered the flesh of a mortal creature of clay in order to save the flesh from its own weakness. Therefore, instead of a genealogy or connection with John the Baptist, John begins with the image of the Word by explaining that the Logos was in the beginning and played a role in the creation. This same Word now creates a new one if people are able to hear it and accept it. Only those who can believe in His Name can receive the power to become children of Yahweh.

John presents an ancient image of a divine being destined to come into the world for the express purpose of birth, death, and resurrection. John the Baptist says: "This was he of whom I said, 'He who comes after me ranks ahead of me because he was before me.'" (Harper Collins Study Bible John 1:15-17).

Amazingly, all four gospels agree on one thing – the identity of John the Baptist: "I am the voice of one crying out in the wilderness," in accordance with a prophecy found in Isaiah. John's role and mission are very crucial to the whole event, and this is something that is obscure today. In the Gospel of John, the Son of Man is actually a bridge between the temporal and historical realms of heaven and earth. He contrasts light and darkness with the 'Logos' and the 'Kosmos'. John's gospel presents more details of the disciples, Elijah, and his disciple's activities and conversations.

John's image is very mystical and esoteric in nature and yet historical and practical to those who had received the higher vision. Nathaniel was one of those who could see greater things due to his possession of the higher wisdom. The 'eyes to see' and 'ears to hear' are common and central themes to all four gospels. John presents an ancient image of an unknown pre-existent being, only revealed to his 'little flock.' The author of Enoch describes a circle of disciples that are like a plant inside of another plant, and they have the 'Logos' or sevenfold teaching given to them.

Alexa wonders if John 8:56-57 is evidence that this figure existed before Abraham. His prayers focus on those saved in his Name, he promises to keep them until the end of the age. He is alien to this world, for it cannot and does not perceive his identity.

By the time Alexa summarized the four Evangels, she caught a glimpse of why the book of Enoch is actually important, after all these years, it just occurred to her that she should read it herself. Alexa never thought she would admit it, but now she knows that any attempt to read the gospels outside of their own indigenous background is, therefore, futile. The gospels present various images of the Son of Man, and this is exactly what we need to get a balanced point of view; there were many more gospels and voices crying in the wilderness, but these are those that managed to survive the ravages of man's censorship and time. In the apocalyptic tradition, the 'little flock' represents the elect that helped to create the new world. They restore Adam Kadmon as they gradually perceive the reality of Enoch's texts. They dwell in the restored garden in secret, as mortals still under the power of 'fallen angels' struggle to see and find the entrance back into the garden. For this community, the Son of Man is the angelic being that leads them back to this cherished Holy Place. The Angel of the Covenant – Malakh Berith, who goes before us to show us The Way.

The Universe continues to suffer under the oppression of angelic powers that oppose the true faith. Facts are like tools needed to combat the errors of the archons, but all fields of knowledge are not necessarily able to deliver the saving 'Gnosis' that leads one back to the garden on their own merit. The Son of Man's role as "suffering servant" is the first step of a two-part process that occurs in historical time. Contrary to popular opinion, for some are still waiting for something that has already happened, the Son of Man is a living spirit who promises to 'be with us always'. The Kingdom remains hidden until we leave worldly conceptions behind in order to 'rise' in the Son of Man. When Elohim says 'yehi' in Bereshit/Genesis, creative thought is born, but still, the effect has to occur in the cycles of time. The death, burial, and resurrection signify a three-stage process; the Son of Man spoke of it as a seed placed in soil which eventually grows up out of the ground into a living tree. Alexa, now rooted in the Tree, begins her new life.

The Tree of Lives

Figure 19 Hall CLXXXI - Rosicrucian Crucifixion
18ᵗʰ c.

This figure depicts the tree of lives contained in the four worlds of the Sephiroth: vegetable stone, animal, and mineral. The Star of David contains the Hebrew letters [YHSHVH] יהושי the three roots of the tree are shown in the letter Shin as a bridge between two worlds. The three realms, permeated with the life-giving essence of spirit or Ruach, begin to move as the Messiah merges angelic events with human prophecies that occur as historical events. Angelic wisdom 'gnosis' enables the elect to enter the Heavenly Temple to be kept in safety from the delusions of error until the End. As seen earlier, zero-point energy enables electromagnetic waves to emanate outward from the center, keeping the chaos of disorder bound through force. Motion will eventually rest in the center and all will become one. The angelic Wisdom is the resting place of Shekinah in the central heart of the elect. Underneath the solid structure of matter is electromagnetic radiation that still has the properties of light. Even the physical body has light (electrolytes) built into its constitution. This is a way to see the manifestation of the Light of the Day One as spiritual energy breathed into the nostrils of every living thing, even though it may not appear so due to the physical properties of matter. Sefer Bahir explores the intricate relationship of 3 & 10 and explains the First Day when the three circles of Light (Who Was, Who Is, and Who Will Be) unfolded as Ayin, Ayin Sof, and Ayin SOF Aur come forth from the 10 dimensions in a special arrangement that permits humans to enter the invisible world beyond time and space. According to Chrapowicki,

Life, in its very essence, is condensed light, crystallized and polarized into matter and manifesting within the sphere of objective perception as tangible forms. (Maryla de Chrapowicki Spectro-Biology 11)

Azazel was once a great angel of light until he falls from his original state of being and undergoes a name change. A name change at times means a letter from the Divine Name is attached to the angel or human. However, when it rebels against the light, there is another change of name, and personal attributes are changed.

Attributes such as hate, greed, lust, violence, apathy, and tyranny characterize Baal, known as Adon, Zeus, Mithra, Apollo, Deus, and Kyrios. These foreign disguises elude the weary passerby who does not look beyond the surface of material existence or the form of the term. The scriptures mistranslated in English are still, to an extent, sealed like the higher dimensions and inaccessible to the average reader. Alexa

186

had not written anything in a long time; she was so excited to share this with Timka; she could hardly wait to see her. Alexa finally recognized that many modern doctrines include minimal amounts of details concerning the Unity of Elohim, which Moses describes in the book of Genesis. This is because the 'Unique' experience of how all these things function together is still unknown, except to those familiar with the history and scientific background based on Wisdom discovered in the 13th century. Another community undergoing duress survived by studying the vast body of knowledge concerning the Supernal Wisdom of Light.

Three Dimensions of One

"There are not three Gods in the Godhead; nor are there but three in One Only; but of One in and through ten thousand times ten thousand, and thousands of the Yahweh-Spirit Power, and that when formed after the model, archetype, or its OWN HYPOSTASIS, or Substance, they become SPIRIT-ELOHIM or sons of God" https://www.christadelphian-origin.org/

Timka sits in silence and remembers the warm feeling she had for Joel after they last talked. She missed Joel just as much as he missed her, but they were living in two separate worlds. She hopes that somehow, they can reconcile their relationship and stop attacking each other. Inspired by the recent peace of mind, she begins to write again after a long dry spell that left her empty and vulnerable again. When Timka writes, it strengthens and renews her because she, too, learns from what she writes. Some of the things she writes about actually manifest in her life. She starts off by writing about the 3 Eternals. Ayin, Ayin Sof, and Ayin SOF Aur are three terms used in Lurianic Kabbalah to explain the three forms, patterns, codes, energy states, or forces that are thought to exist. Ayin represents the 'No-Thing,' Ayin Sof represents the transition stage between Ayin and Ayin SOF Aur – the brilliant infinite light. The dynamics of cosmic strings have a similar pattern and function: cosmological expansion, intercom muting/loop production, and radiation. According to physicists, expansion causes the strings to stretch:

If you draw a line of the surface of the balloon and then blow it up, you will see that the length of your 'string' will grow at the same rate as the radius of the balloon. (Cambridge Cosmic String Dynamics and Evolution P1 para 2)

This corresponds to the process of the Primordial Light in ancient science. The second process involves two strings that can inter-commute and form loops. It is a very 'strange fact' according to the article. Apparently, "a long string can inter-commute with itself, in which case a loop will be produced." Can we learn from the interactions of strings how the Ayin Sof – is extracted through Metatron? If we take a closer look at the relationship between the (3) Eternals, it may be possible to discover much more.

Figure 20 Cambridge Cosmology String Loop

In the above figure, you can see an illustration of how circles or closed strings develop. Cosmic strings and closed strings emit radiation, and when they do, a fourfold structure (quadrupole pattern) forms in the cross-section of the string's interior, which is common to cosmic string radiation (R. Battye & E.P. Shellard P4 para 1).

When strings lose energy, they disappear after going through a lengthy process of intercom muting and eventual decay. The strings become a point that can then form itself into another loop that will then inter-commute with another string and begin the whole process again. This demonstrates the contraction and expansion of Tzimtzum. More importantly, it shows that there is a continuous looping of life, as illustrated in the symbol of a circle.

Three Cycles of Light

The first light symbolizes the soul of the universe in an infinite and boundless breath of energy that radiates as waves of intelligence emanating in six directions throughout the creation. This is similar to the expansion phase of the Superstring theory. Whereas the second light symbolizes the condensation of nebulous matter that produces form inside cosmic vortices. This then sets all the celestial bodies in their proper orbits. This is similar to the intercom muting and loop production phase predicted by string theorists. The final light symbolizes the production of a universe that consists of physical matter continuously receding from its original point of center as it solidifies with every revolution of time. The further away it goes from the point of light from which it was created, the more materialized the creation becomes until its final transformation into matter. This is the final phase of string radiation. Because of this cyclic revolution and separation from the source and substance of reality, humanity must learn to reverse the cycle and travel counterclockwise, as Enoch does in his journey through the dimensions. Humanity has to learn how to ascend through the realms of the heavenly palaces (attributes) until the point of light in the seventh heaven centers once again in the Point or Yod. The letter Aleph (1) extends into the Yod (10); if we look at the two strings as Aleph and Yod, we see why the two loops become one membrane. When the two worlds are one, a new creation is born infinitely; we emerge in the center of the two loops. Eternity and Time intersect in us through our soul, the Center of Being. Listen to how John Oxlee explains the sevenfold teaching regarding the Sephiroth", Timka finds the page and points to the paragraph:

"Not only do the three supreme Numerations correspond to the three divine Persons of the Holy Trinity, as set forth in the Creed; but the seven inferior Numerations, also, have their correspondents in the Energies of the Son of God, or the Holy Spirits, mentioned by the Pastor of Hermas; 41 in the Spiritus Septiformis of Cassiodorius" 42 in the seven burning Lamps of fire before the Throne of God, or the seven Eyes of the Lamb or Word Incarnate, called the seven Spirits of God by the author of the Apocalypse; whose imagery of language is borrowed from the seven Lamps of the golden Candlestick in the Tabernacle, mystically expounded always, as everyone knows, of the emanation of the Sephiroth. Indeed, I hesitate not to declare that such a development of the glorious attributes and energies of the Godhead is perfectly consistent, not only with the writings of Moses and the prophets, but with every part of the Gospel revelation, and that the future Nazarene Church, whenever it shall be established, will do well to cultivate and hand down to posterity the doctrine of the Jewish Cabala, as one of the best human efforts to magnify and glorify Jehovah by intellectual conceptions and the science of metaphysics." (John Oxlee, 1845 64- 65)

"See, there are ten levels of meaning, but we have to think like spiritual archaeologists to decipher the symbols. There is a reason for each plane, and its symbols depict a manifestation of YHVH through Elohim, the archetype pattern. Ruach is the substance and essence that manifests in various forms through Elohim; the Cherub Circle mystics call Elohim the 'Unique

Cherub' who joins our material dimension to the spiritual dimension. The spirit and flesh inter-commute!" Timka just learned something she did not know through logical deduction based on known factors. When two strings inter-commute, an infinite cycle of intercommunion creates motion. This is what Enoch learns during his journey, it is possible to deduct scientific knowledge from analyzing spiritual concepts. The individual that can experience both realms of reality (formless/form) gains equilibrium and overcomes the death of matter (ignorance). Without resorting to earlier authors such as Oxlee, we would remain hopelessly lost in dialectic and materialistic philosophy that moves further away from Medieval Wisdom of Emanation and Light Physics. I recently found out that Isaac Ibn Latif, who lived in Spain and wrote about this in 1240, taught that everyone has a 'Unique' signature in the Avir and that the sephiroth are vessels for the Light Wisdom to expand within us and our arrangement of sephiroth is our signature.

Isaac Ibn Latif, a Philosopher/Kabbalist of the 13th century, set out to demonstrate there is a dynamic motion within the divine attributes that activates an invisible process projected in our mind when we contemplate and learn about the Divine Name. There is energy in the process of learning, and it can enhance our minds. It is possible to actually experience the 'Beginning' (Aleph) and 'Ending' (Thav) through a series of events that emanate one from another. Like the 6 days it took Moses to see the Visions of Elohim in order to copy the pattern of the Tabernacle. Latif and a few other Philosopher-Kabbalists call it the 'Mahashavah' or radiating waves of light and energy that cause an emanation from the Ruach part of our soul to the nephesh of our body, as the Spirit immanence of YHVH penetrates our mind like light particle pierce the darkness. During the account of his journey, Enoch describes a sensation of coldness that begins to freeze his face.

He also feels the sensation of fire upon his face, and later, his face is 'frozen' in order to preserve its 'shape' for the future elect. These changes based on heat and cold are scientific facts the author is aware of, and this period in time was known for its advanced understanding of astronomy, metaphysics, and physics. The duality of energy and matter is evidence that there has been a division of the Unity. Moses recorded particular events and facts to demonstrate the duality and work of the sephiroth dividing the day/night and good/evil; this is evidence to show how light falls into material substances and then begins to generate itself into different patterns of energy. Energy transforms into matter depending on the amount of heat or cold the element encounters, and this dissolves its shape and thereby changes its form. When a person can receive the "Primordial Light" of the AVIR directly from its source, Metatron – The Keeper of the Tree of Life that is the connection – He Who contains the 7 Sefiroth in perfect balance within us, the symbol of the macrocosmic human tree. The three roots, Wisdom, Understanding, and Knowledge, begin to grow down into the soul. The soul can now inter-commute with Ruach (Spirit) as if it were a fertile garden of soil. As the seeds of Wisdom, Understanding, and Knowledge grow, each one reconnects us in the divine circle of Hayyim Ruach/Living Spirit. This is how the Active Intellect inter-commutes with our consciousness, self, and the Universe.

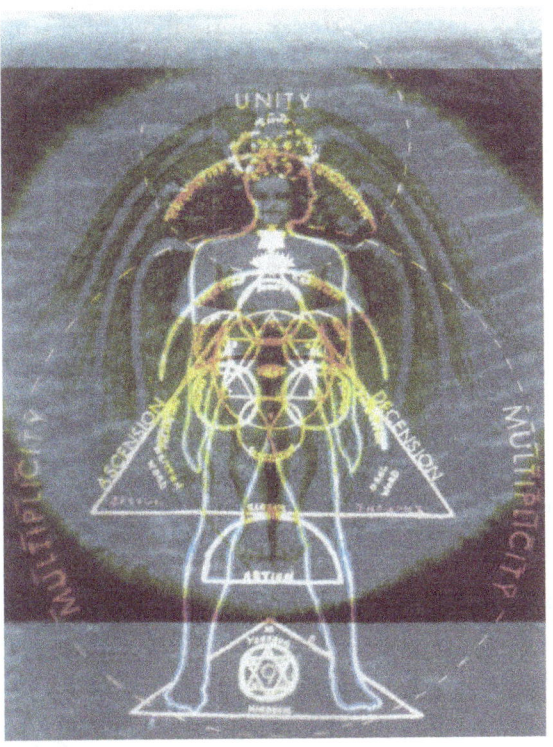

Figure 21 Adams of Angelic/Human Transformation

Veils of Time Become One

A disturbance within the balance of polar energy is what allows life in our Universe to exist. Our world is the result of an imbalance between two forces. The Son of Man joined the two forces (fire/water) within himself, making two substances one new 'firmament.' The sacred Triad is the bond of the Covenant between Spirit and Flesh, accomplished through the birth, burial, and resurrection of the Messiah of Israel, all the prophets described from the visions they experienced and wrote down. Only earthly man can inhabit two spheres at once, this was the uniqueness of Adam. Angelic beings must transform from one sphere into another. Only humans can become both spheres at once, which is our unique property as sentients. However, what science has discovered recently proves it is not unique to Adam but is also pervasive in the entire cosmic universe. Superstring theorists also predict that things can exist at two different places at the same time and that light can exist in either a field of waves or a stream of massless particles. The fact that strings can and do change is what puzzles scientists most. However, in the world of ancient science, mystics expect things to change and form new paths and consciousness's. All of us have a black hole at the center of an active galactic nucleus that has an 'event horizon' that limits our perception and ability to see beyond our personal orbits. The only way we can learn to see past our own horizon is to read the heavenly tablets hidden in apocalyptic texts. These are third Heaven events: Unutterable, ineffable, invisible, ageless, timeless, shapeless, infinity of infinities.

We often assign new meanings to symbols in accordance with our personal views. There are just as many great minds in the world as there are ideas, and all insist they live in an objective reality. Even though physicists believe M-Theory, they have no way of proving or experiencing it except through visual models and mathematics, but they now also use holographic technology. The significant thing is that many premises of M-Theory can be helpful in providing a more detailed interpretation of the scriptures.

Our own senses betray our ability to learn and experience reality because our five senses show us what we want to see, even if it is not there. We, too, must learn to unfold the eight 'shudders' of three dimensions and five senses that blind us to the nature of reality. Until one has actually seen and felt the Presence of the force in the center of the Universe and proved it to his or her own satisfaction, it will remain a nameless being. Scientists know that a holographic image is three-dimensional and contains all the data in each cell concerning the specimen. But they do not know the source of this holographic phenomenon; only looking at the material things of life and denying the invisible things and their innate spiritual laws prevents them from an opportunity to see the deeper scheme and pattern.

Merkavah mystics claim to have traveled through Wisdom, and when one travels, one also gains years of understanding. Our human reason can only comprehend what is useful to navigate through the five senses. Until now, the fourth dimension existed only through mathematical evidence and time. A critical analysis of the Merkabah and Hekhaloth literature will reveal the hidden link between Christianity and Judaism; this hidden connection is a quantum leap into the reality of everything invisible. The type of scientific details embedded in the Torah and Kabbalah proves that ancient civilizations were not brute beasts but discovered and named the details of the Universe, Mathematics, and Physics through an understanding of Light and Astronomy. Others have come to a similar conclusion, so it is nothing new. All those drawn to the ideas in this misunderstood, mysterious ancient literature of Israel naturally see that something definitely happened that left an influence on society since both Christianity and, later, Judaism began to change or rearrange pertinent details at the other's expense.

Both traditions consider their doctrines unique, but are they only extensions of each other like the ever-expanding and contracting Universe? A house divided cannot stand. Moses says all souls were present on Mt. Sinai and heard the thunders and voice; Paul reminds us Son of Man is also a corporate body of individuals not based on culture, race, or religion. Not until we see the true reflection and not just our own perception can we ever begin to interact with the higher spiritual dimensions. Timka looks for John Oxlee's book, and she finds the passage regarding Metatron that she wants Joel to see:

"Suffice it to say that this angel, Metatron, is everywhere described as a Divine Subsistency, corresponding to the second Person of the ever-blessed Trinity; being designated in the

195

Othioth of R. Akiba, 37 The One of all the Sons of the Highest; or, THE ONLY BEGOTTEN Son; in the Sepher Raziel, 38. The Hand of Jehovah; in the Chemdath Tsebi, 39 The Life of the worlds; in the Zohar Gadol, 40 The King of the angels, and in whom as a Body the Numerations of the Godhead are invested as a Soul. That, which I would now more particularly press on the consideration of the reader, is the doctrinal identity of the whole cabalistic scheme of the Sephiroth with the sound tenets of Christianity." Oxlee 64-65)

Timka, deeply inspired by the passage, stops breathing; as her thoughts breathe for her, the clock stops ticking, and music in the background fades away. She begins to listen to her thoughts, increasing and expanding her consciousness, "The reflection starts in the structure of the Universe, and it ends in the fabric of our being. This 'Infinite Being' spoken to by the Ayin from a hidden place within the Supernal Nature of Elohim is the nature of consciousness. After this, the sefiroth begins to emerge from the point or contraction and engage our soul as each one measures and weighs our inner reality.

Neoplatonic symbolism was based on ('awir qadmon) (11 Blickstein), a term for 'Primordial Ether', which is an important background to Latif's system of Emanation. Refer to Gershom Scholem's On The Mystical Shape of The Godhead, a discussion on the astral body comes into a clearer focus when we realize that the 'sapphire ether' is one of the earlier terms used to explain how humans are entangled in the aura of the Aether. The term Avir/Aether is now referred to as 'astral'. Do you see the change and its implications? Scholem also points out how Latif taught everyone has a 'unique' identity, which will never perish. (Scholem, 252, 1991). He connects themes found in Latif's doctrines to earlier Enoch literature and Merkavah doctrines (262), thereby forging a link in the chain that seems to continue evolving since the period when apocalyptic literature was a living experience within humans. He states, "The ethereal body, which belongs to every human earthly body, is now designated by the Zohar as tselem."

Perhaps reevaluating this literature will yield new insights into the human condition; our consciousness lost the concept of the Son of Man, and this place remained vacant for centuries. This was not the only change that took place after the introduction of the Zohar; the term 'Avir Adam' later became associated with an astral body."

Timka is learning from just one passage, many other things that seem to bear no relation to one another; this is part of the panoramic reality beyond the 4th dimension. Timka seemed to connect to the message of Isaac Ibn Latif; she suddenly knew how much he deplored the changes he saw coming in his own time. It did change the nature of the function of spiritual consciousness and the Kabbalah; he devoted his last years to refuting these new trends that sought to go in another direction. His desire to reinstate the original teachings led him to experience a deeper connection with Keter due to this period of tribulation. We must not forget apocalyptic literature helps people during traumatic times to survive; Latif plays a crucial role in the drama of Israel. This was a time of great revolution and political turmoil for the Toledo communities; perhaps it is true that suffering gives us inspiration and power to survive when there is a just cause and reason to search for Truth. "It certainly gives me the courage to wake up each day and face a world that seems so lost," thought Timka. If I did not know that all this is real, I would not be able to get up each day to face the horrors of our world now. The Light fills me up from within; I do not have to go outside of myself to find help and Wisdom. We are vessels of Light created by and through Wisdom; we are its receptacle in living motion – the Word made flesh. Wow!

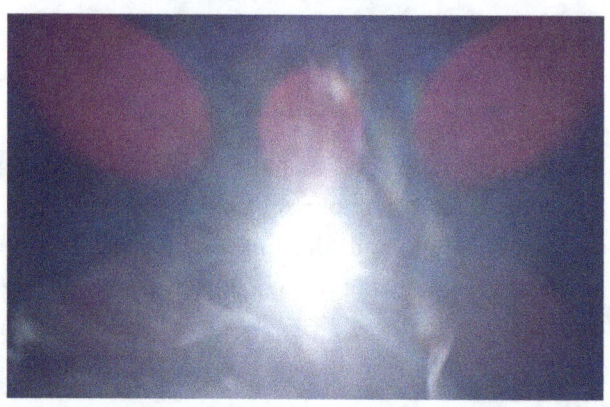

Merkabah has two aspects:

Expansion = Throne Chariot 7 Arch-Angelic Host of the Formless World (Merkabah)

Contraction = Chariot of the 4 Angels in the process of forming the World (Merkaba)

Maaseh Bereshit Esoteric Cosmology Origin of Universe Big Bang

        Maaseh Merkavah Theosophy   GUT M-Theory

        Hidden Aspect   Revealed Aspect

Name Ineffable	Name Spoken
Invisible Spiritual Universe	Visible Material Universe
Secret History within History	Manifest History
(Time is not) Eternity	History (Time Is)

Past	Present	Future
	Tribulation Period	
	Eternal Now	
Prophecies of Dabar		Realized Prophecy
THIS WORLD		WORLD TO COME
(Olam Ha-Zeh)		Olam Ha-Bah)

The study of the Merkavah deals with the division between the formless world and the world of form. The figures surrounding the Throne represent the four archetypes or reservoirs of unbound substance or forces. The forces of Electromagnetism, Strong Nuclear, Gravity, and Weak Nuclear take on material existence in scientific terms, but in the ancient world of science mystics, the Tetragrammaton or 'four letters' symbolize the mineral vegetable, animal, and human kingdoms of the earth. Metatron, as Son of Man, represents the synthesis of the four Kingdoms that become a fifth. When the Hebrew letter Shin (fire) kneels between YH (Sh) VH ,יהושה it forms a new region of existence. It supersedes all the previous concepts associated with orthodox religion bereft of its potent spiritual compound and breaks the illusion of multiple realities, demonstrating just one symmetrical Kingdom of light. Maybe, science may soon find evidence of the fifth force that logic predicts must reside in the four forces. The fifth force gives elements a kind of buoyancy and counteracts the effects of gravity on matter. Inside the Chariot, a veil Enoch calls the 'Pargod' divides between unity and multiplicity. Time is the veil of Eternity. It hides its face from us until we are worthy to enter the eternal holy presence. The fifth force elevates us into the realm of spiritual power. Seven angels that bear a portion of the Tetragrammaton stand behind the Veil. Outside the Veil are four angels that work in the material world of form. The four faces of the Chariot symbolize a spiritual evolution that occurs as the divine limbs emanate the progressive phases of change that form the cubic universe that reflects the six days. Each angel represents a process and interaction of the divine hierarchy. The World of Atziluth symbolizes the electromagnetic force; the World of Beriyah symbolizes gravity and Yetzirah and is like a weak nuclear force, supporting Assiyah, which acts very much like the strong nuclear force that keeps the material creation in a steady state. Timka just allows the words to flow through her thoughts; her fingers type the letter, but each new idea she learns immediately increases her spirit.

Mysterious Soul Power

Joel grows more introspective; he also likes the vibes he feels with Timka when they have a real conversation with each other for the first time in years. He feels different, even a little happy with this Eureka moment that changes his life. Suddenly, he can hear or rather feel and sense a new Voice communicating with him, "At first glance, the 'Mystery' of the soul is very complicated and beyond your comprehension; however, upon deeper inspection and historical analysis of theological issues concerning the meaning and purpose of the term 'Trinity,' it becomes less cloudy. The branch of theology within Christianity solely devoted to the study of Christ, known as 'Christology' is very different from the Apocalyptic 'Gnosis' characteristic of early mystic circles. Many Histologists remark on Old Testament themes in support of their dogmas, but until recently, there has been very little research in ancient Hebrew thought regarding the term 'Memra' and its relationship to the Word/Logos. Justin Martyr wrote about the "Angel" and the

"Word" that perform different functions in the scriptures. He recounts significant events and new meanings of the prophet's visions based on the new Way of revealing the Messiah. He is able to place all of this in a historical context, which is very important to a complete understanding of what is going on in the great debates.

Gerald O'Collins presents various perspectives the early church fathers shared on the Trinity as perceived during the times leading up to I Council of Constantine. The nature of the 'Godhead' or 'Supernal Nature of the Creator' according to O'Collins' analysis of the terms "ousia," "physis," and "hypostasis," is helpful in understanding the issues of the debates. He explains that some groups thought of 'ousia' as a type of primordial substance and 'hypostasis' as a kind of form that has a 'physis' or nature (O'Collins Christology 173). These three terms were the central hub of conflict among different belief systems. The Semitic concept of 'Nefesh, Ruach, and Neshamah' posed no problem within polytheistic groups; they felt these terms referred to parts of one corporeal being. Joel now realizes that he agrees more with Justin Martyr and Tatian, who aligned the Evangels to flow as one text. He remembers when Timka first read the "Diatessaron" and the huge influence it had on her perception of them. It became clear to him that there were many other ideas in circulation at the same time, but they were not all popular with the public. O'Collins' many views and ideas on the nature and personhood of the Messiah were interesting, and Joel could particularly relate to his remarks on Tertullian's Christology. O'Collins says Tertullian was "First to develop the formula 'one substance in three persons'" (173).

This deduction and summary of Tertullian's analogy proves: "The Word (or Sermo) and the Holy Spirit could be derived from the Father without a real separation taking place. He wrote of a root producing a shoot and a spring giving rise to a river, and the sun sending forth its ray" (173). Joel actually appreciated this metaphor, which illustrates a progression of natural growth and development in accordance with the laws of nature. Joel understands now why there is no reason to think it is sacrilegious to use science, as a standard measurement of theological doctrines, to a certain extent, that when scientific theories are 'only theories isolated from human life, they become poisonous to the human soul, berated by its perception of spirit.

The Voice continues, "Let us use the standard of measurement and the law of energy conservation as our guides. If we analyze the element water, for example, we know that it has three states depending on temperature. When we boil water, it transforms into vapor, and after the temperature drops more, it transforms into liquid, and when frozen below 32 degrees, it becomes a solid ice cube. This fact of science demonstrates how one element can assume three different states, and therefore, if we use this analogy, we can see how three different states are but one substance – 'ousia.' This law of nature begins with the pattern that permeates the books of Moses. In the book of Exodus, Moses saw a pattern he used to build a Tabernacle with three rooms that are really one room extended for separate functions. The High Priest performs a different function in each place in accordance with the invisible spirit law of the Shekinah. All three divisions are necessary to operate the single Tabernacle. This idea is also central among the Sabellians, according to O'Collins,

Being merely three manifestations of the one God, three different relationships that the one God assumed successively in creation, redemption, and the sending of the Spirit. (173)

"The Shema is binding on all of Israel forever including the grafted in Israel that Paul says is an inheritor of the precious things of Messiah. "Hear Oh Israel Yahweh our Elohim is One." When our consciousness is pierced with

202

misunderstanding, it is not easy to accept or understand the role of three functions in one operation as many Christological concepts proclaimed." Joel begins to see how the Father, Son/Word, and Holy Spirit are a unity, in the sense that a female is a 'woman' who could also be a 'mother,' 'daughter,' and 'wife.' Joel replies to the Voice, "The past, present, and future are divisions of the one phenomenon we call 'Time,' and yet this seems to present no problem to most people. So why does the idea of a Father, Son, and Holy Spirit seem so hard to grasp – why is there so much misunderstanding?" The Voice replies, "Go back to Justin Martyr's explanation of the Angel, Word, and Logos to gain a better perspective. Martyr's work "Dialogue with Trypho" is an indispensable source and wealth of information. Below is Joel's summary of O'Collins' details of the main groups fighting for dominancy among Christians in the early fourth and fifth centuries. The Kingdom remains open.

Antioch	Alexandria
Nestorians	Monophysites
Logos-Anthropos	Logos-Sarx
Word Man	Word Flesh
Eternal Word Absorbed Man	Word Became Flesh

"The furor initiated by the Nestorian and Monophysite debates over the purpose of the incarnation lasted for a very long time. This early period, characterized by the need to resolve the pressing issues between two natures, divine/human, without undermining the role of the other, was a hard task to perform. The Semitic view does not have to consider the logic of Greek philosophy and reasoning to arrive at Truth or Fact."

One can begin to navigate the confusing waters of religions, philosophies, mythologies, theories, hypotheses, and formulas to see a clear path. The Highway in the desert, which leads us up and out of the confusion through real spiritual validation by experience, is the Voice crying out.

BODY OF THREE

Joel is excited now because he can finally see something he did not realize before, and he is amazed that there really is more to the Mystery than he ever imagined. Yet, he still did not mention anything about the Voice to anyone. Now, when he opens a book, the Voice seems to awaken, and it begins to explain things to him, dropping little hints throughout the day that leads Joel to particular books. Joel goes to that invisible world where his thoughts expand into Wisdom; he hears himself thinking, and "For the Semitic mind the Nephesh, Ruach, and Neshamah were all contained within the one body-soul-spirit of Adam. Maybe it will help us to consider that the attempt to explain the 'how' of the operation confused Christians of the 4th and 5th centuries. The need to reconcile Greek philosophy with Semitic concepts was not an easy task; it still eludes many theologians today. "The debates between Nestorius and Eutyches on the meaning of a dual nature remind me of the debates of modern theologians over the so-called narrative versions of the Old Testament," said Joel aloud. However, no one was in the room. Hebrew scribes did not divide the Torah into narratives; Moses was the inspired author. The division as such is unique to Western Christianity's view on the use of different divine names in the texts of Genesis, Exodus, Leviticus, and Deuteronomy. The argument over the two natures of the Messiah seemed to occupy more importance than the death and resurrection:

The whole controversy with Nestorius, like that with Eutyches twenty years later, continued to shift theological attention away from Christ's death and resurrection to this incarnation. (190)

Timka explained to me many times that in apocalyptic literature, the incarnation is not the main purpose of his birth; the role he will accomplish in a future event is more crucial during the invisible eschaton. The victory over darkness is the hallmark of the message. His death and resurrection were divine signs of his legitimacy as the Son of Yahweh in mystical traditions. In ancient Semitic thought, Yahweh and Elohim are one, and the Councils could not reconcile the polytheism that always sought to infect their religion through Baal worship and Canaanite fertility rites. In that religion, El is one of many Els, and many often stray in the path of polytheism. Many in this age did not fully understand how Yahweh and Elohim were one, so it is easy to see how early Christians inherited the same problem. They could not reconcile the role of a third 'hypostasis' in the sense that Christianity sought to interpret it. The 'Shekinah' was the form (physis) of the invisible nature of Yahweh. The 'Shekinah' was in accord with Ruach Ha-Qadesh or the Holy Spirit, and the rabbis equated it with Wisdom and Power.

For Paul, it is the 'Shekinah' or 'Word' that, according to John, had 'rested' or 'dwelled' in a human being named Yahoshua (Jesus). If we consider the underlying themes in the scriptures along with theological systems, many of the problems of the three transitions might simply vanish. The new debate shifted back to the meaning of the two terms 'physis' and 'hypostasis,' for it seemed very hard to understand how a spiritual nature could be inhabited within a person and not remain separate or assimilated.

This is why it will be useful to see through the 'eyes of science' because the analogy of how an element transforms into a vapor, liquid, or solid is still a viable, functional way to reconcile the problem. During Anselm's era, Greek philosophy lost its grip on the logical development of Christology, and a rise in Roman ethics began to influence the continued development of Anselmian Christology. O'Collins explains how:

'Satisfaction,' a non-biblical term drawn from Roman law and applied by Tertullian to penitential practice, took pride of place in Anselm's theology of redemption as developed in Cur Deus homo. (199)

Joel grows excited with his new increase of Wisdom, and he thinks to himself, "Therefore, we must carefully analyze all the doctrines of this period because they only represent the viewpoint of a small minority of the population at the time. We now know that theological interpretations must always remain within an ancient Near Eastern context to understand the perception of the definer. Many doctrines of Western Christianity have led to the dominance of humans instead of their true freedom to pursue truth because the basic goals of Greece and Rome were to advance and prosper at the expense of the people. Hebrew concepts of tithing and giving to the poor were based on recognizing humans and the need to take care of others, as the Creator cares for us.

During the Reformation, the influence of European Christology began to affect new countries. Columbus opened the door to a new set of questions among theologians, how to indoctrinate all those not 'graced' with Western Christological principles. The Protestant movement shifted the debate away from the dissection of the two natures and into the realm of distributing social justice and Christian ethics to humans besieged with sins:

Paul's sense of the loving initiative of God as the key to human redemption had slipped right out of the picture. (O'Collins 212)

The Voice whispers in his ear, "This is a very important indication that other things might have 'slipped out of the picture' due to theological debates. It seems that many themes already debated in rabbinic circles have also begun to emerge in Christological debates centuries later; however, the main difference is that the Christian theologians do not all share the same understanding or knowledge of Judaism. Nevertheless, modern Christianity tries very hard to define itself through the application of scientific theories and humanistic ontological philosophy, but even this seems to create a new battle of ideas. The human soul is rapidly becoming of less value as humanism begins to dominate society instead of God. Later thinkers like Kant, Albert Einstein, and Max Planck (215) laid siege to the meaning or sacredness of life and determined that most things are relative. When everything becomes relative to us, including truth, it sets the stage for a very impersonal view of the role of Christ in humanity. The rise of Darwinism and the influence of humanism assumed the responsibility for humanity and left a void in our perception of a personal redeemer. Many now believe only humanity can save itself through progressive evolution and science that blindly leads us to the edge of a cliff. John's evangelism follows the same line of progressive thought when he writes, "The Word was in the Beginning and then became flesh and dwelt among us". The early communities possessed a very simple view; for them, humanity's consciousness is how and where the redemption takes place as each person receives an understanding of the mystery of Yahweh." Joel feels as if he will rise out of his body; he does not understand what is happening to his mind; he hears no thoughts and is not aware of the room around him; the music on the radio is now silent, and the clock has stopped ticking.

The Voice continues:

"Whether the Messiah is aware of his own identity as the son of Yahweh is irrelevant when seen against the background

207

of ancient Judaism; the 'Memra' or 'Dabar' both transliterated as 'Word' could instruct, awaken and guide the prophet into the Will of Yahweh. If the Son of Man were not truly divine and human, there would be no point in all the controversial issues that grew over the centuries. These are similar to the issues raised by the Sanhedrin when the early assemblies sought to define the significance of the Messiah for Judaism." Joel suddenly says aloud, "How could the sefiroth or the Memra become flesh and blood? Certainly, this idea is hard to fathom from the philosophical and theological debates at Chalcedon, and it gets even harder when we consider classical humanism. There is definitely a different conception of the Messianic Son of Man in apocalyptic mysticism than what appears in Christology. To start anywhere else but within the native environment of this historical figure ultimately leads to Greek rhetoric and Latin rationale; the 'Mystery' is beyond all secular thought.

So why should we be surprised how scriptural textual alterations have changed the essential meaning of the Bible? Secular humanism leads the way in the twenty-first century. The use of Greek and Latin terms for 'words' often resulted in the loss of their original meaning. The original concepts of the Son of Man are lost in a maze of myth and legend!" "If we consider that all such terms have an obscured history, by time and interpretation, it is possible to escape their constricted meanings. Still, there is something else going on behind the texts.

Timka is right; we must attempt to restore these and many other lost aspects of the ancient ideas behind the scriptures.

An obscure spiritual reality evokes the 'numinous' in us as we search for the original Son of Man described in the book of Enoch. I just experienced it myself, me, Joel, someone who really did not have faith! Since mainstream traditional religions seem to have failed in this area, modern scientists have become the new priests in search of the ultimate Temple - the Universe. How far we have fallen away from true historical facts affects our ability to comprehend Enoch's cosmic reality now that our own natural reasoning has neatly packaged this reality for us. Yes, we need to open the box and climb out of the rabbit hole we created.

Primordial Face of Adam Kadmon

Is there a method or theory that provides a way to experience the 'cosmic reality' hidden from us? The ancients say the 'Word' created 'in the beginning' a pattern in order to transmit a certain 'form' to envision how the Son of Man transcends the veil of the Temple (flesh). When our thoughts can reach out and take hold of the Kabod, it will rescue our consciousness from darkness.

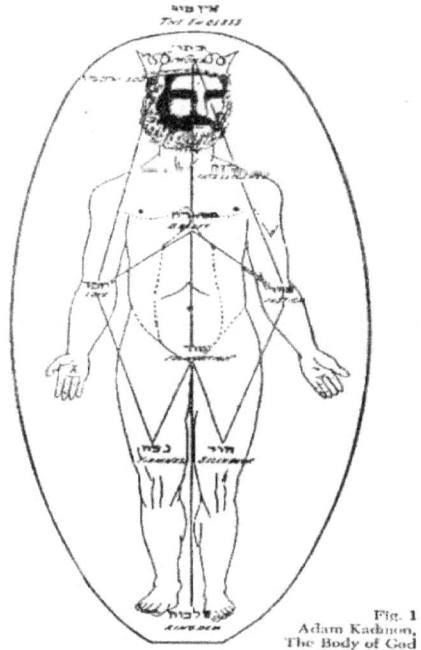

Figure 22 Adam Kadmon from Myers Qabbalah

Alexa is excited to share some of her increasing Wisdom insights with Timka, and she decides to go visit her because she is also concerned that she has not heard from her or Joel. Alexa arrives at Timka's house and knocks on the door. Joel opens the door rather quickly and invites Alexa in with a smile on his face. Alexa really freaked out now, "What is going on here," she thinks. Joel invites her in, offers her some cold beverages, and seems happy to see her. Alexa says, "Well, hi Joel, how are you?" "I am doing great, how are you? Timka goes downstairs; the two of them talking together amazed her. Joel says to Timka, "Did you know that Adam, as the collective body of humanity, created last in the scale of evolution, ironically is the first idea the Supreme Being imagined? Look, right here in this book, it says,"

The Kabbalists explain this when they tell us that the very first ingredient in creation was the thought of Adam – Humanity. Though man was last in the external order of creation, the thought of man precedes creation. He is the original purpose and intention for which the entire building was constructed. The thought of man is called Kadmon, primordial. The first manifestation of God's purpose is thus called Adam Kadmon. The primordial will that preceded all creation and hints at its ultimate goal. (24)

Joel continues to trip Alexa out; she has never seen him this animated. Joel continues, "Our place in the chain of evolution parallels the evolving role of light in the creation. As we now begin to reach the mystical perception of earlier sages, please bear in mind that there were two sets of tablets given to Moses. Ancient lore tells us there was an 'oral torah' and a 'written Torah.' There were two sets of tablets, but the first set was broken, and a second set replaced them with different commandments. How can we once again perceive the 'Face' of the first set? Well, as we examine ancient rabbinic texts and commentaries on the first chapter of Genesis, we find that Adam Kadmon existed before the created material Adam we know.

Thus, Adam Kadmon exists in a potential state still awaiting the ultimate emergence from 'nothingness.' This is the most controversial issue that will ever challenge us, yet these texts claim to have the answers the world still denies. We can actually learn more if we are only humble enough to look at these texts in their original context.

Kaplan explains the analogy between the Tabernacle with nine furnishings and our human body as a Temple to demonstrate that multiple forces can operate successfully as one power. He writes,"

Many mystics "depicted the sefirot as corresponding to various limbs and functions of the human body. For it is the human body, patterned after the anthropomorphic array of the sefirot, that serves as a perfect paradigm of extremely varied forces working in synchronized balance and harmony. (39-40)

Alexa cannot believe her ears; she can only stare at him with her mouth open. Then she feels inspired by his excitement, and she says, "There is a spirit law of transformation that controls everything in the Universe. Hidden in three words in Sefer Yetzirah, an archaic scientific commentary on the book of Genesis, are three 'special' verbs in Genesis that demonstrate a three-phase expansion and growth. The first clue to the secret is found in the verb "Yetser," and Genesis must be read in accordance with the original meaning of these verbs in order to realize what it may have meant to earlier mystics. Carlos Suarez says, "As the Sepher Yetzirah is a commentary on Genesis, it is necessary to read Genesis carefully from the beginning in order to understand the root of the word Yetser" (Suarez SY 44). These roots are proof that Isaiah was familiar with the four worlds: Atziluth, Beriyah, Yetzirah, and Assiyah. Suarez points out that the terms "bara" (to create), "yaass" (to do), and "tsar" (to structure) are verbs that play a major role in the "6 Days" motif in Genesis." Now, Timka cannot hold herself back any longer, she joins them, and all three are speaking together as if they are in their own little secret closets together.

Timka says, "In ancient mystic texts, the four worlds exist inside the primordial Adam Kadmon, who becomes the Tree of Life as his and her solar energy surges throughout each of the worlds (olams). Therefore, Adam contains Eve, the bride, as it was in the beginning. Elohim created them 'male and female' and named them Adam. From Atzilut, the world of Emanation and 'radiation' descends three lower worlds of creation, formation, and production. The mysterious author of Sefer Yetzirah explains how most things come into being through an idea that becomes a concept that is then committed to a blueprint (pattern) and finally becomes a finished product. In Genesis, the creation actually takes place through the Tetragrammaton יהוי, and this is evident in chapter I, verse 26. Here, the 'Name' itself does the work of creating, forming, and making humans in its image. According to Suarez,"

The number 26 is the total of Yod, Hay, Waw, and Hay. Although YHWH appears only in Genesis II, the "idea" of that equation appears simultaneously with the "idea" of the equation Adam. (Suarez SY 45)

Alexa joins the symphony and says, "This is how Adam becomes the image and likeness. Is it only a coincidence that Genesis I: 26 is the very same verse that declares Adam made in the image of Elohim? In case you are wondering if there is any reference to these worlds in the canonical texts of the Bible, consider Suarez's interpretation of a verse written by the prophet Isaiah. He writes: The prophet Isaiah distinguishes the three verbs in question: 'Thus now speaks YHWH who has 'created' you, O Jacob and he who has 'formed' you, O Israel. In the same chapter, verse 7: all those who witness to my Name, all those I have 'created' for my glory, I have 'formed' and also have I 'made.' (Suarez 46)

"Keep in mind that Jacob's name change to Israel indicates a change in spiritual consciousness and awareness. Jacob is the 'created' phase of Adam, and Israel is the 'formed' stage according to the verse. Suarez sternly insists that these three verbs not only represent the three levels of the Tree of Life but they hold the key to the "mystery of the universe"- that people are in the image and likeness of Elohim. The most important point of his analysis is this statement:

We think that the mystery of the universe is impenetrable by the human spirit, but we are in it, we are it, and we have the capacity to study its structure outside and inside ourselves. (46) Suarez concludes that Abraham had this kind of relationship with the Universe and that many humans have it within their capacity to understand more than they realize. Ira Robinson has recently translated a very important 15th-century text by Moses Cordovero known as the Or Ne'erav; he addresses the age-old issue: Where the Kabbalists found themselves divided was on the question of whether the sefirot, taken as a whole, constituted an 'instrument' employed by God for His revelation to his creatures or whether, in fact, the sefirotic realm was God. (Robinson xviii) Many are still confused about whether Elohim is the Tree or an instrument of construction. This question remains unanswered for many people today.

Like the Sefer Yetzirah, we can use a variety of texts as tools to answer questions such as these: "For its adherents, Kabbalah was clearly a tool of great power and sophistication with which to understand the universe. It was just as clearly the ultimate secret of the Torah. This being so, it was by no means clear whether this secret doctrine was to be publicized to wider circles or not. (Robinson xix) Joel joins in again, "This prevailing argument still shrouds this literature in mystery and ignorance. Adam created in the image of Elohim is a very radical concept and yet it is designed to awaken humanity to accept responsibility for the original spiritual covenant and

213

practical application of wisdom and knowledge in the pursuit of harmony and justice between all segments of society. Unfortunately, we are running out of time to accomplish the appointed task.

The distance between primordial Adam and modern civilization is wider than the deepest abyss. As the earthly Adam continues to change, the flow between Tiphereth (Harmony) and Malkuth (Kingdom) alters, and evil threatens to overtake order and bring back chaos. Those who are able to engage in the spiritual battle for the Kingdom are under divine sanctions to study this esoteric science in order to aid in the 'Tikkun.' They just experienced their first trip to the invisible world of thoughts, and its ever-increasing Wisdom power translates them to the invisible world together. They all hear this verse, "Who hath delivered us from the power of darkness, and has translated us into the kingdom of his dear Son." They were all speaking in a heightened state of animation, like tongues of fire; they burned the darkness with their breath, and then suddenly, they all grew silent.

Wisdom of Will

Timka is the first to speak, "Did you guys hear that too?" Alexa answered, "A voice saying something about a translation?" Joel remarked, "Wow that was awesome!" Timka says I feel that something is changing; if you two can hear the Voice, too, something has definitely changed!" She continues to analyze the moment, her favorite thing to do. "Joel, Alexa, I think we might have had a visit from Metatron, the Keeper of Israel; the time must be drawing closer to the full revelation. Salvation is a real event; it is not just a word or something religious or scientific. Wisdom, Understanding and Knowledge are ingredients to restore our soul. Wisdom is a science in Cordovero's text, and Robinson specifies the definition given to Hokhmah. He writes,

Cordovero consistently refers to Kabbalah as Hokhmah, the word medieval Jews used for "science," as in hokhmat harefuah, the 'science of medicine.' It was Cordovero's conviction, and that of some of his contemporaries, that Kabbalah could provide a 'scientific' key by means of which it would be possible to understand the secrets of the Universe (3).

Timka is so excited that she is able to share this type of information with her family and friends; for the first time, they were all brought into agreement by the Paraclete, a Living Spiritual Voice of Messiah! The scientists and religionist have their perspectives, but Timka already knew the 'secrets' concern the nature of the Universe and can ultimately lead to an enhanced scientific view of the structure of the Universe that is more in accord with the nature of spiritual reality. Robinson's passage from Moses ben Maimonides:

The foundation of foundations and the pillar of the sciences is to know that there exists a First Cause, which brought into being all that exists in heaven and earth (47).

"There is no reason why science cannot increase our ability to learn the process and reason of quantum mechanics or why philosophy cannot support cosmological aspects of Moses as taught in the book of Genesis. The pillar of ancient science rests upon a First Cause, and after this experience we had today, our realization permits us to join the angelic hierarchy and begin to study the wisdom of science that can mend the worlds! It is the reason humanity was created. However, not all will be able to comply. There has to be even a handful of humans that desire to receive the message and protect it like a newborn baby. She continues talking, "Cordovero further adds, "These reparations [cannot come about] except through the persistent study of [Kabbalistic] science with the proper intent" (49); the proper intent includes doing it for the sake of the teaching and not personal gain to influence the lives of others or to gain monetary rewards. It is a 'holy work,' "When a man engages in this science, angels and righteous [souls] from the Garden of Eden will accompany him" (88); Enoch claims the 'righteous dead' can still communicate from beyond the realm that veils time, separating us from them. The medium of communication is through the wisdom of prophecy. Do you see now, Alexa and Joel, what has happened to us? We heard the Voice of the Messiah together!

Alexa, reports what she saw in her vision, "The Unique Cherub Circle mystics thought the 'West' contained the souls of the righteous dead. The Unique Cherub shines from the west to the east emanating wisdom to the sons of YHWH.

Robinson points out, "When one clings to the Emanator he will surely be subject to emanation. [Thus], because of this science the world will receive great emanation" (89), the Unique Cherub is the Emanator of a spiritual force that allows the reader to become translated into the Garden of Eden. This may be what the 'translation' or 'rapture' refers to in Paul's letters. Paul hints that something prevents the angelic message from coming to all of us on time and that he will have to communicate, not with pen and ink, but 'face to face'. Paul says,

For now, we see through a glass, darkly; but then face to face; now I know in part; but then shall I know even as also I am known (HNB I Corinthians 13:12).

Wow! Said Alexa that is why more people are not able to see or hear! Paul also said, "And now abides faith, hope, love, these three; but the greatest of these is love." Joel thinks to himself, "We must learn how to find the purpose and plan hidden from before the Earth's foundation. Paul said when we discover the 'Mystery' then mortals will put on immortality as Messiah transforms death back into life." Joel says, "In Paul's own words, 'Behold, I show you a mystery; we shall not all sleep, but we shall all be changed' (HNB I Corinthians 15:51-52). Closer inspection of Cherub Circle terminology and doctrines can assist us in learning the correct interpretations and meaning of the Divine Names found in these ancient texts, as a distinct message emerges from the supposed paradox. Martin Cohen cites a passage from the Shiur Qomah that explains the importance of dissecting the mystery:"

The Holy One says: 'My son you have studied Talmud, have you gazed on the Merkavah? I get no pleasure in my world except when scholars sit and study Torah, and peer and look and study… how my throne stands, and what is its function….but greater than all of these is the study of the Throne of Glory. The highest knowledge greater than all this is the knowledge of how I appear from my head to my toes. (Cohen 58)

Timka explains, "Apparently, the details of the Throne actually contain the 'mysteries of existence' and these mysteries exist for the sake of humanity. The 'mystery' once discovered grants us a safe passage back to the original spiritual consciousness lost by Adam and Eve. A soul praises the Creator through knowledge; Cohen writes, "According to a man's intelligence, so will be his ability to praise Him" (Cohen 64). Cohen explains how knowledge can bring one closer to the Creator of the Universe and this dialogue is a way of showing mutual love and respect. Language, ideas, and concepts constitute what Buber calls the 'I-Thou' relationship. The Hebrew language is divine, for it relates to the divine world of thought; designed to interact with our consciousness. Originally, words were metaphors for translating the experience of life into concepts. Okay, I know it sounds strange, but hold on; let me find something I wanted to share with you. Here it is, listen to Oxlee," she says pointing to the spot with her finger:

"That the third Numeration of Binah or Understanding is the same Subsistence with the Throne of Glory and the Shechinah, may readily be shown. Its identity with the Throne

217

of Glory is thus attested by the author of the Chemdath Tsebi:26 "The term, Peni, Face, amounts by numerical calculation to Hocmah and Binah, Wisdom and Understanding; and so he apprehended the Face of the Throne, the same with Binah or Understanding; and his cloud was over him from the Numeration of Wisdom.

Since the third Numeration is more especially Rashi 27 has an immediate bearing on this question; and plainly proves, that Binah or Elohim is the same as the Throne of Glory: "And the spirit of Elohim brooded, that is, the Throne of Glory stood in the air, and brooded on the surface of the waters with the spirit of the mouth of Elohim, and with His Word, like as a dove broodeth over her nest. That it is the same with the Shechinah or Habitation, is plainly affirmed in the Tykkune Zohar Gadol 328 and as clearly attested in the following passage of the Sepher Kene Hocmah Kene Binah, 29 one of the first and highest Cabalistic authorities: "I will go down with thee into Egypt; and so he says, Wherever they went into captivity, the Shechinah was with them, the Supreme or Most High Shechinah; meaning, the Binah or Understanding; because it is the Habitation of the three first Numerations over the seven days of the Binyan or Building; or, because the Binah is the place, where dwell the six extremities in the mystery of their upper room; and is called the Habitation of His Strength; meaning, the Shechinah which giveth strength to the Numeration of Fortitude." (Oxlee, Three more letters to the Lord Archbishop 62-63)

Tongues of Fire

The Voice of Fire begins to speak to each of them now individually so that each one eats according to taste; they hear different perspectives based on their own consciousness and level of awareness. The Voice says, "The divine world is one of constant revelation taking place in different levels of the human psyche. The World of the Beginning (Bereshit) is entered through a basic study of the origins of not only the divine Name but everyday words you use that are often devoid of a deeper meaning. In discovering the origin of words, with the aid of a good dictionary, you can catch a glimpse even of the origin of Time itself. This 'Word' is not necessarily a book, doctrine, or language. It is also a force of energy. The only begotten Son of Yahweh is the same force of energy, as in the beginning, that created all things. The same 'Word' that transforms into a better and more glorious Tabernacle is now the Soul of this earth and each member of humanity have a portion of it to the extent that they have remembered their origin. The identity of the pre-existent Son of Man is very important for it is the physical evidence of his historical validation. Like a benchmark, it indicates when angelic history actually merged with human history, through the birth-death and resurrection cycle of the Son of Man. People have a right to learn and disagree and debate, but they cannot do this without real knowledge and experience of the true drama; too many are in denial and refuse to believe that something so primitive has any value for the modern world.

The Tree of Life is now the Son of Man feeding all who come to the feast, and yet many will not eat of this fruit, because this doctrine appears to be so unfamiliar to most audiences. This teaching is not of this world, literally and it is hard to enter the invisible concepts. Apocalyptic concepts like symbolic realities on a tree only have to be handpicked and personally contemplated in order to receive the true meaning and fruit. Symbols can transport us into the higher dimensions that contain the invisible mysteries of human existence. Once the symbols awaken in us, mysteries reveal the reality itself. Reality is realized when symbolic parables reflect the Kingdom to us like a mirror image, except the mind itself reflects the invisible reality of its meaning to a place inside our thoughts not seen with mortal eyes." No one said anything now; the experience was so beautiful, peaceful, and calm that they stopped breathing for a while; their thoughts were breathing the Wisdom of Spirit!

As each one slowly heard the environmental noises and clocking ticking in the background once again, they were astonished and just sat there in a daze cherishing the moments they experienced outside of time and space. Timka is elated and ecstatic she cannot believe others are also witnessing the same phenomena too!

She quietly says, "Cohen realized this concept is also in II Enoch Ch. 13 where Enoch describes his transformation during the ascent. He says he saw the "measure of the body, with no measure, similar to nothing and without boundary" (Cohen 80). This literature is sated with esoteric spiritual experiences that exist outside the 'boundaries' of our everyday three-dimensional perception of reality. The Shepherd of Hermas text has encoded messages reserved for the Messianic initiates, yet hardly any remember the codes to break the symbols' influence, which bind us to the world's false wisdom. The author purposely hides transformative agents in the angelic visions and revelation. The transformation takes place via the eyes, mind, and heart, and there is a feeling of sudden knowledge and understanding of the Universe and our place in it. In fact, Cohen believes that every time we read a text again, deeper ideas come into focus, opening the path to higher dimensions of thought (Cohen 119). Timka feels so strong and certain now that others will enter the Timeless Kingdom soon.

Nine Visions of Creation

Before the perfected 'complete' heavenly angel Partzuf Shalem emerged, other primordial men did exist; they were the 'Kings of Ancient Time' in mystical texts. In the scriptures, they are the 'Kings of Edom'. Their level of maturity had not fully developed for mortal thoughts still darkened the light of spirituality. 'Edom' means 'red' and unbalanced force because there was no unity between the positive and negative sides of the Tree, whereas the term 'Israel' signifies balanced sephiroth. The 'worlds' or universes that were created and destroyed before the perfect world was created were all derived from the 'Kings of Edom,' many mystics consider these worlds as types of planets that existed before the earth. They also say these worlds are types of consciousness, not just physical planets or worlds. Many different systems indicate that there were at least 10 separate worlds. This is how the solar day is calculated because 10 x 10 x 10 = 1000. These worlds were not able to maintain the equilibrium needed to sustain their momentum and form. These could possibly refer to the original ten dimensions of the superstring theory.

This may also shed some light on the origin of Enoch's ten weeks motif; at the close of these weeks, the heavenly consciousness is born. The heavenly consciousness is able to enter the Timeless Kingdom, but flesh and blood can never touch the Holy Mountain. Adam Qadmon, created after the Kings of Edom, is Paul's Second Adam. Everyone that joins this new creation becomes 'born again from above'. Before the Big Bang, the World of Atziluth- the archetypal world of pure spirit was contained in the primordial ten forces. This Archetypal World gave birth to three layers of worlds. יהוה is the source and substance of the world Olam Atziluth. Superstring theorists state there are at least ten dimensions and that three superstrings interact to connect all the dimensions to each other in an infinite number of different combinations. Our experience of the Universe may be just one such combination. The figure below shows how intricate the connections of the Universe are and other dimensions appear as geometric designs form levels of connection.

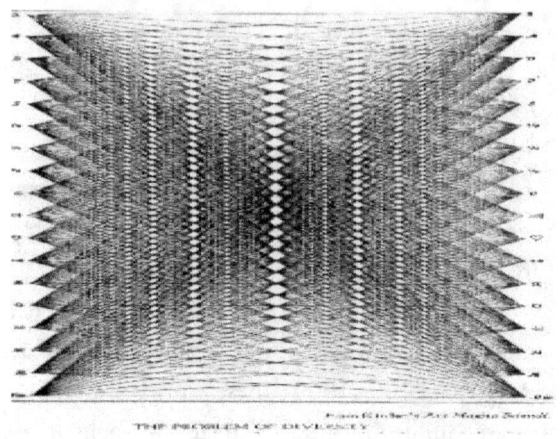

Figure 23 Hall's XV 'Diversity' from Kircher's Ars Magna Sciendi

Diversity represents the world of multiplicity, form, and measurement, a world governed by the box of time. When we discover the Universe is in the image of its Creator, then we can begin to learn how to see the other worlds. We live in a world of reflected light that mirrors the Divine Image.

From this reflection emerged the nine creative acts of Elohim:

KETER Extension/Space	Crown of the Universe is Space
CHOCKMAH Nebula Spiral	Wisdom of the Universe is Helical
BINAH Force/Energy	Understanding of the Universe is Radiant
GEBURAH Vortices	Judgment of Universe is Cyclic
CHESED	Mercy of Universe is Oscillation

Waves	
TIFERETH Matrix	Beauty of Universe is Structure
HOD Laws	Strength of Universe is Order
NETZACH Elements	Glory of Universe is Radiant Energy
YESOD Limits/Bounds	Foundation of Universe is Boundaries

Limits/Bounds

Keter contains Malkuth, and this is how the Kingdom, hidden from the Beginning, is later revealed in the earth. Humanity is contained in the space-time of יהוה the four spiritual dimensions operating through the four forces. Of the four coordinates, three are spatial one is temporal. The whole of physical reality is 'space-time', and the space-time continuum is inside the fourth dimension. In order to transcend the upside-down view of spiritual realities, one would have to be 'translated' back into the World of Eternity or before Time.

Before the Big Bang, Eternity contained the past, present, and future all at once; however, since expansion occurred, an otherworldly dimension developed simultaneously. We can realize this 'other world' through the hidden forces contained in apocalyptic literature. For an exercise in seeing the invisible world hidden within and behind this visible world, consider the following:

Definitions of the Nine Creative Acts of Elohim:

Space has extension in all directions as well as all positions; it is the aggregate of points and a limited extension in 1-3 dimensions (limiters). It can also be a reservation or an interval between two points of time. It can also be an opportunity, chance, or an open area. The Supreme Being encompasses all realities simultaneously.

The Helix or anything of spiral shape winding or circling around a center or pole that gradually recedes from its center demonstrates the expansion. This spiral reality appears as a serpent that has caught its own tale. In mythology, it is the serpent entwined around the Earth. We are caught in its death-like grip, bound by time. The Helix is the movement of the glow that forms when the gaseous properties of a nebula emit light. Some nebulae are bright and some are dark.

Radiant emanations are the result of energy waxing and waning throughout the universe, as it has the function of emitting rays. Radiant rays of light and the reflecting beams of light glowing are like the brilliant and beaming sense of happiness, joy, and love, emitted or transmitted by others. It is the point in the heavens at which the visible paths of meteors appear to meet when traced backward. We, too, must learn to trace our steps backward through the mysteries of Time to meet our future.

Cycles recur in circles and possess a nature of revolution characterized by a ring or closed chain. El Shaddai is a numeric code (314) that circles the universe. The Chain continues to bind the forces of Chaos and will for a succession of Great Years (10,000). This contraction or restriction is what allows material life to exist inside the Tzimtzum. The Vortex, with its mass of liquid, has a whirlwind motion that forms a cavity in the center of the circle. Objects drawn toward its center caught up in its whirling motion and pulled into the depths of the abyss experience the power of the Chariot's Wheels. The Galgillim of the Merkavah also 'caught up' individuals in its motion. It is this swirling motion that creates all things that descend upon the earth.

The Oscillation or swinging back and forth momentum like a pendulum is characteristic of the contraction and expansion laws of the universe. The inhalation **YAH** --- and exhalation **WEH** demonstrate a movement in time and consciousness through the breath of energy. It is aspired in and out of the air each time we breathe. This fluctuation between fixed limits is apparent in ambivalent beliefs and opinions. It also means to vibrate above and below a mean value. The flow of electricity alternately in opposite directions that so characterizes the dual reality that characterizes the Universe in its operation. The positive and negative energy travels in us like electricity.

6). Waves capture movements one way or the other: an undulating or moving ridge on the surface of a liquid such as a body of water or something that swells, has a crest, rises, and falls. It characterizes a period of intensity and unusual activity. One of a series of several events/ a change of atmospheric pressure like a cold wave that causes the temperature to drop, while a single pulse in a vibration disturbance passing through a body (gas or liquid) such as light a simple wave where each particle of the medium undergoes changes through a 360-degree revolution. A wave continues as long as the disturbance lasts. These electromagnetic waves maintain the forces of the Kosmos. Ever becoming and growing in accordance with the will of Yahweh.

Structure provides form. Any kind of arrangement or construction, such as buildings, dams, or bridges, are all constructed with the aid of a blueprint or pattern. An arrangement of parts or organs and types of tissues or particles in any substance that depend on the interrelation of parts, such as the human body, is a structure. There could be no physical existence without structure.

Matrix is a place or enveloping element within which something originates, takes form or develops; it is the natural material that metal, fossil, pebble, crystal, or gems are embedded within; it is that which gives form, origin, or foundation to something enclosed. Humanity originates and takes form in the womb of the Universe.

Order provides a foundation for diversity. It is a line, hierarchy, or a society of persons united by some common rule; any of the nine grades of angels; a harmonious relation in a system; and a customary mode of procedure in debate. Order pushed chaos back into nothingness with the dawn of light. It gives a weaker competitor a chance to even the discrepancy with a stronger opponent.

Matter is where the spiritual laws take place. That of which any physical object is composed; whatever occupies space, that which constitutes the substance of the physical universe, the indeterminate subject of reality seen first as an unorganized experience which, when combined with form, gives phenomena or real objects.

The matter of elements, fire, air, water, and earth envelop us like a womb. Matter: a state or sphere suited to any person or thing also one of the constituent parts of any system, a substance which cannot be separated into substances different from itself by ordinary means. Humanity will always ultimately be inseparable from the energy of the Universe because it is how we live, move, and have our being. We are the Elements and the Element is life [6 + 3 = 9] divine attributes that form three heavens from which emerge seven realms of earth. There are three laws in the Universe: 3, 7, and 12. As it is stated in the Sefer Yetzirah, the three Mother letters Aleph- Mem- Shin created and then formed the seven Doubles or realms of duality that fill the twelve circuits of conductivity.

Heavenly Physics

A Universal Law operates through the two basic energies that first emerged from the Unity. These two energies born out of fire and water are the 'eshamayyim,' a Hebrew term that literally means fire and water, known as Heaven in English. As a seed, Adam is rooted deep in the soil of Assiyah as the letters of the Tetragrammaton lie buried in the tree of his consciousness. (Y) Fire represents oxygen, (H) Water represents hydrogen, (V) Air represents Nitrogen and the (H) Earth containing them all represents carbon. Hesiod and Ovid both say Chaos is a "yawning and void receptacle for created matter" (G.H. Pember - Earth's Earliest Ages 19), and Ovid describes a different version of a creation story than the one found in Genesis.

The ancients used to call me Chaos: for a primeval being am I. See of how remote an age I shall recount the events! This air, full of light, and the three remaining elements, fire, water, and earth, were a confused heap. As soon as this mass was separated through the discord of its component parts, and had dissolved and passed away into new positions, the flame ascended upwards; a nearer place – that is, nearer to earth- received the air; the earth and the sea settled down to the bottom. Then I, who had been but a mass and shapeless bulk, passed into a form and limbs. (20)

Greek and Roman mythology agree that Chaos was the first thing in existence. However, Moses clearly dispels this notion when he says that יהוה 'voiced' existence into being with the enunciation of the command "Yehi Aur!" which results in the primordial light of the 1st day that fought back the chaos with order.

Fire	Energy
Water	Atmosphere
Air	Space
Earth	Matter

Aryeh Kaplan, renowned teacher, scholar, and Kabbalist wrote,

On a somewhat deeper physical level, fire, water, and air represent the three basic physical forces. 'Fire' is the electromagnetic force, through which all matter interacts (Kaplan Sefer Yetzirah 145).

Water will extinguish the fire. Thus, air is the balancing force between the two. Like fire and water, the centrifugal and centripetal forces act together to form and control all the possible combinations of atoms and their physical manifestation. The centrifugal activity goes out from the center then scatters as it goes into space and ceases to be a solid structure. When it gathers in, the contraction takes control of it within its own limits and forms to itself the essence of all being and energy. A ray of solar energy gives it life; it then begins to aspire. This is only at the atomic level; at the sub-atomic level, the activity of strings, particles, and branes totally defies the imagined order of the atom. Particles are in chaos and the forces of expansion and contraction work very differently.

Particles can literally merge into each other. Strings can stretch and expand into great branes or dimensions. Atoms, under the command of strings, combine and form the elements and structures of the material universe. The nine creative acts of Elohim arrayed like the branches of a great tree with rings inside rings is the invisible structure whose creative will directs the laws, forces, elements, waves, and vortices that together comprise the Universal structure of all things.

These systems work together to emanate, create, form, and animate every part of the Universe. It always takes the physical creation (the shadow) to explain the spiritual creation (reality) through light. The physical creation exists in the past (hoveh), and the spiritual creation exists in the future (yihyeh); only humanity can live in both at once in the present. Yahweh is the radiant energy and Elohim symbolizes the vortex that contains the energy channeling it through nine separate vessels in the Tabernacle. Margaret Barker says the term 'Hallelujah also means 'Shine Yahweh' and that 'Hallel' can mean 'praise' but this is the minority meaning. The major meaning is to shine! Things that shine emit rays of light that emanate waves of brilliance and are all useful examples of how Yahweh is in Elohim or how the Father is in the Son. Even light emanates waves of circles that vibrate and cause us to see and our auditory canal picks up sound waves and transmits them to the brain. This vortex is also evident in the cyclic events of the planets in orbit and the evolving seasons.

Figure 24 Hall Grand Man of the Zohar

Today, the discoveries taking place through quantum mechanics and M-Theory have helped us all realize that the Universe is composed of many Dimensions and that all of these multilayered planes exist in the past -present, and future simultaneously, just as the prophets of antiquity taught. The figure in the above illustration has one foot on dry land and one foot in the ocean while maintaining the three heavens or dimensions of the Universe. This structure of a Universal body segmented into realms depicts the perception of the ancient mystics. The Tabernacle of Adam has three sections that Joel reviews in the next chapter.

ADAM of the New World

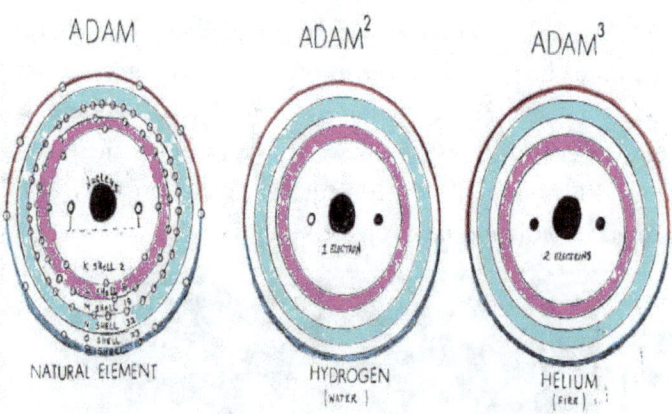

Figure 25 Adam Cubed

The most abundant elements found in the Universe are hydrogen and helium or water and fire. When the 'natural element' or Adam is filled with the water of life and fire of the Holy Spirit it completes the 3-fold Adam, for it is then that the Heaven and the Earth are once again joined through a chemical exchange of energy. The Alchemists searched for the magical means to transform base metals into gold; we have the answers built into our very nature. Elohim is the container of all genes of existence whether they are organic or inorganic, positive or negative, spirit or flesh. Even Time and Space is a creation within Elohim. Elohim is people, locations, and material existence. There is a mysterious code name that can balance the double polarity of the human equation $2 \times 3 = 6$ (the six heavens) resting in Elohim. These dimensions or 'heavens' lie latent in us until we learn how to open the center in our hearts. The center of the soul contracts in the point of a very dense void or 'point singularity' in modern scientific terms thereby becoming a throne for the spirit to sit on.

In rabbinic literature, the figure named Adam has a specialized meaning and a generic meaning. Each meaning becomes relevant only in the context of its purpose. Adam means both the individual person and the whole of humankind without any exception, generically. However, the term 'Adameh le'Elyon' indicates that:

The human person and the human species merit the name 'Adam' only when desiring to resemble God and adhering to the divine attributes. (Hayutman 9)

Hayutman says Adam is the 'quality' that will aid in the coming of the new world: "In fact, it is the increase of the number of people who merit the name 'Adam' which brings the Olam Ha-Ba into Olam Hazeh. What is so distinctive about the people who receive the Glory that Adam lost? How they maintain their individuality (symmetry) and remain within the All is the answer to the Mystery. They emanate light from their center, instead of absorbing the lesser light around them. Hayutman compares Maslow's theory of self-actualization with a spiritual experience in the following statement,

Maslow, who studied human development to its peak, found that the most well-developed humans (those who really merit the name 'Adam') and who have the most universal outlook are really the most individualized and unique (9).

Mirror of Anthropos

Anthropos proceeds from the Son of the Decad. The Ten is a pattern of an 'image', the Hebrew term Demut represents a picture of something. The 'picture' shown to Moses on Mount Sinai is what they used as instructions for building the Tabernacle. In Kabbalistic terms, the Beginning and Ending of Keter in Malkuth are both the reality and the reflection of the

Kingdom. The Hermetic philosophers say, As Above - So Below. Imagine a room full of mirrors we cannot touch and it will be easy to perceive how we are lost in the reflections of ourselves. Since we cannot touch the mirrors, it is very difficult to determine where we are spatially located in the room. This is how hard it is to see ourselves in the hidden Kingdom, even though it is right in the midst of us. We live in the spiritual reality of life, but we exist in our own faulty perceptions of this reality.

In Exodus chapter 24:9-18, Aaron, Nadab, and Abihu witness a transfiguration along with the 70 elders who see the 'body' of the Creator surrounded by a great cloud. After Moses goes into the cloud, he later returns with instructions and a pattern to build the Tabernacle. This is stage one of the process. Matthew then records in chapter 17:1-5 that the Son of Man is transfigured in front of Peter, James, and John, who then ask if they should build three tabernacles. This is the second stage of the divine energy descending into humanity. Both groups see similar things, such as a bright light, a cloud that covers the mountain, and a pattern of the Tabernacle.

Most of us are not aware of these ideas because Anti-Adoptionistic censorship led to the alteration of many original themes behind Paul's Adam motif. Paul explains that the first Adam was from the earth and the second Adam was from the spirit. These two Adams, when combined, became one new man. The Anti-Adoptionist followers teach the idea that an entirely spiritual person devoid of human tendencies represents an entirely new standard for the new creation. Paul never separated humanity from the spirit; he often speaks of the future reconciliation of the flesh and spirit. Many of the alterations affected the way we read Paul's texts:

A similar motivation may have led to the series of corruptions in 1 Corinthians 15:47, in which Paul elucidates his famous notion of Christ as a second Adam: 'The First man was from the earth, of soil, the second man is from heaven. (Ehrman 94)

Instead of accepting both Adams, Orthodox scribes added extra words to Paul's texts: "Strikingly, the reference to Christ as the 'second man' has been variously changed in the tradition: (1) 'the second man, the Lord'; (2) 'the second, the Lord'" (Ehrman 95). The term 'Lord' is a propagandistic ploy added to influence the reader in some way. Ehrman makes this clear when he writes, "Again, it is difficult to account for these changes apart from assuming an orthodox tendency to portray Jesus as far more than human" (95). Ehrman lists a few others who have altered the text:

Several witnesses have omitted the explicit reference to the first Adam as 'man' (Anthropos, lacking in BK. 326 365 Iren at al), perhaps because the contrast with the anti-type Christ might then suggest that he too was a (created) Anthropos. (95)

The primordial image of 'anthropos' will eventually become human. Surprisingly 'anthropos' comes from a Greek term meaning 'one who gazes upward'; for the one who lifts their consciousness to יהוה gains spiritual insight and rejuvenation. These ideas are definitely missing from the way we read these texts today. In II Cor. 6:16, Paul explains how physical buildings have become idolatrous:

What agreement has the Temple of Yahweh with idols? For you are the Temple of the Living Elohim; as Yahweh has said, 'I will dwell in them, and walk in them, and I will be their Elohim, and they shall be my people.

According to Christopher D. Stanley, author of Paul and the Language of Scripture, II Cor. 6:16 echoes the message of Lev. 26:11-12:

"I will set my tabernacle among you: and my soul shall not abhor you. And I will walk among you, and will be your Elohim and you shall be my people" (217).

Many biblical interpreters refer to a passage in Ezekiel as a probable source of Paul's concept of the future Tabernacle. Stanley says that Paul may have used Ezekiel's image of the Tabernacle in II Cor. 6:16: "To express a similar expectation that Yahweh would one day re-establish his earthly tabernacle in the midst of his people" (218). Stanley explains the issues surrounding "intentional adaptations" and concludes that many of Paul's own changes were in accordance with biblical hermeneutics but with a twist that often moves the saving act of grace from the first-person narrative to a third-person soliloquy.

When Humans & Angels Touch

Paul's doctrines expand upon the ancient idea of the tabernacle to include tabernacles made of humans. He claims that each person who sees the 'Mystery' of Messiah transforms from a mortal nature to an immortal nature. The temporary tent or booth is a type of the first tabernacle of the flesh, but the actual tabernacle reared up on the eighth day signifies the tabernacle of spirit. The Temple derives from the concept of the Tabernacle. However, the interchange of these two terms has resulted in a misunderstanding of the texts that contain these terms. Craig Koester, in The Dwelling of God, explains how:

Jewish exegetes could have understood the Tabernacle cosmologically and gradually applied these views to the temple. But a more probable view is that interpretations first given to the temple's furnishings were gradually applied to those of the tabernacle (59).

Koester reports that both Philo and Josephus have a similar view of the Tabernacle's role and its furnishings: "For both, the holy of holies corresponds to the highest realm in the universe and the outer court to lower regions" (61). Margaret Barker adds a very important point:

There appeared very early in Christian writing references to beliefs that are nowhere recorded in the New Testament and yet clearly originated in the tradition we call apocalyptic. As more is known about this tradition, so more and more points of contact can be found between the beliefs of the ancient temple theology and what Christianity became. (Barker 40)

The prophets knew that a more glorious tabernacle of Adam Kadmon was destined in the End of Days. The Temple is an object of great speculation and debate. It is also a prolific topic among the authors of the New Testament, Dead Sea Scrolls, and Apocalyptic texts. Many ancient texts from mysterious places contain the keys to unlock the elusive links of prophecies that will help us to learn the correct 'time', these texts contain more pieces of the puzzle we call 'existence' than we can imagine.

Unfortunately, many of us do not have a chance to investigate these texts due to preconceived ideas about their context. The knowledge of certain mysteries and secrets called 'sod' enhanced one's ability to worship Yahweh and it also provided a way to reach the higher dimensions of the Holy Place. The Son of Man is the New Most Holy Place. The divine indwelling of the Holy Spirit represents the Shekinah that dwelt in the Tabernacle. When the word of wisdom dwelt in Moses, it changed his level of perception.

Moses perceived Atziluth, but only indirectly, as it was refracted into the Universe of Beriyah. Moses thus attained the highest level of spiritual inspiration ever experienced by a prophet. (Kaplan 29)

Kaplan's detailed analysis of the encyclopedic knowledge bequeathed to Moses from the World of Atziluth widens our perception of how the invisible world exists. Atziluth emanates wisdom that is ineffable and beyond mortal consciousness or understanding. Before wisdom was a 'Word', it dwelled in

Keter – the Crown that is within Atziluth. Let us remember John saying,

"In the Beginning was the Word" for it is in and through 'thought' that all things are first known. The equilibrium of the double polarity balances the inner battle of the Ruach (spirit) and basar (flesh) or the yetzer ha-tov (good nature) and yetzer ha-ra (evil nature).

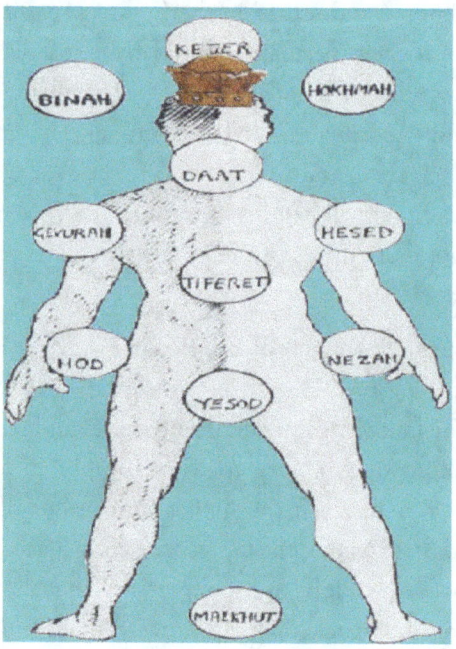

Figure 25 Crown of Adam

Shells of Atom/Adam

Many of the things that Timka talked about began to emerge in Joel's mind; Timka loved talking about chemistry when she took her class. She would always tell him how basic chemistry teaches us that all 'shells' of an atom's interior are filled with the appropriate component before electrons are found in the next shell. The seven shells of the atom have an alphabetical symbol such as [K, L, M, N, O, P, and Q]. In other words, the shells of the outer court do not require fulfillment like the K shell of the Most Holy Place. Joel thinks to himself, "I had no idea the Kingdom is this intricate; most people do not talk about atoms and spirituality together; it seems so odd that she can peer into concepts and pull out meaning; I did not notice." I remember when she had me up all night once, talking about the Lewis Octet theory, and that it opened her mind to understand how stable atoms maintain their energy states. The theory does not apply to all the atoms in the periodic table, but there is something interesting about the relationship between the number 8 and the stability of atoms. Even the smallest atom is under the spirit law of the Universe. Everything created has some type of skin surrounding it, and underneath shells at the lowest sub-atomic level is a string."

"Timka kept repeating it to me. I can still hear her voice saying, "If we compare the shells, called kellipot in Kabbalistic texts, to various layers of the dimensions, it presents a new reality of the heavens that surround everything in the Universe. This may be a way to understand how six higher dimensions or superstrings can exist in such a tight contraction inside us, all around us, and without our realization. The only way to escape their grip is through balance. The ancient mystics knew that everything had these shells and that life emerges from within the constriction. Even the Torah itself has layers we must penetrate before its hidden mysteries and secrets emerge from its vault of esoteric lore. The layers are like a nut with many shells to discard, and of course, the kernel in the center is the desired prize. The Rabbis taught that many stories are garments of a deeper mystical secret meaning that comes to us from a distant time as we peel off the various layers one by one, allowing the raw essence to rise. As physicists continue to look beneath the shells of atoms, they are beginning to discover the intrinsic properties of superstrings, and this is what may eventually lead to a 'Theory of Everything' that can explain how the four forces operate together." Joel begins to regret those days now and wishes that he had listened and supported her more.

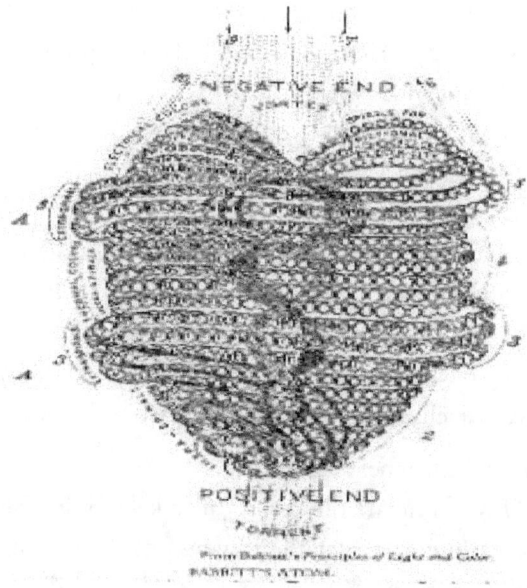

Figure 26. Babbitt's Atom Diagram

He is amazed at how much he has changed by doing this research, and now he cannot seem to stop thinking about all the other things he does not know. He grows curious about magnetism and electricity; he never thought about an invisible world before. He looks at one of Timka's charts in her study room, and he notices that Babbitt's Atom is an amazing illustration. Timka told him that it illustrates an earlier idea regarding intricate internal structures of atoms, she said – "It is a good way to see the detailed work of invisible forces and fields that maintain a circular vibratory motion similar to strings. Even thunderstorms have layers of clouds that conduct electricity and surround a center point of balance known to meteorologists as the 'Eye.' The Eye occupies the calm part of the thunderstorm. Tornadoes and hurricanes have an 'Eye' that is constantly watched by the weather bureau for it also dictates the potential level of a storm's activity. Mystics learn to see the future world through the inner eye of the Torah that opens and watches us imagine." He realizes just how much he loves her again, but now it is a different kind of love. He sees her Light for the first time, and he is confused by how the realization makes him feel.

Who is there that can behold the works of heaven? Should there be one who can behold the heaven, and who is there that could understand the things of heaven and see a soul or a spirit and could tell thereof, or ascend and see all their ends and think or do like them. (I Enoch 93:11-12)

When a person concentrates and seriously ponders certain ideas that catch your inner eye, a wave of insights arises that inspire whoever reads apocalyptic texts to experience the 'face' of the Torah. Torah, like a Bride, must choose to remove her veil and reveal her 'face' before we are permitted to see. Each one of us must face our inner self and that of others. Paul said that he would come to certain individuals 'face to face' and not with pen and ink. The Holy Spirit is a Voice that reveals hidden Wisdom, heals broken hearts, and defends those on the battlefield. The Universe, too, has a 'face', and its structure is a mirror image that can reflect the face of Primordial Adam into our mind. When we see who we are in the cosmology of the Universe, we see Elohim! "We can experience the Mystery of the Son of Man and learn how to experience wonders of the past, though we live in the present, just by thinking. Joel grabs a dictionary to look up the word Atom. He finds out it is from the Greek "a tomos," which means not cut or uncut, indivisible, a particle, jot, or the smallest particle of an element that can exist.

We all come from the original Adam/Atom – like chips off the block with everything already contained within. The perfect combination of atomic weight dictates the linking of atoms with other atoms to transform themselves into molecules. A perfect balance between the two sides of the tree creates a perfect combination of attributes that form the regenerated soul linking it with the souls of others. A very interesting fact is that,

The electrically charged neutral particles (neutrons) in the nucleus add to its mass but do not affect the number of electrons. It, therefore, has no effect. (Brennan Scientific Dictionary 19)

This neutron serves as a mediator [Metatron] allowing the polarity of proton and electron to reach a state of equilibrium. The additional balance adds to the mass and acts as a foundation point for its center. This is only one level of the Atom's true structure. Beneath the proton, neutron, and electron are three tiny little strings that vibrate to a different frequency in a different world where anything can become everything. Around the nucleus of the Atom (center) forms sequential shells, and the 2nd & 3rd periods of the periodic table of atomic weights build up to form completed shells of eight electrons. The High Priest Metatron has eight Garments of Light.

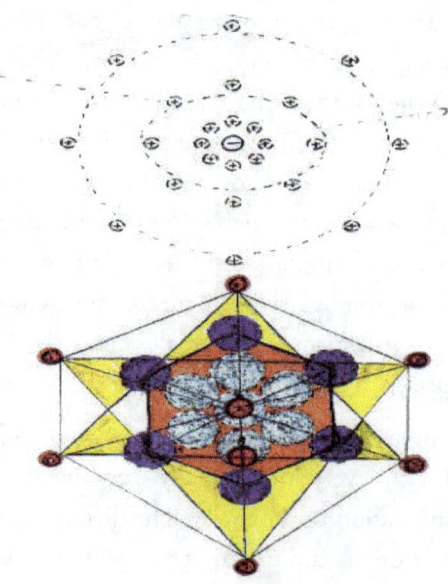

Figure 27 Metatron's Eight Garments

The presence of groups of 8 electrons, for instance, has been explained as an arrangement of electrons at the corners of a cube. (Encyclopedia Brit. Vol. II 1956 646)

Joel begins to feel the absence of Timka; he notices that she has not been around that much lately, "I wonder what she is doing?" He feels strange inside, light, airy, and excited. He hears a Voice say, "Call her." Although he really did not hear a voice this time, he felt the words and knew them in his mind. He puts the book down and calls Timka. The phone rings a few times, and his heart begins to flutter. Finally, she picks up, "Hello, Joel, is that you are you okay? Joel can hardly wait to share that he felt a Voice telling him to call her. Timka says, "Joel, calm down. Are you alright?" Catch your breath." She starts laughing, to her surprise. "Timka, tell me more about the Laws of Nature and the eight electrons; they are a perfect fit for a stable atom, right?" I am suddenly very interested in knowing more about this stuff! Timka is elated but also wary; over the years, she has experienced many reactions from people. She thinks to herself, but I do like the new Joel. "Okay, okay, hmm, let me see, yes, atomic physicists have proposed many theories, but they have yet to offer a reason for the existence of this strange fact of the Universe. It may hold a clue to the meaning of the eight Garments of Metatron. Furthermore, the number 8 is the sign of the lemniscate ∞ symbol of infinity. Eight is also the day of no more time, sun, moon, or death, according to the author of II Enoch. ($2^3 = 8$ or polarity3 = eight) Metatron is also equivalent to 314, which, when reduced to Hebraic algebra, is eight. The circuit of the Sun is a constant rotation and orbiting of the lemniscate of Metatron. The seven days of creation merge into the eighth day of the Beginning."

Genesis Octet

"Joel, did you know magnetic energy results whenever an element does not cancel out, all the pairs of electrons and protons; iron is a good example. The leftover particle creates magnetic energy that will then respond to the earth's magnetic field. When two hydrogen atoms share their electrons, the outer court Shell becomes complete. The outer court electrons aid and maintain the combining power of atoms. The Octet Theory, however, is not the first name assigned to a set of eight things. It is a common theme in Greek stoicism, and the Eightfold Path of Buddhism is a central tenet of that religion. Students of prophecy and apocalyptic also believe that there are eight distinct garments of the soul and eight great works of the Word during the days of Creation. Stoics believe that 'Reason' presides over the eight parts of man.

Reason

Sight Sound Smell

Touch Taste Reproduction

Speech

"The ancient Greeks believed that Reason is the leader of the other seven but according to apocalyptic traditions, we must transcend 'Reason' in order to experience the divine consciousness of the Holy Spirit. In the text of II Enoch, Adam is made of seven natures: (flesh from earth, blood from dew, eyes from sun, bones from stones, intelligence from angels and clouds, veins and hair from grass, and soul from Ruach of Elohim). However, instead of Reason presiding over the lower attributes, Elohim ruled over the Heavens. This is the innate structure of human consciousness in the divine world. There is one very small section of a Gnostic text written by Basilides referred to as 'Fragment A'; it mentions the Octet as "subsistent entities". Bentley Layton translated it in The Gnostic Scriptures: "BASILIDES believes that "justice" and its offspring "peace" substantially exist, being arranged inside an octet, where they remain" (429); it appears that the Octet

Theory had many theoretical applications. Layton adds a footnote concerning the names of the remaining members:

"For the other six members of the octet (parent, intellect, verbal expression, prudence, wisdom, and power) cf. IrBas 1.24.3" (429).

The Sufi Tree of Life also contains only eight attributes, as the outside two are extensions of the Creator, the macrocosm and microcosm. As the spirit wrestles with intellect in order to wrest it from its sleep, the intellect is a delimiter that shuts down our spiritual faculties, blinding us to spiritual things. When the spirit wins the battle, it then transforms the active intellect into the Metatronic consciousness. At least eight electrons form stable atoms and humanity is stable when the eight attributes are balanced. Both sides of the Tree of Life must find balance within three perfect sets of two energies."

I beheld another splendor and the stars of heaven. I observed that he called them all by their respective names and that they heard. In a righteous balance, I saw that he weighed out with their light the amplitude of their places, the day of their appearance, and their conversion. Their conversion was into the number of the angels and of the faithful I Enoch 43:1. (R Laurence The Book of Enoch 1883)

Timka can hear details coming from her mouth, which she learned for the first time; this is why she loves it when someone asks a question; she gets a chance to learn, too. She continues speaking with Joel, "This is an example of how things are 'prepared.'

Yahweh prepared an offering in the form of a Son this Son then prepared places for those who emerge from the ground of Adam's being. Intense ultraviolet radiation (fire) produced by stars in the OB region ionizes hydrogen (water) this then produces energy that transforms clouds of dust that will later become stars. Stellar (winds) create a void or cavity for 'stardust' to expand within its protective concave shape (womb). Then a (wave) pulsates upon the surface of the dust cloud causing it to condense and take shape.

Enoch's numbering of the stars may be a precursor to modern astronomy; it is evident that stars and atoms are very similar in their formative processes. Electrons, like star clusters, tend to form compact little groups. Each group contains a definite amount of electrons just as each stellar dust cloud that swirls into a galaxy contains definite positions from which stars evolve. Not all space within a galaxy can produce the necessary conditions for stars to grow. Similar to this is the fact that not all knowledge is conducive to the edification and growth of the soul that feeds from mysterious esoteric gnosis."

COSMIC TREE OF CREATION

Timka begins to interact with the totality of ten dimensions of attributes, which translates her thoughts to a higher level of spiritual awareness within the Cosmic Tree. Wisdom will now increase the "powers" of her Active Intellect, endowing her with the ability to see and experience the nature of reality and the structure of all invisible existence. This totality of spiritual energy empowers her imagination as it creates her 3D spiritual consciousness within the Avir. Her soul takes on the 'shape' and 'image' of a "fixed structure" (This may be what later Gnostics referred to as the Pleroma). Margaret Barker has captured reality perfectly in her monumental book, The Great Angel, where she quotes an ancient citation:

God appears in his potencies in the trunk and branches of the theogonic and cosmogonic tree, extending his energy to wider and wider spheres. Further, the manifestation was in human form; the symbolism depicts the God of the Sephiroth as Primordial Man, and the great name Yahweh was shown by Gematria to be the same as Adam (Barker Great Angel 93).

Timka writes, "Of course, many doctrines and ancient texts concern the great name of YHWH that is associated with Adam in Genesis 1:26. However, here Barker wants us to pay attention to a debate between Maimonides and Abraham ben David concerning the anthropomorphic nature of the Creator. Maimonides states the Creator has no body, and Abraham says the Cherub figure is proof that there is some kind of body. What does the body consist of? The Letter SHIN ש represents the root of the Tree of Life. The root letter, when inserted between YH & WH, becomes YH (SH) WH or יהושה. This letter has three little 'points' or Yods that form a root that joins the Creator to the Creation. In gematria, the letters Y-H-SH-W-H = 326. 300 is also a very important number in gematria. The Holy Spirit of fire inserted in the midst of the four Living

245

Elements of יהוה indicates a great powerhouse of spiritual consciousness and creative energy. This ancient link between heaven and earth breaks when people forget how to listen to see the living Tree of Life. The Bahir states that "a tree brings forth fruit through water, so the Blessed Holy One increases the powers of the Tree through water" (Kaplan Bahir 45). Superstring theorists predict that certain open-ended strings with two points can attach to a membrane, and that is how matter and light remain fixed to the 'brane' instead of flying off. Underneath the surface of everything are strings and circles that vibrate and stretch into massive branes.

There are ten strings that form 10 branes or dimensions, and these strings possess the key to uniting the "world of the large things" (Theory of Relativity) with the "world of the small things" (Quantum Mechanics), according to Brian Greene in the video "Elegant Universe." The world of 'small things' is a very good way to see that there is an invisible world that maintains the visible world of the 'large things'; it is now possible to see the 'unseen things' all the mystics described." Timka read what her hands typed so quickly that she did not get to see the sentence. She grew anxious, wondering what was going to happen next.

She can feel the Kingdom calling her and transforming her mind and heart, but this seems different, she is interacting with the Wisdom in a way she never experienced before, as if she is also re-created repeatedly. What if I forget where I started the journey? What if I lose myself? She questions the thoughts now since she realized a few days ago that her thoughts are not always her thoughts. Thoughts can enter our minds without our awareness; it is important to observe your thoughts and name them. She decided to rest for a while and clear her mind. She lies across the bed and lets her head hang over one side of the bed. When she closes her eyes, she sees the blue circle open up, and she realizes there is a triangle inside; she can clearly see three points, but one seems to be missing. "What is that?" She thinks to herself, I love that color blue, but it is an odd shape. She opened her eyes and then closed them again to see if it was still there, and this time, the circle began to open, and she felt herself being drawn within the Universe and saw galaxies swirling as she glided along effortlessly with just a thought.

Chaos of Strings

Deep down beneath the electron, neutron, and photon are strings vibrating at different frequencies, creating different wave particles. Within our thoughts, there are different frequencies and signals that trigger memories or feelings that are always our thoughts. Jung wrote about the unconscious self and the collective consciousness. Some thoughts seem to rise to the surface and extend the perimeter of our mind, creating ripples upon the waters. Timka now thinks of the new discovery regarding the string theory, and puts those other thoughts to rest for now. She continues writing, "String Theorists present ideas that are beyond the imagination of many prominent scientists, but since the 1980's when no one took it very seriously except a few people like Susskind, new theories have emerged that actually strengthen the evidence that there are tiny little strings underneath the sub-atomic structure of atoms.

What really puzzled early string theorists is how Einstein's Theory of Relativity could not completely explain the chaotic structure of life at the most sub-atomic level imaginable. At this level, where there is no direction or time, the invisible world of strings matter, time, space, and force have no place; everything is everywhere all at once.

There is no classical order; everything is so chaotic that north is south and west is down, but yesterday is before today. It is the epitome of chaos. Many of the ancient texts discussed describe the same kind of seething cauldron at the center of the

Universe. Directly below the center is the abyss, sealed at each of its six gates with a permutated form of יהוה. The six 'superstrings' wrapped up very tightly, one inside the other, also have an opening that can run either clockwise or counterclockwise. These highly compacted dimensions are responsible for the shape and form of atoms and matter. Ancient science says the fifth dimension contains the path and directions of good and evil and each direction has a very great depth and density. It is the moral realm created to test humanity's perception of the Light. Timka thinks to herself, "The sephiroth are like vessels that convey spiritual energy and consciousness; without our awareness, we are the subject of their creation. Wow! We are the creation! Genesis is about how each of us has the potential to be re-created in the image of Elohim, which is the resurrection of spiritual consciousness. When our soul is reunited to the Cosmic Tree our memory will be restored."

The prototype of all the Sephiroth is Keter as Anthropos is the prototype of the Son of Man. There are six gates with two directions and this gives the sum of twelve. Humanity is subject to six classes: good/evil, up/down, and death/life that perpetuate the human race. Individual capacities to contain and measure the Light determine the quality of each species.

Keter or the Monad is the dense, indivisible state of symmetry or unification. From Keter arose Chockmah, the (Bereshith) that creates the six days (spheres) of the creation process. The creation of multiple life forms expands from the continuing divergence of the four forces. We saw earlier how the four forces were originally in a state of Unification before the Big Bang. The shattering of the vessels occurs because the mortal mind initially cannot receive the 'powers of cosmic energy'; it is a struggle to receive the Wisdom that gives Understanding.

Two Strings of Nature

Mystics taught that the first thing to emerge from the primordial man of Light is two natures: yetzer ha-tov (good) and the yetzer ha-ra (evil) poised within tightly compacted urges and drives until experiences of good and evil awaken the propensity for either to rise from his nature. Could the Tree of Life in the midst of the Garden be another source that proves how an innate matrix exists inside all things that can eventually transform its outer nature? The answer is in this story, but we have to learn how to find it. Adam is not aware of Eve's presence inside him until he has weighed the heavens, measured the earth, and named the creations. He can then realize that everything has its counterpart because he saw it reflected in the things in the environment. Adam, the father of spirit, knew that the true food of the Tree of Life is inside us all. Eve, the mother of flesh (all of us) has to learn how to find the tree within the strings of life. Some scientists are trying very desperately to prove that the Superstring theory is true. One of many new strange ideas involves a Super Symmetry theory that will exonerate the M-Theory. Theorists predict there is a partner for every particle called a 'sparticle', and if the 'sparticle' for 'gravitons' is ever found, scientists might be able to understand and test the M-Theory better to prove their hypotheses are valid. Right now, research points to gravity as the key to how closed string particles can move from brane to brane. Is Eve Adam's 'sparticle'?

Gravity symbolizes the death-like state that falls on Adam, and from this evolves woman from Adam's instinctual longing to mimic everything seen in the Universe. From this division, the unity of spirit and flesh was broken, for Adam could no longer reproduce spiritually but became a physical creator (Lesser Yahweh) who could only win back the lost light of the Kingdom through burial in the matter that he willed into existence. The fall into matter demonstrates the heavyweight or bondage of reproduction and living on earth opposite our nature with sorrow and pain. Adam's dual existence caused gravity to become a stronger force than it originally might have been. Adam's fall into the 'grave' or gravity limited his senses and biological functioning. Each of us has to pass through each of the four kingdoms and forces of energy that scientists are compelled to examine and analyze in the frenzied attempt to travel to other dimensions. The power to rise above the gravity of death lies in the fifth force of love. Like Adam/Eve, scientists must learn to reach for the invisible tree of life that lay buried in the midst of trees. Gravitons form when strings close. The Kosmos exists only through the Sefiroth or vessels of light that physicists call 'strings.' Locked in the cube of materialism, we cannot escape our own selves. Jerusalem above is a double cube with a set of faces that may hold the key to how to enter the garden once again. Timka falls asleep in her chair and enters a place of rest with no thoughts, emotions, or reasons – she just is.

A Vortex of Thoughts

Like atoms and stars, people have charge and spin momentum; just consider the electrical impulses and electrolytes of the physical body, as well as the electrical activity of the thought process itself. Thoughts are never-ending generations of ideas and concepts that form concrete facts when we act upon them. The revolving of our thoughts can be a half, whole, or even three-quarters of a turn. We often say we just changed our mind but it often means we reversed a previous idea and looked at its other side. It is our ability to express these thoughts or ideas in a constructive and positive way with another that completes the dialogue. Often, our ideas and opinions crash into each other like worlds colliding when people approach our internal orbit (personal life). The ability to see another point of view helps us rise above our internal cubic mindset. The circle is like dialogue, each can link us together. Learning to exist with others is a ripened fruit on our internal Tree of Life. Eternal Life begins when the Tree inside begins to expand its roots and takes our mortal thoughts captive. Joel has experienced a few of his own different energy states; he was oblivious to them before he reached a new plateau. He finds he does not have enough time to read and study; there are things he wants to know more about now. For one, he did not realize that First Nation languages contain many traces of Hebrew roots and sounds; whenever he hears Native American music, he notices the permutations of YHVH immediately. "No wonder the two systems have so much in common," he thinks about giving Timka a call. He misses her, she has been away with the kids, her special time to reflect, think, and prepare. Nevertheless, he will give her the space she needs. He will also 'steal the time,' something Timka always says she has to do in order to study. His soul seems drawn to Enoch, but his mind is thinking about other things. He decides to pick up one of Timka's notebooks; this is something forbidden, and her notes are sacred to her. He cannot help it, and he breaks the rules. He just opens it up and finds this page. As he secretly begins to read, he can hear her voice.

"Stars, too, have "energy states" that bind them to a particular position within the galaxy. Strings also need a particular set of conditions to achieve a phase transition; at least ten dimensions are necessary to allow the string to vibrate and transform into a higher frequency. The author of Enoch may have realized a basic scientific view of this reality before modern scientists created scientific terms for laws evident in the Universe. If atomic weight helps to define the chemical law of definite combining proportions, then the weight of spiritual dimensions can help to define the law of combinations in the Tree of Life.

Are electronic scientific instruments the only means available to discover fundamental laws of the Universe? Can a rational order demonstrate facts of natural phenomena and various relationships between them really determine the answers to all of life's wonders? In many ways, natural science has determined to re-evaluate and challenge the very foundation of existence, but it must stay within the realm of all knowledge, not what is exclusively scientific in nature. Ironic as it may be, physicists are beginning to sound like ancient mystic scientists when they describe the invisible world of atoms and superstrings. According to Encyclopedia Britannica,"

Helium consists of four hydrogen nuclei, but its atomic weight is exactly four. Thus, when an atom of helium is built up from hydrogen, there is a destruction of mass and an equivalent liberation of energy. (E.B. -Science Vol 20 -118)

"The destruction of mass redefines the boundaries of time. When we enter the world of eternity, we must learn to embrace the past, present, and future all at once in the fourth dimension. In the world of sub-atomic particles, time continues in three-time dimensions without ever meeting. The past is 90 degrees away from the future and the present intersects the center of the angle in an upward direction that continues to parallel the past and future. A vision of eternal realities in the mind's eye is how spiritual energy liberates the soul from intellectual sophistry."

Angelic Power of the Alphabet

Each symbol of the Hebrew alphabet unlocks the little-known secrets of the angelic alphabet. There are seventy names and twenty-two letters of the alphabet that have ninety-two celestial atoms. These alphabets 'atoms' correspond to the ninety-two elements of the atomic periodical tree. Ancient symbols and meanings assigned to Hebrew letters can show us hidden realities of space and time that still reside in the first three stages. The Sefer Yetzirah contains the formula for arranging the Sefiroth within the Tree of Life. All possible combinations of the Autiot "letters" are contained in the Torah in the form of various names. The Torah itself is one huge Name. Many names derived from one name changed with various permutations designed by visionaries to teach their students how to transcend the flood of thoughts that invade our minds when attempting to study. Carlos Suarez has high hopes for this spiritual science he says,

"I think it will not be long before the Autiot will replace the letters used arbitrarily in physics today. The Autiot, therefore, arrange themselves in equations, not words, which by virtue of their complexity can be studied in several ways, according to the greater or lesser involvement of the Autiot in them" (Suarez Sefer Yetsira 41).

Is this 'numbered code' the same type of code Enoch might have used to measure and analyze the atomic structure of the stars and the universe? Joel feels like he is peering into her soul; he can hear her thoughts and see her visions. "The sefiroth transforms the energy that radiated from photons of gamma-ray transmissions.

They aid in the breakdown process until the radiant Aur light is free in the world as matter. The process began when one force emanated from the singularity point and evolved as the four forces. Suarez says that the two double equations of infinite energy are the "Ayin -Sof" and "Aur-Elyon" (Suarez Sefer Yetsira 53). Ayin Sof represents three concepts: 'No End,' 'Eternity,' and the 'Infinite.' As we learn the meaning of each experience, each concept leads to the next experience. Aur Elyon means the 'Light of the highest consciousness'; it is perceived as a garment of Ayin Sof that shades one from the direct light of Eternity. We live in a world of four dimensions; in our world, knowledge of the measure, weight, proportion, and time of the Universe is what gives definition to the "nothing" ex nihilo of all that is. The Unique Cherub shades us from the direct light of the Ancient Unseen Essence.

Through the limitation of infinite and primordial substance, "limiters" or Arms of the Universe set up boundaries. The four directions, plus above and below, are the boundaries that shape and form our life on Earth. The Great Name [YHVH] of the Heavens and Earth sealed the creation with six spatial directions, thereby giving life through form and constriction. Each gate sealed with a different permutation of the Tetragrammaton keeps chaos bound in the abyss. The various permutations of YHVH are various states of 'Being,' most commonly known as the Four Hayyot, that travel in one direction. Joseph Dan explains that יהוה does not refer to the Supreme Being but to the name of the Glory that created the heavens and the earth. He wrote,

"The name YHVH refers to the Kavod, a divine power which came into being during the process of Creation and cannot, therefore, be regarded as the Creator himself" (146);

Enoch describes this creature as Adoil, a figure full of light that comes from the belly of another figure. Is this another remark concerning the process of emanation? Dan connects this figure with Metatron, "This demiurgic dimension is found also in the description of the transformation of Enoch into Metatron. He explains how the Unique Cherub transforms into the various manifestations seen by the prophets that account for the controversial anthropomorphic activity later scribes and editors later censored or reworked. Many denied these aspects, but this group seemed to possess an earlier doctrine of describing the Cherub, not based on the Kabbalah of the Bahir or Zohar.

There is another source that I find very interesting concerning the identity of Metatron from 1845",

"His praise, the universality of His dominion, the adoration of His person, and many other attributes incompatible with a mere mortal, the predicted Messiah is declared to be from above - to be capable of imparting from His lips the spirit of prophecy--to be miraculous in His counsels -- to know the very inmost recesses of the human heart to be free from sin—to be the vehicle or chariot of Jehovah in preference to any angel — to be Jehovah in the more eminent acceptation of that term— to be the Author of all righteousness to man - to be the mediating God — to be the angel of the great council --to be the angel of the covenant, and the lord of the temple. But all these titles and prerogatives are celestial and divine. They can comport with no other being than the Metatron, the second Subsistence of the Godhead; and, therefore, the Metatron and the predicted Messiah are one and the same personage." (Oxlee 69)

"Look at the last two sentences! Did you see that? Metatron and Messiah is the same person, according to this author. The letters are also these books of people who looked for Messiah centuries ago, and they found Him! That is what brings all these teachings together. Even Joseph Dan wrote about it here, "The secrets of Creation, and the 'letters by which the earth and the heavens were created; are given to him" (147); here, Dan implies that the figure possessed the ability to create and form various types of flesh and substances with the use of Tetragrammaton, otherwise known as Formula 26. Suarez expressed the 'Aur' Formula like this: Aur (aleph-vav-resh) with an atomic value of (1.6.200) equals the operation of how spiritual light moves into matter. Aleph is infinite energy in motion. Resh represents the elemental physical foundation of all that exists. The Vav is a letter that acts as a link, joining two into one. Son of Man is poised between the spiritual Universe and the earthly Universe as a reconciler of the two opposite charges of energy. Holiness and unholiness exist side by side as one expands the other contracts. New discoveries in X-Ray

Astronomy show that energy ejected from black holes is not only sucked in as originally thought. The energy emitted from black holes can escape the 'event horizon,' and this could be the evidence needed to see that the sefirah are concentric circles that both expand and contract during changing energy states. At the center of every black hole is an active galactic nucleus or AGN; when one breathes in, the other breathes out. Joel drops her notebook and falls to the floor, dumbfounded by what he just read. He actually began to see what Timka was describing, and then he noticed that if he looked right in the center with his eyes closed, he could see the center swirling around a central point, and it felt as if he were moving forward through this center into the Universe!

Mysteries of Magic Numbers

Strings can only vibrate properly in either 10 or 26 dimensions. Michio Kaku says,

Strings can vibrate self-consistently only in 10 and 26 dimensions" (152),

this is a very interesting idea considering how significant the numbers 10 and 26 are. Hebrew letters Aleph to Yod symbolically and numerically express the numbers one through ten and illustrate how energy begins to descend through the first letter, Aleph, then goes through each letter until it rests in Yod, the tenth letter. Again, we see a pattern of themes that involve emergence and motion. Aleph-bet lore explains how Aleph expands and then unfolds into the letter Yod. This is how the divine energy travels through the four worlds, changing its shape and form in each realm until it finally becomes material.

The four-in-ten riddle is a very ancient concept shared by Pythagoras and many other early philosophers. It is a good example of how there are numbers hidden inside numbers. Let us keep in mind, according to the mystics; the four dimensions hidden in six indicate a compacted meaning. The sum of the numbers 1-4 is 10. (1) + (2) = 3 + (3) = 6 + (4) = (10).

The numerical values of the letters Y (10) H (5) V (6) H (5) = 26, but the letter Yod represents the totality of 10 itself. The 10 is contained in the 26 as the 10 dimensions are contained within 26 dimensions, but sixteen are compacted very tightly inside the others. The equation יהוה (26) or 2+6, when further reduced, is the number 8 that symbolizes dual energies that have a reciprocal relationship. Now we can see perhaps a connection; to the 16 dimensions, each contains a set of 8! 4 x 8 = 32 this is the number of paths in Sefer Yetzirah! These dimensions must work together somehow reciprocally producing and emanating energy or aether.

Dan quotes from another ancient text that describes how the name יהוה relates to the creation:

The first day corresponds to 1, the second corresponds to 2, the third corresponds to 3, and the fourth corresponds to 4, 1, 2, 3, and 4 combine to the number 10, which is the first letter of the name of Glory. Then He put up the luminaries and gave light to the celestial and the earthly, in the day in which he completed to sign one letter of His name.

The fifth day corresponds to 5; the sixth corresponds to 6, so he had signed YHV, three simple letters, which He selected for His great name; he indicated His name in the first letters [of the words] 'the sixth day and the skies were completed; half the name in the Creation of earth and half in the Creation of the heavens. (Dan 148)

Perhaps the 26 dimensions consist of two pairs of 10 dimensions balanced by the remaining neutral dimensions. If sixteen of the dimensions are in a tight coil, are the other 10 dimensions symbolic of the lower half of the name that created the earth? Is this the 'golem' or 'formless mass' formed by the 'thought-less light'?

Kaku says that each string can vibrate infinitely and produce infinite structures. According to mystics, the letters of the name vibrate the energy of each letter and its healing powers result in multileveled realities experienced as heightened consciousness or heavens. Thoughts can change, but knowledge remains the same. Strings can change from an electron to a proton and then a graviton simply through different frequency rates. Physicists understand that strings cannot move in three or four dimensions, there have to be at least 10 or 26. The Sefer Yetzirah contains a very stringent law about the number of Sefiroth and warns the reader not to accept nine or eleven, but only ten as the correct number. Apparently, Da'at fell from the original structure and became the eleventh sefirah. After the Tikkun, this attribute will return to the other ten and the lower dimensions inhabited by humanity now realign with the higher dimensions when the fallen attribute is restored.

Light of Life Before the Big Bang

What does this have to do with the beginning of time before the Big Bang? Maybe it has to do with everything. If physicists are correct, they will soon have a complete 'Theory of Everything.' Here, Kaku says scientists are actually going back in time in order to reconstruct what happened. The Big Bang, as we shall see, perhaps originated in the breakdown of the original ten-dimensional universes into four and six-dimensional universes.

Thus, we can view the history of the Big Bang as the history of the breakup of the ten-dimensional space and, hence, the breaking of previously unified symmetries. (195)

The Lurianic Kabbalah revolves around the motif of breaking vessels that result in the shattering of light. This concept parallels modern scientific theories of cosmology and might be evidence that there was a death of some kind at the foundation of the world. It occurred when the original symmetry was broken, and the Unity fell into 'many ones.' Light immersed in the darkness of time waits to be discovered through our consciousness of Eternity.

The lamb slaughtered at the foundation of the world takes on cosmic proportions in light of today's cosmology. Light gave a form of its life to us as particles and waves so that we could exist in time and space within a different type of light.

YHVH	Most Holy Place
ELOHIM	Holy Place
YHSHVH	Outer Court

All three forms of Light are dependent on the previous emanation and produce the Iota or Yodh of Thought that gives us the ability to think and act. Each aspect of Light turns in its own orbit and has the same manifestation within each of the three levels of our state of being (terrestrial-celestial- spiritual). Each Thought is a sample of Will (Keter Crown) at work, but unless the Thought is acted upon, Will does not orbit the intent to perform the Thought, and you do not act upon the idea; there is no manifestation. There are many potentialities, but only particular Thoughts we connect with will bring the concept into physical expression.

SIX GATES OF CUBIC UNIVERSE

The six days of creation represent the geometrical progression of numbers and sounds that result after the fall and scattering of the original light. The six days are the six faces and edges of Jerusalem symbolized as a cube to typify the structure of the material Universe. Adam Kadmon, bound within the six metaphysical arms of the cube, waits for the great day of deliverance. Three faces of the cube are visible, and three are invisible. The two sets of faces illustrate how heaven intersects earth within the six gates of space. One face looks up toward heaven, and the other peers down toward earth. Leonora Leet's monumental work, The Secret Doctrine of the Kabbalah is an encyclopedia of ancient wisdom and science of Sefer Yetzirah mechanics.

Leet says that 26 is an intermediate number that lies between 13 and 52. Here, she says the 'heart' represents the intermediate place of Adam:

Considering the number 26 as the geometric mean between 13 and 52, we should note the further Kabbalistic association of Tetragrammaton, the Gematria equivalent of 26, in terms of the Tree of Life Diagram. Most significant is the assignment of the divine name to Sefirah Tiphereth, the Sefirah also associated with the cosmic heart of Adam Kadmon. (Leet The Secret Doctrine of the Kabbalah 121)

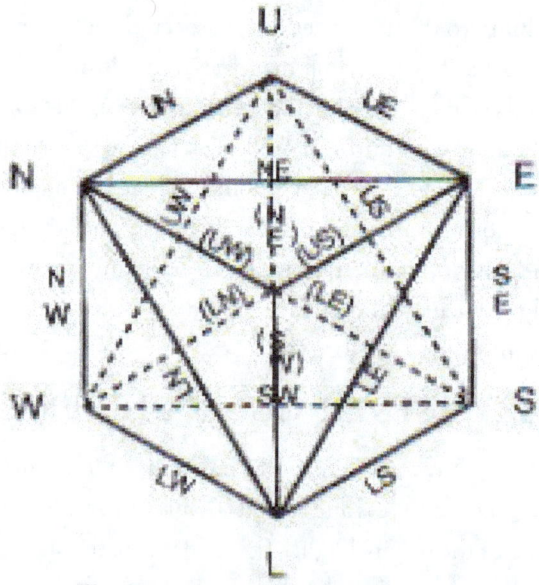

Figure 28 Leet Atzilutic Cube of the Six-fold Tree

The two faces show how heaven and earth intersect each other in geometric proportion. Each of the edges assigned a direction shows that energy scatters in all directions even when contained. Particles and strings also react in a geometric environment and field of energy. If you focus right in the center of the cube in the above figure, something amazing happens to its lines and angles. This meditation device is very ancient. Even this is not new, but there is something new and 'unique 'about the mysterious number 26. A very important mathematical fact involves the 'unique' qualities of the number 26. Ouaknin explains how special it really is:

Fermat noted that 26 lies between two numbers, one a square ($25 = 5\times5$), the other a cube ($27 = 3\times3\times3$). He then sought other numbers that were positioned between a square and a cube, but he could find none, and he asked himself whether 26 was, in fact, unique. (Ouaknin Fermat's Last Theorem 393)

The square is symbolic of a door, and there are symbolic descriptions of a cube in the Book of Revelation. Both symbols represent a form of restriction and materiality. The double cube is really two boxes joined at right angles. Each right angle forms a Y intersection. These rivers are the water of life on the outskirts of New Jerusalem. The cube of spatial directions also has boundaries and faces in which the letters of creation are engraved. The names on the twelve gates are various permutations of the Tetragrammaton. Peter Hayman describes the design of the Universe in "Some Observations on Sefer Yetsirah: (2) The Temple at the Center of the Universe," where he states:

We have here, then, in SY an apparently cubic universe, a sort of box or room, with the Temple set in the middle. This picture corresponds closely to the description of the last six sefiroth presented in para 15, where the author offers a demythologized version of a well-known myth about God's sealing of the abysses at the time of creation. (176)

Matter is the 'box' that contains all the ingredients of life that is sealed in the particles entangled within Avir/Aether. It is no coincidence that the earliest Superstring theorists have discovered a chaotic world of disorder below the subatomic level of atoms. This confirms the ancient belief that there is a seething abyss at the center of the Universe. Strings obey no rules and have no laws at the sub-atomic level it literally appears to be a boiling cauldron of possibilities. Everything is a possibility, and therefore, nothing can ever become realized. North can be in the South, and time is immeasurable because everything absorbs other things. In the four seasons of the year, the 'Great Revolution' of the galaxy demonstrates purpose and order. Ezekiel's Chariot and four living beings must face each its own direction, never entering that of another, in order to maintain the order of creation.

The four directions of the Chariot illustrate the emergence of order and form, and it symbolizes the gates of the Sun as it prepares a way out of the darkness of 'disorder' and 'nothingness' (Ayin) characterized by night. Night is the chaos of strings at the lowest level of existence. Chaos looks like a bubbling stream of erupting bubbles and explosions that result in nothing less than more bubbles. Chaos is similar to the first phase transition as order is to a smooth-flowing transition.

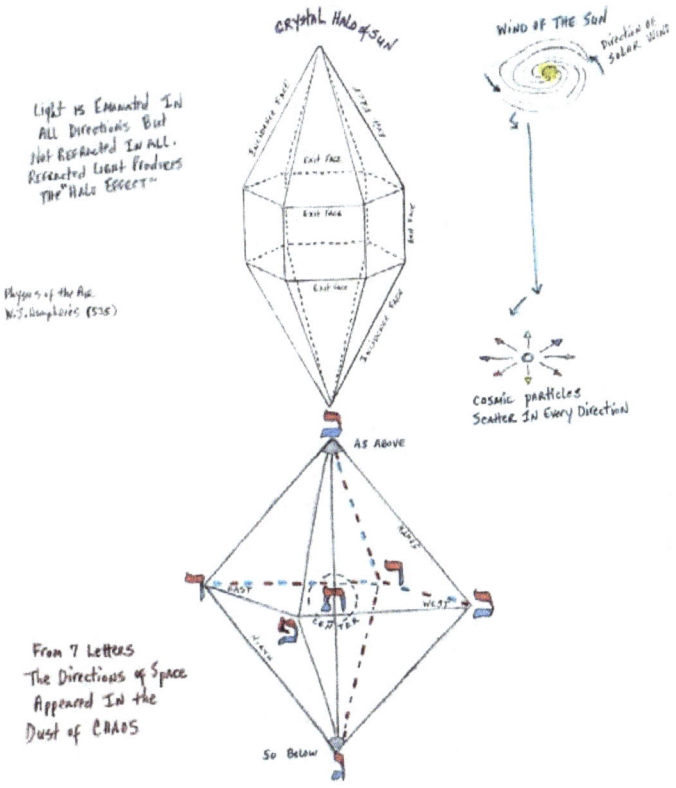

Figure 29 Halo of the Sun

The 64 points of the Chariot is similar to the halo of the Sun. In the above illustration, the 'Incidence Face' is where the ray of light enters in, and the 'Exit Face' is where the ray leaves. The refraction and reflection of Light are evident in the angle between the two faces, although we see light traveling in a single path in a straight line. Actually, when light hits an object, its rays project in a different direction, and we catch the reflection in our eye. This is how we visualize our outer world. Sunlight on the water reflects in many different directions before we finally catch it with our eyes. Most of our entire reality is a reflection or refraction of an object approaching our view. You see, without the Light, nothing can be seen. The light of the sun is scattered in all directions but the living beings of the Chariot always go forward in the same direction. A change

263

in the Face of either pair of the angles will result in a change of Face in the corresponding pair. Each of the four camps situated around the Tabernacle were designated three tribes. Include the twelve apostles and we see the twenty-four elders. The twelve tribes represent the past, and the twelve apostles represent the present, while the twelve gates of the city represent the future. The Chayyoth (living beings) of Ezekiel's vision each face in its own direction. There were 64 sides in all. The tesseract also has 64 sides represented as eight cubic boundaries. The diagram right above the Halo of the Sun is a comparison of the similarities of the sides and dimensions of the cubic figure described in the Sefer Yetzirah. Amazingly again mathematics seems to favor this system because 32 x 2 = 64 obviously there is an underlying formula and system that still remains elusive to us now.

This text contains many mysterious terms that describe how something is constructed. Gems embedded in quarries require picking, chipping, sanding, and polishing as part of the refining process of minerals or stones. In the Sefer Yetzirah, the human soul is like a stone that has to be refined by the transformative properties of fire. The stone, in its embedded, raw, and refined states, is like the states of the soul.

Box of Time

Refined	Pre-existent	Neshamah	Future
Raw	Alive	Ruach	Present
Embedded	Existence	Nephesh	Past

The nephesh is our material existence and is embedded in the flesh for its sustenance; it must learn to grow. It only learns after things have happened in time through constant reflection on the past. Ruach is the raw, pure consciousness that motivates our desires, drives, and instincts; it is what gives us the illusion of being alive and the sense of 'Now' in our present. Neshamah is the pre-existent spiritual experience refined in the fire that transcends time and space, giving us a glimpse of the ineffable face of our future. Each of us has to break out of the quarry of disproportionate senses and emotions that lead to conflicts in our actions and statements. We have to leave the 'square' and enter the 'circle'. Earth is a symbol of the Cube that contains all energy and matter exhausted in the creation of the physical earth (Adamah).

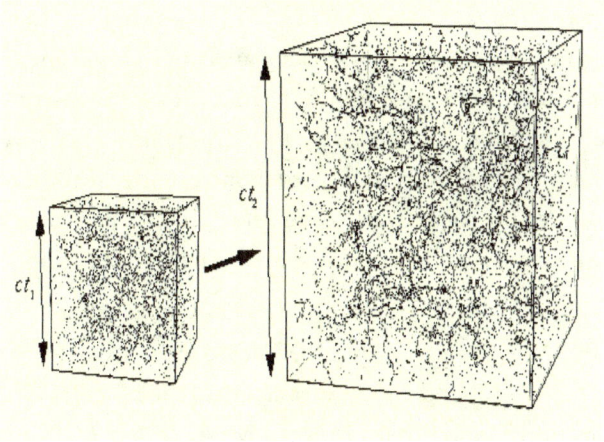

Figure 30 Cambridge Scaling Cube of Strings

The Woman or earth is contained in the Male heaven. Pandora's Box was "safe" until it opened, and then all chaos was set free upon the earth. This is a Greek expansion on the mystery doctrine of 'four,' the Tetrad of ancient wisdom. Life on earth exists contained within a box of logic and science. All things live to escape the confinement of materialization. The above illustration from the Cambridge Cosmology String website shows that when we reduce the size of space, the strings still react in the same way. They tend to form a geometrically proportional alignment with other strings. The planets in our solar system orbit in geometric alignment with each other, and this is how many ancient sailors used the geometry of the stars and constellations to navigate the seas at night. Everything 'created' is contained in something else. Thus, the term 'apocalypse' refers to the continuous revealing or emergence of life.

Apocalyptic literature is more than a genre; it is the nature of the spiritual experience of life. The Ruach is the immanent force that frees life from its solid state by allowing the soul to transcend its container. Light is the force that gives life its freedom from death. The four corners of directions [North-South-East & West] exist in one circular motion and yet there are four points, a square circle. That symbolizes Eternity (circle) entering Time (box). There are twenty-four time zones where the experience of time is different for every zone of the "noon" shadow. This proves that everyone experiences a different type of reality and that no one can ever really explain his or her life experience to another unless one enters that person's reality of the "noon" shadow. Time is the shadow of Light.

The Sun travels along a definite circuit according to II Enoch 13:1-15, and we see various paths and circuits the Sun makes on its grand tour of the Universe. Enoch measured its path of travel according to the constellations of the stars. The sun turns on a circle in a (circular orbit) on wheels (Spheres or Ophannim). Its solar energy gives life and momentum to the circular movements of the planet's spheres. It provides a type of solar blood, oxygen, and carbon dioxide in its process of cleaning the Universe. The heat-light- and chemical transformation of the Sun fluctuates with the seasons, and that is why it is intense in summer and weak in the winter. Everything has its own particular time, even the circuit of the Sun. The Son promised to be with the Bride (Earth) until the end of Time, even through all the seasons and changes. Yahweh changes not; unlike the Sun, the Moon goes through various phases when certain parts are hidden from view. Unlike the nature cults, the ancient prophets taught time is linear and moving towards a particular purpose and goal. This was an innovative thought, for most of the then-known world felt it was an unending cycle of cycles with no outcome. The Son of Man, like the Sun, battles with the night and is victorious in his rising during the Omega. The Sun goes forth progressively towards the West. Then, it turns back in the opposite direction from the six gates according to the occurrence of the seasons.

The sun rises and is responsible for the different parts of day and night, which continually evolve; the constant struggle between light and darkness is won with every Sun/Son rise. The journey of the Sun signifies the journey of life and death that everyone must take. Each hour is like a day or gate and we must cross its threshold, never to return to the place from whence we come. We must continually move forward through time, unlike the Sun, which completes its journey every day. These are the Great Gates of the hours of the year. The circle symbolizes how heaven's intersection is the line of time. The cube symbolizes the earth and its boundaries. Carlos Suarez explains the significance of this,

When this psychological East is understood, we can follow the cabbalistic "Spatial Cube," introducing the human being in an inner space constituted by the first four sephiroth and in the outer space made of the six other sefiroth, every one of them pointing to one of the 6 directions of that space. (Suarez 85)

Suarez says the first four sephiroth (four forces) give form to the 'Inner Space' (Quantum mechanics) of Adam Kadmon. At the same time, the next six sephiroth (six days) give form to Adam Kadmon's 'Outer Space' (General Relativity Theory). Adam's face points in the East direction of Metatron's Cube. Standing upright, his head can reach the fifth sephira, as the sixth sephira becomes a footstool. Adam then gazes at the seventh sephira while the eighth supports his rear. One hand extends towards the right, pointing at the ninth sefirah

(South), and his left-hand points to the final one (North). Suarez believes that the six directions of space are 'sealed' like the surfaces of a cube.

The "directions" of space are the 'Arms of the Kosmos' for they seem to reach out and give shape and structure to the Universe.

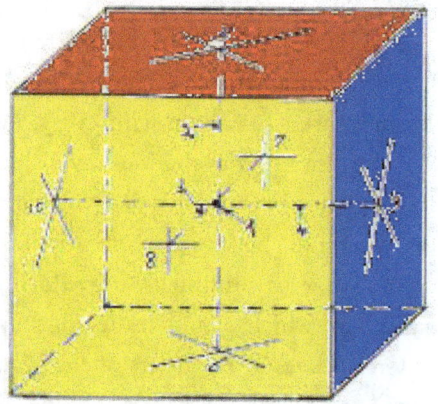

Figure 31 Suarez Cube from SY

Joel thought to himself, "Are we responsible for keeping the energy of our personal universe bound and fettered with our lack of spiritual consciousness?" M-Theory predicts that six densely compacted dimensions lie within a fifth dimension and are actually responsible for providing shape and form to living things. Suarez sums it up,

"Everybody lives inside an enclosed and bounded cube locking inner space in a package" (Suarez 87).

Until we allow the tree inside us to grow and expand, we will remain misshapen. He thinks aloud, "If humanity is able to challenge questions, ask statements, and lose assumptions, it can find a way to experience life 'outside the box.'" There is a force in the center mass of atoms, and at the center of our soul is a unified harmony of force and energy that radiates love. At the center of all things is a hot, fiery, burning core waiting to burst itself upon the outer perimeter of its Shell/Sheol in order to break free from the solid death state of matter. M-Theory has confirmed that this is exactly what all life of substantial essence does in its struggle to become free of form. Ancient mystics discovered this through deciphering the symbolic images found in geometry and astronomy. When an Adam/Atom or Monad is subject to the holy fire, its internal structure changes, and due to temperature changes, the sephiroth resurrects from the death-like state of cubic structures [six gates]. Their baptism in the liquid sea of Avir, the emanating mayyim or sea of Elohim, prepares them to be freed from the grip of material limitation." Joel can hear and see these things clearly in his mind, yet he realizes that it is acquired because he is not the initiator. He does not realize that he shares properties with an atom in a chamber; when the Holy Fire breathes upon us, our soul is free to rise above all containers.

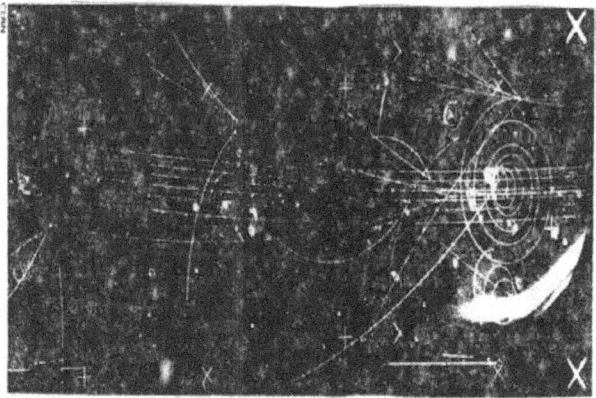

Visible sub-atomic particles such as the electron can be 'seen' when recorded in one of the many thousands of three dimensional photographs taken during an experiment on atoms in a bubble chamber—a device used by nuclear physicists. Here the clearly shown spirals are electrons, which can be knocked out of the atoms in the bubble chamber liquid (usually hydrogen) by incoming high energy particles which are moving near the speed of light.

Figure 32 Atomic Bang Science Encyclopedia

Joel looks at an illustration from over thirty years ago; scientists captured spirals of electrons as they bombard atoms with energy. He can see how electrons escape from atoms as

269

heavy energy bombardment bangs them into other particles. Freed atoms can literally 'pop out' of death's grip as gravitons can float off a membrane into other dimensions. Amazingly, they form spiral circles upon releasing the electron. This is due to the law of the second-order phase transition. Consciousness is a form of energy that is also bound and in need of release. When Adam – the material man, learns the significance of the equation, then freedom will be unbound for Adam – the spiritual man.

Formula #26 and M-Theory

Joel instantly learns things now just by thinking about certain ideas; the more he contemplates, the more his ability to see logically that there is an invisible world. There is nothing mythical or mystical about it anymore; he can see Truth demonstrated in the Cosmos. He is amazed at how the Strings change phase position in 10 or 26 dimensions, and Aleph-Yod represents the numbers 1-10 or the process of energy descending into matter. The Voice gets louder and clearer now as if his thoughts were tuning into a specific channel. "As pointed out earlier, the four letters YHWH are numerically equivalent to 26. This mysterious 'number name' is one of the 'magic numbers' that may hold very relevant information for future researchers of M-Theory. The lore of "magic numbers" is very intriguing, as Kaku points out,"

We will see that these self-consistency conditions force the string to move in a specific number of dimensions. In fact, the only "magic numbers" allowed by string theory are ten and 26 dimensions. (155)

"The mystery of 'magic numbers' is something the mystics were aware of, for many scientific laws were encoded in these numbers. The strings require an adequate amount of room or space to develop and transform. All living things have a string-like system that governs existence.

All things are dependent on the DNA chain of protein molecules that wrap around each other to form double strands of the DNA ladder. When the Helix unwinds in a helical turn, it closely resembles the spiral of the electron in motion.

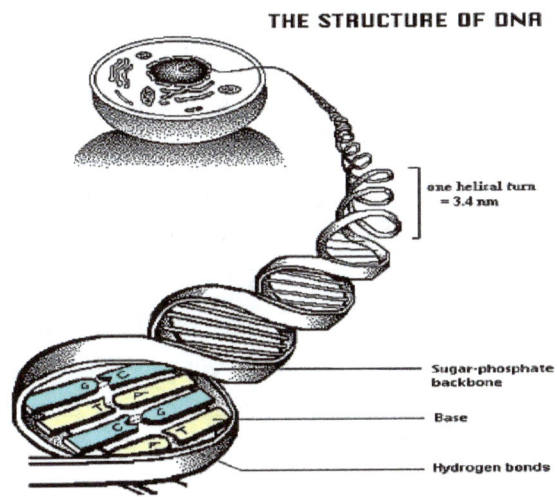

Figure 33 DNA Helix Diagram from Medical website

Michio Kaku builds a case for the connection between strings, human biology, and genetics,

For living things, nature uses the double strands of the DNA molecule, which unwind and form duplicate copies of each other. In addition, our bodies contain billions upon billions of protein strings formed of amino acid building blocks. Our bodies, in some sense, can be viewed as a vast collection of strings – protein molecules draped around our bones. (156)

Kaku theorizes that the fifth dimension contains compacted, contracted dimensions. What is even more enlightening is the connection he makes between the Big Bang and the strings,

In conclusion, the symmetries that we see around us, from rainbows to blossoming flowers to crystals, may ultimately be viewed as manifestations of fragments of the original ten-dimensional theory. (159)

"The world you live in, Joel, is the debris left over from the shattered original ten dimensions. This idea not easily accepted at first in scientific communities, is finally coming of age.

Even at the time Kaku wrote his book, there were still arguments over the five different string theories. Until Witten developed M-Theory, string theory was a joke, but he tied up the loose ends, and Superstrings were back on the scientific agenda for exploration. According to Kaku,"

It was soon realized that, in dimensions other than ten or 26 dimensions, the theory completely loses all its beautiful mathematical properties. But no one believed that a theory defined in ten or 26 dimensions had anything to do with reality. (168)

The Voice resonates in his ears, now filling the room, "Many critics still dismiss the 10 and 26 levels as ludicrous and insignificant to reality. At the time Kaku wrote Hyperspace, Witten's M-Theory had not been born. Many baffling questions still plagued early superstring theorists. How could there possibly be 26 dimensions? Kaku says a brilliant Indian mathematician named Srinivasa Ramanujan discovered another "magical number," the number 24. Physicists added 2 to Ramanujan's "24" and got 26,

Since physicists add two more dimensions when they count the total number of vibrations appearing in a relativistic theory, this means that space-time must have $24+2 = 26$ space-time dimensions. (Kaku 173)

In the following equation, we see that $3 \times 8 = 24$, and with duality, it gives us a total of 26. A strong point of evidence for the significance of the Octet Theory, as discussed in previous chapters, is the following fact:

When the Ramanujan function is generalized, the number 24 is replaced by the number 8. Thus, the critical number for the superstring is 8+2 or 10. This is the origin of the tenth dimension (173).

Joel begins to concentrate on one of the things he hears. He wants to call Timka and tell her all about it, but he is so drawn to the experience and trying to figure it all out he changes his mind and continues to study. He has learned how to deny the 'archon thoughts' that seek to distract and interfere during his study time. He begins to take a few notes of his own, "The numbers eight and two may continue to be significant to research in Quantum mechanics in the future. Spiritual concepts can elucidate and complement scientific concepts. When asked by audiences why nature might exist in ten dimensions, physicists answer, 'We don't know' (Kaku 173). There are certainly many more questions about the how and why of the Universe, and science can never answer them all alone. Another startling discovery about the 'mystery number' is that it has an 'unknown' shape. The following citation from Mysteries of the Kabbalah explains the dimension of 26,

From a geometrical point of view, a square is an area, and a cube is a volume. Perhaps 26 was a dimension other than an area and a volume; more specifically, a dimension that made it possible to pass from an area to a volume! (393)

This dimension has transformative properties that seem to function similarly to strings vibrating back and forth from an electron to a graviton and then back into a proton. Furthermore, the development of matter in space involves the movement from a point, line, plane, and triangle; this demonstrates different states of energy fluctuations in transition during their transformations.

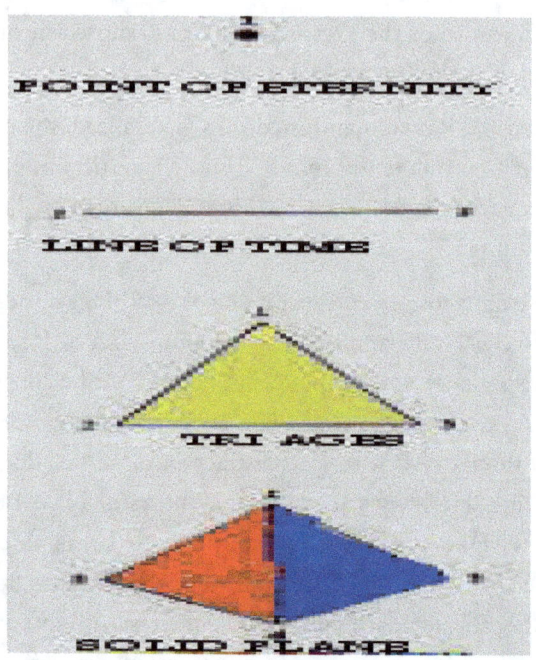

Figure 34 Motion in Time

The point represents zero, the line is one, the plane is two, and the triangle is three. Together, they form a solid plane of four.

From the zero or the Ayin come the three or the Father, Son, and Holy Spirit or vapor, liquid, and solid.

The Decad of Pythagoras seems to play a role in understanding the connection between Spirituality and Science; geometry, fractals, sacred mathematics, and astronomy are the mediums to translate spiritual energy and forms into material reality. Could equation 13-26-52 contain the instructions for how to travel from dimension to dimension? According to the author, it might be:

The number 26 would thus be a fourth dimension, enabling the transition from the second dimension to the third. It could not refer to the time since the time dimension is also necessary to pass from 0 through 1 and from 1 through 2. (Ouaknin, 394).

He grows intrigued by the number 26, which may open the fourth dimension. There are many analogies to show the scientific and spiritual relevance of the number 26 and the number 8. Besides the fact that it is the same number that was present after the Big Bang, this number may be the code or formula for the transition of matter into energy. There were ten dimensions before the Big Bang; sixteen are compacted, and ten remain. Each set of ten functions in two ways: one end of the strength moves clockwise and the other counterclockwise. The sefiroth also have a law binding on how they interact with each other. Attraction and repulsion or contraction and expansion create a momentum that sustains its infinite evolution. The attributes also have a positive and negative influence on the ascending and descending energy that circulates through each circle or emanation of our thoughts. At the very lowest sub-atomic level, where there is no fluctuation and momentum has ceased – zero-point energy continues to radiate tons of energized particles into our part of the Universe. Zero-point energy totally defies modern scientific theories that once taught all energy comes from the force of momentum. The singularity point may hold the clue as to why created things come from inside a structure of some kind. It is evidence that there may be more to the rest that occurs at the end of the six days; this rest from motion results in a state of equilibrium between the positive and negative polarity of forces. 8 is the Day of Eternity restored.

El Shaddai & the Sword of the Cherub

Figure 35 Hall CXXV Cherub of Ezekiel

Timka and Alexa have not seen each other for a while; they each have the same idea and try to call each other at the same time. It was as if Timka answered the phone before it rang, "Hi Alexa, is that you? Alexa replies, "Wow, how did you know it was me calling you?" Timka laughed and said I don't know!" Then she says, "I wanted to share something with you that I just learned about the Genesis narrative of Ch. 3:24. Do you remember where it states, "So He drove out the man, and He placed at the east of the garden of Eden Cherubims, and a flaming sword which turned every way, to guard the way to the tree of life"?" This shows us that Cherubim guard the entrance of Eden with a revolving sword. The Medieval mystic Gikatilla describes a Cherub circling the Universe with a sword. The circle of the sword maintains the constriction or 'El Shaddai' that allows material existence to take on form and live. Originally, Abraham, Isaac, and Jacob recognize the Supreme Being as 'El Shaddai,' but Moses learns a numerical equation that results in the act of emergence from one plane of existence to another. YHWH or 26 emanates or fluctuates in our waters, giving us the power to rise and expand in order to escape the contraction of 'El Shaddai' (3.14), the metaphysical Egypt and state of darkness called Ayin or Abyss.

These two Divine names parallel the two-phase transitions we discussed earlier and demonstrate the action or work of moving from one level of understanding to another higher level of knowing! Each Name contains a self-existent power that communicates with the soul of man. The redemption of humanity occurs in stages with the revelation of the divine names created to form us in the image of Elohim. It creates a circle of light around us because of the swirling sword that quickens us to try to conquer the supposed limitation that faces us from the West. The West in Enoch's literature represents the land of death, and the East is the rising of Light. Humanity learns how to rise through the movement of divine breath: we must breathe with the divine breather.

As we inhale, we pronounce [Yah], and as we exhale, we exclaim [Weh], filling our lungs with the air that rises throughout the body. Nephesh signifies the spirit or breath of life at 'rest' in the human tabernacle; Ruach holds all the emotions, memories, dreams, and future destinies that always seem to change.

Ruach acts like a barrier between neshama [infinity] and nephesh [void]; it is like a circle that contains the psychological life we experience in biological bodies. Marc-Alain Ouaknin, French Rabbi and author of Mysteries of the Kabbalah, explains the significance of the term "Tzimtzum" and the nature of the Universe,

To summarize the theory of tzimtzum, the space occupied by the world is created by an emptying or withdrawing of the infinite and by a force that maintains the light of the infinite at the periphery. This force is called Shaddai. (370)

El Shaddai, translated in English, means roughly, "that is enough," and its numerical equation relates to the contraction of

space and the origin of limits. Ouaknin has found many parallels between the number 314, the contraction, and El Shaddai. Ouaknin cites a passage written by Gikatillia, a sixteenth-century author, that sheds light on the relationship between the circle and the name El Shaddai. Ouaknin says Gikatillia,"

Affirmed that 'the circle is constructed on the basis of the name of Shaddai," which, as has been explained, is the force that maintains the limit between infinity and void at the core of infinity. (372)

Alexa replies, "Yes, and Abraham, Isaac, and Jacob recognized the Supreme Being as 'El Shaddai,' but Moses learns the numerical equation that causes emergence from one plane of existence to another. יהוה signifies the power to rise and expand in order to escape the contraction of 'El Shaddai' or metaphysical Egypt and its state of darkness or Ayin. Physical life is the bondage of Egypt, and the vague apprehension of the Supreme Being as a source of sustenance and protection reflects the spiritual sleep of Nod. Humanity is able to rise from the stupor of ignorance through the movement of divine breath and the pure thoughts of Elohim. That is how we enter Canaan, a symbol of the Promised Land. Shaddai, circle, and the line lore are very ancient mystical concepts. The author explains that,"

"If we perform 'Hebraic' (or "algebraic") mathematics, the respective numerical value of the letters of Shaddai are 300, 4 and 10" (372).

Timka says, Yes, Wow! The 3.14 is the mathematical symbol for (π), which equals 314 or Shin (300) Dalet (4) Yod (10) in Hebrew symbolism. Notice that Shin, symbolizing the

Holy Spirit of fire, equals 300, Dalet, the 'door,' equals the number 4, and the 'hand' or Yod, forms 10 fingers. Do you see the invisible Body at work creating us from the inside out? The symbolism of letters allows us to see that the Holy Spirit of fire opens the door to the hand, which shapes and forms us in the image of the divine, completing the Circle of all Circles.

Circle in a Circle

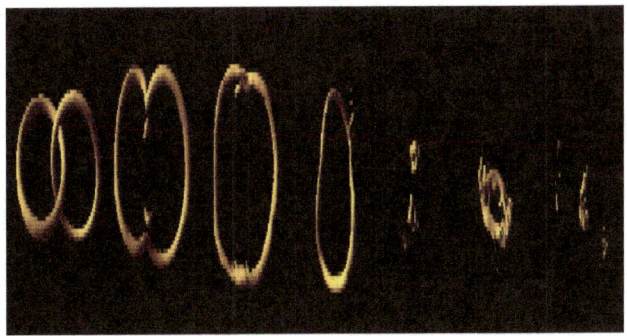

Figure 36 Cambridge Cosmology Illustration of
String Intercommuting

When strings intercommute, the two circles, as seen above, become one string that can give birth to another string infinitely. We exist within this, breathing in and breathing out of the cosmic circle of life. Superstrings in the process of decay, as in the above illustration, demonstrate how two forces emerge from a single point and then form a new string that returns to a single point. This is evidence that new things created from 'nothing' expand and extract from within a dense point to project outwards. M-Theory proves that during string intercommuting, the two circles become one and then vanish back into a point. This is evidence of centralized energy that perpetuates dynamic contractive and expansive forces that continue to breathe life into the material universe. We live, move, and have our being within the expansion and contraction of the living Word that spoke in the 'Beginning' results in Divine energy becoming materialized as the material creation. Ouaknin points out another very important relationship between the point and the circle:

The Greek mathematicians, especially Archimedes, attempted to use science to resolve the problem of the circle (or limitations permitted by the world) and the radius (or diameter) that retains the void around its center. That is how they found the value represented by pi. (372)

The value of π in arithmetic is 3.14; Joseph Gikatilla also recognized the link between 314, the contraction (tzimtzum), and El Shaddai. 'Shaddai' is a constriction of something in either time, space, or the Universe; he writes, "Shaddai is an important name that governs the balance of the forces of nature between order and disorder" (380)

Angel of the Circle

Joel breathes in and out and feels his lungs filling up with air, and as he breathes out, he imagines there is a release of negative energy from his body. Now, he is ready to interact with this Wisdom on another level of awareness. Through the constant contraction and expansion of our thoughts and lungs our life is sustained, and Ruach can continue guiding our inner life. Ouaknin has found a reference to an angel who guards a sacred entrance with a revolving sword in front of the entrance of the Garden of Eden. Ouaknin says that Gikatilla describes the angel in the act of circling the Universe with a sword thereby maintaining the constriction or 'El Shaddai'. Joel's heart begins to pound harder as he reads how Gikatilla

"Refers specifically to the episode that ends the story of the Garden of Eden: an angel stood at the gate and brandished a sword with which he traced the circle of the universe" (372).

He had never thought of it this way before, and he realizes that according to this interpretation, the point of constriction began in the center of the Garden of Eden. He thinks to himself, "Are the four rivers that surround the Garden symbolic of the four forces that evolved from the singularity point after the Big Bang? Did Moses receive the power of knowing how to hear and see the limit and boundary of El Shaddai with this numerical key? Did he find a means to escape the darkness of disorder and chaos when he learned the meaning of Ayah Asher Ayah? Yes, and perhaps we too can 'become what we will become' if it is in accordance with the laws of the Universe." The circle is a great source of balance. Ouaknin states that Shaddai is:

An important name that governs the balance of the forces of nature between order and disorder. It is also at work in the tzimtzum, the withdrawal of the divine, and has been much commented upon and compared with Pythagorean preoccupations. (381-382)

Divine names have more scientific and sacred mathematical value than Joel previously imagined. The numerical equations form realities; one reality is Chockmah or Wisdom. The Angel of יהוה is the Cloud by day and the pillar of fire by night that can still lead us up and out of Egypt into higher thought.

Center of Cherub Contraction

Wisdom found not a Place on earth where she could inhabit; her dwelling, therefore, is in Heaven. Wisdom went forth to dwell among the sons of men, but she obtained not a habitation. Wisdom returned to her place and seated herself in the midst of the angels.

From the point of the center, the Universe evolves from all that is hidden. The Cherub restricts itself so that material life comes into existence. This angelic being contains all the forms and shapes that show the movement of energy through geometry and physics. The Garden of Eden lies hidden in the midst of the angel only until we prepare a place for Wisdom's return. Until the place is prepared for Shekinah, we must learn to find a lower wisdom among the angels. The Cherub appointed to lead us back to the beginning of the Garden appears in Genesis several times, but all this might appear rather far-fetched to the uninitiated. It is not because people are not looking and searching for her; the Shekinah Wisdom is mysterious by nature. What many just do not realize is that cherished biblical texts are missing that would help to explain the role of wisdom.

The fundamental ideas associated with the term 'Chockmah' have been compromised or just plain ignored. The other factor is that 'Wisdom' is destined to be withheld until the 'end days'; this is a word/sign Margaret Barker explains in more detail:

Although the Book of Enoch preserves material from many periods, the Wisdom material is consistent throughout. Most is known elsewhere, but 1 Enoch adds that the gift of Wisdom/resurrection was to be a sign of the last times. (Barker, The Revelation of Jesus Christ 208)

Our own age is the ripe time for eating from the Tree of Life that contains the 'Wisdom Science' of resurrection and immortality. Earl Ellis, author of Prophecy and Hermeneutics, describes the role of Wisdom at Qumran. He says the Maskillim: "were skilled in 'wisdom' and taught in the community 'knowledge' in the mysteries of (God's) wisdom and participation with the angelic spirits of knowledge" (34). The ambiguous meaning of 'resurrection' is clearly defined as a 'spiritual experience' that derives from Wisdom. Rudolph Otto explains in Idea of the Holy how to understand one aspect of the 'resurrection':

We can only get beyond the opposition between supernaturalism and rationalism by frankly recognizing that the experiences concerned with the resurrection were mystical experiences and their source, 'the spirit.' (223)

Like Jewish mystics and Gnostic initiates, Otto agrees that the "higher knowledge" can only come from the 'Spirit' and this knowledge (Da'at) is the agent of the second resurrection. Otto says, "It is the eye of spirit, not the eye of sense that beholds the eternal things" (223). Wisdom is a medium of communication between the spirit and the senses. Chockmah, or Wisdom, is the first attribute to emanate from the Crown. Reuchlin takes us on a tour:

The second gate, after God, is the archetypal world, and, according to the Jerusalem Targum, it is called 'Heaven created in wisdom by God the Tetragrammaton. For 'in the beginning, is substituted 'in wisdom' surely confirming what we have said, that in wisdom God the Tetragrammaton created the heaven, the hall of angels (253).

Figure 37 Ark of Covenant Door

Joel really likes how Reuchlin explains that the letter 'Dalet' symbolizes a 'door,' the Kabbalistic symbol for Hokhmah or Wisdom (325). This image of Wisdom hidden in many Christian symbols, such as the door and gate, is not usually apparent. John says the Father's house has many mansions, and Wisdom is the mother of prophecy in many New Testament books. The Gospel of John states, "He that enters not by the door into the sheepfold, but climbs up some other way, the same is a thief and a robber" and again, "I am the door: by me if anyone enters in, he shall be saved and shall go in and out, and find pasture." What does this all mean, and where does Wisdom live?

Margaret Barker says, "Wisdom stands by the heavenly throne (1 Enoch 84:3) and gives Enoch eternal life, which enables him to "see" his visions" (208).

Mystery of Wisdom

Did the early assemblies know this hidden Wisdom? It is very likely, and an analysis of the evidence to support the fact they had knowledge of Merkavah physics is in Margaret Barker's work. Here, she details the similarities Origen found between Ezekiel and Jesus:

Origen compared the baptism of Jesus to the experience of Ezekiel" he is referring to the Chariot speculation known to have still permeated the early 1st century. Barker writes, "Origen implies that what the prophet saw, Jesus also saw. (211)

The direct allusion to the enthronement of a prophet and the Chariot is not apparent in the New Testament. Again, we must rely on Margaret Barker's analysis:

The Gospels encode this information in the account of the temptation in the wilderness. Jesus was 'with the creatures and the angels served him' (Mark 1:13), immediately recognizable as a Merkavah experience. (211)

Many will think, yes, it all sounds interesting, but I do not have time to sit and study all these texts, and besides, what has Wisdom to do with my daily life? This condition demonstrates the parable regarding the vision the prophet Isaiah saw: People sitting in the darkness, not comprehending how Light comes into our inner world. There are many references to Merkavah concepts found in the Gospel of John and throughout the New Testament, but they are camouflaged with later additions to

Christological doctrines that came after the death of the earliest members and eyewitnesses. According to Barker, "Wisdom writings exhort the reader to consider the raz nihyeh, the 'mystery of existence,' or perhaps it means 'the mystery to come'" (117); she explains how Wisdom enables the seer to see into the past, present and future to witness who will gain salvation or damnation. This wisdom makes them worthy of the esoteric gnosis that exudes the 'sod' a 'mystery of existence' while giving them a peek behind the veil of time.

Barker explains that the Messiah is the sacrificial lamb destined for the altar prefigured in various prophecies of Enoch, Ezekiel, and Isaiah and, indeed, is the same lamb of the Book of Revelation that overcomes the veil of death. Wisdom can help us find our identity and place in the Book of Life, but we must first find the Malakh prepared to lead us back to the Tree of Life. Most of us see English words when we read the Bible, but these merely camouflage the original languages in which the New Testament was composed. Adams reminds us of the most important issue in 1 Corinthians:

"The dominant theological perspective of 1 Corinthians is an apocalyptic one" (Adams 106),

And if the text is to be read accurately, some of the concepts associated with apocalyptic themes must be analyzed to learn the history and meaning of the term within its own cultural perspective. The ultimate mystery is how to discover the real identity of the LOGOS. Before Eternity, when the Father and Son existed as a kind of 'Knowledge,' Wisdom did not play the same role. 'Wisdom Gnosis' enacted the six days of Creation and it is continually becoming until it is finally made; it is an ongoing process until the circle is complete. Moses describes it in the term Bereshit, for hidden in the word itself is Reshit – Wisdom.

Rudolph Otto, in The Kingdom of God and the Son of Man, describes the spirituality of apocalyptic books,

"This religion is already conscious of itself as a missionary religion, and as one which is destined not only for Jews but for the 'children of the earth,' here Otto refers to a prophecy from the book of Enoch. He claims the highest mystery of the Son of Man is disclosed when Yahweh and his Son walk together with humanity, "with those who walk in the ways of truth, and indeed during their lifetime. You will have peace. Rejoice, ye children of truth!" (212).

Even now, the Son of Man comes in search of the lost sheep. Otto says it means even more than we imagine, "The Son of Man is active and operative even now, 'during their lifetime.' As peace comes even now, so the Son of Man comes even now with his Father" (212), 'peace' is what Wisdom brings immediately. When we realize the meaning of our spiritual identity, each of us becomes a type of the Son of Man and part of a corporate body in the heavens. Moreover, when we realize the meaning of the mystery, we will see the Son of Man who is always 'coming' to take us to the mansions of the Father's house. Joel wonders how the mansions of Olam Ha-Bah – the future world of spiritual consciousness, will help him to realize eschatology.

SECRETS OF THE FUTURE WORLD

Enoch prophesies of the peace to come "in the name of the future world," and Otto explains what this future world is,

From the very beginning, all peace has gone forth from something which does not yet exist at all, which is only the future, which is the future world", and this future world is always coming into actualization because 'having a dynamic directed backward, the final reality is already operative (209).

"So, this is what Timka is talking about when she says that the Name is not yet existent. The term for the 'future world' is 'Olam Ha-Bah,' and many believe it is a faraway place during an age to come in the future. This is not due to willful neglect but to lack of exposure to concepts found in the missing literature. The world to come is operative and waiting for guests. "It seems to me that the Greek rendering: "En to aioni to rehome" (97) [time in the next world'] does not reflect the quality of always becoming; this is the fundamental meaning of 'Bah' (the 'coming'). Peace gradually enters our world in stages until the gestation period transitions us to a time of maturation.

The world we live in now really is separate from the divine world, even though it is potentially the only place where we can realize the divine is imminent and always spiritual transformations are always occurring. Many Christian doctrines are saturated with the idea of the 'end days' that they associate with the end of the world; very few of these theories are based on any actual biblical scholarship. People being left behind or taken up to the clouds while driving their cars are a few of the concepts taught today. Some are still waiting for a rapture event, but so far, they are still here. It is no wonder that religious fanatics continue to reign powerfully over those who dissent. Zealots in the time of Messiah believed it is might that is right, not the light. Joel becomes very interested in what Dr. Hayutman explains regarding 'Olam Hazeh,' a world of alienation from God and from nature, a world where God is hidden" (6). Hayutman says the 'coming' is a process, not a one-time event,

It is true that the legends of the sages about Olam Ha Ba and even the prophet's descriptions of the end of days, as exciting as they might be, are not so convincing for the contemporary reader. But it is the very quality of Olam HaBa – precisely that it is the world of the "Coming" and what is 'coming.' Hayutman claims that what is 'coming' has a quality: "Which is so concrete (mamash) – this is the very quality of concreteness. (7)

Keep in mind that many mystics attribute a sense of 'heaviness' or substance to the Kabod as the Shekinah materializes; this anthropomorphic language refers to the appearances of Yahweh. The 'Olam- –Ha-Bah' or 'world to come' arrives when humanity can recognize its own history as being a part of divine eternity. This is how the angelic pre-history of apocalyptic literature re-enters the mortal history of humans. Once Wisdom enters, the human world of time will rest in the center of Eternity.

According to Dr. Yitzhak Hayutman's World, Adam and Adamah,

The concept of the world is called in Hebrew 'Olam' and appears with the Jewish sages of the second Temple period, and they distinguish between two types of Olam: Olam Haze (This World) versus Olam Haba (Coming World) (Hayutman 4).

Hayutman defines history as a transition from one Olam to another: "The meaning of history, according to our sages of blessed memory, is the passage from another kind of Olam-world" (4). The total Olammim continues for six thousand years or three periods of two thousand year segments. We are currently in the age called 'the days of the Messiah,' and it extends into the Olam Haba. Even though this hidden dimension can enter our world at any time, it indicates that access to the quality of the new world is now available to humans, but some impediment is blocking their entry. Other authors describe an 'In-between world' such as Paolo Sacchi, who declares the opposite. He describes a reality that already exists and insists the Kingdom has dawned. Death has no more power, but because time still rules over the material world, there are yet events determined to occur at appointed 'times.' Nevertheless, from the apocalyptic viewpoint, the Kingdom has already dawned, and its citizens are partially in heaven, although they are on earth. Meanwhile, these 'human angels' share a glimpse and taste of this 'in-between world' during their physical lifetimes as a witness and testimony to the authenticity of the Kingdom written about by all the prophets of Israel; the 'vision' provides strong faith and stability to endure the tribulation.

Barbara Thiering refers to this time as the "Future time of visitation" in her analysis of scrolls found at the Dead Sea near Qumran. It is her understanding that humans do not approach heaven, but heaven will come to earth, and humans will have a chance to become angelic if they receive their inheritance- the hidden dimensions of the Third Heaven. Thiering explains how events many think will take place in the "Future time" are actually taking place during our lifetimes:

Nevertheless, in the future, the difference in the conflict will have been removed. The reunion of inward and outward will be unlike anything known at the present time – in this respect, it will be a supernatural change – but it will be a change within the physical order, not a change from a physical to a spiritual order. (B.E. Thiering, Redating the Teacher of Righteousness 68)

A major theme in I Enoch is how heaven and earth, now divided from each other, are destined to reunite in a 'future visitation' during the reconciliation of the angelic and human worlds. Paul's letter, II Corinthians, contains many apocalyptic themes only fully understood against the background of early Jewish-Christian apocalypses. Adam claims that: "Reality is sundered by the cosmic duality of heaven and earth (5:15), the temporal duality of this age and (implicitly) the next age (4:4)" (233). In Adam's opinion, II Corinthians is more apocalyptic in nature, "The main elements of the apocalyptic viewpoint are thus evident in this letter" (233), and if this is true, then modern Christian interpretations are not in accord with the fundamental concepts behind the terminology of Paul's letters. This is why many people today are still attacking Paul and do not understand his position on many important themes of realized eschatology. Joel now realizes, "This is why the Kingdom remains hidden, how can we wage battle with wickedness and deception when our knowledge of the scriptures, our tools of survival are blemished with so many errors of thought?"

He begins to see the drama of the conflict that has such a tremendous influence on Timka. Just then, the phone rings and the intrusion startle him. As he picks up the receiver and hears Timka telling him about something she had just read. He finds it very strange that Timka begins to say, "Adam points out an error: "The underlying Hebrew term (Olam) in post-biblical Hebrew underwent a development in meaning from "age" to "world" (109). When the concept of 'age' was lost and the term 'world' began to acquire more significance, the meaning between the two terms became distorted, and the idea of two distinct worlds was lost. Adam shows that many apocalyptic texts describe the two ages:

The dualism is explicitly expressed in the classic Jewish apocalyptic writings, 4 Ezra and 2 Baruch. 4 Ezra 7:50 states that 'the Most High has made not one world but two.' (109)

Timka explains to Joel how these books dictated to humans by angels show how there are two worlds: one will contain many, and one will contain few: "This world was made for the sake of the many; the world to come was made for the sake of the few (8:1). The dividing point between the two worlds now rest in a 'future time of visitation.' The term 'judgment' refers to discernment and decision, but we often associate it with ideas of condemnation or punishment. Hayutman explains the significance of 'judgment' in the Olam Haba through critical analysis of a Kabbalistic doctrine,

The seven lower Sephirot ('the sephiroth of Binyan' – building) are ascribed to Olam Haza, whereas the Sephira above them, the Sephira of Binah (Understanding), is ascribed to Olam Haba. Bina- understanding is thus a quality of Olam

Haba, and her penetration into Olam Haze is through the quality of 'Tvunah' (the Malkuth of Binah, roughly 'intelligence". (7)

She continues to explain how Hayutman defines three stages of development that correspond to the three ages: The first stage of 'Tohu' that Hayutman refers to as 'wondering' others have associated with the 'Chaos' of the very Beginning. The second stage is the Torah and the need for instruction. After these two initial steps, a type of dialogue is established. He says that at this point in the development there is, "autonomic navigation in the domain of knowledge until complete mastery." He also describes what will happen if one can gain entrance into 'Binah' or understanding, the same thing as "The domain of Olam Haba where all information comes as if on its own accord without striving and resistance" (8).

Timka is almost out of breath as she gasps for air and tries to say, "How can humans find this hidden dimension before it is too late?" Joel says, "How is it that you called me and said this at the same time I was studying? "I just read earlier that Adam says it corresponds to two different viewpoints. She is very surprised at his eagerness to share this with her. They talk a little while longer about household things, and they both say, "I miss you," before hanging up. Joel is more determined than ever to understand this process better he goes back to Reuchlin for more answers. In Medieval and early Renaissance mystical doctrines, Johann Reuchlin explains the two ages and the divine Name Yah:

"So, when two ages are mentioned, the letter Y signifies the future age and the letter H signifies the present age, that is, this world (315).

The 'world to come' is in front of this present age, not after it; this is the great paradox.

The Greeks called it aeon; we call it 'age,' 'eternity,' where there is neither body, nor place, nor vacuum, nor time, nor age, nor change (Reuchlin 197).

Aristotle, Plato, and Socrates, all influenced by Pythagoras, were pioneers in experiencing the 'world to come.' According to Reuchlin in On the Art of the Kabbalah, philosophers perceived our physical body as limited by flesh and senses and our life in this world as imperfect; Pythagoras says, "When you cast aside the body you come to the free aether, you will be a god and immortal" (197). The Gnostics also expressed considerable disdain for the flesh. However, the Son of Man restores the value of the physical body, as shown in the resurrection narrative in the New Testament. He shows the disciples the wounds he sustained in his material body. This was a very innovative concept for that period of history, and not many were prepared to accept the supernatural idea that the body would survive death.

Medieval Talmud and Kabbalah students did not always see eye to eye on methodology either, but they did agree on one important thing: "That there are two worlds. The one is intellectual, called 'the world to come' the other is physical, being the present world" (97). Reuchlin provides an insight into the structure of the 'two worlds':

"Kabbalists posit two worlds, one physical and the other the visible and the invisible; one of the senses, the other of the mind" (101). In the fourteenth century, Reuchlin and Pico Della Mirandola both wondered how the two 'worlds' exist simultaneously and yet the entrance to the 'world to come' is hidden. Many have pondered this very mysterious idea, but few have actually realized its place. Wisdom is like love, sought by many and found by few.

Little does Joel know all that is about to end; the Kingdom is anticipating the final act of the drama. The seer of II Esdras envisions the future world as just a curtain away. The present world of time has a narrow entrance that opens into a wide Great Sea. Only through the narrow road of life can one pass through to the open wide sea of endless Eternity. A narrow dangerous road with fire on one side and water on the other side is what Esdras describes as the barrier that exists between this world and the next. In our world, love is not really the love of the divine world. We have a fallen love and fallen wisdom until they are quickened through the Holy Spirit. Our everyday life is the place we must cross in order to enter the real world of love and wisdom. This explains why there is so much pain and suffering in the world, even though people have wisdom and try to love. Without reliance and trust in the word/signs and an understanding of inner experiences that occur with studying and contemplation, there is no way to breach the gap.

Reuchlin declares the real purpose of knowledge is to aid humanity in making the transition from one dimension to another, "It is rather the passage from a life of action to a life of contemplation, consisting in peace of mind setting ourselves apart from the trouble." We learn to move out of the constriction of Egypt and into the freedom of Zion.

One gains entrance into the Heavenly City of the Kingdom by passing through the Angel of Time. The Angel of Time guards the Garden of Eden with a revolving sword so that only those who have transcended material reality can enter the domain of invisible realities. The future world to come is for those who persevere and learn to eat of the Tree of Life. John wrote about it in Rev 2:7, "He that has an ear, let him hear what the Spirit says to the assemblies, to him that overcomes will I give to eat of the tree of life, which is in the midst of the garden of Yahweh."

When Heaven comes to Earth

Medieval Christianity depicts a fallen world judged and oppressed along with Adam/Eve and the generations of human life; it is no longer the 'good' world originally created by Elohim. Instead, there is a desire to punish and imprison those who dissent from mainstream authoritarian edits. On the other hand, some Gnostic texts demonstrate aversions to 'basar' a Greek term for the flesh, merged with biased Christological doctrines of the ascetic divinity of Christ and suddenly, our human tabernacle, the promise all the Hebrew prophets wrote about and longed to see now appears 'sinful' in Christian doctrines. This is something that grew out of time and distance from the 1st-century community who taught a doctrine called 'The Way.' This was not always the case in biblical texts. Eventually, our 'garment of flesh' became the beast that opposed the spirit, and it seemed sacrilegious to think that mere humans could enter Heaven or be associated with spiritual realities. The traditional Christian view is apparent through the method used to interpret Genesis and the fall of Adam. Many of us are ambivalent about learning 'gnosis' and things that sound 'strange,' and therefore, we do not venture into the 'unknown' world of ancient texts for fear of religious reprisal or bizarre ecstatic trances that show us things of the unknown.

The 1st-century community had a vast amount of literature; they were people of the Book. Burning books does no good because the Logos is the Revealer and the Word that replenishes the All.

Many people throughout the ages feel the same way; you can read this, but not that one and you can think this thought but not this thought. In the end, we forget how to think for ourselves. Heaven comes to earth when we learn to see the hidden mysteries of the Kingdom in all the scriptures and a rich variety of texts and concepts concerning the Kingdom prepared for us from the foundation of the world. This term 'foundation' is the sephira 'Yesod,' and the term 'sod' indicates a secret substance of Wisdom. We received the second set of tablets written after the first set was broken, through the anger of Moses when he realizes that many will not join the exodus out of the material world; they simply cannot find their way without laws and rules that prohibit freedom. Another interesting thing about Wisdom is the relationship it shares with Shekinah, the Presence known to inhabit human beings. The concept of the Shekinah underwent drastic changes. It, too, is associated with the Presence or Name of the Creator. The great existential reality continues to elude the weary passerby, who forgets that the Name is a garment that permits us to envision the Creator. This vision currently takes place in the human mind, but in the Olam Ha-Ba, the vision becomes your own reality and place in the Kingdom. How this Vision of Wisdom exists is revealed in the eschatological age that happens during the tribulation, as spoken of in Matthew 24,

Taken strictly, the meaning is that He Himself would not really exist until the End. His existence is at first only that of the NAME, which is "Named" before Elohim in the earliest beginning. (Otto Kingdom 188)

The book of Genesis describes the descent of the Shekinah and the manifestation of the invisible Creator in 'Adam,' a generic term for humanity. Adam receives the Name on a white stone and is renewed, but first had to endure the tablets written against the 1st Adam before the 2nd Adam would manifest as the Son of Man.

AZILUTH	Y	Realm of Eternity (Primordial Light)
BERIYAH	H	Realm of Creation of Time (Thoughts)
YETZIRAH	W	Angelic Realm (Senses, Feelings)

ASSIYAH	H	Mortal Realm (Material Body)

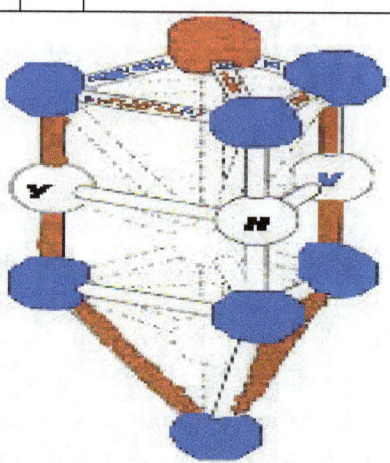

Figure 38 3-Dimensional Tree

The four worlds depict a three-dimensional paradigm known by many as the Tree of Life symbol that mystically comes to life in us. The Messiah, our 'Branch' of the Tree of Life, preserves the Light Wisdom. The river of light that angels bathe in emanates and circulates throughout the universe of the macrocosm and the microcosm. Knowledge of the Tree of Life (Son of Man) is the only source of contact with the true Living Eloah, who is unutterable, ineffable, and amorphous. The Son prepared the Way to enter and leave in peace. The Son of Man restores the Lights of the Sephiroth in the Kosmos. The Ayin Sof is the invisible Keter that Crowns the Universe. Chockmah (Father) and Binah (Mother) give birth to the Son of Tiphereth (Balance). The Son of Man is the only human being who is capable of balancing Geburah (Judgment), which resulted in Da'at, with Chesed (Mercy), which results in Life. None can go to Keter (Father) but through Tiphereth (Son). Tiphereth contains the six sephiroth in balance through the Middle Pillar. Joel realized this also describes the six days of creation. Before the 8th Day, Tiphereth is in chaos, but after the 8th Day, Harmony is restored. Traditional Kabbalah has a different view of the figure on the Throne, which is a central theme in Merkavah mysticism. However, the Throne's occupant is the Mystery of the Kingdom for Paul and Enoch.

John Bowman and Margaret Barker are the authorities in this area. More recently, April Deconick's Voices of the Mystics includes a brilliant analysis of the conflict between Merkavah mystics and John's circle of believers. It is indispensable in providing details of the issues of many different doctrines in circulation among Merkavah groups. John opposed those who taught that others had already entered Heaven through angelic assistance. According to DeConick, John states only 'One' has ascended into the place of the Father. Other Merkavah mystics did not actually reach the tenth heaven through the usual methods discussed earlier. Apparently, this might be one reason why Merkavah mysticism receives such a negative image; many mistakenly believed they should abandon its strange theories without first putting them in perspective based on cultural and religious viewpoints. Buried under dogma and ritual trappings that many unaware readers never escape from is the 'Saving Gnosis' prepared for us from the beginning of time – a Da'at or Knowledge of the Messiah.

The only path that will help us to find the way out of the forest of discrepancies, rigid orthodox views, and cultural prejudices against the Son of Man is to approach this material with the innocence and awe of a child who learns to read the sacred meaning of symbols. Dan explains why,

As mysticism cannot be expressed by sensory or intellectual means, upon which speech and writing are based, the mystics need indirect means of expressing their experiences by symbols, by the expansion of the meanings of words to realms beyond language. (Dan 39)

The Son of Man parables demonstrate the power to create with words because he found the method to teach invisible concepts through images from nature and everyday life experiences in order to relay hidden spiritual laws and reality. Many of the elements of the parables contain prophecies and moral exhortations; ethical maturity is a prerequisite for entry into the Kingdom, and the sephiroth increase through exercising their functions in our daily lives. The ability to distinguish the light from the dark is only the first step; obeying the light has always been the real test of man. Real love hurts and heals at the same time, for each stroke helps soothe spiritual afflictions. There is a battle, many have lost, and some of us still have time now. One must overcome the world of material wisdom and values before the inner world of transformation can begin; there is wisdom of the world and Wisdom of the Spirit.

5th Dimension and Da'at

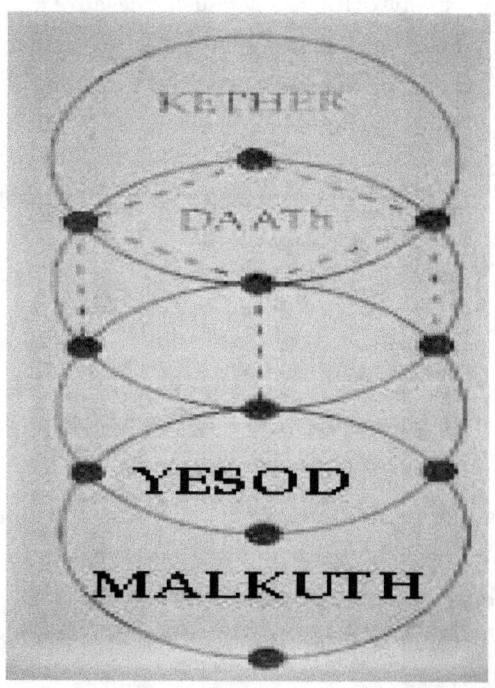

Figure 39 Circles of Da'at

Joel suddenly has an insight regarding the eleventh dimension. He thinks to himself, "We see three dimensions

298

emerge outside the cube: length, breadth, and depth. Time is the fourth dimension, but now M-Theory predicts there are six more dimensions. Ancient mystics wrote about the six dimensions, and they knew that two poles of good/evil are contained in each. The ancient mystic scientists taught Da'at is a fallen sefirah destined to find its place once again within the Tree of Life. This shows that Adam/Eve fell away from a higher evolution into a lower state of consciousness and could no longer access the Garden of Eden. In ancient rabbinic lore, Da'at, the sefirah of knowledge, fell from the Tree of Life and became ensphered as an eleventh attribute; it exists in order for humanity to have free will. It represents the fall of energy into matter and the death of spiritual consciousness. Da'at must be very important.

Joel feels tingly inside, and he can feel his thoughts reaching out for something, even though he does not yet know what it is. Suddenly, he hears a whisper in his ear, "The fifth dimension contains six contracted dimensions according to the Superstring Theory; ancient science of the Sefer Yetzirah taught that the realm of good and evil have great depths beyond measurement. These realms in the fifth dimension, known in Lurianic doctrines as the Moral dimension, have two directions called good and evil. Depth seems like a strange term to use here, but each sefirah has a depth and height. The fifth dimension contains the six "depths" of the human propensity to practice good or evil. One can also ascend to the 'heights' of the Third Heaven; Paul is an example, along with others who followed the Way. Stephen saw the heavens opened and the Son of Man sitting on the right hand of the Father. Joseph Dan provides an excellent analysis of the fifth dimension in the literature of the Unique Cherub Circle. Ancient science mystics of that age believed that human consciousness could either help restore the unity of light or further divide it. Dan's research into the hidden Cherub Circle is a valuable contribution to the interpretation of Sefer Yetsirah. In the book, he describes ten directions and how the Creator dwells in the center of the Universe. He writes:

To these six, the two directions of time are added (the fourth dimension according to modern physics): the beginning and the end. The last two directions, representing a fifth dimension still undiscovered by modern science, are good and evil, the ethical dimension. (44)

Joel sees now how science can actually help to explain ideas found in ancient cosmological teaching, and all the deep mystics and prophets that describe the properties of the fifth dimension according to M-Theory. "Timka would be excited about this," Joel thinks to himself as he recalls some of the arguments Alexa and Timka used to have over science. He finds that it is important to remember that this text is not a religious text; it is actually a cosmological text, according to Dan. Who writes, "Sefer Yetzirah is essentially a work of science. It is an attempt to discover, analyze and present in a systematic manner the laws governing cosmic existence" (Dan 44). This ancient science sought to explore, test, and confirm the observable and the unobservable natural and supernatural phenomena of its age. Enoch says some of the stars disobeyed and altered their orbit by not coming out at the appointed time, thereby creating conflict and chaos in the operation of the solar system. This act of self-will still influences our lives. Kaplan says the reason for the eleventh sefirah is to provide an opening of choice to give humanity a chance to experience good/evil and develop a conscience by exercising free will. The angels are also subject to laws, and when they break the law, this activity influences the human potential for either good or evil. Boccaccini explains the details of the event,

On the fourth day of creation, the angels of the seven planets that revolve around the earth carried their planets outside the orbit ordained by God, damaging creation from the beginning. Adam was put into a universe already contaminated. (Boccaccini Mysteries & Revelations "The Contribution of Italian Scholarship 40)

The heavens are ruled by archons, fallen angels, and wicked powers of the air; humans are accused and persecuted and can only understand the nature of the battle by gaining the necessary knowledge (Gnosis) to engage in the battle. The archons work through powers and principalities that hold the world and humanity in bondage to poverty, war, and death. Kaplan writes about the origin of this war: "In discussing the death of the Kings of Edom, we pointed out that the shattering of the vessels began with the quasi-sefirah of Da'at knowledge" (85). Self-will characterized the Kings of Edom, and therefore, there was no balance. Superstring theorists noticed there is an eleventh dimension that appears to be there, and then it does not, but it is there under certain conditions. Supposedly, our string, separated from the higher strings, is currently below the higher dimensions that remain beyond our reach. Our Post Big Bang Universe is the result of an imbalance in the forces that brought matter into form. Our Universe exists under a particular set of circumstances.

Kaplan explains why there is an eleventh sefirah, "This is the only time that eleven sefirot are mentioned as constituting one unit. It is only in the Universe of Tohu that Keter Crown and Da'at – Knowledge are both present simultaneously" (86) Tohu represents 'chaos' and the Crown represents the Divine Spirit, never had these two come so close. Da'at, the fallen sefirah, wards off evil and cures plagues. Kaplan reveals a long-lost secret: Moses had a special mixture composed of ten spices that were pleasant and one that was bitter. Galbanum has a foul odor, so they mixed it with the rest of the spices in order to repair it. Our dimension may be mingled with the higher dimensions in order to repair it in some way. How the ten sefirot parallel the ten Dibburim of Creation can add further insight into the eleventh dimension.

301

The eleventh Dibburim is also very peculiar; Kaplan states, "The eleventh saying of creation was introduced by God's statement that 'It is not good for man to be alone'" (86).

This eleventh 'saying' may indicate that we are alone on the eleventh dimension, cut off from the higher spiritual realities. This, too, is in agreement with an ancient doctrine about an eleventh sefirah that falls from the tree; its name was Da'at, which means 'knowledge of experience,' but Christian doctrines depict the tree of knowledge of good and evil as 'sexual knowledge.'

Kaplan says the fallen attribute represents self-will and isolation from the Divine Presence it is destined to regain its place within the structure of the Tree when heaven comes to earth. Da'at's place in the Tree is restored when the Son of Man sits on the Throne of our consciousness, emanating waves of spiritual power, love, and maturity in the Kingdom. Until then, one fluctuates back and forth between knowing and not knowing, what one learns – one soon forgets. Eternal Light is permanent spiritual consciousness and awareness.

Knowing and Not Knowing

Timka begins to recognize that things she once knew, she later forgets, and yet the Voice continually reminds her of what is happening when she cannot see or hear. There are times when Timka cannot see or hear things from a higher spiritual consciousness, and then daily life and her pain grow in proportion to her sadness. Sometimes, she feels so strong and filled with Shekinah, and then she feels weak and empty, but her mind remembers the pleasant experiences as if they were a dream. She is just beginning to realize that her state of being affects her conscious awareness; she tries hard to stay awake, but the flesh is weak. She does not know that Ruach, like the wind and our breath come and go, we have no control over what we are or know. She thinks to herself, "When someone is

302

being negative towards someone else, everything you know about that person becomes negative, but if you are positive towards the same person, everything you see will reflect that positive state of mind. She realized that we could have all the knowledge in the Universe and still hate others because all the knowledge would be turned in the wrong way toward that person. Negative emotions, especially anger, will always arrange one's idea of Truth in the wrong way. Truth and Error can never see eye to eye. Until created in the divine image, we are not really 'living' in the biblical sense, and this lack of spiritual consciousness continues to keep us out of the Garden of Eden, a spiritual consciousness of which our soul takes root like a seed in the soil. It may be the gate between Heaven and Earth."

"If superstring theorists are correct and the predicted structure of parallel multiple dimensions is true, perhaps we really are in the eleventh dimension right now. The fallen attribute Da'at, where the battle between good and evil plays out, maybe our earth. The Apostle Paul says there is a battle that begins in our soul once the resurrection starts, and from this point on, the believer must battle his or her own material self to gain the freedom our soul desires. Therefore, we are up one day and down the next; we know one moment and have faith, and then we are confused and lost in the face of adversity; both forces fight for supremacy. If we do not learn how to observe our thoughts and emotions, it could be the end of humanity as we know it. If there is falsehood in our intellect and emotions, we cannot really see clearly."

She remembers something written by Leonora Leet, a brilliant English Professor. Leonora presents us with ancient keys to rediscover the hidden dimensions in her revolutionary research in Kabbalah and Science. She details what and how each dimension exists in a quantum cosmological constant that enters our world through the concepts of the Tree of Life. Her monumental work, The Secret Doctrine of the Kabbalah, demonstrates the synthesis of spiritual and scientific ideas that can teach all of us how to realize that these dimensions exist now inside all of us. Leet also believes the fifth dimension contains the realm of good and evil, and here she shows the importance of Sefer Yetzirah in understanding Genesis,

If the Sefer Yetzirah key to the higher dimensions can be accepted, and we can identify the fifth dimension ("a depth of good, a depth of evil") with the fifth cosmic world, then we are led to a curious coherence between the number of dimensions and the number of the world they define that must cause us to examine the question of dimensions still further (Leet 393).

Somehow, there must be a way to help others learn how to examine these dimensions; that is the only way to find the key and open the higher dimensions outside our immediate awareness. When the spirit emerges from the flesh and the resurrection moves into the final stage, perhaps we all will once again join the higher spiritual dimensions. However, according to a view put forward by Boccaccini in Mysteries and Revelation, the fundamental nature of 'apocalyptic' is not about secrets and fantastic journeys to other realms. It is more about the choices that humans must make and accepting the responsibility and consequences of those choices. Boccaccini writes,"

It is possible to identify its core in a peculiar conception of evil, understood as an autonomous reality, antecedent even to humankind's ability to choose. This conception of evil is not simply one of so many 'apocalyptic' ideas; it is the generative idea of a distinct ideological tradition of thought, the cornerstone on which and out of which the whole 'apocalyptic' tradition is built. (37)

"Boccaccini respects Paolo Sacchi's work in the field, and he is convinced it is the most revolutionary work of its time for the advancement of apocalyptic literature, Sacchi in the Italian edition of and commentary on the Old Testament Pseudepigrapha, the 'apocalyptic' tradition has become a familiar and indispensable notion for understanding those ancient documents. (37)

Sacchi proves the important decision of the hour lies in the ability of people to choose a higher spiritual life and live. Ruach is the level of intellect and reasoning, and it can be materialistic or spiritual; it all depends on the individual. As Ruach strives to overcome the abyss, it manifests as an earthly Adam or a heavenly Adam. The earthly Adam relies on natural biological drives, intellect, and reasoning faculties that originate below the abyss. The heavenly Adam is able to use the spiritual faculties of an activated intellect and increased intuition to help Ruach rise above the abyss, thereby becoming the Ruach Ha-Qadosh (Holy Spirit). This whole idea of protecting our Ruach is lost in modern Christianity, and many do not understand the function or meaning of the soul. Movies that deal with concepts of the soul are often dark, demonical, and psychologically gruesome. How will people ever have a chance to know the truth? The continual rise and fall of our spiritual consciousness as it travels to inner dimensions and then back again is how we evolve from 'nothing' into 'something' on a daily basis. All this and more lies buried in esoteric wisdom of apocalyptic thought." I am so thankful, Father, for this life, she wrote and then closed her notebook.

Adam's Vision Light

Ancient Near Eastern groups such as the Mandaeans, Samaritans, and Iranians possess documents that describe a 'First Man' or prototype of Adam. However, Adamas, filled with light and heavenly gifts from the 'First Man,' gives birth to the 'Son of Man,' and it is this symbiotic relationship that is the center of discussion in many ancient texts of the Near East. Nag Hammadi texts found in Egypt and the Dead Sea scrolls, found at Qumran both describe an 'original Adam'. A central idea involves how a human creation rises from the image of a previous spiritual creation. Frederick Borsch provides a comprehensive summary of this figure in The Son of Man in Myth and History; Joel is reading a very interesting verse from a book that describes how the 'Man of Light,'

He is seen as a cosmic figure, made in many sections so that he might even be designated as a city or perhaps a prototype of human society. (Borsch 63)

As seen above, this figure has several functions: a cosmic being that is both city and society. Joel thinks, "If we understand more about this primordial figure that arrives through the Son of Man, then we will be able to enter the city." More of his research uncovers an ancient saying popular among the sects: "Man exists, and so does the Son of Man" (63). Apparently, the Son of Man restores the link between the pre-historic Adam and modern humanity. Some do not understand the term 'Son of Man,' and again, each theological doctrine will describe the figure differently. Joel finds it interesting that the Book of Enoch contains many details regarding the Son of Man, which many people have never seen. He begins jotting a few notes down as he listens to his heart, "In the tree of life pattern, Tifereth [Harmony of Beauty] represents the Son of Man reconciling the upper three attributes with the lower six attributes making the two separate realms one. This results in a balance of harmony or the symmetry of the 'beginning.' Ruach manifests as a false sense of importance (Ego), and the Id (Drives) can change its face over the years, deceiving us with the veil of time. Like the moon, it is always changing it has no unity or continuity. The lower side of ruach, Da'at, is the illusion of self-knowledge and is, by nature, temporary, but the Son of Man overcomes the Ego and Id and remains connected to ruach for us." This is Metatron (The tree of good/evil is symbolic of the lesser ruach, while the tree of life symbolizes the greater ruach. Knowledge represents the form of an idea. Realization of an idea, both scientifically and logically, helps us to accept it, but then immediately, the essence of the fact breaks up and goes back to the abyss after we learn it. The thoughts we hold on to become what we are. If we do not hold onto constructive, positive thoughts, then a legion of negative thoughts will bring reinforcements and tear us apart!"

Joel begins to speak, and his voice grows stronger, "Things in our daily life come into existence in order to be created in time, but once its purpose is fulfilled, it returns to the 'chaos' or ocean of possibilities. This is not true of the spiritual world of Ruach, for things you create there last forever. The invisible things are the real source behind the visible world of particles in a solid state; we see ideas in our minds, and we think with invisible thoughts that influence our feelings and emotions. We live in an invisible world that very few can imagine, and none can deny. How can anyone explain this to others? I see now why Timka looks so worn and tired; when you see things, you become responsible for those things. Eternal life is a wisdom that provides understanding and knowledge of how the Son of Man breathes upon believers, giving them the power to see invisible realities.

The first three sefirah are really one. Keter the Center represents 'Knowledge,' Chockmah

Space represents 'The Knower' and Binah Time represents 'The Known'; all three are extensions of the same reality. Keter represents the Monad that contains the secret center in the heart of the Universe, Chockmah is the space that provides a place for Binah to grow and develop in time. Time then descends into the six lower sefiroth that rule over the six days of creation and the six edges of the cube. Time will cease when Da'at finds its original place within Tifereth (Harmony), and it is within the power of human consciousness to transcend the fallen attribute and go back to the center of Divine consciousness. Malkuth is when the Kingdom of the Decad is the full expression and realization of the Monad manifested through the Beloved community.

Seven Thunders of the Voice

Joel, filled with tingling sensations in his head, feels his body gently vibrate from within; his face and head shake lightly as he begins to write down what he just experienced and saw. He is amazed at what is happening to him of his own will; he does nothing but think about a particular idea. As he writes, he speaks, "John infused with aetherial energy on the Isle of Patmos is told not to write what he hears as the seven thunders utter their voice. What are the 'Thunders of Heaven'? Are they something you can touch, feel, taste, or know? Is Truth like thunder? Is it possible that nature will combine forces with supernatural angelic forces to rescue the innocents from a devastated environmental condition created through the pillaging of the earth's resources? Thunders can be constructive or destructive: "And there were voices, and thunders, and lightning; and there was a great earthquake, such as was not since men were upon the earth" (Rev 16:18). Whenever thunder occurs in verse in the Apocalypse of John, great events and signs happen in the earth and sky. When the first seal is broken, thunder and voices can be heard (Rev 6:1-2):

Out of the throne proceeded lightning, thundering, and voices, and there were seven lamps of fire burning before the throne, which were the seven Spirits of Yahweh. A mighty angel clothed in a cloud with feet of fire, and a rainbow for a hat opened a heavenly book and began to preach aloud like a lion: "And when he had cried, seven thunders uttered their voices. And when the seven thunders had uttered their voices, I was about to write: and I heard a voice from heaven saying unto me, Seal up those things which the seven thunders uttered, and write them not. (Rev 10:1-4)

Joel saw that John was not allowed to write what the seven thunders (days of creation) uttered, and he sealed the meaning that will manifest on earth only in the end days when those with "eyes to see and ears to hear" will understand the (symbols) and decipher the mystery that still silently shouts. The Apocrypha and Apocalyptic literature represent the '70 hidden books', and 'Sod' is numerically equivalent to 70. Is apocalyptic literature part of the seven thunders that were sealed in accordance with John's vision? Daniel the prophet was also told to seal up the vision; he says the 'Maskillim will 'shine like the stars' and receive this great wisdom in the 'end days.'

Thunder is not just the sound effects of a storm in the scriptures but is a very central symbol of spiritual intervention on the earth and in the affairs of humanity. Moses stretched his rod up to heaven, and Yahweh:" sent thunder and hail, and the fire ran along upon the ground; and Yahweh rained hail upon the land of Egypt" (Exodus 9:23). When Yahweh's Voice is heard from the top of Mt. Sinai, it sounds like thunders and lightning, so many people persuade Moses to intercede on their behalf to escape the dreadful voice of Yahweh. Many people today, after centuries of discovery and conquest still horrified by thunder cowering in fear. Storms are very formidable opponents now that the earth's ecology dwindles away. Many ancient prophets mention the storms that will be of such ferocious nature that nothing and no one will be able to resist their powerful assaults on the earth. Therefore, weather wars and geo-engineering will roar its voice as one of seven phenomena that will come upon the earth when the Lion roars its message.

When the atmosphere is in balance, there are no weather disturbances such as tornadoes, hurricanes, or cyclones. When warmer air currents mix with colder air streams, it creates a major imbalance; many variables play a role in why we will suffer unpredictable weather conditions in the future. El Nino is still a factor that meteorologists must contend with as the warm surface water of the eastern and western jet streams continues to heat up the ocean floor. For North America, El Nino means hurricanes with wind velocities that will continue to accelerate as the jet stream knocked off its orbit continues to cause havoc. This means many places will experience wind gusts of over 120 miles an hour. What happened in New Orleans is just the beginning of many ferocious hurricanes that will cover North America. As technology enters the losing war against weather, huge machines, as predicted by H.G. Wells, designed to change our atmosphere, will make life on Earth one big storm. When laws of the atmosphere become unbalanced then unpredictable weather patterns are inevitable on an international scale. There are some types of areas more susceptible to the influence of what modern man calls "EL Nino".

The Thunder of El Nino

The term "El Nino" means 'The Baby Boy,' a term to refer to the phenomena. El Nino is still the supposed culprit of the mysterious and deadly fire wind that heats the ocean floor. Many blame the core in the center of the earth and some attribute it to the greenhouse effect or the depletion of the ozone layer for lack of a better explanation. Recent research indicates that, perhaps, it is a combination of all these problems. Clearly, it is evident how temperature imbalance and wind velocity are a dangerous duo and can have very catastrophic effects on large areas of each continent. Did any of the ancient prophets have anything to say about this strange occurrence?

The following verses present a different outlook. Chapter 66:4-15 contains one of the prophecies shown to Enoch and Noah regarding the chemical poisoning of the oceans and atmosphere. The author of Enoch prepares his future descendants for the coming plagues on those who will harness the ability to alter the weather. Once fertile waters covered the earth and were the source of health and prosperity, Enoch foresees how the same waters will become polluted and destructive. For instance, here Enoch says, "I beheld that valley in which there was great perturbation, and where the waters were troubled" (Lawrence Enoch 66:5). Enoch says that a strong sulfur odor mixed with the waters and then began to boil the oceans.

The fallout from mixtures of sulfuric acid formed in the atmosphere from carbon dioxide spewed from factories and automobiles has no other place to settle than on the ocean's floor. Many rivers and streams in North America and Canada are dead from the amount of acid found in them. Meteorologists know that El Nino is directly causing the oceans to heat up, thereby causing the jet stream to move off its normal path due to the aberrational rise in temperature. This path is used to prevent Atlantic Ocean hurricanes from growing even more dangerous. Enoch 66:88-10 is very explicit in its description of the abuse inflicted on the oceans through business, trade, commerce, and ships that utilize its great trade routes and health benefits. Here, he explains how the same waters will become a snare:

In those days shall these waters be to kings, to princes, to the exalted, and to the inhabitants of the earth, for the healing of the soul and body, and for the judgment of the spirit. Their spirits shall be full of revelry, that they may be judged in their bodies; because they have denied Yahweh of Spirits, and although they perceive their condemnation day by day, they believe not in His Name. As the inflammation of their bodies shall be great, so shall their spirits undergo a change forever (Lawrence Enoch the Prophet 81-82).

In verse 13, there is a direct allusion to El Nino: "In those days shall the waters of that valley be changed; for when the angels shall be judged, then shall the heat of those springs of water experience an alteration" (82). While verse 16 states that very few will be able to see or believe the effects:

For these waters of judgment shall be for their healing and for the death of their bodies. But they shall not perceive and believe that the waters will be changed and become a fire, which shall blaze forever. (82)

Have we misnamed what is really happening in the oceans and the atmosphere to our own demise? Enoch offers the testimony of a witness who has seen what will happen when the weather becomes Earth's fury. The book of Genesis does not relate how Noah went to visit Enoch concerning the flood and received 'saving knowledge.' What was the information that Enoch gave to Noah, do you know where or how to find it?

The figure of Enoch is like a tree that contains branches of the many appearances of the Angel of YHVH, a.k.a. Metatron, the Keeper of Israel, demonstrates the manifestations of Elohim in the world of Spirit, whereas the Son of Man entered our physical world and performs acts of salvation in this material world. Son of Man (Ben Adam) represents the human Tzaddik on earth who receives the Holy Spirit for the world and distributes it with his very own person. The figure of Enoch became immortal in our very time and age with the onset of the storms he wrote about in such detail. He also mentioned the seasons would change, and winter would begin to change its cycle. This ancient prophet represents the guardian and protector of those living in the 'End Days' specifically and claims his 'books' will be a source of light and understanding as the inhabitants of earth become disillusioned due to the loss of real Love and Wisdom. Joel continues to take notes as he reads chapters from Enoch that describe the ultimate condition of the oceans. He thinks, "Unless we do something very quick to avert the tragedy, this is what might happen one day very soon"

I beheld that valley in which arose a strong smell of sulfur, which became mixed with the waters, and the valley of the angels, who had been guilty of seduction, burned underneath its soil. Through that valley also rivers of fire were flowing, to which the angels shall be condemned, who seduced the inhabitants of the earth. (Laurence -Book of Enoch the Prophet 82-83)

Could this be a reference to the same river of fire in the New Testament book of Revelation, where Satan, his angels, and wicked humans will be condemned after judgment? Revelation 20:10 declares the Devil that deceived them was cast into the lake of fire. Will humans create the great fire that will be the doom of all life on the earth? There is evidence of fire in the oceans, and there are many dead zones with no oxygen; if you add more chemicals to the existing methane levels, the scenario is not hard to imagine.

Clouds of Change

Margaret Barker, renowned author and researcher of ancient Temple Studies, also wrote about the vision Moses experienced:

"When Moses on Sinai was commanded to make the tabernacle, he had to replicate on earth what he had seen in his mountain-top vision (Exod.25.8-9, 40). Later texts indicate that what Moses had seen was not a heavenly temple - although some do say that that is what he saw. Moses' vision was the six days of creation, which he had seen when he was within the cloud of glory for six days (Exod.24.15-16). This vision is now the opening of the first book of Moses, Genesis chapter 1. A comparison of the six days of creation and the stages of erecting the tabernacle (Exod.40.16-33) shows that each day of creation was represented by one item of tabernacle or temple furnishing. The sixth day, when Adam was created, corresponded to the laver of water in which the high priests

313

purified themselves before approaching the altar. Thus, the creation of Adam represented the high priesthood. This pattern of correspondences is a complex and fascinating topic, but one that we cannot explore in detail today." Margaret Barker (Adam the High Priest in the Paradise Temple (pg. 2) 2010)

Timka says, "There are various distinct views on this particular book called Genesis, so imagine a multitude of people from all walks of life who have different doctrines arguing their points of view; nothing is positive about the encounters; it only creates more confusion. Each group attacks the other, neither one respects the other's point of view, and the public is at the mercy of two never-ending wars of indoctrination by both scientists and religionists. Moses wrote Genesis from a divine revelation and vision; we have to acknowledge this before we can understand the symbolistic dynamics used to convey the idea that both heaven and earth were made in One Day, not six days. The actual vision of Moses was of Elohim. When we learn how to interact with this vision in our mind it will change our hearts and, on the 7th Day, dwell in our cloud of spiritual consciousness. When we understand the 6 Days represents our physical lifetime, we can then Rest in our Understanding. Without a vision, the people perish; without the meaning and understanding of Hay/Life, there is Chosekh/Darkness. Do you see that, Alexa, there is a way to solve the paradox of time that divides religion and science.

My mother actually had a book she read many times, written by Reverend Samuel Kinns, called Moses and Geology (1895). I can prove to you that Moses really did have a vision. She runs upstairs to her other secret library and hurriedly searches through several boxes, looking for the book. She yells, "Here it is right here. I found it, listen!"

"It is probable that when Moses was on Sinai's top, God communicated to him these events, and I think with Hugh

Miller, McCausland, and others, that He might have done so by a series of panoramic visions, for there is a vividness in the statements which would perhaps lead us to suppose that Moses saw what he has described. There is another confirmation of this view in the patriarch's being told to construct the Tabernacle according to the pattern God had shown him while on the mount of this Tabernacle, then, he must have had a panoramic view, and indeed, he could not receive only verbal instructions from an architect. If, however, any other plan was adopted, it would not at all affect my argument of the scientific accuracy of the order in which the events occurred." (Kinns-Moses and Geology 17 1882)

All these individuals, very independent of each other, understand the same event actually took place as a vision that re-enacted the creation of the earth and heaven in a period of phases, not actual solar days. Kinns further explains what really happened to Moses on Mt Sinai:

"At the close of this second revelation, which was a commentary upon the Decalogue, Moses was summoned to the top of the mount and was hidden from the people for forty days. Seated in that holy place, he had the high privilege of conversing with God "As a man convers with his friend," and, after receiving from Him still further laws in reference to the ritual to be observed by the Israelites in their future worship, the Past History of the World was communicated to him, and he probably was then shown visions of the six great Epochs of Creation before mentioned. Casting his eyes upwards, he saw the cloud that surrounded him moving, and soon a pitch-black sky was above him; whilst wondering what this might mean, he heard the same voice of God saying——— "Let there be Light and there was Light," (Kinns 19)

"Do you see how these six days are stages of specific events that are like a schoolmaster to show the Way out of one type of consciousness into another higher consciousness? Other levels of knowledge and awareness emanate from just one idea, with a simple thought. This demonstrates we will go out from one situation, into another situation if we follow the three steps or phases that lead up to Yahveh Elohim. The time of change is very near; scientists and environmentalists know that the ice at the North Pole is melting at a rapid rate, and oceans will continue to rise in temperature as the combined effects of the ozone layer depletion and radioactive decay steadily change the composition of the atmosphere. Moses states in Genesis how the waters separate and divide; the atmospheric clouds are the 'waters above' and the oceans are the 'waters below.' The clouds and waters are a symbiotic family and what happens to one affects the other and vice versa. All aboriginal cultures respect this balance and understand the dangers of changing the composition of the earth and its atmosphere.

Several cultures of prophets, especially Native American prophets foresee many types of storms and electromagnetic disturbances that will affect the entire earth and its inhabitants. There will be anomalies in the sky and erratic changes in weather that all will witness.

The process of precipitation, evaporation, and condensation is a prime example of how water obeys the universal spirit law through various states of transitions as it moves from a vapor to a liquid and solid corresponding to steam, water, and ice. The loss of form results in the element's return to raw energy or 'symmetry' before time. Human energy and emotion interact with the ecological biosphere and create symbiotic chaos of events." Alexa was just standing there looking at Timka speechless. She could see now why Timka is so fascinated with science, geology and astronomy; these fields can actually show us the background details that support the vision of Moses. Wow! That is amazing! I can see it now: the Universe was extremely hot at the beginning of the expansion when the Point of contraction gave birth to Avir, and then Light exploded and lit up the Universe with Yah! Yehi Aur!

Later, the plasma cooled down, and then particles entangled in Aether, creating atoms that formed molecules that moved the planets and matter through the fluctuations of aether upon the perimeter of space. Everything is subject to the law of heat and cold. Heat and temperature play a major role in the formation and composition of clouds that, in turn, play a role in shaping the atmosphere, and this is what creates the various types of precipitation. For Enoch and the ancients, these meteorological factors result from angelic forces acting under the jurisdiction of Elohim. The atmospheric clouds are not the only region where hurricanes and tornadoes take place. It is possible for the clouds of our mind to become bewildered and then to seek rest from the storms of depression or anger. This confused state can come from an imbalanced mixture of thoughts and feelings then compounded with extenuating circumstances that result in explosions and murders as deranged minds storm the earth." Timka replied, "Yes, yes that's it, Alex, you can see it too! Timka has to raise her voice because she feels like she is underwater, and her ears are like caves the waves are crashing into; the Ruach was lifting them both up into another level of awareness; they were experiencing a transformative event together.

Timka continues shouting, "These storms that Enoch saw will be very volatile in today's fast-paced society, where no one has time to stop and reflect or think clearly. People are in their own personal storm wars, and their hearts explode with fear, hate, and confusion all over each other. Some of these explosive mind states induced with drugs, chants, dance rituals, or sex evoke alternative states of consciousness. The authentic transformation does not come from outside of us; it happens within our center of perception. Nevertheless, things derived from negative thoughts pollute Wisdom and Knowledge,

317

emotions can alter what we perceive and believe, and lies become a reality when we see life through sad, negative eyes that look for bad things and feast on them.

No faculties of the human mind can free the mind to hear the spiritual thunders that Moses saw and perceived through a pattern and constructs of thoughts and ideas contained in the Sephiroth, which provide structure and form within our own divine attributes." Yeh said Alexa and many young people use drugs, DMT, and other hallucinogens to escape the horrors of life. Others use pharmaceutical drugs or treatments to shut down the central nervous system so there are no more emotions and explosive feelings. Ironically, our emotional states intensify with stimulants of any kind, and then emotions will generate more literally, heating up our metabolism. This raises blood pressure and our heart rate as the body works to restore its balance; the heat is what leads to sexual crimes, murder, and oppression.

The modern world frowns on the Wisdom of ancients they deem unsophisticated truth, yet the truth remains in many things that seem simple or irrelevant to others. Just read the daily newspaper to see the extreme results of people exploding everywhere, every minute of every day. People have hurricanes within that can wreak havoc on the minds and hearts of everyone they meet. There is a great pressure hanging in the air; the barometric pressure is so heavy sometimes I can hardly breathe; everything seems to be attacking our source of breath. Oh, Timka, what is going to happen to everyone?" Timka replies, "Did you know that if you are in a bad mood that will change the way you feel about what you read? Our emotional state will arrange how we perceive things; anything we learn can be tainted by a mood, which perpetuates unbalanced emotional states. If we have bad attitudes and wrong attitudes about others or low self-esteem, it affects our ability to learn; this is why even if we try to share any of this, many will not

318

hear it correctly. Each person is so used to false thinking and artificial logic they are disconnected from reality by false thoughts that become shapeless illusions they fear or hate. Our energy and state of mind trigger bad moods and dispositions that take over and smother the Spirit within. Lies from the legion of negative entities feed the false personality; the Essence of Spirit suffers from the artificialness of life. The soul aches and groans for deliverance."

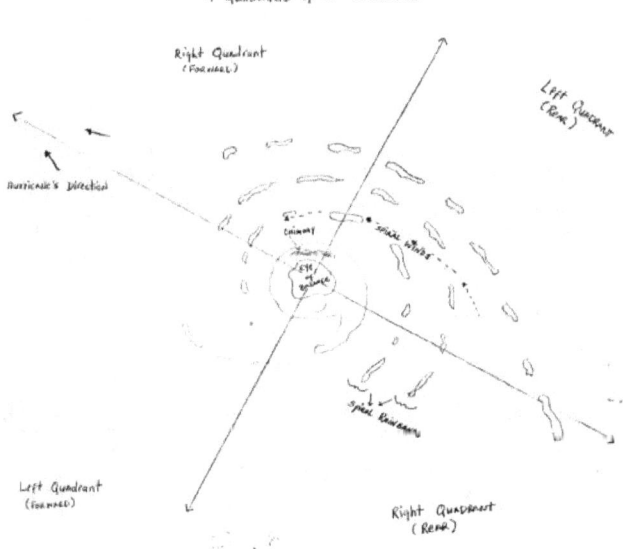

Figure 40 Eye of Hurricane

The swirling circular motion of vortices holds important clues about the formation of protogalaxies of our early universe. Cloud layers surround the Earth and form atmospheric eddies and vortices. Hurricanes fully developed consist of atmospheric eddies hundreds of times larger than those above tropical islands, such as the hurricanes of Canary Island.

El Nino is changing the location of these hurricanes as the warm oceanfront continues to move around the globe causing havoc and destruction in its environment. Whereas spiral galaxies are a trillion times bigger than hurricanes both begin the same way from some type of vortex. Are the wheels of the Chariot the forces that support the constant revolving of the Universe, galaxies, planets, and even hurricanes? The mysterious author of Sefer Yetzirah tries to demonstrate the comprehensive structure of the Universe and our atmosphere. Keter or the Crown symbolizes the whirling force and movement of the sefiroth as divine energy begins to surge down into its roots.

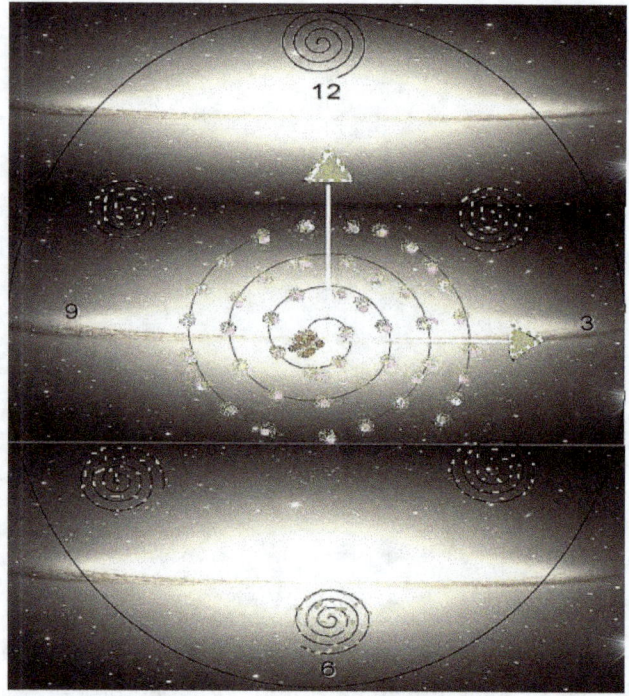

Figure 41 Swirling Sword of Thoughts

When a person tries to connect to divine energy and is not prepared, a swirling and turning of thoughts begins, which is like the sword revolving in front of the garden blocking our entrance to the unity of thought. The figure above illustrates how the dimensions of time exist in a hierarchy of aeons that emanate from the center of the vortex. The Son of Man shows us how to bypass the revolving sword of thoughts and time in order to achieve a state of rest and balance between the physical mind and spiritual heart. The peace of the Son of Man comes the first time a person is able to turn off the cyclone of thoughts that invades the normal conscious state. The Gospel of Thomas says that we will become 'amazed' and then 'disturbed' before learning how to 'rule' over the world of conflicting emotions and thoughts. When we overcome the six days of creation, we become lions that hear the silent voice of the seven thunders roar.

SON OF THE NAME

Is there a Way to walk, a Truth to experience, and a Life to gain that can help us learn how to protect our loved ones during the coming tribulations? The New Testament writers tell us this 'Way' is a path to walk upon in the darkness and that the 'Truth' shows us the nature of existence, while 'Life' is the prize we win if we run the race. Joseph Dan explains how we can find the path, "A person must reach the Throne of Glory and pronounce the names of the Heavenly family and the names of the angelic ministers in order to pass through safely" (Dan The Ancient Jewish Mysticism 35-36).

According to the ancient Shema, the family is designated Echad, meaning 'Unity' of the Divine Presence. The family consists of:

YAHWEH	Father
ELOHENU	Word/Son
YAHSHUA	Holy Spirit

The Gospel of Philip contains an account of how spiritual reality and mystical understanding take the place of ascetic rituals. Believers learn to perceive invisible realities or 'gifts' that result in the right knowledge and action. The author of this text warns readers that the names used to refer to the Father, Son, and Holy Spirit are incorrect and that it leads to great deception. Archons, a.k.a. fallen angels, exchanged the original names with names from the various nations' deities, and thus, many people inadvertently worship what they know not. This event has actually happened; it is historically evident through research of the etymology of names such as God, Lord, Jesus and even the word heaven.

The author of the text believes the discovery of hidden errors saves one from the death of ignorance. The hidden meanings discovered in the etymology of words exist because words often have several meanings in different languages. Meanings that many of us are not even aware of, but we accept the face value of what we see written. Fallen angels, known as 'archons' in Gnosticism, supposedly responsible for the miscommunication, can be overcome when we challenge the discrepancies and resolve the errors regarding the original meaning of words. Elaine Pagels writes,

But those malevolent lower powers who seized upon truth's gift and stole the "names" intended to transform them from a means of disclosing truth into an instrument of deception. (Pagels Nag Hammadi 50 Years Later: "Ritual in the Gospel of Philip" 284)

Her commentary may be even truer than we realize. Pagels says the things meant to bring about our salvation: names, baptism and knowledge, now lay disguised and hidden from us in errors that bind us to the archons rather than releasing us from this supernatural influence. The author of the Gospel of Philip writes:

Names given to those in the world have a great deception, for they separate the heart from what is established to what is not established. Thus, the one who hears the name "God" does not perceive what is established but what is not established. So also, with the "father" and the "son" and the "holy spirit" and "life" and "light." (Pagels 284)

Pagels explains the importance of 'names' in helping us realize symbolic truths,

While 'names' are necessary to teach truth, Philip notes that, when implicated in deception, they may also teach error. The power of 'types and images' do much more than words; they do more than teach; instead, they alone, Philip says - convey divine reality (288).

The divine reality comes into the world through 'types and shadows' disguised as names, and our perception of reality is clothed with them like garments.

Garment of Glory

The ancient divine name, יהוה, composed of four letters, not only forms the shape of a figure with arms and legs as in the below illustration, but it has more history than the world itself, and yet we know so little of how it exists in the structure of our lives through the Universe. Moses, the author of Exodus, says no one knew the name יהוה until its revelation to him.

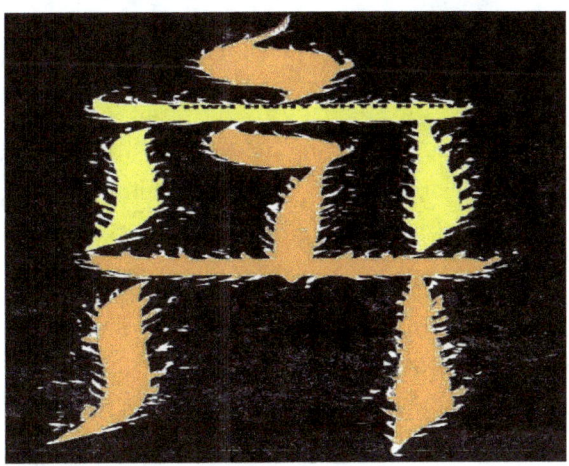

Figure 42 YHWH Man

Before that time, men called upon El Shaddai, which we saw earlier means 'enough' and is usually translated as 'Almighty Provider' in English. The patriarchs called upon El Shaddai the energy of Abraham, Isaac, and Jacob, who spoke from time to time. Was it only a four-letter name that a small minority of people invested their lives in, or is it proof of the Presence of the Creator investing its creation with life? Dictionaries define the name YHWH as 'ineffable' or 'unutterable,' and thus, the connotation of silence has enveloped the Name's voice. Perhaps the only way to comprehend the Name is to embrace it through its garments or role.

Remember, we saw earlier how the attribute of 'Wisdom' is the 'Beginning' of all things created. Wisdom creates us in the divine image so we can comprehend the invisible things from visible things. Wisdom is the source of the essence of the name 'Yah.' The name is a descriptive device used to convey hidden memories of the time before Moses. Once the symbol activates our memory, the essence of thought takes the form of ideas that later become concepts that eventually become our own wisdom. From concepts, all things emanate, but only in the attribute of 'understanding' were things created. John says, 'The Word was at the beginning with Yahweh, and the Word became Yahweh.' this still happens, for we all start at the place in time called the 'beginning' where the Word dwells. Joel relates this to what he read in Johann Reuchlin's The Art of the Kabbalah, about how the Tetragrammaton creates both the earth and heaven.

Then Reuchlin quotes from Maimonides' famous Guide to the Perplexed: "From the beginning, when nothing was, there was nothing besides the Name of God and his wisdom" (253). Wisdom is nothing without comprehension and comprehension is fruitless if not practically applied to help guide one's life. The whole purpose of wisdom is to help guide us out of the darkness of despair and confusion. What is so hard about that, Joel thinks to himself, "Why do I fight so hard against Timka's views and revelations? Most of the time, I do not even listen to what she says before I disagree and try to tell her my own point of view. How pathetic is that?" John says the 'Word of Wisdom' became flesh and dwelt among humanity, but humans could not comprehend how this even takes place.

For Yahweh sent his Son into the Kosmos not to condemn it, but that the Kosmos through him might be saved.

We have forgotten how our own minds and hearts condemn us first, and our actions testify of the soul's fruit. We still live in the darkness John describes as long as we inhabit our fleshly tabernacle and live in lower thoughts that make us envious, jealous, judgmental, and self-righteous with others. Only the Son of Man possessed the correct formula of names and the geometric equations, which, when put in their proper order, produced mystical and miraculous events needed to combat the lower forces that Paul calls 'powers of the air.' The archons create oppression and a heavyweight each individual must bear as cruel economic and social injustices of worldly kingdoms exert powers over every living thing, creating a daily hell. Most importantly, the earliest disciples and assemblies understood how the Father, Son, and Holy Spirit heal us with stripes of chastisement; as Isaiah says, the same one that kills makes us alive. Many religious doctrines, hymns, and liturgy of the ancient world heavily saturated with divine names, oaths, rites, and rituals take the place of genuine inner spiritual transformation. Priests, rabbis, healers, sorcerers, miracle workers, and soothsayers all operate in diverse contexts and have varied spiritual outlooks, yet all have one thing in common: the use of the Tetragrammaton.

Four Worlds of YHWH

The term comes from two Greek words, 'tetra,' meaning four, and 'gramma,' or letters. It became a great symbol in Kabbalistic doctrines for the divine name given to Moses. Hugh Brownlee's important research of W.G. Waddell's The Tetragrammaton in the LXX explains why we usually see a different term in its place,

In the earliest Septuagint manuscripts, the Tetragrammaton was written in paleo-Hebrew script, but the pronunciation of the word as Kurios led to its substitution in later manuscripts. Strictly speaking, this was not a translation of the sacred name but of its surrogate (Adonai). (Brownlee 289 note# 2a)

The Name endowed with great mysterious energy and power reveals itself gradually in stages. Brownlee says,

In each case, moreover, one must reckon the fact that the translators of the Septuagint, and the Massoretes, as well, misunderstood the original sense. Far more important to the Hebrews than the etymology, as important as that may have been at one time, was the nature of Yahweh as they came to understand it through a long history of revelatory deeds. (291)

Both of these facts are very important to help us understand the Name's function. Originally, Power and יהוה had become synonymous. The ancient records and history books show that the discovery of the Name of a thing-person-place also gave one control over it. There are other divine names that perform particular acts the Tetragrammaton was specific to the restoration of Adam.

People still believe and practice this unconsciously. Egyptian mythology, Babylonian astrology, and Greek mystery religions owe their foundation to the Name. These magic arts based on 'muttering' names of different deities were often hybrid versions of יהוי smeared with Greek and Latin roots. The true name is a living divine energy that evolves with us in the same way that the energy of the Universe continues to evolve with and sustain living things. Ironically, the Bible, in its present form, lies stripped of its life-giving properties as redactors in attempting to eradicate the magical element that had grown up alongside the Holy Name, also wiping out the evidence of the Name's very Presence.

Eventually, it is forgotten how the Name itself is a representative Ambassador of the immeasurable, formless Supreme Being. Wainwright's observation explains it better, "Shekinah (Glory) was used like Memra as a reverential substitute for the divine name" (Arthur Wainwright The Trinity in the New Testament 37). He says that even the word 'Glory' is a euphemism for יהוה. The name is literally clothed in other names.

Should We Be Curious about Kyrios?

Hekhalot mystics wrote about the ability to 'ride the heaven of Araboth' on the name יהוה, while Psalms 68:4 declares, "extol him that rides upon the heavens by his name YAH" (Gideon New Testament). The true purpose and function of the Names, forgotten and distorted beyond recognition, have left the world steeped in name rituals and rites that have little, if anything, to do with יהוה. Even, Freud drew the obvious conclusion of the similarity of Aton and Adon in his book, Moses and Monotheism. Where he explains how Adon = Lord whereas Adonai = My Lord, this was the name used in Egypt, but in Israel, it is Baal. The Septuagint version of Adonai is Kyrios.

Hellenism affected Palestine primarily in the arena of language; specifically, it brought the Kurios title, a title which could refer to anyone who exercised authority (Capes 32)

It is more like a generic term for an official position of authority in the worldly sense; this is not how the early assemblies perceived the original term. יהוה is a type of mnemonic for the divine Name and its functions. Capes comments on Paul's use of Kurios,

Given the fact that he preferred the LXX, in which Kurios represented the divine name, his application of this title to Jesus must have meant that he considered Jesus to be more than a man. (32)

Cape concludes the issue by saying there is no evidence important enough to warrant looking beyond Palestinian Christianity: "Kyrios title stands within the religious milieu of first-century Jewish practice. There is no need to look beyond Palestinian Christian experience" (33).

Joel thinks there is much to learn from the ancient device of substituting one word for another. He reads in another source from Martin Hengel, who says, "Kurios, in fact, was generally not used in the mysteries" (31), and he maintains that no evidence exists to suggest the circulation of mystery teachings in Syria in the first century. This is evidence of an obvious displacement of original ideas. If Kyrios did not come from the mysteries of Greco-Roman religions, where did it come from? Perhaps the answer goes back to the days of the prophets who fought against the Baal cult, or maybe it goes back to the Hebrew occupation in Egypt when Adon replaced Baal.

According to Ehrman:

Early scribes were far from averse to extending the names and /or titles of Jesus in the texts of scripture. This applies not only to the terms 'Christ' and 'Son of God' but also, in particular, to the title 'Lord.' (161)

Often combinations such as 'Christ Jesus, 'Lord, Jesus Christ' and others were added to Paul's epistles in order to cement the relationship between the second Adam and Christ as a non-human redeemer so that the phrase, "Jesus Christ our Lord' is regularly attested as a corruption among the New

Testament manuscripts" (161). The idea that יהוה is manifested in the form of Kabod is so far away from this perspective that now the idea of the Chariot has nothing more in common with Kabod than the idea of a Throne. Due to various theological debates and controversies over the divinity or humanity of the Messiah, many erroneous titles and functions camouflage the scriptures in order to accommodate the views of the doctrinal majority.

Another problem that blocks our path to seeing the divine image is the distinction between the Father and Son blurred in modern Christianity due to a lack of understanding regarding the names. For example, Paul writes to us in Ephesians 1:21 about the most important thing a believer must do to be in the Messiah. It is very simple, yet difficult for many: "Naming the name is what makes one belong to Messiah." The sum of the entire gospel hinges on the concepts of Father and Son (or 'Grace' and 'Peace' when seen through the eyes of Qumran). Yahweh is the dispenser of 'Grace' and Yahshua receives the 'Peace' that is delivered to those able to receive in accordance with their own faith. None of this is realized when we read the terms in our Bible when the High Priest pronounced the name thousands of years ago; even then, it was muffled or muttered, so it wasn't heard correctly. This ancient practice is still with us today as dictionaries and people continue to proclaim the impossibility of regaining its true pronunciation. Tetragrammaton is not ineffable phonetically, but its spiritual experience is ineffable and indescribable by the mouth.

There were also those who used this Name, then and now, as a weapon against imagined enemies. Great penalties placed on offenders found in a text from the Dead Sea Scrolls, the Manual of Discipline, states that one so accused and found guilty of cursing a person with the Name could never return to the Community of worship. In the backlash of this confusion regarding the fate of the divine force behind this power base, it became easier to twist and contort its original image and essence rather than deal with its mysteries. Eventually, fear, shame, and offense became the garments of this precious Holy unction instead of courage, honor, and forgiveness. Some taught that the removal of the Name was a form of punishment as the Grace and Truth began to leave people's consciousness. Only ancient mystical literature has retained any traces of the importance of the Name. Christian Kabbalists such as Pico Della Mirandola of the fourteenth century and Johann Reuchlin attempted to restore the Name to its proper place but met with great resistance from both Jewish and Christian sources.

Y represents the Future

H represents the Past

V represents the 6 Days of Time and the 6 directions of space

H represents the Present and the ability to enter the realm of Eternity

From Ayah Asher Ayah comes forth:

Hayah – was

Hoveh- is

Yihyeh- will be

John says in the Apocalypse, "Grace to you, and peace, from him which is, and which was, and which is to come; and from the seven Spirits which are before his throne," evidently the distinction has a purpose. The seven spirits animate the seven days of creation. We have lost that distinction and need to find it to find our own identity. For the sake of the Name, the right hand reveals a Great Arm in the world. This arm or 'branch' is the Messiah that appears as the Kingdom approaches, and the importance of knowing the Sacred Name יהוה becomes a right hand of power that forms the process of salvation. No prophet, priest, or king will get the victory.

The right arm of Yahweh will fight the battle single-handedly. "Behold Yah-Yahweh will come with a strong HAND, and His ARM shall rule for Him; behold, His reward is with Him." Isaiah 40:10-15. The name of the Hebrew letter Y is Yod, and 'hand' is the symbolic meaning of the letter; therefore, the Name is likened to a hand that can shape, mold, and form a creation,

'He is his Name and his Name is He' follows that the knowledge of Elohim (God) granted to the mystic in his ascent to the throne and vision of the glory will consist of knowledge of the names. (Eliot, Through a Speculum That Shines 182)

Is the Divine Presence lost when we remove the Name and its Glory? One of the angels mentioned by Enoch is Semyaza, whose name and nature are changed. In an eighteenth-century pamphlet, Proper Names in the Book of Enoch, Reverend D.A. De Sola restored the ancient Hebrew/Chaldee interpretation of the names found in the Enoch texts. According to De Sola:

"Samyaza is from Yalisha (salvation) and Shem (name) which when combined renders a phrase 'the saving name'" (De Sola London 1852).

We learn that when we add or remove a divine prefix or suffix an angel's nature is changed. When the divine name יהוה, hidden ehind disguises, is unrecognized, human nature is forever changed.

331

HIDDEN JOSHUA CIRCLE

There is another secret 'life circle' of events surrounding the figure known as Joshua, son of Nun. The circle of Joshua is so secret that very few people even realize it exists. Very few recorded details point to this figure directly, but what is available reveals a hidden side that is too secret to utter. There is reason to believe that the Angel of יהוה that helped deliver the Israelites from Egypt also transformed into a cloud by day and a pillar of fire at night. Enoch knew this figure as the 'little יהוה' or Metatron. Moses may have known the human form of the Angel of יהוה as Oshea of the tribe of Ephraim and a descendant of Joseph. He has no genealogy; often, the descriptions of the Glory of יהוה and the Angel of יהוה are almost identical, and this figure appears in the cloud surrounding the tabernacle. Moses goes up to Mt. Sinai with Joshua, son of Nun, who enters the Tabernacle when the cloud of the Shekinah shines upon it. Very little research exists to establish the identity of this figure, but there has been an extensive amount of research on the Angel of יהוה. So, let us start there.

Angel of YHWH and Joshua

The Angel of יהוה bears a portion of the 'Name' and prepares the path through the wilderness of Sinai. Bear in mind that the Son of Man came to show the 'Way' to the path. Carl Judson Davis provides a good resource for other parallels with this figure and he finds a connection between the Angel of יהוה and the Son of Man. Davis found a reference to this angel in Hellenistic Synagogue Prayers that he cites in his book, The Name and Way of the Lord. According to Davis, a "Christian interpolator identifies Jesus as the name God caused to 'encamp among us'" (57). The Shekinah is the Glory that resides in the Tabernacle and the Temple and it can reside in humans. The mystics of the Unique Cherub Circle were certain

332

that the Cherub was the Angel of יהוה and that it could assume human form. Was Joshua the human form?

Joshua fought the battle of Jericho and he can even make the sun stand still. Davis reports on the research of other specialists in the field,

Fossum suggests that Samaritanism amalgamated the angel of [the LORD] with the glory of [the LORD], and then credited him with the destruction of the Egyptian army during the exodus. (57)

Evidently, other people have seen a connection between these two figures. Davis sees the full array of figures that seem to be the same entity at work, but it is too hard to prove theologically how it can be true. He finds many parallels between Melchizedek, the Angel of יהוה, the Glory of יהוה, with the Word, the Logos, Metatron, and the Son of Man. However, many still find it inconceivable how or why the Creator could become human; for Davis, the debate has become a wet blanket on the significance of these parallels. He writes:

The question we raised over the significance of these parallels is a difficult one since the New Testament writers identify Jesus with both Wisdom, Glory, Word of God on the one hand and as God's chief agent on the other. One could argue that it was either understanding that underlay the New Testament application of such Old Testament passages to Jesus (60).

Justin Martyr also saw these parallels and wrote extensively about them in many of his own works. There is evidence and documents demonstrating the importance of this figure known as Joshua the son of NUN and Moses' Minister. For instance, Saul Levin's work The Divine Patronymic contains a valuable analysis of scribal alterations and how one particular alteration replaced HVH with NVN in order to suppress the fact that

Joshua/Yahoshua was the Angel of יהוה. Levin proves that several references to naue, nave, and nun used as variants of Joshua's surname derived from the substitution of HVH for (NVN). From the very beginning, the scribes were at war with יהוה and went to great pains to conceal the secret identity of יהושה at that time. According to Levin, with the prefix 'Yod' removed and the remaining letters HVH changed to NUN it is evident someone sealed a very important fact from public view. The very letter that Moses assigned to Oshea deliberately edited and lost from public access is a piece of evidence that time and history could not bury forever.

Joshua and Elders of the Chariot

Perhaps the mysterious meeting of Abraham and Melchizedek took place because each had in himself an element of the name (YAH). Hoshea, son of NUN, received the Yod or 'hand,' and Abram, son of Terah, received the Heh or 'breath.' Jacob/Israel as a nation of nations was to receive the Vau (W) to symbolize its dual nature as a "womb" and "link" between Yahweh Elohim and the Gentiles. These four types are linked with each other for some particular purpose because they each bear a portion of the Tetragrammaton. The Angel of יהוה contains the Name.

In Merkavah lore, humans take the place of the four angels that surround the Chariot Throne. The gospels of the New Testament follow this four-fold pattern. There are laws to the pattern, and therefore, we know numerically NWN is also incorrect for יהוה= 26, and this is a sacred mystery. Letters are substitutes for other letters of equal numerical value. There also had to be a particular amount of letters per verse. We learn from Malachi that some scribes have written down things falsely and that if even one "jot or title" goes; it would break the unity of the whole text. Joel's research demonstrates how this unity has been broken a multitude of times. As a result, few people think of the scriptures as 'sacred' or relevant enough to address the issues we face each day. All this proves there is a literary "Son of Man" figure pushed under the rug of debate, and this is historical evidence to support the fact that there is a hidden Messiah as prophesied in the books of Enoch.

Enoch Genesis Effect

Sacchi explains the significance of the Son of Man and provides us with a very likely explanation of the relationship between Enoch and Yahoshua/Jesus. Sacchi writes concerning the Son of Adam,

He in fact was created before things (1 En 48:3) and did not have a name. This probably favored the assimilation of his figure with others: the Gospels identify Jesus with him; a Jewish interpolation of the Book of Parables (1 En 71:14) identifies Enoch himself with him (Jewish Apocalyptic 248).

Who is this figure 'created before things' and why does Sacchi identify Enoch with it? This is evidence of early traditions we know very little about that describe a figure created before time. We must search the scriptures diligently to find the Word, Wisdom, and Way of the Beginning - Reshit. The protology of John demonstrates the attempt to fuse this ancient figure of the 'beginning' with the Logos now dwelling in the human Messiah. Paul says that the Messiah did come from the 'order of Melchizedek, who had no birth or genealogy. This is in reference to his being born from the 'beginning' before time; the Semitic concept of time is necessary to understand that the past is always in existence. Due to this kind of bizarre paradox, many consider this literature too fantastical to be of any practical use. Sacchi's own explanation demonstrates the point,

Enoch sees the structure of the cosmos. But 2 EN is even further removed from the apocalyptic genre. Everything becomes a story, if it were not fantasy, it would seem history. (249)

Even Sacchi says the story is 'fantasy' but seems like history. Joel finds many of the elements in this literature more historically credible than mythical. He understands a little better why not all are able to comprehend how these things are true without an understanding of ancient Semitic thought. This may have been part of the dilemma facing the disciples when asked the question "Who is the Son of Man?" It is the same dilemma that each of us will face. Peter is the first to learn the secret identity of the Son of Man. It does not come from his own understanding; the 'Father Above' reveals it to him. The Son of Man is actually hidden in an 'unknown identity' that can only be revealed to believers by going back to the 'beginning' (Genesis). Once again, we see a pattern of exchange between three different phenomena.

When Shekinah shines on Kabod, it reveals its nature to the Unique Cherub, who then, in turn, reveals it to humanity and the ten angelic realms. The Unique Cherub doctrine of the thirteenth-century German circle did not exist in ancient literature; it is a later development of a much older tradition that proves they did believe in a figure from the 'beginning time' that continues to animate all of humanity with its image and likeness. Enoch symbolizes the movement of eternity through time, and the figure demonstrates how the light shines into the darkness of time through the spiritual consciousness of believers. When believers find comfort from the words of all the prophets, then they are brought into the circle of eternity, and time and history stand still, giving us a glimpse of the meaning and fulfillment of prophecy.

The mysterious Unique Cherub Circle developed their ideas regarding this figure during the twelfth and thirteenth centuries in Medieval Germany. The social climate was at odds with its central doctrines. Gershom Scholem believes the term 'Body' as used in Shiur Qomah texts, relates to the "Creator of the Beginning" he links with the doctrines of the Unique Cherub circle.

Scholem also describes Merkabah mystics that "Speak of a 'body of the Shekinah' and of a 'Creator of the Beginning,' yoser Bereshit, who sits upon the Throne and in this manifestation has, as it were, number and mass" (Scholem Origins 210). Scholem declares that some ancient texts actually state the Divine Presence is capable of measurement and has a weight that can be named. It represents a human presence on the mystical Throne of Glory and Scholem solves the mystery of the Trinity when he explains how the figure is not the Supreme Being who has no shape and form, but something altogether different:

In the Kabbalistic fragment, this demiurge is a more external manifestation of an inner soul that dwells within him and which is itself in no way identical with the First Cause but represents the third sefirah, Binah. (210-211)

Scholem argues that, in the Cherub Circle, they identify the human figure with mass and weight as the Angel of יהוה and that the only innovative thought they possessed was the "New idea, that this cherub has an interior aspect, a 'soul': It is precisely this soul that constitutes the realm of the sefiroth" (211). Perhaps the soul of the Cherub is the Tree of Life, as argued by Philo.

Metatron One and Two

Harry A. Wolfson's work on the pre-existent angel in the doctrines of the Magharians shows that this is not a new concept. It existed centuries before the Cherub circle even lived. What intrigues me most is why there are two different figures called Metatron. Scholem says that there is a higher form of Metatron:

The author must, therefore, have had in mind a higher Metatron whose power was invested in Enoch, the son of

Yared, after his ascension. It is not so surprising, then, that we later find among the Kabbalists of the mid-thirteenth century, and perhaps already in their sources, the concept of a 'Great Metatron,' Metatron Rabbah, contrasted with the Metatron who exercises, as Prince of the Countenance. (Scholem 212-213)

As Joel pointed out early in his research on the Genesis narrative, he saw evidence of two different stages of growth and he parallels them with the stages of Enoch's transformation. Bear in mind, that in early apocalyptic circles, the human figure named Enoch transforms into an angelic/human named Metatron. However, in the New Testament, Paul describes this same person as the heavenly and earthly Adam. The first Adam is 'material' and the second Adam is 'spiritual'; Paul incorporated this process from the Enoch saga. Scholem states that "the figure on the Throne is the 'Great Metatron' and the 'Little Metatron' is the human representative; both are connected to each other through the 'soul' or tree of sefiroth." He also tells us about a special 'Cherub' that directs all prayers on our behalf:

Pray in such a manner that his prayer be accepted before the Creator, praised be He, by the power of the 'particular cherub' who was emanated and created from his great fire which consumes the fire. Just as the Creator emanated ten sefiroth and the cherub is one of them, and everything is united in a unity that is complete and without distinctions. (215)

Those not familiar with these ancient mystic doctrines would naturally ask what significance they bear to the Father and Son motif of the New Testament. Borsch explains the significance found in Pseudo-Clementine literature. He writes,

Here First Man, Adam is once more glorified. His initial sin is even denied, and Adam and Jesus, the Son of Man, are closely related in thought. The true prophet first manifested in

Adam and later in others was finally known in Jesus Christ (Borsch Son of Man in Myth and History).

That the 'first man' continues to surface throughout the generations of times in different individuals is a 'bone of contention' that still prevents many from understanding the role and function of this mysterious hidden Savior. It is a mystical sense of timelessness that one is born into when the divine image has formed its image in our souls; we are then new creatures existing in a spiritual state of regeneration. Some view this as a form of reincarnation, but according to ancient traditions, not all humans reincarnate; only the soul of the First Man continues to live throughout the generations. This First Man dwelled in Joshua ben Nun. When this First Man dwells in Enoch, he becomes Metatron. John points out a very important message in Chapter 31 where his protagonist explains his identity and relation to the Father.

The Father who sent me has himself testified on my behalf. You have never heard his voice or seen his form, and you, because you do not believe him whom he has sent. You search the scriptures because you think that in them you have eternal life, and it is they who testify on my behalf.

Here is the New Testament equivalence of the distinction between the Kabod and Unique Cherub or between the Father (Greater YHWH) and Son (Lesser YHWH) in Christian terminology. Yahweh the Father has no shape and form, and many have not ever heard his voice; humanity is under the tutelage of the Unique Cherub, here known as the Messiah or Anointed. John continues the protagonist's soliloquy: "I have come in my Father's name, and you do not accept me; if another comes in his own name, you will accept him. How can you believe when you accept [glory] from one another and do not seek the [glory] that comes from the one who alone is El?" This is a direct identification of the Name and the Glory associated with the Angel of יהוה in Exodus. However, as Joel previously discovers, this tradition almost completely eradicated from the Western concept of Christianity, is practically mute, smothered by ancient creeds and bans. Those who do not consult the ancient identity of the figure do not seek the Glory (Kabod) of the Cherub; they depend on their own glory (wisdom of understanding) and the glory of others.

Apocalyptic Time of the Beginning

Another crucial piece of evidence that links the Son of Man with the Angel of יהוה reveals the connection between the first Joshua and the second. The Son of Man asks what seems to be a cryptic question, "If you believed Moses, you would believe me, for he wrote about me. But if you do not believe what he wrote, how will you believe what I say?" Moses records the events that lead up to the creation from the 'Beginning' and Enoch records the events that lead to the 'Ending' of the new age. John sees a vision of the 'End' from the 'Beginning' of the Creation, all three testify of the same event from different vantage points and times. The Son of Man claims to be the Light of the beginning Day – the true Light of the Kosmos not the Sun of the sky, but the Son of the Divine Presence. In 'pseudipigraphic and apocalyptic time', even though Moses lived after Enoch, he is still able to communicate with him. James Charlesworth provides an excellent summary of how time operates in this literature. He writes,

Although an odd idea to moderns, the sages easily conceived of Enoch quoting Moses who lived millennia after him" and this is possible because the apocalyptic author can reverse the time period of different figures so that "Moses can antedate Enoch. (Delamarter Scripture Index 5)

Wisdom surpasses all designated times and can reveal information to every generation regardless of when a person actually lives on the earth. Wisdom contains the events that have already happened and the ones that will happen again. It is the same story re-experienced in the same way as the same energy and atoms of the Big Bang continue to vitalize and maintain the material world. Charlesworth draws a very salient conclusion, "The Pseudepigrapha thus placard a human truth: 'story' displays how wisdom and vision transcend time" (5). The only way humanity can transcend time is through re-entering the sacred 'story' of the Son of Man. Scholem confirms what Hoeller surmised about the three Joshua's being a process or ongoing creation. Here his analysis of the three initials in Adam's name demonstrates it is a process:

The name of Adam is an abbreviation (ADaM) of the three forms of existence of this soul in Adam, David, and the Messiah. This would imply that the Messiah has to pass through various stages of incarnation so that his essence 'always lives among us' in one form or another (460).

The above statement definitely indicates that there is an older hidden doctrine of the Son of Man buried in forbidden literature, but it did not originate there. It has been assimilated from even older traditions.

Life Cycle of a Secret Circle

The secret circle of 'Joshua' is very wide, yet its circumference is unknown. Stephan Hoeller provides some very interesting theories on the Joshua circle in his book Jung and the Lost Gospels, where he says Joshua, son of Nun, the Teacher of Righteousness, and Jesus are different phases or states of transition of one ongoing process. He finds many links between the Teacher of Righteousness of the Dead Sea Scrolls and Joshua, Moses' Minister. Hoeller affirms,

The first of these links concerns the Jewish hero whose name the Christian savior bore. Joshua, or Yehoshva, son of Nun, the successor of Moses as leader of the Jewish people, was a remarkable man. Josephus, calling him by the Greco-Latin name Jesus, son of Naue, describes him in terms of the highest esteem. (49)

He also recounts the mighty acts of Joshua, from drying up the river Jordan and knocking down the walls of Jericho to making the sun stand still. Joshua is responsible for sealing and storing the 'hidden books' in order to preserve them for future generations. Many perceive his role as a great lawgiver and second Moses.

Hoeller sees a very important connection with how the 'hidden books' are handled among the Essenes. He writes, "Amazingly, even the mode of the concealment and preservation of the Scrolls affected by the Teacher of Righteousness seems to have followed the example traditionally set by Joshua, son of Nun" (50); Hoeller then quotes a passage from the Assumption of Moses that describes the same mode of preservation as evidence for a relationship between the two figures. He points out a cycle of relationships between Joshua, Teacher of Righteousness and Yahshua/Jesus that is very crucial to our destiny in the Kingdom. Hoeller says,

Again, Jesus brings a new law, or Covenant, and foretells his own second coming for a future period when the final battle between good and evil shall take place. As the first, two Joshuas hid their secret doctrines and sealed them hermetically, so that only the right people might discover them at the right time. (51)

It sounds far-fetched, but there may be some truth to it. Books have been sealed and stored away for those individuals destined to find them at the 'right time'. There is a prophecy in II Esdras that describes how '70 hidden books will be read and understood during the tribulation.

The knowledge contained in the books becomes a source of food and protection for those able to read and comprehend them. The real thrust behind apocalyptic is a plea to humans to learn how angelic history relates to human history. The true history altered and confused by fallen angels that write their own books to shape and form humans in their image and likeness has to be searched for like a buried treasure. Apocalyptic seers attempt to bring back the original teaching to people living in the future through the symbolic imagery of a great battle between forces that takes place in our souls. For the mystics of the Unique Cherub Circle, the difference between this idea and reincarnation or 'gilgullim' is that the same Cherub is the 'world soul' that performs the work of salvation making each of us a real human being.

One Spirit-Three Threads of Time

Hoeller leaves us with another way of looking at the obvious three-step process stamped on the figure of Joshua,

The three Joshua's have an organic connection with each other- they are conquering, revealing, sacrificing, dying, and re-appearing images of a Gnosis that ever seeks its expression, irrespective of the adversities and vicissitudes of human history. (51)

Hoeller is correct to find a Gnostic relationship between the Gospel of Phillip that claims the true mystery concerns the Hebrew name of Jesus יהושה. The letter 'shin' signifies the Holy Spirit when inserted between the two parts of the Tetragrammaton, it forms Yahoshua יהושה (Yah's Salvation), which is common knowledge to Christian mystics. It is nothing new. Hoeller suggests that the insertion of the 'Shin' indicates that a fuller manifestation of holiness has appeared in the Messiah,

Sanctified by the power of the holy letter Shin, the original divine tetra morph now receives a differentiation that it previously did not possess. In psychological terms, one might say that Yahweh becomes conscious in Jesus and that this process of the creator's growth toward consciousness proceeded from Joshua, son of Nun, to the Essene Teacher, and finally culminated in Jesus as understood by the Gnostics. (52)

Joel sees how this understanding is what actually can open up one's spiritual consciousness so that it becomes possible to experience the true human and angelic history hidden behind mistranslations and time. It was a common fact that Israel expected to have a visitor from the Heavens, and the book of Enoch is not the only apocalyptic text that has this hope. Many of the apocalyptic texts were in circulation right along with the scrolls of Moses and the prophets that also describe this mysterious personage. One particular verse in Enoch states:

He sat upon the Throne of his Glory; and the principal part of the judgment was assigned to him, the Son of Man. Sinners shall disappear and perish from the face of the earth, while those who seduce them shall be bound with chains forever. All their works shall disappear from the earth; nor shall there be any to corrupt; for the Son of Man has been seen, sitting on the Throne of His Glory.

These were promises the oppressed could live by, assurance that justice would not go unbalanced forever. The figure of the Son of Man serves to edify and build a nation of prophets; all who can see the complex simpleness of this figure could aspire to become like it. Vision is a source of creative power and is capable of transforming humans into angelic beings in the Timeless Kingdom. Just as Moses, Abihu, and Nadab, along with the seventy elders, saw the anthropomorphic form of Elohim, others, particularly the three disciples who witnessed the Messiah transform in front of them, saw the anthropomorphic structure that Moses and the children of Israel witnessed on Mt. Sinai. Some refer to it as Wisdom others the Angel of יהוה and even Metatron, but all these titles or attributes refer to the same emergence of a hidden spiritual consciousness that was lost when Moses broke the original tablets. Remember that the original assembly and community in the Wilderness begged Moses to be their intercessor because they could not bear the thunders, light, and numinous Presence of the Supreme Being. Many seemed to have been guilty of pushing the Divine consciousness, which resides only in His Palace/Name, out of His Holy Temple. Perhaps this is the true meaning of the Tikkun. All must return to the Original Thought (Word) or be lost in their own vain imaginings. Will vain imagining consign us to the river of Acheron as we become hopelessly lost in our own ideas and forget our true origin?

Abraham	Source and Substance	Father
Isaac	Matrix and Vortex	Son
Jacob	Various manifestations	Holy Spirit

Jacob represents the center of balance in the Age of Grace where Yahshua has fully ascended to the Father and has restored the world Soul and Equilibrium. On the Tree of Life this is the central pillar that balances the two outer pillars of 'Geburah' and 'Chesed' or judgment and mercy. It would seem that our state of consciousness is much more powerful than ever imagined. We insist on not believing anything previous generations have handed down unless it fits in with the current preconceived notions of the time. We all must individually also become aware of the ancient thread that binds us to the wheels of life and time in the past. Rudolph Otto says the Son of Man,

"spoke of a 'new thing' now at hand, which neither righteous men nor prophets of the previous era had been able to see, was now to be seen and experienced" (Otto Kingdom 162).

Joel begins to wonder how anyone can understand the relevance of the 'new thing' if we do not know the 'old thing'. This is something he had always wondered. The misinformation covers the new work of the Son of Man like a blanket of water, drowning the spiritual consciousness of sincere seekers. We have to seek the Son of Man hidden from before the foundation of the earth but we have to be determined to escape the confines of mortal thought and human error to succeed. The act is a declaration of war on the powers and principalities in high places. Joel realizes a person must be determined to find and know hidden truths found through the errors left in the records of human authors who recorded their own version of human history. The fact that words and ideas are changed becomes apparent through comparing scientific and spiritual documents with each other. Truth is stronger than error; the biggest battle already won is the victory we each personally make of it.

LITTLE FLOCK OF ANGELS

That day or its light does not set. If anyone becomes a son of the bridal chamber he will receive the light. If anyone else does not receive it while he is in this world, he will not receive it in the other place. He who has received that light will not be seen, nor can he be detained, and none shall be able to torment one of this kind even if he dwells in the world. And again, when he goes out of the world, he has already received the truth in the images. The world has become the aeon. For the aeon is for him a Pleroma, and it is in this manner: it is revealed to him alone, not hidden in the darkness and the night but hidden in a perfect day and a holy light. (Gospel of Phillip P134:1-18)

In The Date and Unity of the Gospel of Philip, Barbara Thiering, a pioneer in the field, has researched many ancient texts of the Qumran texts found over fifty years ago. She is concerned with the true cultural identity of the people

346

mentioned in the scrolls and their relationship with members of the earliest Jewish Christian communities. Thiering believes there is no certain evidence that texts such as Enoch, Baruch, or the Clementines originally derive from ideas in the New Testament, yet critics of these texts use this as their main argument. On the contrary, excluded texts seemed to have preceded the canonical gospels and the Pauline letters by a couple of centuries. Thiering claims the Gospel of Philip written in the early part of the first century A.D., is vital to understanding the activity of early assemblies. By saying they derive from other texts it places them in a secondary position, instead a complementary relationship.

The argument of illegitimacy based on the miscalculation of historical dates gives modern society the opportunity to cast aside the duty to explore this lost heritage. Some argue that later Christians wrote them for propagandistic reasons; thus, another reason to dissuade many readers from taking the documents seriously. Our very lives may depend on learning the facts hidden in footnotes, commentaries, and scribal interpolations. Thiering argues that it is due to a lack of knowledge on the part of modern researchers that they fail to see the unity and structure found in the 'cast out' gospels. She writes,

"It may be that we have not had the information to see the sense that links the sayings" (105); her deductions in support of this argument are diverse, but all work together to lend a sense of credibility to her assumptions. Most importantly, she states that many other texts besides the canonical scriptures have been given a much later date of composition than they were actually written.

Thiering's own view is that the Dead Sea Scrolls hold the key piece of evidence that a division existed between a larger community of Jews that left Jerusalem to settle in Qumran and a smaller group [Little Flock] within that group that believed

347

the 'true interpretation' or 'pesharim' had been handed down to them orally from the Teacher of Righteousness. Out of this spiritual dispersion grew many documents and texts; the New Testament represents only a single view in its current form; it has been edited, censored, and altered to cover up the relationship between Enoch and the Son of Man. What is the 'true interpretation'?

She gives us a taste of its fruit through carefully prepared analogies as she interprets the text in light of their native background.

A familiar concept found in the New Testament and the Gospel of Philip is the distinction between a "slave" and a "son." Those under the old law were 'slaves' and those who had accepted the Son of Man were "sons" gaining an inheritance and spiritual maturity as opposed to the infancy of "slaves" who did not receive the full inheritance.

There are two 'heirs,' heirs to "living things" and those who inherit "dead things," those gentiles that practiced any of the old laws were considered 'dead' and full initiation into the teaching was denied them. Gentiles that accept the Son of Man receive a lower level of life, than those fully initiated were often times excommunicated or considered 'dead'.

Men Walking as Trees

The author of the Gospel of Philip makes the Garden of Eden its central core as the divine ideal of the "promised salvation" that can be won if the new teaching is eaten and accepted as the new 'Tree of Life'. The Dead Sea scrolls contain similar imagery of the Tree but in a different way; the author of the "Hymns of Thanksgiving" (109) describes a person as the source of the water that fertilizes the members that make up the Garden. Members of this group symbolized and compared to trees growing through the doctrine of the Teacher of Righteousness. His teachings are like water from a spring that comes out to water the garden of human trees. The Garden of Eden contains trees that are actually human angels. The Son of Man prepares the soil in the Garden and the disciples are the trees that grow and actually bear new fruits.

The New Testament has a similar theme wherein its members collectively conceive of themselves as a Temple, another symbol of the Garden. The fact that Paul teaches the Temple of Yahweh is now presented in the human body revolutionizes spirituality and it may be inferred that the "paradise" planted by "Joseph the Carpenter" was really the development of an institution that prepared initiates for instructions in this new teaching. Was it really a 'new' teaching? Was it a reform movement designed to remind the latest community of an ancient teaching associated with a secret 'plant of righteousness'? We see now how the Garden of Eden signifies a circle of students filled with Shekinah or Wisdom, and from them, the water flows to the four quarters of the world that surround it.

The human part of us has a mystic thread connecting us to the primordial Adam, but we are not always conscious of it. The Son of Man is aware of the mystic thread connecting his identity with the 'beginning'. The 'beginning is an embodiment of 'powers' that were once only principles and forces contained in the Father. Sirach describes a figure that will encompass and manifest the 'powers' of the Father as water pours from his mouth. This is how humans come to 'rest' in the motionless ageless wisdom from the 'beginning'. Rudolph Otto says the Son of Man, "Spoke of a 'new thing' now at hand, which neither righteous men nor prophets of the previous era had been able to see, was now to be seen and experienced" (Otto 162). It is mainly due to his research in the early nineteenth century, that modern society began to take the important link between Enoch and the Son of Man seriously. Otto writes,

Here is a greater than Jonah and Solomon," and he places 'Jonah' in the sefiroth of Understanding from an earlier age, while Solomon occupies the place of Chockmah, the Wisdom of the Ancients. He states, "Both faded away before him who was more. (Otto Kingdom of God and the Son of Man 163)

We stumble trying to understand the 'more' of this superhuman figure able to overcome a frail human nature and the fear that keeps all of us from being truly alive. The nature of our daily reality is itself a shadow of what Is, for the very substance of the shadow is the physical world. The source of the shadow is the spiritual world. While it is true that many manmade religious concepts are 'likely tales' we should not assume that the Son of Man is just another tale: "Everything depends on the worldview that controls the "facts" it brings to light and to which it gives meaning" (Smith 115). Sometimes censors manipulate facts to suit a particular worldview and this is what Smith wants us to recognize.

Joel knows now that theologians must begin to stand up for the facts of faith instead of joining the ranks of scientists who must have tangible mortal evidence. If more religious leaders were as serious about the scriptures, critical scholarship, and social justice as scientists are serious about antimatter, multiverses, and quantum physics, society would be better prepared as members of a nation. They would be able to derive hypotheses and form theories in the application of practical spiritual laws and education designed to deliver the disenfranchised from ignorance. This is the true role of the Elect and the social consciousness of the early communities that left us a legacy of humans striving with the angel of life.

When the pearl is cast down in the mud it does not become dishonored the more, nor if it is anointed with balsam oil will it become more precious. But it has its worth in the eyes of its owner at all times. So with the sons of Elohim wherever they may be. For they have value in the eyes of their Father. (Gospel of Phillip 110:17-26)

Sacrifice of Elect

The word 'Elect' has come to be associated with a group of 'special' 'chosen ones' destined for crowns and promised the inheritance of a Kingdom. However, the Greek word for "Elect" has many other connotations. It originally signified a group destined to fight the forces of the fallen angels and archons that currently rule the Kosmos. They are not special or elite; no extra privileges are given to them. Instead, many of them, marked by terrifying visions of the future, seek solace in solitude. When they are not fleeing from the horrific tribulation woes inflicted on them by 'rulers' in high places, the fire of the mystery burns deeps within causing a longing that never stops. The Son of Man sacrificed his earthly life for the Elect's sake, and thus, in exchange, he is due the Elect's sacrifice as the 'first fruits of his death'. Enoch describes the Elect one in more detail than any other text, how this mysterious figure remains hidden and whose existence is only potential still waiting to manifest. The early Disciples claim they not only saw, heard, and walked with the Logos who appeared at the end of the seventh week.

Moses Cordovero explains the specific role of the Elect in each generation:

Rabbi Simeon and his colleagues were superior to the others in their generation by far. [Thus] he said we seven are the eyes of God: This refers to their constituting a foundation for the seven higher sefirot. (89)

Those who study spiritual science become 'eyes' in the sense that their own perception of divine reality reflects the divine light of understanding into the world so that it can see the Kingdom. The Elect give their life as a gift to serve others and keep the flow of divine Wisdom directed to the earth through visualizing the Kingdom in the 'world to come'. Olam means not only world and forever, but more importantly, it signifies consciousness of the 'divine reality'. Through Wisdom, the elect experiences the future while living in the present and dying in the past. This is their specialized role and function.

We cannot communicate true spiritual experience with mere words anymore; words and language contain many barriers, as we have seen. A person can only experience divine reality through an intimate knowledge of the identity of the Son of Man. We have the sequence of the days of Creation and then, of course, the generations of Adam as guideposts to show us how the Son of Man becomes Metatron, the Eternal Scribe, and Author. The Author, if understood correctly, can show us a faraway land through visual imagination of things in the 'world to come'. The elect learns to experience the 'unknown' until it becomes the 'known.' This is why those things considered 'taboo' hidden away for the sake of the elect come at the end. Torah has a face and will not reveal it to one who is not prepared mentally and spiritually while others cannot, by nature of the revelatory law itself, ever see all the hidden wonders shown to the elect.

Angelic concepts, spiritual language and the destiny of history are tools to help us begin a dialogue with divine reality. Ezekiel has a prophetic experience and visualizes a 'great stormy wind' that disturbs his thoughts, as if, a pebble dropped in a pond of water and disturbs the once placid surface with a ripple of waves. The storm can occur in life as problems or trials that disturb our security and peace of mind; but they can also be spiritual trials that affect our consciousness. It is the way these trials are perceived and dealt with that determines our worthiness and holiness. Most of us cannot handle the times of isolation from without and even within that often comes with the spiritual experience and therefore, not many can walk the path. We know we can walk the path, if once our trials confront us and the result is for us or against us, and the determination to persevere is strong; then the secret and invisible things behind the events of daily life will become evident, as Wisdom lights our path.

Daniel sealed the secret of how the elect become like stars shining in the night of darkness. As violence and crime become the new mother and father of our time on earth, more people with damaged psyches and hatred for society will continue to breed more misinformation until we learn to acknowledge that spiritual realities are essential to our lives. Gravity accelerates each particle of air down in a vertical direction. Atmospheric pressure exists as the air particles resist the force of gravity. Gravity compresses the atmosphere by its own weight. Love can fall upon itself when anger wins the upper hand. Fear quickly pushes down our peace of mind and as the Holy Spirit resists its thrust, pressure builds up in one's soul. Anger swallows love by its own nature. Unless there is a balance between these two emotions, that generate more heat than any other emotions, a person is liable to become imbalanced mentally and emotionally. There is a scientific law that explains why:

The hydrostatic equation expresses the state of exact balance in the atmosphere between these two forces. The force of gravity acts vertically downward. The pressure gradient force acts upwardly. (Encyclopedia Britannica 354 1956)

When these two forces are out of balance, the vertical downward movement of gravity gets an advantage and looms downward at such an increasing rate of acceleration that it can form "vertical displacements of air" which become a vortex or vortices. Such as an 'air in air' vortex, this is exactly what creates devastating tornadoes. This demonstrates, both physical and mental, that everything created has at its very core a waging war that requires the need for balance between polar opposites. The elect, invested with the skills to overcome the struggle inside, begin to project a renewed higher consciousness into the Universe as they gradually learn to adapt and evolve. Joel believes that there really is a constant interchange of energy that is demonstrated in the up and down of all polar phenomena. The various atmospheric conditions are a type and shadow of the varying states of consciousness experienced by the average person every day, such as dreams, desires, fears, hopes, hates, or confusion. How can the average person battle these powers? No one can ever really win alone. The Son of Man has to rise within our hearts and minds in order to strengthen our spirits:

The existence of the Son of Man was two-fold: He will exist in the future "with power," yet He has not yet come "with power" but is still hidden with the Father (Otto Kingdom 192).

Our own restricted consciousness is what blinds us and binds us to the lower forces. However, the elect seek, find and know the experience of His 'power'; Paul exhorts us to remember the Gospel seems hidden only to those who refuse to see. There is no 'chosen' race anymore; it is a universal decision everyone will make; the elect are not special but have been appointed by Yahweh from the 'beginning' to "receive" a revelation of the Word in themselves. The elect from previous generations projected the spiritual wisdom into the future; when we 'receive' the knowledge, the circle is complete.

The documents available to us now in the form of fragments from ancient mysterious times are mere shadows of the true teaching.

Grace Saves

It is not something that any of us can plan or prepare for; the 'saving event' is something that will take place outside of Time, we have to have that 'beginning time' in us through cognitive data. This invisible reality reveals the first stage of its presence in the physical world through the 'beginning' (prophecy) and the final stage manifests the 'end' through historical events that parallel the events of the 'beginning'. It becomes a part of everyday life as the Olam pervades our present world and the Son of Man 'receives' Glory in the Kingdom. Even though the elect still inhabit fleshly tabernacles, they envision the Son of Man in Heaven through visionary imagination. Albert Schweitzer comments on the elect in Mysticism of Paul the Apostle, "they paint with supernatural colors, but it is only a glorified transfiguration of reality" (76).

The invisible Kingdom hidden within and without appears as we begin to see the analogies that exist between the invisible Universe of mystical concepts and the structure of the visible Universe.

If we apply the scientific method as a 'yardstick' to perceive prophecy through, it can measure where we are in the historical events that reveal hidden 'mysteries' to the world. The 'primordial beginning' is the harbinger of the heavenly kingdom in which humanity participates through the mind's eye. The traumatized, rejected, despised, humiliated outcasts are given just enough Power and Glory to "exist" (76) amidst the anguish of mind, body, and soul in the tribulation. No one can enter this battle and be successful without first being born into the world of celestial time. Paul left the facts on record in the epistle of Ephesians, where he says that one born of the world is of the world and one born of the heavens is of the heavens.

We live in two worlds. One is spiritual, the other is cosmic; the 'in-between world' is where the battle has already come to an 'end', but in our world, the battle continues. Powerful forces of the Universe are at work in our lives, and each of us is in a battle just to live every day and maintain our humanity.

There is nothing whimsical about a 'faithful person' relying on feeling, intuition, spiritual knowledge, and facts to understand life, for faith is the evidence of things not yet seen. This time of 'grace' is a short period given to the disadvantaged to even the battle. The Kingdom is not about gaining new 'gnosis' or even a consciousness of supernatural truths, it is about a real war with the principalities and powers that rule the spiritual world 'olam' hidden from us. Once the elect enters back into the 'beginning,' they wake up in 'heavenly places' in the Son of Man. This transposition of spatial and timeless realities is the crux of the matter for this is how the inhabitants of the earth become heavenly citizens while still on earth. This seems to be a total contradiction of what we learned all these years regarding the geographical location of Heaven. Heaven began to come to earth through the 'beginning', and it now is in the earth during the 'end'; understanding this secret helps one to escape 'time death' by knowing that heaven is right here on earth.

These 'principalities, dominions, and archons' are 'places' of great wickedness that mimic the three 'places' shown to Moses in the pattern; they conspire to destroy anything sacred or meaningful. Nihilism is the accepted doctrine of the day, and disenfranchisement is the fate of those who dissent. The scribes of the Middle Ages, both in Christendom and Judaism, softened the activity of the angelic heavenly realms into mythology and fairytales they do not even believe anymore. In reality, there are two sets of angelic realms where the 'unholy angels' live to create obstacles for humans. They live on fear, hate, anger, and suspicion.

Daniel explains how an appointed guardian angel of each nation protects its patrons from these invisible enemies, but humans have to realize they are there.

Mystics and Hidden Existence

The mystic, according to Joseph Dan, goes in search of hidden esoteric symbolic truths that are, in reality, the true nature of existence. The elect sees the secret mysteries of the construction of the universe in a multi-layered structure that has a 'beginning' and an 'ending' that is mirrored in the first and last week of Enoch's apocalypse of weeks theme. All of the divisions that take place in Genesis during the creation converge into one point of balance, and this is how the spiritual and material worlds are intuitively and mystically "known" and "experienced."

We can enter this experience if we learn to see the image of the 'Father' in the Son of Man. Dan says,

When the one who descends to the Chariot stands to the right of the Throne of Glory, he is given the opportunity to see how ELOHIM runs the world, and as a result, he can know everything that will occur in the future. (Dan 85-86)

The ability to see the 'image' empowers a person according to Dan, "This knowledge is not merely passive, but raises the person to a new level in terms of his personal powers" (86). The knowledge enables one to enter the 'in-between world' that is "full of good things". Apparently, the Future World to Come 'Olam HaBa' is for those who persevere and eat of the tree of life while they are still only mortal beings. It is a very narrow and straight road to the Garden of Eden and only one can walk upon it at a time. The two sides must coalesce before we can go back into the Garden; as the Gospel of Thomas states, 'the two become one.'

The 'unified two' refers to the nature of the inner life. The information is always there just waiting for people to receive it from angelic mediation that teaches them the unutterable and ineffable mysteries of time and history. The elect receive such a revelation, and their induction into a living, moving, and vibrating secret that is so controversial the world would be destroyed if it were uttered before its Time takes them into the 'place' that only angelic humans can go. The only way into the life-giving sources of the Secret is through inner knowledge and wisdom that actually transforms human nature into an angelic existence.

Sacredness and holiness accompany the Presence of the Shekinah, but there is also a great sadness, and most mystics that really experience the spiritual rarely write about it. It is usually only taught through oral tradition to those considered capable of really helping to restore the world. It may be that some groups choose to remain anonymous in order to study freely without the restrictions and bans imposed on this type of literature. Sacchi writes about the reticence of these ancient circles,

Anderson is right in advancing the hypothesis that the Book of the Secrets of Enoch is the product of a fringe sect. According to Anderson, in order to resolve the mystery of the Book of the Secrets of Enoch it is necessary to identify this group. But it is the very Book of the Secrets of Enoch that identifies it, even if it does not give its name. (238-239)

Does the hidden Son of Man tradition remain hidden throughout the centuries, buried in an encrypted script of the Enoch texts that only the elect ones of earlier generations can decipher? Maybe not, the prophet Isaiah also knew the 'hidden tradition', it is recorded in Isaiah 49:1-6

Listen to me, O coastlands, and hearken, you peoples from afar. Yahweh called me from the womb from the body of my mother he named my name. He made my mouth like a sharp sword; in the shadow of his hand, he hid me; he made me a polished arrow; in his quiver, he hid me away. And he said to me, you are my servant, Israel, in whom I will be glorified.

The idea of spiritual pre-existence and, finally, material existence saturates this text and is the missing key to its interpretation. Many obscure passages in Isaiah are hard to fathom without apocalyptic literature to help fill in the gaps.

Enoch prophesied the inability to learn the ancient mystery hidden from before the ages because many would abandon the true knowledge and learn the ways of the fallen angels. Apocalyptic books are testaments that document the supernatural events destined to occur on the earth. Enoch, which signifies 'initiation,' has become the Witness that Yahweh of Spirits willed him to be against a wicked and perverse generation. There is much more to this than obscure truths and complicated symbolism, these Son of Man myths are human stories of becoming. These 'hidden groups' may have shared a common purpose – to experience and process the Chockmah or wisdom science of the Son of Man known by some groups as the 'sod'. Terms like visible/invisible, revealed/concealed and physical/spiritual were all concepts used to reflect the six days of creation and its twofold divisions that form us in the image of Elohim. The riders of the Charlot could penetrate and transcend the veil or 'vilon' of Time and bring back communications from the upper dimensions. The concept of an elect body of believers and a hidden Messiah who exists proleptically as a Name may prove to be the very evidence that gives credence to the historical value of this literature.

This battered, bruised, tested, and tried little 'flock' is destined to be the 'first fruits' of the Son of Man in fulfillment of the Father's promise to the Son. The elect are the inheritance of the Messiah. What gives them this ability? Could it be because they knew his genuine identity? An author's identity was not always a prerequisite to 'receiving' and believing a divine message in these fringe sects, the knowledge gained from the ascent experience was always more important. Many of the pseudipigraphic texts contain genuine spiritual experiences of real people who later attempted to preserve some of what they saw in scrolls. There were many other groups who did not write it down, for they practiced strict secrecy and silence. It is really a wonder we have any texts at all.

Seven Eyes of Time

In the Apocalypse of Baruch, the author mentions one of the many roles of the Elect:

The present world is not the end and the glory of God does not abide in it forever. For this reason, those who had power prayed for the weak, but the day of judgment will be at the end of this age and the beginning of the immortal age to come, in which corruption has passed away... No one will then be able to have mercy on him who has been overcome... (Sacchi 244)

There is only a certain amount of time designated for the elect one and his elect, to intercede on behalf of humanity. Once the time is up, humanity will have to face its own limitations and lack. The prophet Zechariah says the seven eyes of יהוה roam through the earth; a reference to the elect who will shine like lights in the darkness like candles of the Menorah and the seven days of creation. Daniel calls them the Maskillim and notes how they will teach righteousness and non-aggression towards enemies. They will try to live the words, not just read them out of the book. They receive the resurrection in their lifetimes; the once dual realms of non-being and being coalesce into a different form of existence called 'Eternal Life' in the Kingdom of Light. The anonymous author of Enoch mentions many admirable traits humans can attain, but the most important one is 'Patience' according to Sacchi:

Patience too, the capacity to bear misfortune with serenity while knowing oneself to be just, is a fundamental virtue for our author. Perhaps only the just, precisely as such, is capable. (245)

Thus, to overcome the evil thoughts and illusions in the world is to overcome the human bondage to fear and hate. Until humanity can do this on their own, then figures like the elect will always be necessary, until the end of the age. The new world, or Olam Ha-Bah, where justice and peace replace corruption and war, will be delivered from a great cosmic battle only through divine intervention, but humanity does have a role to play – it must stay awake, look above, and see. Sacchi says,

Really, the just/elect do not have sufficient justice for themselves in order to reach salvation. God will have to give to the just 'eternal justice,' which evidently is not human justice. (115)

Enoch says the 'Just' will not receive the 'eternal justice', until after the seventh week when the sevenfold wisdom oozes out of the mystery of divine reality into a 'life-circle' or 'plant' of individuals hidden in a fringe sect. Joel begins to wonder about the identities of this group of early disciples that gather around the Son of Man; as they follow him, they, too, perform great works and possess great faith. They receive keys and the seven-fold teaching. Luke wrote about them as the 'Seventy' that could perform miracles and healing in the Name. This is another guidepost to determine the historical reality of the Enochic heritage.

There were many groups studying the texts; only a few really experienced the power of the Ruach Ha-Kadesh or Holy Spirit until after Pentecost. Even then, only the immediate circle and the '70' found in Luke made any real progress in the hidden Son of Man יהושה – Yahoshua ben Yosef het Yaacov. This set of names found on a 'bone box', is the latest piece of archaeological evidence recently discovered and sold to the highest bidder.

It is not that there is no information available to us to find out more about the Son of Man, there is more and more knowledge coming to the surface. Actually, the gnosis or 'spiritual intelligence' is already distributed and we may well be living in the last part of the eighth week when evil grows stronger as the face of death and hands of violence mask the world. According to Enoch 91.14, "In the ninth week the world will finally be destroyed, 'and all people shall direct their sight to the path of uprightness" (115). The old world, the 'olam ha-zeh', must give birth to the new world through great pain and anguish, delivering its children to the dragon waiting outside the womb to devour them.

How can wisdom and sefirot transform a mortal into an immortal? Son of Man becomes the Logos over again in each of us for his words are Eternal Life. As the Father declares 'Yehi' (Be light) and there is life in light, the Son's words sustain that life. We are as human tabernacles built to contain the light/life in a tripartite relationship; a three-fold unit is more central to the core of the hidden identity than thought by earlier Councils, in a mad frenzy to dissect the flesh from the spirit. So much pertinent information is missing it is no wonder, so few believe a spiritual world even exists. Aryeh Kaplan, author of Inner Space, explains why books like the Zohar, Sefer Yetzirah, and the Bahir became closed books sealed from the Western world and Christianity. He says,

What had been written down remained, as the Torah had been in its time, a closed book. The keys were to remain oral. Just enough had been written down to ensure that only someone familiar with the tradition would understand. (5)

Apocalyptic 'secrets and mysteries' do not open the door to inner inspection; correct consciousness is what opens the opportunity to unlock the seal of mystery.

There is a tradition of knowledge 'not written', but is known through having one's memory restored of spiritual intuition developed periodically throughout the centuries, both before and after the advent of the Messiah. Certain strands of knowledge and doctrines forbidden by different circles and groups literally created a 'war of words'. The Son of Man rebelled against the carnal, earthly stringent laws and taboos; he taught the twelve disciples at the level they could 'receive' as he taught the multitudes what they could 'receive'. Any who had ears to hear and eyes to see could do so. "If the gospel is hidden", says Paul, it is because we do not open our hearts to it.

Yod Connection

Kaplan explains the true validity of יהוה, without all the flash of modern hype esoterica and complicated gematria or repetitive definitions; he shows how it represents authentic charity, not the kind seen by others. Kaplan explains that the Hebrew letter 'Yod' is tiny, round, and resembles a small coin; the letter 'heh' represents a hand and 'vav' is an outstretched arm giving a 'coin' and the final 'heh' represents a hand receiving the 'coin.' We must put forth our hand to 'receive' what is hidden from us before we are further ensnared in the power of capitalism,

The letter yod at the beginning of a word denotes the future, something that is still in potential. So, also, at the level of yod existence is still hidden and unavailable. There will be no access to it until a hand is created to receive it. (Kaplan Inner Space 11-12)

None of us can embrace our spiritual identity and destiny unless we put forth a hand to find it; this is how our own lost light recovers our spiritual comprehension. It is how to comprehend an invisible source of light we lost sight of when we cut ourselves off from the ancient ones; nevertheless, we must put forth our thoughts now to see the tselem 'face to face' instead of in a 'mirror'. The Word/Dabar takes shape and forms through reflection that activates human consciousness to respond to mystical images. The Dabar reflects human consciousness into 'bereshit' time. The wisdom of the ancient ones transforms us invisibly as our soul ascends into the intelligence of light and then descends to the understanding of life. Each of us has a heavenly counterpart – it is our true 'soul mate.' Scholem offers a comprehensive view of the sefirot:

The eight 'limitations' qesawoth, that is, the principal limbs of man that nevertheless are only seven, since 'the torso and the [reproductive organ] only count as one.' The ninth and tenth would then be the two 'ofannim of the Merkabah, designated in the Bahir with an expression borrowed from Isaiah 34:10, as the nesahim. Nesah in Hebrew means 'duration,' 'permanence.' The lowest of all these powers is also designated, as nishono shel 'olam, the duration of the world, a power that 'inclines toward the west. (160).

Above, Scholem compares human limbs to the divine attributes that contain water from seven different streams; they become channels distributing water to the world, according to Scholem:

"The Righteous is, therefore, a channel through which all the brooks and streams of the superior powers flow into the sea of the Shekinah or the mystical 'heart'" (160).

Angelic Gnosis

Without the mediation of human advisors, angels themselves will teach a group of individuals through divinely appointed heavenly books. These individuals actually enter a different kind of time zone, where the story of Genesis comes to life in each one until it finally rests in the all. Modern scientists belittle the creation story due to the fantastic explanations and interpretations as to why there are two stories of creation in the Genesis narrative. The modern interpretations so far removed from the cultural milieu of the literature have virtually camouflaged the spiritual value of the text. Sefer Bereshit and Genesis have little more in common than the mutual content of words and punctuation. Primitive texts contain genuine experiences of a spiritual world and its structure, and the literature of many obscure circles confirms that many texts were inspired by actual 'secrets and mysteries' learned firsthand.

There is a growing body of research on encrypted codes in certain 'phrases' that act upon the consciousness; thus 'telling' an individual what and how to think in order to gain entrance into the spiritual realm of experience. One function of the Memra is to instruct and tell saving acts. Sacchi comments on the work of his fellow colleague Anderson, regarding the 'scientific validity' of the Secrets of Enoch. He says the:

First attempt to make science and faith agree on a valid explanation, except that, unlike a person today who strains to find such agreement, the author of the Book Of The Secrets Of Enoch sees or reads in the structure of his 'scientific' knowledge the unfolding of the great work narrated too briefly in the Bible. (246)

Anderson realizes that portions of the Enoch text detailing the structure of the Universe are not really developed in any detail in the Genesis narrative of the creation. These outcast scriptures supplement the accepted canonical texts. They evoke an experience designed to awaken the heavenly image above that parallels how the Shekinah will shine on it from the West.

EAST OF THE GARDEN OF EDEN

In this age, we face the east, and only the Shekinah (female side of Creator) can access the place of 'blessings', the apocalypse revealed in the body, otherwise symbolically known as the 'west'. Dan writes,

According to the Baryta and the treatise following it, Kedushah resides in the West, which is traditionally regarded as the abode of the Shekinah, while the greatness, the Cherub, resides in the East, and the light of holiness shines over it from the West to East. (57)

The East is associated with the sunrise and going forth, but more importantly, it refers to the position a person faces; the East is always before "Bereshit in front of us like a fence or veil.

The term 'kedam' is associated with Kadmon, the 'primordial' existence before time. In the New Testament, the term 'anatole,' one of the initials of A.D.A.M discussed in II Enoch, represents the East. Matthew 24:24-37 is an apocalyptic section that mentions one of the signs to watch for, "For as the lightning comes from the east and flashes as far as the west, so will be the coming of the Son of Man" (Harper Collins Study Bible 1903).

There is another reference to how things flee to the West in the Pistis Sophia when Messiah and twelve disciples stand at the four corners and pray in the secret place to keep the seals bound on the gates of the abyss. A portion of the Psalms retains the ancient idea of the 'secret place' and is an indispensable source of this mystic Gnosis. Peter Hayman points out the relevance of this scene in his analysis of the Temple in the center of the Universe.

"Ironically, similar to the evolution theory of emergence, there is another meaning associated with the term East; it is the word 'rise.' In eschatology, spiritual evolution parallels how the Son of Man will 'rise' from the centralized loins of Judah and spread out over the entire land from the East to the West."

If we converge all these images into a focused center, we can see a progressive movement outwards, for even the treks from Egypt to the Wilderness and then to Canaan land demonstrate a migration and progressive evolution from a low place to a higher place.

Our Sun is subject to the same kind of process as it ascends through three hundred and sixty degrees called 'gates'. With each sunrise, the sun travels through gates or geometric points in orbit that are responsible for the different parts of day and night. As night and day engage in a constant struggle between light and darkness, the sun always rises victoriously at the end. The hidden primordial light of the 'beginning' will rise in the Son of Man in the midst of a great tribulation, forcing Adam [humanity] to rise out of its fleshly tabernacle until it eventually dissolves and its divine energy is released. At first, all of us see only our own face or 'self' in the Garden of Eden. Humanity will eventually learn to see the divine face through its own reflection, but first, it has to turn towards 'destiny' and face the Unique Cherub.

We all naturally face east, but the holiness 'kedushah' resides in the west and contains blessings and gifts; according to Dan, "Rabbis called the West Oria, or-yah" (70). There is more to the West than just a resting place for the dead, according to Boccaccini. In Mysteries and Revelations, he tells us the location of a place in the West where souls of the Just and unjust still wait for eschatological redemption. He says,

"It is from here that the souls will come forth at the time of the Last Judgment, which will ratify for all eternity the state of both the blessed and the damned" (1 En. 22).

The previous verse helps explain this mysterious biblical phrase 'The Son of Man will come when lightning, shines from the east to the west.' The Son of Man brings the 'thought-filled' light of redemption that shines from the East to the West; divine light shines into the darkness of death and overcomes its hold on human consciousness. When the divine light shines on humanity represented as the east (spirit) and west (flesh) then will the heaven and earth be one. We continue to face the east since our departure from the Garden of Eden, but it is not the 'real world' we reside in; we live in the land of Nod [sleep].

Boccaccini comments on this: Already in his lifetime, the individual lives in a two-dimensional universe. Its real world is not this world but the one in which his soul will continue to live. This world is dominated by evil and will be destroyed in the end. (41)

Visions of Salvation

The startling connection between the Enoch literature and Cherub Circle mystics is their common view on the condition of the just in the evil world; they are 'already saved' while they live in the world waiting: "to reach the valley in the west where there is no longer suffering or sin" (41). The Qumran community and the Cherub Circle thought they were already 'blessed' and redeemed. Boccaccini's view on Enoch 25:6 asserts the same thing; I think it does agree with the conditions set down by the Cherub Circle, except for one main difference. Boccaccini writes,

The better world is no longer far away in the West, open to the souls of the just, but is placed at the end of history and destined for those just who are there in that moment of time. The concept of the immortality of the soul loses importance. God will save humanity in this world and not in a spiritual dimension. (41)

The Elect can see the nature of this reality through vision and revelation. However, humanity sees through the 'things that are made' in the earthly world. Paolo Sacchi, author of Jewish Apocalyptic and Its History, writes, "For the ordinary person, there is another way: finding God in things" (247). How can we find the Creator in things? One way may be to look at the way historical events and scientific facts complement and substantiate metaphysical and spiritual concepts about the Son of Man. Moses Maimonides says,

Everything produced comes into existence from nonexistence; even when the substance of a thing has been in existence and has only changed its form, the thing itself, which has gone through the process of genesis and development and has arrived at its final state, has now different properties from those which it possessed at the commencement of the transition from potential to reality, or before that time. (178)

Everything seems to move out from a center; therefore, we must start by extracting our inner light from the same center. We can see that there is a progression of events: Elohim creates a system of forces that unite in the Son of Man, who then projects the true nature of the Father. Some unknown, mysterious 'little flock' receives the tools needed to navigate in the dangerous world around them.

The progression continues throughout the ages as revealed truth, the 'realized eschatology' takes on form and shape in the age to come. It is the role of the Cherub to distribute the 'hidden wisdom light' buried in our hearts of stone.

Light of the Cherub

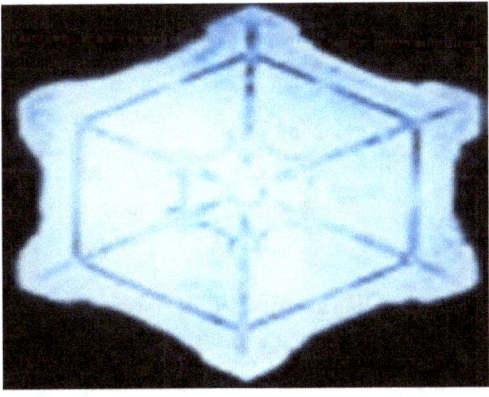

Figure 43 Kepler Snow Flake

Johann Kepler also noticed an 'angelic being' in many of his works. In one particular work, Six Cornered Snowflake, he says a "divine fashioner or former" is the agent responsible for the physical structure and geometry evident in the design of the universe. Dan's recent research into a figure in the Shiur

369

Komah called 'Unique Cherub' is proof of rabbinic speculation regarding an archetype model from which everything else derives its shape and form. He says the 'Unique Cherub' is responsible for the creation of the angelic realms and dimensions, not the invisible, formless Supreme Being. The invisible essence and energy of the Supreme Being does not change, it is the 'Unique Cherub' that is subject to change. It, like the Logos, functions as a channel to distribute the breath of life and form to the multi-leveled universe. Dan says, "It seems that these formulations represent a mature and self-confident concept of a multilayered divine realm, even though the very idea was hardly several decades old when this text was written" (Dan The 'Unique Cherub' Circle 110). Dan quotes from an ancient text that describes the creation of the Cherub that precedes all previous species:

For him [the Unique Cherub] he created an image and a form, and a human form, and eyes, and hands and 'from what appeared to be his loins upward; and on his forehead is engraved 'Yah Akhatriel' and phylacteries are on his head and it is written about him 'And what one nation in the earth is like thy people, like Israel; and he has the Shiur Komah of Rabbi Ishmael; in His image Man was created, and he sits on the Throne of Glory, and he is above all the proud ones, which are the four kings of the earth, eagle, lion, bull, and Man on the four sides of the throne. (Dan 110-111)

Enoch reads the 'Pargod' a curtain of time that enables him to see the same Kingdoms as the 'directions' of the cube he travels in during the journey. As he travels from the 'beginning' to the 'end,' he tells the reader what he sees in each geographical region of the west, east, south, and north. Joseph Dan believes these regions did not only represent directions:

The Cherub is sitting on the Throne of Glory, surrounded on three sides by the pargod, and open only towards the West, from where the spiritual divine power of the Kavod shines upon it. (113)

The curtain covers three parts of a structure that has only one opening in the west. He explains the relationship between the Shekinah in the west and the Cherub in the east (108-115); the Glory of the Shekinah shines on the Cherub quickening it to shine its light in our world.

Cherub of the Circle

One of its main roles is the distribution of Wisdom. The Kavod, according to the Unique Cherub Circle, has two parts. The top half looks up at the Shekinah and the bottom half looks down toward the Unique Cherub. The female Shekinah receives the divine emanation and then distributes it to the Unique Cherub who distributes it to the earth. The process results in a circle of communion that parallels how the 'beginning' protology looks down to the 'ending' eschatology when the two aeons become 'one'. The Universe shows us a world of circles inside circles and waves inside dimensions that can teach us a means of attaching ourselves to the strings of the Cosmic Covenant.

Figure 44 Superstring Cross-section

In the above illustration, we see a cross-section of a superstring demonstrating that it has circles inside circles. The sefiroth have circles inside circles and like M-Theorist, ancient mystics believe there are ten dimensions that parallel the divine attributes.

We have to raise our thoughts higher than the lunar influence that surrounds the Earth. Although plants and animals have no problem receiving the full benefit of the Sun, humans have a defect that predisposes us to become black holes, and like the black holes of dying stars, we have the potential to implode.

Joel can now see how even his own gravity (ego) acts as a self-destructing agent that can dismantle its genetic code structure. We can undo our own peace with the antimatter of negative thoughts about ourselves and other people. The Hubble telescope and modern physics have given the world the ability to imagine the invisible universe of energy, motion, force, atomic nuclei, and even stardust, but only the scriptures can give us the chance to see inside the hidden inner spiritual world of Adam. The discovery of the laws that govern these invisible realities is what has given scientists an understanding of the depth and width of the Universe. Martin Cohen says, "The Shiur Qomah can be read as a 'scientific' proof of the validity of anthropomorphism" (Cohen 68). The "Unique Cherub" also has an invisible spiritual essence. The role of the Shekinah belongs to Wisdom. If we combine and individually assign all the duties to each respective figure, a clearer picture begins to emerge of how the Shekinah and Unique Cherub function as a unit.

Shekinah	Kabod	Unique Cherub
Presence	Throne	Image

In the Unique Cherub Circle, they interpret these three terms very differently than mainstream circles.

They were a fringe sect that remained anonymous and we know very little of their identities or how they developed this unique doctrine. Dan's research is the most detailed to date as he describes how these 'mystics of the book' all work together as a unit, like the phantom and cherubim surrounding the foot of the Throne. He cites a very interesting description according to the Barayta:

Surrounding the Throne of Glory on which (resides) the Unique Cherub, there is a cloud from three sides to separate it from the Holy Beasts, except for the fourth side, which is the West, from which shines in the abode over the Unique Cherub, and His Glory shines there, and this is why our Rabbis called the West Oria, or-yah. (70)

They believe the mysterious figure on the Throne in Ezekiel's account of the Chariot is the 'Unique Cherub' and even more interesting, in contradistinction to the Tetragrammaton, Elohim is the "Supreme divine name" (68). Elohim is a title and Yahweh is a name.

Elohim of the Ancients

This is something they have in common with the Samaritans and Magharians, who also consider the divine title, Elohim, the source of the creation. Here, Elohim is a presence and existence before creation:

In Sefer Yetzirah, this terminology seems to be based on Gen. 1:2, a verse that was understood by the author of this text to describe existence before the actual Creation. The 'Spirit of God' hovering above the water was the divine power present at that time; therefore, it must be prior to Creation and independent of it. (68)

The term occurs ten times in Genesis, this is common knowledge, but the Cherub Circle had a different idea of the Creator. They consider 'divine speech and Creation' as the same power (Dan 69). The members of this circle believe the world was 'spoken' into existence by a voice that has no form, shape, or visibility. The Dabar or 'speech' can participate in our world and lives.

The reason for this belief is that the Cherub Circle mystics rank vision secondary to the voice. These mystics believe the immeasurable, unseen source and substance of energy need no form or image, but humanity does. Dan explains the function of 'vision' among these obscure mystics who managed to maintain a spiritual link with the ancient past. He comments here on the role of 'vision', "It became meaningful only when Man was created, at the end of that process" (69); the 'end' of the process is designated eschatology in apocalyptic literature. An understanding of the 'last things' gives us the ability to see the hidden vision. The Shekinah did not create us in her image symbolized by a secret that covers the essence of the true spiritual reality. The Cherub Circle mystics believe "Man was created in the image of the Cherub, not in the image of any superior divine power" (69); this solves the paradox of whether or not the Creator has a body or form. The actual essence and energy of the Universe withdrew and what remains is the residual background radiation that awakens the Shekinah's existence as light.

We, on the other hand, made after the image of the Cherub, are, by nature, estranged from the divine presence hidden inside. How does the creation of the Cherub differ from our creation? Dan explains,

A divine element, originating in the Creator, reached the Cherub by a process of emanation and resided in it. This element did not reach the Cherub directly but by the mediation of the 'Shekinah of His Glory.' (69)

In other words, Light [Shekinah] influences the life and being of the Unique Cherub. This angelic being created from the breath and fire of יהוה, especially 'prepared' to be the Son of the Father, is found in the missing books. There is evidence

374

in many old texts that humans will transform into angel stars, but even so are still subject to the 'time of tribulation' that comes upon the earth. However, the Son is beyond the angelic hierarchy for he ascended to the Father in the tenth Heaven. As Paul says in Ephesians about the 'work' of the Father, "Which he wrought in Messiah, when he raised him from the dead, and set [him] at his own right hand in the heavenly [places], meaning other dimensions unknown to us at the time.

The third heaven is where Paul heard things too mysterious to repeat to others. The next verse explains how the Cherub is still in charge in the 'world to come'. Notice that in Ephesians 1:21, Paul comments on the levels and locality of its power, "Far above all principality, and power, and might, and dominion, and every name that is named, not only in this world but also in that which is to come." The Son of Man goes before the angels in the 'beginning' and returns with the ten thousand angels during the 'end', according to Jude 1:14-15. Even though there will always be people who consider this literature dangerous or only for the elite few, there are still others who would attempt to overthrow the existing kingdoms of the world and force the hand of heaven. Thanks to the secret, sevenfold teaching there will also be those who consciously realize they are in a hidden spiritual Kingdom that far exceeds the boundaries and depths of good and evil. They realize the literature helps aid a broken creation.

Joel understands now that there will always be voices that like to shout about the 'end times' and scare people with horrific scenes that continue to haunt their futures. He sees why very few find the hidden Kingdom inside the world of 'wisdom light'. No matter which view we take, a small group of individuals destined to become the Son of Man community, along with the Son of Man in heaven, is destined to enter the Book of Life. It is their fate to help heal the world as they learn a new way to control their thoughts and feelings and focus on the coming of the Kingdom.

TIME CONSCIOUSNESS & PERSONAL BEING

Does consciousness have an influence on our personal experience of time? Carl Jung's Synchronicity theory states that humanity shares an unconscious connection with all the concepts, symbols, dreams, arts, and language of every human. Leonora Leet says there is a 'synchronicity' factor that influences reality in the fifth dimension. At this level, a higher sense of divine determination is at play in the Universe and justice prevails over unrighteousness. On the other hand, Rudolph Steiner suggests there are hidden [Akashic] records that contain all human thoughts, discoveries, and impressions in accordance with his theory. Others believe it is a supernatural ability to tap into the various dimensions of cosmic consciousness and interact with entities and other life forms.

The mystics of Enochic literature know there is an ability to tap into 'Wisdom Consciousness' that emanates Eternal Thoughts that awaken the divine attributes sleeping in us; these are the places Paul calls 'heavenly.' Angelic beings can manipulate these places inside us, some turn Ruach towards the 'light' and some towards the 'dark.'

The Dead Sea scrolls contain accounts of the war between the Sons of Light and the Sons of Darkness battling for the souls of man. Many ancient Near Eastern nations believed in a system based on the correct proportion and depth of a soul based on the extensions of the sephiroth that need to take root and grow. A personal scale determines the amount of light or darkness. Apocalyptic authors describe the war as a battle inside human consciousness and they say the Torah of the Name is our fortress. If the human consciousness is brimming with darkness, it manifests that darkness in its environment. The consciousness of light can enlighten our surroundings and the lack of it can darken our horizons. We are on the brink of total destruction, anarchy, and despair globally. Yet, the biggest battle of all is not weapons of mass destruction, but thoughts.

Can our thoughts influence time? When humanity's consciousness is dark, then the effects of death (gravity) can roam freely, this has an effect on how we experience time. As gravity eats space, time is born. Everyone knows that time flies when life is fun and exciting, and in contrast, how long events seem to last when life is hard and scary; time seems like it lasts forever. This hour will seem like an eternity to those persecuted and killed in this unnecessary sacrifice. In this dire hour of world wars, chemical weapons, tsunamis, earthquakes, and viruses, humanity's consciousness, bombarded with the finiteness of time, falls under the flood of fears that sweep the earth. Unfortunately, the two tools at hand, 'religion' and 'science' that could be the light and wisdom of these dark days; are instead at war with each other.

Some scientists use time as a tool to chisel away the credibility of a pre-existent being destined to come according to Enoch. Time and spirituality, inextricably bound together, are so much a part of the religious experience in many different faiths that it seems very strange that science interprets time in such a way as to say a Creator cannot exist within time. Some say a Creator does not exist in a personal relationship with anyone or anything because we live in time. This is not the idea found in Semitic scriptures but in Greek philosophy. The Greek Platonic concept of 'ideas' and the Hebrew concept of 'attribute' both stem from a belief in an 'archetype' force that exists in Time.

Jung believes that while humanity shares basic common thoughts and experiences, these are all bound to the limits of life within time. The unconscious is affected by 'archetypes' that are timeless and from another place outside humanity.

Danah Zohar, physicist and author of Through the Time Barrier describes his 'archetypes',

But the memories and experiences that fill the collective unconscious are of a very special sort- they exist as archetypes or formal patterns of psychic energy that structure the shared sense of meaning for mankind as a whole. (Zohar 108)

These 'archetypes' are not subject to human consciousness; human consciousness is subject to them. Jung taught there really are living 'ideas' that exist outside of time, and every now and then, humans have a personal experience of them. However, the common state of human consciousness, inextricably linked to the impulses, desires, fears, and aspirations of the age in which we are born, cannot easily escape its shape. It is almost impossible to escape the effect of humanity's strong thought patterns and whole countries and nations can be convinced of different realities by appealing to the human sentiment. This is true of great thinkers, orators, and scientists who seek to persuade their society in some way or other.

Timeless Mind

Joel finds that many of the arguments Einstein has against a personal deity have caused the scientific community to reconsider the importance of a Creator that seems so helpless and impotent against the vast parsecs of the Universe. Time is not the determiner of life it is only a measurer of events. Life is in the ingredients of the fallout of the big explosion called Time before there was anything and nothing more behind heaven's door. Humans are more than the atoms, molecules, cells, and organs that make up our body; we occupy space and time, and we are more than the chemical compounds that maintain metabolism and vital energy. Humans are more than the stardust and flesh that clothes the mortal soul; we are free to travel into the past and future with the blink of an eye in the time of a thought. Mind over time is more important than mind over matter.

For Einstein and many others, only the 'real' is substantial to research and explore; this realism blinds them to the value of imagination. Imagination allows the first scientist to question his surrounding environment. It is imagination and intellect that help a doctor perform surgery, and the chemist discovers new chemical compounds for potential pharmaceutical products the public buys. Science definitely provides us with things that are very necessary and valuable in today's modern society. Should scientists be both jury and judge? Einstein oversteps his boundaries when he allows his scientific judgment to sway the public's opinion on the kind of spirituality humans embrace. He has the right to his opinion, but his opinion should not be held up as the ideal in the face of society because of his role as a respected scientist and scholar. Yet his religious outlook and opinion have had a profound impact on the way science views religion. Weizenbaum, author of 'What Are We?' explains it like this,

When we explain personal relationships, we do not use the terminology of electrons, protons, atoms, and molecules but talk about emotions, intellect, and volition. The two aspects do not belong to the same class or category. (101-102)

This is the area of greatest ambiguity, and the problem with the way science and religion relate to one another right now. There are other obvious problems with religion and its recent impact on the world and terrorism, but this is not the result of education but of ignorance of the inner tradition hidden in the scriptures. The way scientists have tried, tested, studied, and formulated theories that are now scientific laws is similar to how the editors and writers of the scriptures transmitted their own laws through observation, trial and error, and real-life experience.

379

Is the current conflict really between scripture and science or is it between ideologists versus ritualistic religious practices in the world? Science is a by-product of the human intellect, like all other human qualities, nothing more and nothing else. Creativity is a result of human intellect and imagination working together. Can intellect (science) and imagination (spirituality) ever really work together? Weizenbaum provides part of the answer, "The parts cannot be confused with the whole and the real cannot be reduced to the observable" (102). This is because there are so many dynamic laws and forces at work in the universe and in our immediate world that we are not even capable of perceiving the multidimensional realities that pervade our very existence. It would be shortsighted to let any particular ideology invade or alter the main tenets of other domains; to do so is to invite the return of chaos.

The new research in quantum mechanics and M-Theory has taught us how intricate our world of multi-dimensions really is, and yet we cannot see the invisible realities with our naked eyes. Superstrings exist, and scientists can prove it mathematically with five different theories finally unified as the theory of 'Everything,' but they still cannot demonstrate 'strings' to the naked eye. Time eludes the naked eye, and it is just barely captured in a clock, but we never doubt its existence. Weizenbaum comments on self-awareness,

In self-awareness, we realize that we are both the subject (the thinker) and object (what is being thought about): not only the responder to sensations but the interpreter and organizer of such an experience. (103)

We alone do not possess the capacity to reflect on our own Being-ness, sense of morality, relationship, or communication with life. Einstein argues that humans worship their Creator through altruistic acts and that, eventually, self-actualization may help a person to seem religious. Psychologists do not believe humans are moral because of religion per se, but at some point, they experience a sense of ethical maturity that can lead to positive personal development that can help foster healthy communities. Community is closely associated with scripture, but it is not supposed to take the place of scripture. Spirituality is not just about community, worship, religious practice, or personal salvation. It is a process of evolution in the same way that material substances change with time. Humanity's self-awareness also changes with time and never remains the same; no one is ever the same person from year to year.

Even the values of society change with new events and conflicts, nothing seems to be permanent about morality except when it suits a purpose or serves as propaganda. However, morality and compassion are the very fabric of spirituality and the goal of most religions in theory. Everything about community is very personal; how can thinking skeptical humans really relate to an impersonal Deity that must be appeased through prayer and mortification? This is exactly what Einstein suggests when he argues for abandoning any idea of a Personal Creator. Weizenbaum points out a very important fact about the significant difference between a spiritual and scientific viewpoint when he writes,

The atoms that make up our bodies continually change over the years but the arrangement of them remains the same. The continuity of identity is not in the atoms themselves, which the physicist studies, but in the pattern. (103)

Joel thinks his theory of identity and pattern is an actual scientific law intrinsic to how we view reality. Thoughts are like atoms and once an idea is considered, a concept forms, just as molecules combine into organs. The concept itself is a pattern of the idea. Realism and nominalism are conceptualization as an object, and its reflection is two sides in a mirror. The mind's ability to grasp reality through an image or concept is innate to human nature, just as the five senses filter data from the

381

physical environment, translating it into data the brain can read. The ability to visualize ideas is invaluable for productive creativity. Unfortunately, these are things science cannot measure, weigh, and label, so they become suspect, and like the pattern of the atoms, they, too, are eventually ignored and finally not seen.

Existential Science

Images, concepts, patterns, words, and communication are the building blocks or atoms of human consciousness and conceptualization. According to Einstein, "It is the attempt at the posterior reconstruction of existence by the process of conceptualization" (Essays In Science & Religion 1). Joel becomes very curious about Einstein's premise that science is based on the 'after' or the result of the 'big bang,' for science knows very little about before the 'big bang' directly, but it is advancing every day. The creation, according to the author of Genesis, is an afterthought, or an event that takes place 'after'; for example, the Hebrew term 'hayah' is the past tense of the infinitive 'to be.' Both science and religion acknowledge creation to be an unfolding of its Beginning…. into an "after". This is just one agreement between science and religion; there are many others, but for the way that some scientists interpret the facts.

For Einstein, doing 'good science' means using systematic thought to classify the material world of nature in order to identify, examine, and understand its various parts. Einstein's above statement indicates a pattern of his scientific thought; it is up to the reader to discern its import and intent. The word 'posterior' means 'coming after,' later in time, later in origin, and simply 'behind.' The word 'reconstruction' means being 'made again', or renewed in Webster's dictionary. Interestingly, the word 'existence' has the implied meaning of a 'continued – repeated manifestation or actual occurrence where actual implies 'spiritual' or 'material', organic or non-organic sustained growth. Similarly, Einstein seeks to renew or reconstruct existence by examining what happened 'after', since the time before time. He intended to use the traces of ancient cosmic quarks, stardust, and the spins of electrons to determine the path of space and time but neglected to find the invisible 'ether' so many sought in the early nineteenth century.

Now we know that zero-point energy does exist. The need to go back in time to discover the origin of the Universe is inevitable. Humanity has to come face to face with the Face of the Universe. The Universals are to Science as the Torah is to Moses, and yet the two ultimately meet in humanity. Universals exist in our minds as subjects of discourse or as laws that can aptly describe reality. Realists believe that the universals exist outside the mind. Conversely, others say, "I Think, Therefore I Am." Then, Conceptualism comes along and states that objects of sense perception are real in their own right. They exist with or without human recognition. Einstein is saying that science is duty-bound to be preoccupied with reality, scientific proofs, and theorems as opposed to idealism, speculation, or 'vain imaginations.' Realists must think and act in the light of things as they are while denying visionary imagination any base in reality. Five 'universals' are literally the very foundation of scientific materialism, race classification, and basic cosmological doctrines.

Genus, species, difference, property, and accidents typically categorize and classify the various forms of life, but they are terms philosophers, and some theologians use to describe what we call 'existence.' Both camps agree that things have a birth, race, sort, class, order, shape, and form and that there are noticeable variations among species. This, too, is in agreement with most biblical cosmological themes. However, there is a major flaw; Einstein believes time contains everything, including the Supreme Being. In the Semitic view, time is a created thing and will have an end; therefore, even it cannot contain the Supreme Being. This is the ancient argument that provoked the early Christian communities to conflict regarding the divine humanity of the Messiah; many found it impossible to understand how the Logos/Dabar/Memra, something that is outside of time and space, manifests in time and history as the Son of Yahweh.

Mind out of Time

For Jung, the 'archetypes' exist outside of time, yet inside the human psyche, they are able to elicit powers of precognition, clairvoyance, and, most importantly, awareness. Nevertheless, prophecy comes from the Holy Spirit and derives from Eternity. Zohar's research on ESP, Physics, and Precognition has opened new pathways in how science and religion view these 'supernatural' powers latent in human consciousness. She defines Jung's position,

At those moments when we possess these faculties, we are experiencing, he says, not the perception of events in the outer world of objects arrayed in the fiction of space and time; rather, we are in touch with something deep inside ourselves. (Zohar 108)

The 'archetypes' are personally experienced even though they lay outside of time if we learn how to awaken our inner selves. This is how eternity comes into time through our consciousness.

Due to Einstein's personal ethos, he must subject the study of religion to the scientific criticism characteristic of his era. He must find a way to explain how the Creator can fit in his own personal concept of time, a concept supposedly proven by mathematics, logic, and human ingenuity. He makes very sweeping, generalized statements about thousands of years of historical events and documentation compiled during the growth and evolution of the scriptures. He belittles the enigma of time and the creation. In Einstein & the Transcendent God, he admits his perplexity about the systematic process of various religious doctrines. He writes, "I can never under any circumstances bring together, even to a slight extent, the thoughts of all those who have given this question serious consideration". At first, Joel thought he meant religious practices in general and various religious factions and parties that battle one another over ideas and beliefs. Eventually, he comes to realize that Einstein may be condemning various religious doctrines of time and eternity that continued to be subjects of debate among theologians and philosophers.

Perhaps Einstein and other scientists who accept certain aspects of reality wanted to find some underlying logic or order of development among the many religious controversies and conflicts that occur when different belief systems mingle. He is not able to find the same safety nets he has used in science, i.e., tests and theories that are tangible and real. Things measured, weighed, and labeled appear more absolute and/or authoritative and practical. Einstein's own need to explain the order and a grand unified theory of the four forces of the universe forced him to reject a personal Creator. Following Einstein's theory, time itself is relative to subjective experience. Psychologists tell us our own perception is as real as individuality is in our own mind, but Joel realizes the Creator is not an object that exists due to our conceptualization or perception.

The universals describe the creation or evolution of nature, not the nature or essence of Elohim. The universal substance is not dependent on the life it sustains to sustain itself. The innate essence or nature of Elohim does not change by any material phenomena. Paul Tillich agrees:

The concept of a 'Personal God,' interfering with natural events, or being "an independent cause of natural events, makes God a natural object beside others, an object among objects, a being among beings, maybe the highest, but

385

nevertheless a being. This, indeed, is the destruction, not only of the physical system but even more the destruction of any meaningful idea of God. (Tillich A Discussion with Einstein)

Besides 'Time,' the other constant conflict between science and religion involves the personal aspect of the relation between Elohim and the creation. As long as science denies possibility beyond the yardsticks of its measurement, it also denies its ultimate purpose- to know the immeasurable. Einstein categorizes worshippers according to religious practice, the ability to transcend self and ego, and the extent altruism is a purpose and goal. Is this all there is to religion; is it only a substitute for psychological morality in an amoral society? Einstein thinks so; he writes,

For science can only ascertain what is, but not what should be, and outside of its domain, value judgments of all kinds remain necessary. Religion, on the other hand, deals only with evaluations of human thought and action; it cannot justifiably speak of facts and relationships between facts. (Essays 1)

Joel notices how he subjugates any personal aspect of Elohim to impersonal and incomplete classification based on scientific philosophy. Joel thinks, "This is ironic when science claims to study the 'what is' in contradistinction to the 'what should be.' They seem to be telling us what we should believe, not how to use science to discover all possibilities of reality. Nevertheless, his views are both enlightening and condescending. Still, he does make a useful observation concerning his perceived role of religion in this statement, "But science can only be created by those who are thoroughly imbued with the aspiration toward truth and understanding. This source of feeling, however, springs from the sphere of religion." Joel feels that Einstein's statement about being "imbued with the aspiration" is just another way of describing what the prophets experienced when filled with inspiration; both act from a very deeply personal experience of existence.

386

Yet, Einstein asks the scientific community to give up a "Personal God" in exchange for a static, timeless, impersonal, altruistic self-actualization. This argument, too, is empty. Energy is not dependent upon our self-actualization because the source of energy and life is independent and separate from us through its very nature. However, we can study energy and, to some degree, measure it within our biology and psychology. Negative energy in all its forms is life-threatening, and positive energy in all its manifestations is life-vitalizing.

Paradox of Mystic Lore

Timka and Alexa have a little time to reconnect, ever since they started studying together more often, all kinds of problems plagued all three of them. Joel and his work situation, Timka and her health issues, and Alexa, more aware of things in the world, she feels overwhelmed and cannot sleep at night. Life is a paradox. We live in two realms: one is oblique, lacking depth, angles, and measurements, and the other is straight, obvious, demonstrative, and parallel. "Alex, how are you doing? You look tired," said Timka.

"Yes, I am. It has been hard to sleep lately; I just keep thinking about everything that is happening in the world today, and I can't seem to turn off my internal television. I feel worried and anxious and I never had a problem sleeping before." Timka looks at her eyes and can see that she knows. Alex knows that things are about to change, too; the realization can be overwhelming at first. "Alexa talk to me, or should I just share something on my mind instead?" Alexa said, "Yes, just share something with me. Timka, how are you doing? How are your neck and back? Did you find a different chiropractor?" "No, I wish I did not have to go anywhere; I can alleviate some of the pain with exercise and hot baths, and of course, when I study and write, I feel nothing but lifted up.

The pinched nerves are my biggest problems, but we all have a thorn in the side, right? She smiled, but her eyes showed their sadness.

"Alex, you know how there are a variety of religious practices in the world, and the attempt to classify spiritual experiences distracts scientists from seeing any kind of a system of development in spirituality. Spirituality and Religion are two different things entirely. As religious groups and sects fight one another for supremacy and kill and murder innocent people, surely the "still small Voice" that spoke to the prophets of old is barely audible to them in such a psychological atmosphere. Did you know the very first chapter of Genesis involves a process of classification; each division between day and night further defines an order and goal? The six days of division between light and dark finally rest from motion when they settle in the center of seven. This is not apparent in many modern Christian traditions anymore. Some Christians find themselves in disagreements about its contents and meaning due to a loss of the original Semitic understanding of the text. This is one reason Genesis has become a bulls-eye for the darts of skeptics, both scientific and religious.

Realists deny the reality of anything perceived only by the mind's eye, while a nominalist will argue that things perceived by the mind are real in themselves regardless of human thought. This creates a contradiction for anyone attempting to understand religion as a system. Realism, in the scientific sense, is strictly concerned with reality and material substance, as opposed to idealism and intuition. Some scientists claim to be curious and inquisitive about reality and nature, which is innate to the scientific method. On the other hand, in terms of spiritual introspection or positive idealism appears childish, immature, or gullible. They have no imagination and neglect to wonder at the beauty and mysteriousness of the supernatural world. Does our perception make our spiritual experience real, or are they real on their own?" Alexa says, "Einstein denies that religion can deal with facts and relationships because he cannot see the underlying structure of systems or conclusions of this kind using the five universals. He is stuck in his own theory of perception, as many of us are. His view of religion, based on scientific, psychological theories of altruism, self-realization, and moral perfection, is lacking in sympathy with the true condition of the human consciousness and psyche. Religion may be the method to attain many of these things, but they are not the end or purpose of religion.

Many of us are guilty of imagining a very impersonal reality and that change is solely in the power of the individual to evolve. It is similar to Darwin's theory of the 'fittest' in this respect. Evolutionists see reproduction as the catalyst for a continued or sustained manifestation of living things. However, the scriptures never really claim that the Creator is the sustainer of the physical manifestation of creation." "Right," said Timka. She picks up where Alexa left off, "Instead, the Ruach 'brooding' over the face of the waters in the 'beginning' impregnates the earth with its seeds of light. This image of the process of creation illustrates a sustainer of eternity and the soul through an emanation of energy and Light. Adam is dual in nature, inhabiting both heaven and earth. The biological side of existence is temporal and must use visual and auditory senses to measure its reality. However, one cannot measure imagination and realization within the human personality, a prerequisite so crucial in science; but is missing from their equations."

Alexa replies, "Einstein's theory of the properties of time and how they react differently outside earth's atmosphere in space-time is the subject of Paul Davies' latest book, About Time – Einstein's Unfinished Revolution. He explains theories on time before and since Einstein. He clarifies the issue with this argument,

The core of the debate is the daunting problem of how to build a bridge between God's presumed Eternity on the one hand and the manifest temporality of the physical universe on the other. Can a god who is completely temporal logically relate in any way at all to a changing world, to human time? (Davies 24)

"He, too, points out that even theologians and philosophers do not seem to agree on how it is possible for the Creator to exist both in time and outside time. Timka, do you really think Elohim has revealed the Mystery to us? I do feel different, even though I cannot sleep; that is my body's natural reaction to stress, but my mind and heart fill full and brimming with desire to know more and understand everything there is to know."

A Time of Eternity

Alexa, yes, I think it is possible to understand the Mystery. The Son of Man is the Mystery, and when He is come, we feel the light inside us. The Son of Man is not subject to space, time, or material reality, but through Logos, all these become one in Him.

Two worlds become one inside of us, which is the mystery revealed of how Time can enter Eternity. When the Spirit dwells in flesh, Eternity and Time come together, and an explosion of Wisdom and Understanding is our Big Bang," she said, laughing. Alexa smiled a little at her attempt to be humorous. She replied, "Einstein's theories of relativity, time warps, gravity, and a blending of past, present, and future into one big gob of space-time has had a negative impact on the fragile relationship between science and religion. Davies further points out that because of Einstein's ideas, many scientists are convinced there has to be a beginning, "If time is flexible and mutable, as Einstein demonstrated, then it is possible for time to come into existence – and also to pass away again, there can be a beginning and an end to time" (17).

Paradoxically, Davies refers to the "origin of time" as the "Big Bang". Time, the mainstay of Judaic-Christian doctrine whose foundation is based on historical validation, is an alternate instrument that science implements in its quest to disavow a spiritual reality based on Truth. Time was once the tool of the ancient prophets' attempt to maintain order in civilization, planting and harvesting, and to recount significant pre-historical spiritual events unfolding within human history."

Timka does not feel her headache or back pain anymore; once she gets started and her thoughts shake off the darkness, there is no more awareness of all the earthly troubles she wakes up to each day. "Alex, according to the Semitic view, Time moves forward in a linear progression towards a definite purpose, as opposed to the cyclic revolutions of nature religions that attribute growth to seasons, instead of a spiritual creation... However, for Einstein and some Quantum mechanics theories, time is not quite so predictable or determined; instead of past, present, and future moving into the other, Einstein says there is no past or future in real space-time. The future remains denied; they do not believe it exists until events occur in time. This is entirely opposed to the spiritual reality of Time and Eternity. Does this necessarily negate all the Wisdom of the ancients? No! Perhaps we really experience three types of time.

There is the time of infinity that exists in a 'heavenly place', the time of conscience that can think, perceive, and reason about the limitation of life, and the time of measurement that we try to capture in clocks. Time consists of a past, present, and future because that is how we perceive the passage of time on earth. It is all about the state of the physical creation, not in general or absolute poles. The physical condition is

391

temporary, not permanent – only invisible Eternal things, according to the Greeks, are infinite." Alexa says, "They really show they do not understand basic ancient principles. Gravity binds us to Earth, and our view of time segments our perception of past, present, and future; they have a misconception of how time actually behaves outside the realm of Earth. For example, even the Heisenberg Theory of scientific perception vs. creative potential beyond individual perception is very valuable in pointing out this little-understood principle. We are only as good in our estimation as to what we already know. If there is something you do not know, your estimation will not be accurate. Science, blocked by its own perception of what is true, remains disconnected from a larger context it is not aware of and is impervious to learning it 'all'. However, this does not mean that time is only experienced as past, present, or future." Timka agrees with Einstein that Time has no linear progression, but she can also see that from a historical perspective, time can be broken into different parts. She replies, "According to Zohar's study,

If all events are looked at within the framework of General Relativity, they become timeless phenomena in four-dimensional space-time, stretched out along the curved contour of our spherical existence as a static, changeless whole. Such a picture implies that everything that ever 'will be' now 'is,' i.e., that the future is already written and is as fixed as the past. (Zohar 118)

For the prophets to experience, the presence of the Creator is to transcend historical time by remaining in the now or the present within the center of being. This is what many mystical schools both Western and Eastern, base their most fundamental principles upon; the ability to escape time and experience the reality of Wisdom and Understanding of spiritual reality is very ancient." Alexa says, "Perhaps the 'immeasurable' enters into historical time whenever humans perceive or realize the moments of eternity in their daily lives. Is traveling at the speed of light the only way to make time stand still? Maybe not; we have been able to transcend time conceptually, whenever we are not bound to material or artificial events and principles, nor driven to future despair about possible 'accidents' or incidents of life that may never occur."

Consciousness Lives in the Past

Alexa can feel her mind relaxing; she really does enjoy studying and sharing ideas with Timka, and it takes her away from feeling helpless and vulnerable. It is ironic, actually; Timka initially suffered panic attacks. She replies to her friend, "When learning to live in the 'now' and really experience the 'now' becomes a main goal in our life, this might be the whole 'point' and importance of understanding singularity. Do you get it, Timka – the point of everything?" she said, laughing. Timka laughs and continues ministering, "Many of the verbs and terms for creation (bara) in the book of Genesis all refer to a past event, such as "It was good," "It was made"; perhaps life, as we know it (in a limited state), is merely an afterthought or reflection of the eternal now. The English name Eve does not accurately reflect the truth of 'havah.' Her name, in Hebrew, is a term indicating 'life' in the past tense. What if eternity is the now and what we think is life is really our own perception of time already lived? 'He Who Is, Was and Shall Be' [Present-Past-Future] may be another way of expressing the reality of time in terms of our own consciousness and being. Time, as measured by scientists, might have nothing whatsoever to do with proving the origin of human life, determining the existence of Elohim, or the age of the earth.

Time is subject and not subject to human consciousness, but in the world of quantum mechanics based on humanism and Cartesian dialectics, it only operates in space-time in the ways scientists calculate and observe the nature of reality."

Alexa says, "Maimonides, in the Guide for the Perplexed, says the problem with time is that it is not fixed:

It is not a fixed property; on the contrary, its true and essential condition is not to remain in the same state for two consecutive moments. This is the source of ignorance about the nature of time. (171)

"He is saying that time is always moving and life alters with its momentum, and it seems as though time, itself, is the great determiner of events, but this is an illusion. Maimonides explains that: "we consider time a thing created; it comes into existence in the same manner as other accidents" (171); it is actually a part of the creation, not a separate phenomenon. In contrast to what Einstein thinks, Maimonides thinks the Creator did not create the Universe in time. He says,

"For this reason, viz., because time belongs to the things created, it cannot be said that God produced the Universe in the beginning" (171);"

Timka replies, "In the Sefer Yetzirah, the mysterious author says the 'Beginning' is a symbolic term for Chockmah that indicates the divine attribute called 'Wisdom.' If we consider that 'in the Beginning' does not necessarily refer to the creation of the Universe and earth, there is no incongruity. The first sefirot is the force that emanates the 'beginning' reverberation of energy through the lower attributes. As stated in the 'beginning,' Elohim created 'Wisdom,' and all things concerning the nature of the Universe and humanity are contained therein. Chockmah, or Wisdom, is the womb, and Binah, or Understanding, is the seed that comes to fruition through the portals of time. As we comprehend invisible things through scientific concepts, we manifest the destiny of time.

The Son of Man ascending and descending through realms or heavens in order to accomplish a specific purpose demonstrates the principle of transfiguration. This is the main theme found in all this literature, and the message seems to be that humans must continue to evolve and develop through a series of historical events that determine and form their consciousness."

The latest scientific research demonstrates a new explanation of how other dimensions exist that agree with the ancient concept of a multi-structured Universe. Quantum mechanics shows that the Universe is composed of many dimensions; these multilayered planes exist in the past, present, and future all at once. The prophets of old knew this and often referred to the Creator as 'He Who Was, He Who Is, and He Who Will Be'. Is the three-dimensional life we experience proof that our Universe contains the past and the future? Then perhaps we occupy the presence as our 'now' outside of eternity in the 'big bang' known in M-Theory as the eleventh dimension.

This may explain why ancient Gnostics were extremely interested in their 'origins' and destiny. Somehow, those who possess knowledge of the 'beginning' find the 'ending' and are transformed into angelic beings in the 'eighth sphere' where there is freedom from the chaos of the seven lower spheres. Plato wrote about the Ideo or world of Ideas, this higher type of consciousness known in Jewish literature as 'Mahashavah' (Pure Thought) that we can only enter through meditation. Just a thought about the mysteries of the Universe can lighten our higher consciousness as a light bulb lights up a dark room."

When Time Becomes Myth

Timka is emanating with the glow of Wisdom. She has found her niche and stands strong in what she knows are real demonstrations of a different reality based on perception. She explains to Alexa that recent research shows time actually expands in three vectors, as if a cone shaped cylinder determines how it flows within paths infinitely in different directions. Instead of just the x and y axis, there is a third 'z' axis that projects the present in a different direction. "Before the beginning of time, there was no past, present or future; this casts a new meaning on Isaiah and Paul's declaration regarding 'Today' and how to respond to the ancient Voice of יהוה. There will come a point in the development of time when there is no more 'Today'; the distinction will not be necessary. So, if you can hear the still small Voice, even 'Today,' you will be able to escape the confines of space and time and travel to the Kingdom. Scientists believe that after the Big Bang, time divided itself, and the emergence of material substances and forms were able to come into existence. Time is the 'limiter' that measures out events already written in Eternity. Ancient prophecies are like glimpses from the Day of Eternity, shown to Hebrew prophets for the express purpose of having them recorded for our benefit. When the prophecies unfold, and we understand the significant historical events, then eternity enters time.

It is this realization that gives credence to the concept that there is an angelic history hidden from modern society. We are the processors who must weigh and analyze the duality of the data our senses receive on a daily basis. We are, in the end, the scientists of ourselves as we peer out into the vast expansion of the spiritual Universe. The ancient texts of Judaism, Gnosticism, and Nag Hammadi portray a cosmic battle of immense proportions that not only takes place on the earth but also in the heavens, and it enters the realm of human thought through the conflicts that occur on earth during the tribulation period. Some particles have a very short spin life, and new research indicates how spin angle determines the life span of atoms. New angels or messengers (programs) that compel the creation written within a mega second of one of our thoughts are constantly renewing the world. All of this is nonsense based on mechanical scientific notions. Some mystics claim that after meditation on the spiritual structure or macrocosm reality behind the physical world, the soul leaves earth-time, and when it returns to earth, it seems that only moments have elapsed. This concept is demonstrated in the movie Contact, based on an astronomer in a space capsule.

For what seemed like a few minutes to observers, actually, she experienced a longer sense of time; and was somewhere else during an experience of alternate reality. Our personal consciousness does allow each of us to experience time differently. Not only are there different time zones, but there are time dimensions that intersect at right angles, forming the past, present, and future. The authentic spiritual experience allows one to transcend time. In the realm of Eternity, where gravity has no power and time has no depth, there are no boundaries or limits, only freedom and expansion. A person does not have to escape the physical gravity of the earth in order to escape time; one has only to escape ignorance. True Gnosis is an understanding of how nature and reality truly exist, but we have to find its realization in the realms of science and spirituality. The battle of Time and Eternity has to be reconciled through humanity's expanded spiritual consciousness."

Is the Universe Conscious?

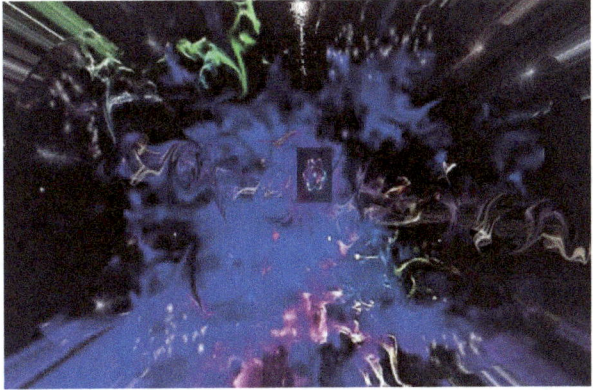

Figure 45 Rays of Light

397

It is through consciousness that the life of the universe can be studied, and consciousness makes the most intimate contact with nature by the sense of vision. It is normally through the small range of electromagnetic waves known as the visible spectrum that we make this contact. (Sutcliffe 13)

"Alexa let me show you what Sutcliffe thinks about the electromagnetic spectrum as a mere "ribbon" compared to the range of waves we see! There is so much more to the reality of the Universe; it takes many perspectives to see the multi-dimensional reality of this magnificent Kosmos. He asks us a very important question, "Why should not consciousness be able to contact this wider range?" (13). Sutcliffe tells us in The New Astronomy and Cosmic Physiology that the universe is an organic whole that sustains life through a circulatory process that unites every atom, molecule, cell, and planet together. His early studies in physics and Eastern philosophy demonstrate that every atom has a duplicate in the sun and that there is a stream of energy flowing in both directions from them. The irony is that he wrote the book in the early nineteenth century before all the scientific advances in physics had begun. He believed DeBroglie and other physicists of the time already knew "that such rays, or lines of force, consist of a sheath and a core, the velocity of the core being in general greater than the sheath" (24). Now, this may shed light on our previous discussions, and it may be evidence that early physicists recognized 'superstrings' way before the recent Superstring revolution! What do you think about that? Check out this illustration from the Cambridge University Physics website that demonstrates a visual representation of a string interconnecting with itself.

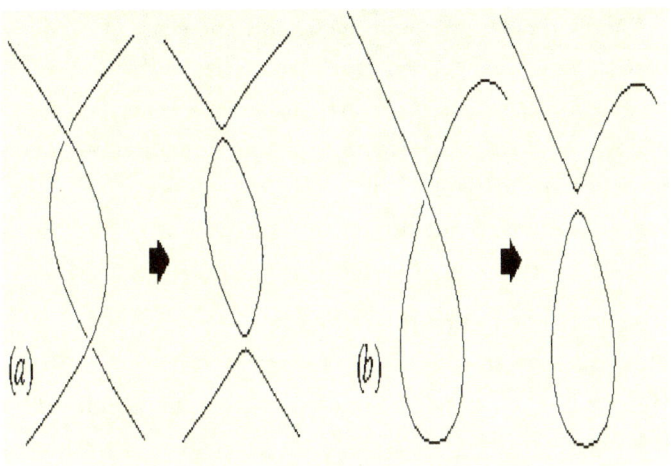

Figure 46 Illustration of Strings Movement

In String Theory, the myriad of particle types is replaced by a single fundamental building block, a 'string'. These strings can be closed, like loops, or open, like a hair. As the string moves through time it traces out a tube or a sheet, according to whether it is closed or open. (Cambridge Relativity: Quantum Gravity P1)

"In Sefer Yetzirah, the attributes are living 'realms' that interact with each other in a number of ways. The elusive Da'ath, sometimes hidden and sometimes seen, caused the injunction that there are ten sefiroth, no more and no less, and ancient scientists bound by this law understood its importance for envisioning a genuine view of the structure of the Universe. Similarly, these 'superstrings' hidden from our immediate view are the very foundation of our Universe. Big Bang theorists maintain the further back in space we go the hotter it gets, so hot that matter is no longer in the form of matter. Cambridge Cosmologists state,

With increasing temperature, we see a succession of phase transitions for water in which its properties change dramatically: the solid phase – ice melts to the liquid phase – water – and then eventually boils to the gaseous phase – steam.

"Alexa, there is no doubt that energy and elements undergo three states of change, and as we saw earlier in the discussion, the dynamic law of energy conservation is an important factor in how the creation, formation, and action of the material earth occurred. The earth was not only 'created'. It was also 'formed' and then finally 'made.' The author of the article points out an important fact to note,"

You should notice that steam is 'more symmetric' than water, which is, in turn, more symmetric than ice. And so it is with matter in our Universe; it begins in a unified or 'symmetric' phase and then passes through a succession of phase transitions. (Cambridge Phase Transitions in the Early Universe p1).

Alexa gets excited now. "Wow, she says, "The evolution and devolution of energy parallel the divine energy that 'emanates' the Kingdom in gradual stages of development that coincide with our ability to grasp and comprehend hidden esoteric 'gnosis' from 'ungnosis.' A hidden world of celestial mechanics runs parallel to our own terrestrial world yet remains unseen through normal sensory channels, just as the different dimensions of Superstring theory are also hidden from our senses. There appears to be a sequence of steps that lead to a series of events that culminate in a product.

Sutcliffe also grappled with this idea:

Matter, which appears to us as the very embodiment of continuous existence, is not so in reality, but that each atom of which it is composed is a phase in a cycle of changes. In another phase of the cycle, it is a light wave or some other form of electromagnetic wave. (33)

Timka interjects, "Amazingly, this is precisely what M-Theory also predicts because physicists know strings change from an electron to a graviton through frequency fluctuations. It seems that metaphysical ideas have finally found their place in modern physics. The model of divine 'attributes' found in the Tree of Life can be seen as different waves in the electromagnetic spectrum. The things that are physically observable in the Universe are part of a pattern of an invisible spiritual world that really maintains the 'Kosmos' as we know it. Sutcliffe examines the relationship between the contraction and phase transitions. He writes,"

In fact, these cyclic transformations may be regarded as the causes of the contracting and expanding spheres, each electromagnetic vibration being a beat of the atomic heart, which keeps in circulation the cosmic lifeblood. (63)

She continues speaking, and her voice grows louder; she hears the roaring of the waves and feels the warm oil pouring down upon her head with every word. "The cosmic life of the living Universe sustained through an expansion/contraction process; manifest and creates the various electromagnetic waves on earth. The 'attributes' or 'sefiroth' have a positive and negative aspect that opens or closes each sefirah. Each 'sefirah' empties itself into the 'sefirah' below it. This cycle then repeats itself in an upward motion, thus causing an exchange of energy and motion. Beyond a doubt, there is more than one way to understand evolution and devolution in science and religion. Although the two cannot occupy the same space or place without proper preparation, this should not prevent the attempt to understand one field from another field's point of view. Science should not try to influence public opinion and religion should not continue to go unexamined by critical scholarship. The two must become like two forces. When one expands, the other contracts, and when the other contracts, the first continue to expand.

"Blessed is he who is before he came into being. For he who is, both was and shall be. The highness of man is not revealed but is in secret."

"What is the importance of the above verse in relation to our discussion? The Timeless Kingdom is here right now but covered in mysteries of human ignorance. Some of the mysteries flee when we understand what they are through the Wisdom Science; Knowledge is power in the world. This is why so much is kept secret on purpose. The Greek term 'Pneumatikon' used so often in Paul's epistles denotes all realms of spiritual activity on earth and heaven, but how these various realms cooperate and exist together is what we lost sight of when we forgot our 'origins' in the higher dimension Paul explored."

Cosmic Body of High Places

Alexa likes this topic, "Paul envisions the new spiritual creation of the second Adam as something that restores a lost pristine awareness. He claims these are things that cannot be uttered with tongues of flesh or imagined by mortal consciousness hidden inside a spiritual conscience; the 'gnosis' has to evolve to the earthly copy of 'paradise' located within our own thoughts. The true perception that projects our consciousness into the Kingdom lies hidden in our ability to 'love' Truth and Wisdom and then Shalom peace of completeness must follow. At the time Paul wrote this, the Kingdom had just begun. Many still stand now in reality without consciously knowing how or why. A central Kingdom theme involves ancient patriarchs, matriarchs, prophets, and saints falling asleep in the Messiah, who are destined to rise with the elect of the tribulation period. Only those who have received the 'pneuma' Paul writes about will have the supernatural power to withstand the oppression of the 'archons,' 'powers', and 'principalities' that rule over the corporeal world.

The spiritual person is one who walks by the 'spirit/pneuma,' which is considered a 'supernatural' consciousness, as opposed to the physical person who walks by the 'flesh' of mortal consciousness. Paul says our true divine purpose hides from us not only in time but also in our carnal egotistic nature. Destined events only happen when it is the 'correct time', and those who possess knowledge of the true calendar know how to calculate heavenly time. Angelic prehistory, [prophecies] are actually benchmarks in time designed by our spiritual ancestors to point out the true 'time'. Supernatural power is our heritage, but the power hides from our consciousness; the 'way' to awaken it comes from visionary activity according to 'holy men' of the ancient world." Timka joins in, "A certain kind of 'gnosis' is integral to the visionary process; many ancient scientists were engulfed in foreign Gnostic and Hermetic ideas based on ascent and transformation. When Greek stoicism met Hebrew visionaries, many of the Hebraic apocalyptic ideas were engulfed in a sea of mystery rites and sacraments that have nothing in common with the 'Adam of Light' figure." "Yes, said Alexa, "I agree Judaic, Hermetic, and Gnostic sources agree that knowledge is important, but they seem to disagree on many other things. This is a problem not with spiritual texts but with interpretations. I think this is why Einstein and others view religious fringe groups as not finding agreement. Even though the biblical concept of transformation first developed in Exodus when Moses and many others witnessed an 'appearance' on Mt. Sinai, there is very little mention of it in traditional orthodox circles of Western Christianity. John J. Collins mentions this in A Throne in the Heavens,"

A description of a heavenly ascent in the Hebrew Bible is in the Sinai narrative in Exodus 24. There Moses, Aaron, Nadab, Abihu, and the seventy elders 'went up, and they saw the God of Israel. Under his feet, there was something like a pavement of sapphire stone. (45)

Timka says, "Yes, right, only a few saw this mysterious 'Body'. What kind of 'body' they see is the key to understanding this cryptic verse. Was it a human body, an angelic body, or a pattern, maybe even a plan? The 'Body of Measure' known as the Shiur Komah in ancient texts, is a pattern and blueprint that would eventually become the matrix for all Hebrew knowledge. The pattern demonstrates how all divine and earthly things connect with each other and that there is a mode of operation built into each section. Not all knew the operation of the Tabernacle; it was secret information shown to Moses, who recorded it in hidden books." |Remember, Moses receives instructions on how to design and construct a tabernacle that illustrates the order and operation of the divine tabernacle of the universe.

When he is on Mt. Sinai, a cloud surrounds him, and it is there that he witnesses the creation of the tabernacle. The Universe is the penultimate Tabernacle, according to the ancients. Joseph Dan's research confirms this,"

Ancient Jewish mysticism saw the mystical powers of God not only in the celestial realm of the Merkavah but also in the cosmos itself, in its intrinsic structure (305).

Carlos Suarez associates the Tabernacle furnishings and the light of the Menorah with the "Cube of Ayin Soph Aur," a term he coined in his commentary on Sefer Yetsirah (92). He writes,

As it is said in Exodus XI, 24.5, the light was put in the meeting tent: He put the light in the meeting tent, opposite the table, on the southern side of the tabernacle, and lit the lamps in front of YHWH, as he had been ordered. This lamp was of pure gold and made in one piece. It has six branches, three on one side and three on the other, like the six faces of the cube, High-Low, East-West, North-South, in opposite pairs. On each branch were three chalices, corresponding to the three interior axes of the cube; with its four chalices, its buds, and flowers conveyed knowledge. (92)

"This geometrical design theory did not begin in Greece but possibly dates back to the time of Moses.

Suarez's most significant point regards the force in the center that emanates outward. He writes,"

There were seven lamps: six corresponding to the six faces of the cube and the 7th corresponding to the 4th Sephira, Esch Memaim, or as the inner light, to the 1st (92).

Alexa replies in a thunderous voice, "The heart of the physical body also serves as light and a source of heat, similar to the way the menorah functioned in the tabernacle and the Sun functions in the Universe. The Tabernacle, Temple, and Merkavah/Chariot are terms that describe three-tiered structures that depend on each other to operate effectively; an example is the human body, a structure that relies on each of its nine biological systems to survive. The image of the physical body, held in high esteem in Hebrew literature, found enemies in some Gnostic authors who wrote so furiously against the flesh that it eventually had a negative impact on how Christian doctrine deals with issues of the flesh. Another important thing to remember is that there is reason to believe that the Universe is a kind of 'Body', a living Being, that is manifesting itself as a system of cosmic physiological processes." Timka says, "Remember, Sutcliffe's theory in The New Astronomy and Cosmic Physiology is that the Universe is an organic whole that sustains life through a circulatory process that unites every atom, molecule, cell, and planet together. He writes,

The atom is not the physical unit; it is the terminus of a line of force, the other terminus being in the body of the sun. The real physical unit is these two termini with the line of force between them. (23)

"Here, Sutcliffe explains the interchange of energy between strings binds the atom to its corresponding atom in the sun.

He was convinced all atoms have a duplicate atom in the sun that constantly exchanges energy in both directions (23); he considers the process a 'completed circuit' that acts like a cable across the galaxy." These lines of force are the veins and arteries for the flowing life of Nature and constitute the basis of Cosmic Physiology. (25)

"Keep in mind that Sutcliffe was writing at a time when very little was known of Eastern philosophy in the Western hemisphere, and his ideas were not readily received in the early nineteenth century. The revolutionary concept of how the Divine immanence flows throughout the material universe, filling it with life, was ahead of its time. The Universe, in his estimation, is actually a living Being. He proves what the mystics have always said, that we live, move, and have our being within it, and it lives within us. Sutcliffe says, "The ocean of space is swallowing the drop, but the drop is also swallowing the ocean of space" (38). This sounds similar to the Pauline motif that the Creator is in everything, and everything is in the Creator. Sutcliffe was not even vaguely aware of the Superstring theory, yet he seems to have written about 'strings' as he describes 'cables' extending across the galaxy. The Universe is a living three-dimensional 'Body' in the material world but ten-dimensional in the spiritual world. How it exists outside of time and within time is a great 'Mystery! The two concepts of 'Body' speculated in the Shiur Qomah texts and associated with the figure known as Angel of יהוי are not always accepted by mainstream Judaism, even though the books of Moses related these accounts directly. Speculation on the dimensions of the 'Body' found mainly in fringe groups that practiced Merkavah mysticism in secret, oozed into Hermetic Gnostic texts and twisted and contoured to suit each one's own point of view. This is the dynamics of religion and philosophy batting heads with mythology. Anthropomorphic concepts often troubled orthodox circles, even though the idea flourished among many different mystical groups. Joel Rosenberg wrote about this in "Biblical Traditions: Literature and Spirit in Ancient Israel,"

In what was very likely a Gnostic turn of thought, rabbinic interpreters likened the commandments of the Torah to the limbs and sinews of the human body (Mak. 23b). (86)

"Both Gnostics and Merkavah mystics developed systems of knowledge regarding the various limbs and names of the 'Body'; many knew how this 'gnosis' could induce an ascent experience. Cohen found evidence of this doctrine in II Enoch Ch. 13, where Enoch describes a visionary process that results in his own transformation. First, he sees the "measure of the body, with no measure, similar to nothing and without boundary" (Cohen Shiur Qomah 80). He later sees how matter transforms back into raw energy. Without form and boundaries in place, things of the 'created' realm cannot exist in the material world. Material things contain light through electromagnetic light propagation. We are riding on a wave of light! If we fail to realize this important symbolical interpretation of (form/boundary) in this context, the hidden Kingdom will remain hidden from our consciousness.

Merkavah mystics describe a feeling of burning eyes coupled with a sensation of 'knowing' receiving data, images, concepts, voices, sounds, and colors floods their mind. Words on the printed page begin to grow bigger and seem to vibrate and move as strings of sentences. There is much more to the invisible and visible worlds than is perceived because not everyone perceives things in the same way; it is almost 10 billion to 1 odds that someone will be able to experience these things unless they find that special arrangement of sephiroth which is the key."

Our Universe a Mirror of Light

*Figure 47 – As Above So Below – Hall Secret
Teachings of All Ages*

Joel is intrigued by what happened to Ezekiel, who saw the Merkavah Chariot reflected in the waters of the river Kebar; he was also looking at the reflected sky in the river. The Universe is like a giant mirror that reflects the invisible world to the visible world. Words reflect invisible data into our thoughts, and thoughts can reflect our moods and emotions to others. The human brain, under stress, does not perform the same way; the body will demonstrate the effects of stress on the brain. Therefore, we can see a cause and effect in simple things; we can study the Universe now that astronomers have the means to take pictures of the past. The elect reflects a positive force of consciousness into the cosmic abyss of shapeless things as they assist in the re-creation of the Universe.

Even though Metatron, the pre-historic (Son of Man), is described as the Teacher and guide of Moses, he was also thought to be the Angel who prepared the way as a pillar of fire by night and a cloud by day. This Angel leads Adam/Eve back into the Garden of divine Consciousness, where true being only exists in the originality of things. Language and the origin of words can reveal hidden truths about changes in meaning and associations; when one language is transliterated incorrectly, it affects time and civilization. The experience of the Merkavah was like skydiving for ancient Hebrew mystics. The ability to transcend time and space without movement is the ultimate secret of the Kingdom. Ascent techniques based on the relationship the mystic has between the 'world above' and the 'world below' were numerous, but this is not the same type of idea found in the Son of Man tradition. Many mystics often reported a feeling of rising and a sensation of moving forward.

Some even actually experience the sensation of falling downwards and going into a deep sleep. A reciprocal relationship exists between the seer and the Merkavah. Joseph Dan describes it in the book, "Re'uyot Yehezel (The Visions of Ezekiel):

Ezekiel saw the divine Chariot reflected in the waters of the river Kvar; he was looking at the reflected sky in the river. (291)

Joel realized that ancient mystics, philosophers, and scientists envision the Universe as a giant mirror that reflects the invisible world to the visible world. An invisible reality that we can only see through another medium, such as parable, analogy, or metaphor, is common in Judaic, Hermetic, and Gnostic traditions. Dan says each Chariot proceeds from another Chariot until it reaches the tenth hall or heaven. He can see that four sets of wheels animate the Chariot, each bearing the face of an Eagle, Lion, Ox, and Man; each wheel represents a process of creativity. The four worlds are inside of us all, but since we lost 'Glory,' the connection between the worlds is gone. Now, we live in a dimension below the higher dimensions. Our gravitons have a different weight than gravitons of other dimensions. This means that discovering the hidden laws of gravity is the key quantum physicists now strive to find.

He experienced another 'reality' out of our reach in the 'heights' that Paul calls the Third Heaven. The Ophites left traces of this in an ancient diagram found in Kurt Rudolph's infamous work, Gnosis. The 'other world' exists in the center of the 'Glory' Kabod and those who are able to visit there bring it down to earth. The 'Glory' resides in the 'in-between world' where history has already closed, the spiritual Kingdom is fully operative, and the war is over. Ancient Merkavah mystics thought the only way to repair the breach was through vigorous ascetic rituals, purification rites, and constant Torah study. Others are beginning to realize that whoever can master concepts about invisible principles and how they operate in the visible world can also have an experience of what she or he learns. Dan says,

The reader of the biblical book may learn from the text that God has a neck, hands, and feet, but the Shi'ur Qomah explains that his hands are not like human hands. (296)

Cohen writes,

The single most characteristic feature of the Shi'ur Qomah is the description of the divine body and the revelation of the names and dimensions of the limbs and some of the internal organs of the Deity. (99)

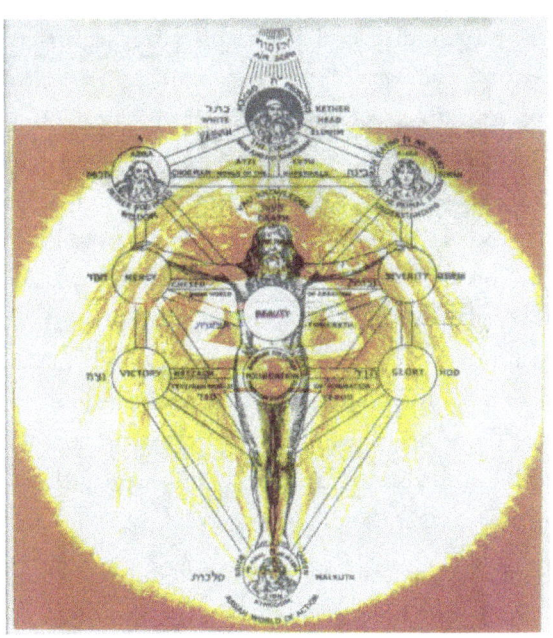

Figure 48 Chariot Tree

Joel examines the various 'limbs' and learns how they function individually; it is important to know they can only operate together as one unit. A central motif throughout this literature is the unity within the multiplicity of names, concepts, and processes; the one object is the One – the many reflect the functions and powers of emanation and radiation of Aether in the world. This is behind all the 'mystery' associated with the Kabbalah. It was a given that energy is a real phenomenon. There was no need to deny the Aether, but instead, some scientists embraced the concept of 'vacuum' to use the same phenomena, but with a different label or name. The 'riders of the Chariot' had to know this information in order to ascend or descend in the Chariot. What is this information? The information consisted of celestial mechanics of emanation theory and the radiation of light waves and particles, of course.

In the first century, many taught that 'hekhals' or 'palaces' were heavens ascended by mortals and descended by angels.

411

Yet, there was another level of interpretation sequestered kept locked away. The heavens were symbolic of the attributes, limbs, or 'sefiroth' according to later Jewish mysticism of the thirteenth century, according to Solomon Gabirol and Isaac ibn Latif. Schaya says, "The heavens are the orderly steps of the 'ladder' which is 'set upon the earth, its top reaching to the (supreme) heaven" (77). According to Leo Schaya, author of The Universal Meaning of the Kabbala, Chariot mystics believe the transformation from human to angel occurs gradually, at the end of a spiritual journey. However, the author of Enoch decides to frame his view of the ten weeks as an apocalypse. In contrast, Dan focuses on angelic folklore and guardians one must show special seals or amulets to pass by.

This journey, including the names of God, the names of the guards and their functions, and the description of the obstacles to be overcome, became the basic description of a mystical experience not only for the Hekhalot literature. (298)

Joel, can see clearly how this is not in accord with what Paul describes regarding the nature of the Son of Man implied in the book of Matthew. Especially in regards to the infamous Chapter 24, whose main theme includes the 'mini' apocalypse at the end of the age, also because Paul says Messiah has the 'dynamis' or power over 'principalities and powers.' Dan points out how this alternate concept of transformation had a great impact on "later Jewish mysticism" and continued to exert its presence throughout the eighteenth century (299). The central motif of the Sefer Hekhalot is the rise/fall and ultimate translation of an ancient biblical figure named Henokh (Enoch), who is taken to heaven to walk with the angels according to Genesis 5:24. His disappearance is elaborated in the Hekhalot literature as a human figure known as Enoch, that later becomes transformed into a 'superhuman' named Metatron. For instance, C.R.A. Morray Jones states in

Transformational Mysticism in the Apocalyptic-Merkavah Tradition,

Metatron is, in fact, referred to as the 'Lesser Tetragrammaton' (YHWH Ha- qaton), and it is said that 'his name is like that of his master' or that he embodies the Name of God. (8)

Joel can see more pieces of the puzzle falling in place through his examination of various doctrines that depict how a human being's nature transforms simultaneously as one learns how to walk back into angelic history. Dan explains how Enoch is the designated human witness to pronounce judgment on the fallen angels. He saw the 'Day' thousands of centuries ago when he was allowed to read the angelic tablets of pre-history. Dan says,

The divine power Anafiel was sent to earth to bring him up to the divine realm to reside there and prove that the harsh decision of God concerning the deluge was justified. (300)

"Hmmm," Joel thinks, "How interesting, that Anafiel is a name derived from a word that means 'branch', and some think this refers to one of the titles assigned with the Son of Man.

If it is, then we can assume the above verse informs us the 'Son of Man' will take us to a 'divine realm' to show how the 'judgment' of the fallen angels is justified. However, Dan says on the way to announce the 'judgment,' something happens, and instead, Enoch undergoes "a process of transformation" as he becomes the angel Metatron (300). Morray Jones confirms this,

There is evidence, then, of the early existence of a tradition concerning the ascent to heaven of an exceptionally righteous man who beholds the visions of the divine Kabod upon the Merkavah and is transformed into an angelic being. (10)

What happens when Enoch sees the vision of the 'Body' that initiates the transformation? According to Sefer Hekhalot,

Enoch's flesh was turned into fire, his dimensions grew until they became full of eyes, a fiery garment was put around him, and he rode a Chariot of fire driven by fiery horses. (300)

These are all ideas reminiscent of the gigantic 'Body' found in the Shi'ur Qomah texts, but the element of fire plays a more important role. Fire is a symbol of the divine presence, and to be clothed in it entails a transformation. The 'eyes' echo the mysterious phrase in Zechariah 3:9,

"For behold the stone that I have laid before Joshua; upon one stone [shall be] seven eyes: behold, I will engrave the graving thereof, says [Yahweh] of hosts, and I will remove the iniquity of that land in one day."

Eyes of the Secret Place

Joel thinks he figured it out because his eyes began to tear a little when he learned certain things. Sometimes, his eyes would grow large as if he had seen something strange, but it was due to something he realized that caused his eyes to change. Joel understands through experience that 'Eyes of Fire' gives us the ability to perceive the Kingdom in various dimensions through an intellectual exchange that also affects emotions, consciousness, and the sockets of human eyes. Keep this in mind as we continue to locate the 'place' Enoch sees during his vision. Many ancient texts found in Egypt, Palestine, and Syria contains descriptions of the pre-historic life of some primordial figure; even though they have their own distinct doctrine, most all agree the figure gradually comes into power of a Kingdom. Dan says in Semitic doctrines, the epitome of transformation is knowledge, "He received divine knowledge; he knew every secret above and below, including the secrets of the process of creation" (301). This knowledge is conveyed to those of the 'plant,' a small inner circle of disciples that contain and distribute the 'secrets' like water becomes the 'anointing oil' that transforms the sons of Adam into the sons of Yahweh. In the Sefer Yetzirah, an anonymous author describes the meaning of the sefiroth. Dan says,

The ten sefirot are the six directions of space (up, down, north, south, east, west), the two directions of time (beginning, end), and a fifth dimension called here 'good' and 'evil'. (303)

The very names and words used to describe the creative world are capable of great things, "The power to create is inherent within the language and, when used in the proper way, can be employed for the purpose of creation" (304). Bereshit is a process of creation that recurs in those people who hear and obey the divine Hebrew terminology found in the scriptures.

In this sense, the transformation is actually a result of an ongoing creative process that began in a distant time. People try to take the Kingdom by stealth, but it is given it cannot be taken. The power of confusion and falsehood used to destroy is just as potent as particular words and thoughts, people abuse each other with, and they become poisonous arrows shot at perceived enemies. The ability to invest positive and constructive power in the spoken word is still beyond the control of most, when negativity is cherished. The Son of Man is our witness to the re-unification of the Creator with the creature. He has the power 'to do' the words, not just speak them. Mark's Gospel describes a supernatural Son of Man who has secret knowledge and powers over nature. These supernatural traits go back to the ancient Primordial Man of Light traditions. Christian and pagan traditions have influenced hermetic and Gnostic ideas of transformation. These traditions deal with issues of knowledge and self-development that can only come from discipline and willpower, according to Greek stoicism. The concept of 'self' is a very large part of the Gnostic and Hermetic traditions. Ascetic purification rites and practices and the reciting of chants were the means of ascent. Gnostic and Hermetic concepts deal with the development of the 'self' in relation to oneself and the social environment. The pagan view (like science) does not accept the possibility of the divine Creator intermingling with the 'fleshly' creature either,

For a pagan thinker, it is unbelievable that, in its perfection, the superior turns itself towards the inferior, the model towards the image. (Filoramo 138)

Joel is amazed that the earliest 'Christians' or Nazarenes (for lack of a more appropriate term) sought an experience and presence of the Creator; it was their form of worship. For Gnostics, the self-defined as consciousness of the ego and selflessness or selfishness represent two options an individual can exercise. In Giovanni Filoramo's "The Transformation of the Inner Self," he states, "The position of the Gnostic and hermetic process of conversion is located between these two extremes" (138). Both sought direct knowledge of 'gnosis'; they saw it as the foundation of the transformation. Filoramo states, "It flows that at the center of the process of the gnosis, we find the transformation of the self" (138). The introspective Gnostic is in search of the ultimate self and tends to become very individualistic in outlook. Filoramo adds, "The Gnostic tradition, like the pagan, ignores a real concept of person" (139), whereas, in Semitic traditions, the person is considered a 'world or universe', and to destroy a person is to destroy a world. The wise and mature believer seeks to lose the self in order to embrace the self of the Creator. The give and take or the up and down entails an evolving and devolving relationship between two parties. Filoramo states that,

Unlike the pagan, the Gnostic and hermetic process of transformation of the self can be described as the outcome of a reciprocal relation between the Supreme God and the hermetic or Gnostic. (142)

The pagan outlook did not include a personal relationship with a force outside one's self. Filoramo describes the 'rituals of transformation' and points out that "As with hermetic regeneration, it is a process which coincides with a vision which, simultaneously, is an illumination" (142). Merkavah mystics describe it as a vision of heavenly things finding their place in the constitution of man. Filoramo explains the Gnostic concept of the Messiah,

In effect, he is the spiritual cause of the birth of a new anthropological reality, the man of light, who will be the result of the process of interior transformation. (143)

Joel feels stronger now after studying and meditating on these ideas. He thinks aloud for the first time in a few weeks since he was laid off, "We are getting closer to finding the actual point of entry, for we know that there was a transformation, which first took place in the Son of Man, and it can ultimately occur in anyone that can see. The vision ultimately leads to a 'gnosis' that transforms its recipient. Filoramo says, "The formation of the new man is an ethic process which prepares and culminates in the intellectual acquisition of gnosis" (143), and this explains how a 'body of immortality' reforms within the inner self. Joel hears the Voice whispering, but it is not as loud as before, "The body of 'immortality' invisible to physical sight can only appear through spiritual insights. This is where the 'seven eyes' come in because it is only through these 'eyes' that your limited eyes can see the various levels of vision. In Hermetic thought, "The vision enables the disciple to be assimilated by what he has seen, that is, the eternal generation of the superior world" (145); in this way, the disciple actually becomes a part of the Universal Self. In Hermetic transformation texts, a figure named 'Hermes' represents the teacher, and 'Tat' is the student, whereas in Gnosticism, the role of the resurrected Messiah is the central theme. Filoramo writes, "The resurrected Christ plays the same role of initiator towards the disciples played by Hermes towards Tat" (146), both traditions reflect a reciprocal

417

relationship. However, Semitic literature does not share the same properties of Gnostic or Hermetic interpretations. It is distinct. The figure Metatron receives eight garments that initiate the transformation,

With these robes, he can now ascend to the supreme places where he will take the two robes of the Ineffable and of the First Mystery. (146)

The goal seems to be the same: escape the 'archons' rule over the seven days of creation, but the terminology of the robes is different. Pistis Sophia is a Gnostic text that contains questions and answers of real seekers and "Aims at revealing the new reality which has been formed in the disciples" (146); these texts function similarly to Hekhalot texts that describe the psychological experience of the practice. Once the disciple receives the 'gnosis,' the initial phase of the transformation begins, but only through understanding the 'vision' can the process mature. Do you understand Joel? The reciprocal relationship of looking through a mirror of concepts enables one to experience a vision, or in Pauline's terms, the 'pneuma' restored to the believer grants life and light to its bearer. This results in the final stage of a process that Filoramo says happens, "As a result of this transmission, a new reality is now acting in him: the man of light" (147). Finally, the recipient is one consisting of male and female, spirit and earth, energy and matter, particle or wave. All terms reflect a duality of forces that are finally reconciled.

Going to the Hidden Place

The Voice continues to lift Joel up; sometimes, it lasts for a few minutes, and other times, it could last for hours. Joel is so happy and comforted to hear it again, and he listens carefully now with full attention. The Voice gets a little louder now as a result. "The Gnostic desires to regain the heavenly part of him or herself. However, in contrast with Hermetic concepts of self-perfection or altruism, Gnostic texts claim the full 'glory' awaits the disciple in the 'eschaton' or new age to come. The term 'eschaton' embodies a dual meaning of 'end days' and 'things to come,' but some Gnostic interpretations differ from Paul's. Many ideas often merged in the ancient Near East when Greek civilization became more and more dominant. Philosophy merged with Biblical principles and began to go on a different path. Joel, remember Paul describes a transition between one stage of physical development and another stage of spiritual maturation. Recent Pauline scholarship reveals the influence of many Enochic concepts and themes regarding the Son of Man. One common theme is that each stage gradually leads into another until the transformation takes place. Claude Tresmontant explains it as a "passing from a natural to a supernatural order" (Tresmontant Saint Paul and the Mystery of Christ 51).

Furthermore, he reiterates, "It is impossible to understand St. Paul unless we look at things from this cosmic standpoint" (51). What is this important cosmic standpoint? In M-Theory, there are phase transitions with varying vibrations that change the nature of strings. Strings and waves are constantly losing one form and gaining another as they sustain the matter of creation. Matter is a natural part of human life as is energy a formless part. Tresmontant sees a pattern and system within Paul's letters. Therefore, he emphatically suggests that it is not possible to understand Paul's ideas out of their peculiar context.

The foundation of Paul's doctrine regarding the transition between the first and second Adam is the peculiar context. For Paul, the first Adam was from the earth, and the second Adam was from heaven. The flesh is essentially natural, not evil, and it was not 'born in sin.' Gnostics such as Manes and Marcion taught, "The flesh is evil; it is the body in which the soul is shut up as in a filthy prison" (55). This type of ideology influenced the development of Western Christianity, and subsequently, the perception of the human body became distorted. Paul speaks about a 'new self' that arrives when the disciple is 'clothed' or created in the image of the Creator. Tresmontant renders Col 3: 9-10 as,

You must be clothed in the new self that is being refitted all the time for closer knowledge so that the image of the God who created it is its pattern (54)

He does this by replacing the correct English rendering of Greek terms according to their cultural context and milieu. Tresmontant's outstanding research suggests that whereas the Gnostics held the 'flesh' or Greek (sarx) as evil, biblical prophets acknowledged the 'flesh' of all living things as intrinsically natural and Tov 'good.' He says, "Once again, in the Bible, the flesh does not signify a part of man; rather, man is flesh" (55). Joel, it is easy to see how the alteration developed in later religious systems. In the Semitic view, "The flesh, then, in the biblical sense, is this biological order, quickened, living and conscious" (52). However, Paul believes the spiritual Adam comes after this Adam of 'flesh' and the spiritual order is 'from heaven', that is, supernatural, and he says it comes 'afterward'" (52). Genesis states the first man is made 'of dust' from the earth. However, "The second mankind, the second Adam, will be of heaven, by a transformation" (52).

Who will participate in the transformation? Is it only for Christians, Jews, or everyone? M. Eugene Boring asserts that Mathias Rissi's research on Paul's epistles suggests,

The whole of mankind will become the body of Christ and for 'the redemption of all creation into God's consummate kingdom', without any indication that there is anything to the contrary in Paul's thought. (Boring The Language of Universal Salvation in Paul 272)

Joel thinks to himself and reflects on everything he hears. "Paul's idea of the transformation always includes the resurrected Son of Man as the Head of a restored, glorified humanity. In The Great Angel, Margaret Barker explains how the 'sons' were associated with the angelic hosts, and the Word/Son was the leader. According to Barker, this same Yahweh figure "Could be manifested on earth in human form, as an angel or in the Davidic King" (3). Now, she points out the identity of the Sons of Yahweh:

All the texts in the Hebrew Bible distinguish clearly between the divine sons of Elohim/Elyon and those human beings who are called Sons of Yahweh. This must be significant. (10)

Barker's remarkable research points out an older tradition within ancient Judaic apocalyptic, esoteric, and mystical texts regarding the identity of the Sons of Elohim that is more informative than the usual Christian doctrine. Segal states,

It seems likely that this enigmatic human appearance of God discussed with appropriate self consciousness in the Bible, is related to the so-called Son of Man. (99)

Another meaning of 'Son of Adam' is simply Ben Adam because the term is Hebrew for 'man', and this may be another indication of the ancient association in Paul's use of the term. Segal asserts,

Yahweh himself, the angel of God, and his Glory (Kabod) are melded together in a peculiar way, which suggests to its readers a deep secret about the ways God manifested himself to humanity (100)

In this interpretation, Segal tells us how the actual appearance of the Kabod becomes an agent of transformation within the Creator and the creation,

His immortality and glorious appearance were something Adam possessed in the Garden of Eden and lost when he sinned. Paul, as we shall see, uses all these traditions to good advantage (100)

Morray Jones contrasts the view of the gospels with Paul's view of the term 'Glory':

Whereas the synoptic tradition speaks of Jesus sitting or standing at the right hand of the Power or the Glory, it is clear that in the Pauline and Johannine literature, Christ is the Glory. As such, he is God's 'image and likeness. (11)

He hears the Voice explaining, "In another ancient text written by Ezekiel the Tragedian, the mysterious figure is called 'light.'.', "The figure on the throne is called 'phos gennaios' which is a double entendre in Greek, since phos can mean either 'light' or 'man' depending on the gender of the noun" (102). Segal points out the importance of 'light' once again and demonstrates important parallels between the Son of Man and the figure on the Throne. This is evidence of a definite parallel between the Son of Man 'sitting on the right-hand side' and Metatron 'sitting next to the Throne', and future research in this area may lead to a clearer understanding of scriptural allusions regarding the relationship between the Son of Man and the person named Enoch in the book of Genesis."

Hierarchy of Human Angels

The origin of Paul's transformation theory comes from an ancient biblical reference in the book of Daniel, and we must interpret it in light of this background. Seyoon Kim, Alan Segal, and Claude Tresmontant have contributed a vast body of research in this area. Segal boldly states, "The sectarians that produced the visions in Daniel expected to be transformed into stars" (104). He boldly connects the transformation experience in Enoch 71 with "The experience of an adept undergoing a transformation prophesied in Dan. 12:3" (104). The transformation involves the restoration of a lost part of the human soul. Segal explains how the lost soul restores itself through a new set of 'clothes':

Go and extract Enoch from earthly clothing and anoint him with my delightful oil and put him into the clothes of my glory. (105)

So obviously, the 'new clothes' are synonymous with the 'Glory of Adam.' Segal argues that the clothing appears to function as or symbolize Enoch's new immortal flesh for Enoch, as they are immortal clothes emanating from the Throne room, not from Earth. (105)

Thus, "For Paul, as for the earliest Jewish mystics, to be privileged enough to see the Kabod or Glory of God is a prologue to transformation into his image" (Segal 111). This image is the second Adam. Ultimately, "Being in Christ, in fact, appears to mean being united with his heavenly image" (113), and many support the idea that this is the same heavenly image identified with the creation of Adam. Joel noticed that all biblical prophets, mystics, and saints experience suffering and alienation due to their roles as seers; indeed, it is the trademark of most apocalyptic visionaries. However, Paul states that all believers will also share similar fates due to their identification with the image or 'body' of the Messiah. Segal clarifies this fact here, "The persecution and suffering of the believers is a sign that the transformation process has begun; it is the way to come to be in Christ" (114). Suffering is what characterizes the present age; however, "The glorification follows upon the final consummation" (114). Dr. Marvin C. Pate explains the importance of suffering, "The reason for the community's inheritance of Adam's glory is its righteous suffering" (Pate Adam Christology as the Exegetical & Theological Substructure of 2 Corinthians 37). Pate quotes a Dead Sea Scroll about the righteous:

Because of their purity and righteousness, they suffer persecution from the dominion of Belial: 'all their afflictions and the set times of their troubles are under the dominion of his hostility' who attempts to 'trip up the sons of light.' (37)

When Joel learns that his suffering is for a reason and is part of the transformation, he begins to relax, and his thoughts are clearer. He knows that he will find another job; he cannot let events that happen in the world have such an effect on his life. He knows now that this 'time' of suffering extends to the whole world, for as in Adam, all men died, so too will all experience the suffering of a changing world plagued with misery, sickness, and death. Political turmoil, economic struggle, mental conflicts, emotional tumults, and physical infirmities all play a major role in the ultimate transformation. It will become a challenge for consciously aware readers to be able to surmise what political and historical events really mean, and it will be hard to know who and what to believe. Mystics are often worthy of eschatological secrets unknown to other circles, and they are able to see the Kingdom because they have experienced the 'hard lessons' that open the mysteries. Knowledge actually transforms the knower, so many of the texts shrouded in secret codes become open and 'unsealed' as the hidden 'gnosis' imbibes the seeker with power to bind the forces of chaos (troubles, afflictions) with seals of truth and certainty. In contrast, as the 'books of life' are unsealed, darkness and chaos bound by the Light of Wisdom and Understanding is conquered another day. Eventually, all suffering will transform into victory over mortal history as angelic history reveals our origin, and the books of life appear to those who were once not able to read them

Our Center of Being

Life is a continual apocalypse or revealing of things not known. The future is always coming towards us until we experience the past as the present. Wisdom can convey spiritual realities to those of us capable of realizing and protecting the sacred inheritance buried in words. Peter

Hayman's article "Was God a Magician? Sefer Yetsirah And Jewish Magic" is very important in that he brings a fresh viewpoint on the role of the Sefer Yetzirah and readers. In the article, Hayman carefully explains how the Creator is located in the center of the Universe, sustaining the six directions; the center is where the Creator 'rests' in the seventh 'edge' or point. Big Bang theories call the time before the creation the 'singularity point,' and therefore, expansion symbolizes the unfolding or evolving six days of creation. However, Hayman includes a quote from the Sefer Yetzirah that explains a formula for sealing the seven 'edges' of the universe with various combinations of YHW, and he determines that this magical device is used to protect the area from evil forces.

Apparently, the most dangerous area is where the seventh point rests in the center below the Temple site. Hayman writes, "The threat of the emergence of chaos is greatest: below the site of the Temple, the pre-eminent symbol of cosmic order. (230)

Cube of Strings

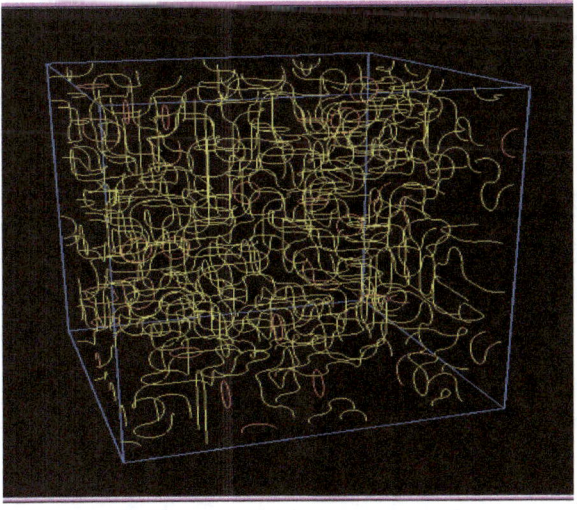

Figure 49 Cube of Strings Cambridge Cosmology

Timka and Alexa talked about so many things that neither one of them is aware of their problems anymore. They feel light, airy, free, and full of hope for themselves and others in the world, and they especially pray for children globally for the strength to endure life wherever they are in the world. They both know all too well that life on Earth in Da'ath contains us all within a box of time with six gates of space: Light/Darkness, Above/Below, Right/Left, North/South, Good/Evil, and Life/Death that determines all events and journeys that will occur in our lives. All things live to escape this confinement. The illustration from the Cambridge Cosmology String website shows us that even if the size of space is reduced, strings still find their previous geometric alignment.

Strings tend to maintain a geometric proportional alignment with other strings. There is an interesting account in the Pistis Sophia that parallels this alignment.

The author narrates how the Son of Man and the twelve disciples aligned themselves in a cubic structure to seal the gates of the abyss. In ancient mystic lore, this evil force continues to wage battle against the seals, preventing chaos from roaming free again upon the earth. Hayman points out another parallel to this idea in the Pistis Sophia,

As Jesus was saying these things, however, Thomas, Andrew, James, and Simon the Canaanite were in the west, with their faces turned to the east. But Philip and Bartholomew were in the south (with their faces) turned to the north. The rest of the disciples and women disciples, however, were standing behind Jesus. But Jesus was standing before the altar. (230)

This hints at the enormous significance this knowledge had in that age. It also demonstrates a gathering of worship with a High Priest. We have lost the ability to understand how these concepts operate in our own inner worlds. Hayman says,

So far, we seem to have here a kind of magical séance involving Jesus and his disciples, with some of the disciples symbolically placed at the four points of the compass while

Jesus stands beside the altar and proclaims a prayer which, though in Greek, contains three of the permutations of the divine name which appear in SY 15. (230)

Timka explains to Alexa that she does not really think it was a 'magical séance' at all; this type of interpretation demonstrates how this literature is not always understood through the eyes of the Hebrew Wisdom but, more often than not, is seen through the eyes of other theosophical teachings. One way to gain a new understanding of an old worldview is to explore the significance of the words used to seal the abyss. The Divine Name, the Tetragrammaton, transforms into three permutations that seal the abyss.

Hayman explains the significance of the three forms, iota (YHW), alpha (HWY), and omega (WYH), in sealing the universe. He says,

"This is its interpretation: iota, because the All came forth; alpha because it will return again; omega because the completion of all completions will happen" (230).

This sounds similar to the expansion concept of the Big Bang theory: iota is the expansion, alpha is its return or contraction, and omega represents the completion of a circle of cycles. In another scene from Pistis Sophia, a great battle ensues, and the heavens, aeons, spheres, and all the archons run to the west,

And Jesus with his disciples remained in the Midst in an airy place on the paths of the way of the Midst which is below the sphere… (231)

He and the disciples stand in the center of the universe, poised for battle with the forces of chaos in the Midst or Makom of the Aether. The real battle involves overcoming all various interpretations and interpolations of Gnostic and heretical traditions that opposed the early community of the

1st century. Another interesting link Hayman sees is between SY 15 and Genesis in that:

Both offer the reassurance that there is a God who has carved out of chaos an ordered space in which human life is possible. His constant presence is necessary in order to keep those ever-threatening forces of disorder at bay. (231-232)

Both girls transformed in their minds and hearts, no longer fearing the battle and wars of the falling angels. They can see this Universe appears to be a very chaotic battlefield in which the cosmic forces of good and evil are constantly at war, and this reality takes place right now in our own lifetime as it did in the 'Beginning.' There is literary evidence that the 'prepared space' tahiru is where humanity dwells in safety in the midst of a great battle. The Son of Man said, "I go away to prepare a 'place,' and as Messiah, he informs us it is a 'place' that we can inhabit only after this 'special' preparation.

This foreshadows the work of the six days, in which the Son of Man goes to prepare the void to receive the light. As the terrible cataclysmic events of 70 A.D. occur during the first stage of the tribulation, the archons make a dramatic strike that manifests in the destruction of the Temple. In Hayman's estimation: "The loss of the Temple tore apart the union of heaven and earth, God and the Temple, Yahweh and Israel" (232). It is prophecy fulfilled, even though something negative was turned to our good.

Since the destruction of the Temple in 70 A.D., there has been an attempt on the part of scribes and sages to preserve the ancient practices of Temple worship. Hayman thinks language was a way ancient sages attempted to save the formula of the Universe: "The Hebrew language replaces the Temple as the key to the unity of man, God, and the universe" (232). He asserts that extraordinary attempts to preserve the Temple functions by replacing them with words, concepts and language in texts such as Sefer Yetzirah itself. Therefore, it appears that Sefer Yetzirah is a text designed to preserve what might have been the first ancient attempt at formulating a scientific account of the Universe. The unknown author assumes the reader knows how to transcend time, space, and history in order to view the invisible structure of the universe. This indicates a strong possibility they possessed techniques for envisioning the Kosmos, and it was probably much more popular than we imagined. Maybe this idea was not just a mystical secret among a few groups it may have been a hot topic of debate in scientific yeshivas. Hayman points out that our waking reality is not always what it appears to be:

As in SY, so in the Mishmash there is no historical dimension at all. Both texts are situated in an ideal realm outside of history. They tell us how things really are if we shut our eyes to observable historical reality. (232)

Our human eyes still hold the reins and control the soul-carriage we must steer correctly. What we choose to see or not see, limits our experience of the journey. These texts hold valuable clues regarding the location of a secret 'place' that existed before our history. This is exactly what Bereshit mystics also set out to accomplish in order to ascend the seven heavens or days of the creation. Bereshit mysticism focuses on the 'work of creation'; it is an ancient system used to teach about pre-existence and existence.

Language of Light

Timka enjoyed the long visit with Alexa. She felt like a Merkavah mystic 'riding the chariot,' and she realized that, they too, were recipients of the vision, and they became part of the 'living beings' that surround the Throne. Dan's research proves Sefer Yetzirah is not just a mystical text; he describes it as a scientific document that details technical data used to classify and instruct others concerning the cosmological structure of the Universe. Hayman accurately notes the distinction between the SY and so-called 'mystical' texts. SY does not describe a mystical, spiritual experience; according to Hayman,

In SY, and not infrequently in other texts that we assign to the mystical trend in Judaism, there is no reference to any kind of spiritual experience. (233)

Timka goes to her special place more frequently, she has fewer panic attacks, her relationships are richer, and she is grateful for everything. She still thinks about her loved ones, who are no longer nearby, but she feels their love in a different way each day. Often, she may dream and remember encountering them; sometimes, she does not recognize them until she wakes up and thinks about aspects of her dream. She knows that science and spirituality are important allies; together, they are stronger but separated, and each loses an aspect of crucial reality.

Sefer Yetzirah is a scientific manual used to capture the great Temple teachings. Besides Merkavah and Bereshit mysticism, some circles possessed 'letter' secrets of the alphabet and how to systematize numbers, letters, and human consciousness in such a way that it enables the reader to envision invisible realities. This modern research of ancient texts reveals a tripartite of cosmic proportions that envelop the entire Universe. The more she learns about it, the more she can enjoy experiences beyond the world of physical things.

Timka takes her notebook out before she forgets what she just felt in her heart. She writes, "The 'living words' not only operate outside us, they operate inside me too, brooding upon the surface of my mind. Even though Dan argues the scientific value of 'words,' his concept is underestimated and overlooked by current scholarship and continues to suffer neglect. He says, "Suffice it to say that the main concept is the development of the idea of creation by language into a scientific system" (22); in this statement, he describes how the (sefer) book conveys knowledge to give its bearer power to 'experience the Creator.' Hayman says the success of the text parallels the spiritual evolution of the believer, the exalted status given to humankind, and the microcosmic image of the universe (macrocosm), which is the real secret of the success of SY. (234)

Timka describes how we are little copies of our cosmic universe, and if we can accept the truth that seems 'offensive,' the experience of learning the hidden secrets of the 'written word' can transform its recipients into 'living epistles.' She talks about Luke recording things Son of Man taught regarding negative things happening on earth, which will cause many people to become offended by each other during the tribulation. Luke records how the Son of Man set a 'blessing' against a 'curse' by setting a precedent not to be offended by what is learned, "And blessed is he and she, whosoever shall not be offended in me." (Luke 7:23). Timka knows she has found the Way to share this information; it starts in her heart and in the heart of all others crying out for deliverance, justice, and Truth.

The truth is so controversial today, opposite to world events, and seems so otherworldly that very few will be able to believe the report. Hayman presents evidence that Sefer Yetzirah's real success results in our ability to: "Think God's thought after him, and hence in a real sense to experience imaginatively what it is like to be God" (234). In other words, a person is able to be in the divine thought, within one's own thoughts, through a higher spiritual level of understanding. For example, in SY, Abraham, the protagonist, realizes the existence and use of scientific laws in the universe. He then becomes a knower or 'magician' "who by his knowledge of the correct formulas can compel the gods to appear and do his bidding." In the excerpt below, we find evidence of a cosmological text that classifies and defines different constructions of various symbols used for the dimensions.

Notice the designations assigned to the 'seven double' letters that parallel the seven days. According to Westcott's interpretation of Sefer Yetzirah,

These Seven Double Letters point out seven localities: Above, Below, East, West, North, South, and the Palace of Holiness in the midst of them sustaining all things. These Seven Double Letters He designed, produced, and combined, and formed with them the Planets (stars) of this Universe, the Days of the Week, and the Gates of the soul (the orifices of perception) in Man. From these Seven He hath produced the Seven Heavens, the Seven Earths, and the Seven Sabbaths: for this cause, He has loved and blessed the number Seven, more than all things under Heaven (His Throne).

Again, we see that a certain kind of knowledge reveals a long-lost secret about the mysterious seven days destined to give humans the ability to see the image of the Universe. For Hayman, this: "is the real secret" (234). Enoch is born the seventh from Adam and is the figure that 'walks with Elohim' during his earthly life, going back into the realm of the heavens.

Hayman notes that Philip Alexander sees a correspondence between Enoch and his role as a 'knower' or 'magician' of the Universe. According to Hayman, Alexander says Enoch,

Was a human being who had been elevated over all the angels, and was living proof that man could overcome angelic opposition and approach God. (236)

What does it mean to overcome angelic barriers, and why must we do this? The lower forces of the Kosmos took control of the chaotic consciousness of our ego, and ever since then, compulsive 'drives' have ruled us instead of the spontaneous freedom of intuition. In Hayman's view, Enoch comes to know what Adam and Eve realized. However, he brings back the way to overcome the fall. When he sees the tree of good and evil and is able to put the two together, the hidden path to enter the Garden of Eden appears. Hayman says Alexander underestimates the event,

I would put it a little more strongly than this. 'Doing an Enoch' offered the possibility of coming to know what God knows or obtaining the 'knowledge of good and evil' and hence becoming 'like one of us.' (Gen. 3:22) (236)

Meanwhile, Joel is now determined to find the 'secret place' also, and he is certain Hayman's observations provide important clues to the connection between the ancient figure of Henokh and the science of Sefer Yetzirah; somehow both play a role in the development of Lurianic Kabbalah. Joel thinks his head will burst with awe as he envisions Hayman's article and his explanation of how the Kosmos is shattered before Creation by a cosmic catastrophe that happens when the vacuum created by the withdrawal of the Creator is incapable of maintaining the weight of the creative light (236). We live in the era of 'restoration' or 'tikkun' when the 'shattered vessels of light' come together as one. Adam Qadmon is the epitome of the unification of the Sephiroth of the Crown as the Divine Thought harnesses the seven forces of color so the white light of Wisdom shines from one unified eye into the world of darkness.

Alpha - Omega & Bereshith Mysticism

Timka, Joel, and Alexa play different roles that seem to merge eventually, and they begin to see and hear each other better, too; their whole life seems more meaningful, and they look forward to the time when the Kingdom dawns permanently. All they had to do was look for the 'Beginning.' Bereshit is a place and location before time; and is also a person with a historical identity. A person once known as Metatron with divine creative motion that will eventually rest in the 'End' in our world of consciousness. Maaseh Bereshit texts

433

consist of various theories regarding the seven days of creation, and Maaseh Merkavah texts explain how to use the divine center of the Throne to travel to cosmic dimensions beyond this age and box of time. The eighth day signifies the 'world to come,' a world of freedom and truth. Moses told them about a peculiar cloud that would follow them by day, and a fire showed them the way at night during their journey in the wilderness of Sinai. The trio begins to understand each other better, and their memory is restored when they learn about the secret identity of Metatron – they found their place in the Kingdom.

Gnostic Memories

The Gnostics, very interested in knowing their 'origins,' taught that learning one's destiny is to know one's 'origins' and to know that is to know one's end. Christology calls the same 'origins 'protology the 'knowledge of before' and corresponding to 'destiny' is the study of eschatology or 'things of the end.' This means, in Gnostic terms, that knowledge of our 'beginning' and 'ending' is the transformation. In the Pistis Sophia, there is evidence that Alpha and Omega signify more than just two letters of the Greek alphabet. Hayman also believes "alpha" signifies return or cycle, and "omega" points to the rest or completion of all the returns (230). All proceeds from the Iota infinitely and this is conveyed in the Hebrew letter Yod, which actually represents a cycle of ten days. Enoch's ten-week apocalypse parallels not only the ten dimensions of M-Theory but is a clue to deciphering the meaning of 'beginning' and 'end' as we examine the divine week. Zechariah says the seven days are like seven eyes,

"For behold the stone that I have laid before Joshua; upon one stone shall be seven eyes: behold, I will engrave its inscription thereon" Zechariah 3:9. We know so far that there were six days of division and a seventh day of rest from motion.

However, there is an eight-day followed by two more days. We now live in the duality of the six arms of the cubic Universe.

Day 1	Day 2	Day 3	Day 4	Day 5	Day 6	Day 7
Light/Day Dark/Night	Waters/Above Waters/Below	Sea/Land Seeds/Trees	Sun/Moon Star/Galaxies	Creatures of land/water and air	Adam in image of Elohim male and female	Rest from motion
Beginning Protology Aleph/Alpha	Up/Down	Right/Left	Good/Evil	Spirit/Flesh	East/West	Ending Eschatology Tau/Omega
	Genesis	Exodus	Leviticus	Numbers	Deuteronomy	

They learned how six days shape and form our experience and perception of life. As they live through the difficulties of daily life, obstacles take on a new meaning, and they see there is a purpose behind what seem to be random events in life. Our inner Adam/Eve dwells in the midst of a constant battle that takes place in our lower nature for six days before the spirit rests in the center of our soul. They learn from the author of the Gospel of Thomas, who explains the way to overcome the 'archons' is to seek the correct interpretation of certain verses found in Gnostic texts. The understanding of secrets and mysteries of the Universe opens the gates of the cube, permitting them to find the means to escape from the six days of motion as their earthly consciousness is balanced between the ever-swinging pendulum of good/bad, up/down or life/death events. As they rest from the six days of motion, each one longs for the seventh day of rest, destined to bring liberation and equilibrium.

Once the seventh day awakens us, the fifth dimension opens our awareness, too, and we see how events connect in a strange form of justice that operates in accordance with reality. Leet has detailed many interesting aspects of seven of the higher dimensions; one particular one is that she believes the fifth dimension has two different experiences of time. One she refers to as the 'charmed life force' and the other as the 'strange life force' (405). Both have different influences on our experience of life and the meaning of events.

We began to see how the six days really do influence our lives and it is then that Adam begins to emerge from the darkness of 'nothing' to the light of 'something' shaped and formed through trial and error. Now, we live in the duality of day and night. We experience joy and pain, but on the seventh day, we find rest from the struggle to become aware of our situation, and for a time, we see everything and it is good.

Two Lights of Time

The light of the 'Beginning' (Aleph) shines ahead of us and behind us (Tav), drawing us towards the center of our inner firmament (Yodh). That point of condensed Light (Aur/Avir) as it emerges from within the point Aether takes on an outward form and an inner form that emits particles and waves. Waves undulate in an electromagnetic field as particles of photons travel in massless streams of energy. Pancoast describes how Solomon learned from the wisdom of 'illuminated time' that Moses learned in Egypt regarding the nature of light. He writes,

The 'wisdom' it enunciates is claimed to be that taught to Moses in Egypt. It describes God as Illuminated Time; no origin can be assigned to Him; He is engulphed in his own glory, 'dwelling in the Light which no man can approach unto.' Creation is stated to have consisted in emanations from Him, which dispelled darkness, the antagonizing element to Light, as Evil is to Good – the one fleeing as the other makes its presence felt. (Pancoast The Kabbala Or True Science of Light 20-21)

Humanity does have an 'origin' and 'destiny.' Our lives, measured by time, have a limit, but the energy of the Universe is timeless. Pancoast explains the deep significance of Sefer Yetzirah, which he refers to as "The Book of the Creation." Here, he quotes an eleventh-century Rabbi named Yehuda ha Levi, who not only explains the doctrine but also gives a concise summary of the book. Levi wrote:

The Book of the Creation, which belongs to our Father Abraham, demonstrates the existence of the Deity and the Divine Unity by things that are, on the one hand, converge and harmonize, and this harmony can only proceed from one who originates it. (22)

Pancoast explains that the author of Sefer Yetzirah tries to:

Declare a system whereby the universe may be viewed in connection with the truths found in the Bible in such a way as to show by tracing the gradual and orderly process of creation and the harmony that characterizes its details and its perfection. (21-22)

The power and awareness of ancient science deserve to be re-examined. Harmony is thought of as an order of visible things; these two poles characterize Alpha and Omega. When we learn how to line up the material things in our environment with the thoughts (letters) of the divine alphabet, we re-create the order and harmony of the 'beginning' that leads to the existential creation symbolized by the creation story recorded in Genesis. The extraordinary insight of Neil Douglas-Klotz, author of Genesis Now, examines the Hebrew tradition of Bereshit in terms of Syriac terms not translated correctly in our English Bible. Klotz presents research that leads Joel to believe the Messianic Kingdom parallels the creation story in Genesis. Here, he describes a quality of the Kingdom that continues to influence our daily lives as it pushes us forward to meet the mystery hidden within and without; he says the Kingdom,

It is not a static condition or a primordial or apocalyptic place beyond time, but rather a dynamic reality included in the creative act of the divine in Genesis 1, which can continue to affect the life of the experience in the present (Klotz Genesis Now 6 P2).

The Messianic Kingdom of the Gnostics is much more vibrant and alive and gives the reader a chance to participate in the mystery. Some argue that John and Thomas were at odds, but Klotz clears up this ambiguity by demonstrating that the mistranslation of Syriac terms results in a forced interpretation of foreign texts.

He reveals a cosmological mystery of the Image that is present from the 'Beginning' of creation; the same image that creates Adam creates the Son of Man. There is a primordial 'place 'called Makom where the hidden 'Beginning' resides in a garment that masks its glorious face. Klotz says,

To the Semitic mind, this place is not a 'space' out of time but a mode of existence. It was another word for the 'seat' of the divine at the protological moment of benefit (Klotz Reading John in Bereshit Time 12).

Klotz states that there is a living spiritual 'place' accessible right now if a person is born again in the 'Beginning.' The light of

Gnosis projects us into the Kingdom, showing us our origin and destiny. In this tradition, Alpha represents Keter, the Crown that emanates Ayin Sof that divides itself, and its leftover substance stretched out upon the Universe becomes the 'firmament' of our mind as it expands to contain the Word of Knowledge. The Universe literally wears a great garment of light radiation that has a 'beginning' and an 'ending.' Light is the energy that generates life and motion. Bereshit generates light from an older light that emanates nine waves that spiral down the string of cosmic energy, forming what we call the electromagnetic spectrum. Pancoast points out that Solomon Ibn Gabirol, another eleventh-century author, had a similar understanding of light. Pancoast says,

He speaks of the unity of Light as it arises from the throne of the Most High, which subjectively becomes divided into nine categories. (23)

The nine creative acts all take place within the Light. The sefirot are couched in Ayin Sof and represent the Unity of the nine spheres, "whence the number 10 is called a 'perfect number" described as the number 1 enclosed within a circle "representing the unity and synthesis of creation" (23). The 'One' and 'Ten' represent respectively, protology and eschatology. Light can be a waveform (protology) with eight steps or a self-sustaining particle (eschatology). Pancoast identifies the two forms of light:

The Kabbalists represent the properties of Light as dual, calling the parts the two hands of Deity. Although it possesses duality, it maintains its unity and harmony. (25)

True unity and harmony only exist when two opposites evenly balanced by a third, rest in the center. These are just a few of many analogies found between the symbolic terms Alpha & Omega and light Aur. Aleph is the breath that breathes life into the Universe, and Resh symbolizes the 'beginning' or head. The letter Vau balances the two sides, and as a result, the Hebrew term Aur- light evolves. The Hebrew term for light would, therefore, be equivalent to 'In the 'beginning' the breath and head are one' or the solar radiation contained all within itself. The Semitic view of the 'Ruach' implies there is a solar cosmic breath vibrating powerful forces that radiate energy to all that is living. The initiation cycle of a year is at the head (Resh) of the year in the spring season as the Sun gains its momentum and ends toward the feet in the winter. The human embryo begins from an invisible cloud of genes. As it evolves from the fertilized egg, every other organ develops from the heart (center). Historical evolution takes place as events coming from eternity enter a dynamic time that continues to unfold through the ages of time. The Angel of Time continues to measure the Kingdom with a rod that determines our days, hours, weeks, and years. When the [beginning] (Heaven) rests in the [end] (Earth), then the Angel of Time [firmament/fourth dimension] will lay down its sword and time will be no more.

Enoch's Timeless Journey

Enoch's journey through the dimensions involves mysterious geographical sites that many researchers assume to be mythological imagery. Some recent Enoch scholars have designed maps that depict a schematic view of different regions described in the astronomical portion of the text. The latest researcher, Kelley Coblentz Bautch, presents new insights in, No One Has Seen What I Have Seen', where the author compares Enoch's journey to ideas found in other cultures of antiquity. Bautch writes:

Just as a Mesopotamian regent would be known by the royal epithet 'King of the Four Regions,' so too was Enoch's God sovereign over all the cosmos. Following the visit to the heavenly palace where God gives Enoch a powerful condemnation to deliver to the evil watchers (1 Enoch 16), the tour of 1 Enoch 17-19 reminds the audience that sites related to judgment, punishment, future reward, and God's return have already been established and are powerfully present, though not yet accessible to anyone but Enoch. (Bautch A Study of the Geography of I Enoch 17-19 190)

Joel thinks these sites may exist in an 'In-between world,' another dimension that is right here with us, but because our consciousness is still 'stuck' in the time of human history, we have to learn how to regain this vision. More of Batch's research reveals Enoch's view of the Universe includes three realms of concentric circles that divide the earth into three parts. One-part humans inhabit, one part has water, trees, and darkness, and the third part surrounds the Garden of Righteousness or the 'third heaven' Paul describes. This is the 'third heaven' that provides an opening into seven mountains. (199) Bautch assures us that,

There is every reason, I believe, to read 1 Enoch 19:3 as a testament to Enoch's unique status. Only Enoch has seen the geographical extremities as well as the heavenly mysteries. (154)

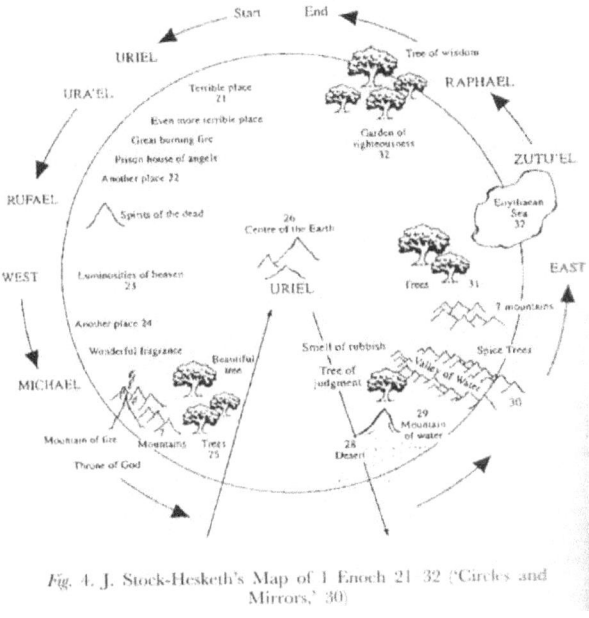

Fig. 4. J. Stock-Hesketh's Map of 1 Enoch 21-32 ['Circles and Mirrors,' 30]

Figure 50 Map of Enoch's Journey

John argues that only the Son of Man first ascended into heaven because he first descended from heaven. Is Enoch's journey only an exploration of geographical locations or a testament to the unique status of the Johannine Son of Man? This idea is demonstrated in the journey he experiences as he sees the 'Alpha' and 'Omega' of time. In the above figure, the map drawn by Stock-Hesketh indicates a 'start' and an 'end' of Enoch's journey. The 'start' of the journey begins when Enoch sees 'death' fall into the human realm.

The 'end' of the journey is when Enoch sees the location of the 'Tree of Righteousness' and the life destined to be given to the children of Yahweh in the 'end days'. This theme parallels and echoes the evangelism of John's account of the Son of Man's resurrection, from death to life at the end of a journey. Joel is certain this map may hold evidence for the idea that Enoch has traveled through time and not necessarily to different physical locations in space.

Eden: A Circle of Mirrors

These mysterious 'places' are located in our own world, and yet no human is able to perceive how or ask why. Only the Son of Man can make the dangerous journey from life in heaven to the death of earth and yet live to return to the angelic existence; Messiah comes to us through words/signs that accumulate energy and substance called faith. Mirrors and circles play a big part in the journey for our life is a reflection of the divine image built into the geographical structure of the Universe. This is evidence and a demonstration of how Divine Light is the 'All in All.' Kelley Bautch analyzed the map of Stock-Hesketh and summarized his theory:

He argues that mirrors and circles are the key structures that underlie the symbolic universe of 1 Enoch 21-32. He also suggests that the fundamental structure of the world in 1

Enoch 17-36 is enantiomorphic. By enantiomorph, he means the mirror image of an asymmetric figure, like the two parts of the yin-yang symbol. (181)

According to Bautch, he is actually explaining how the geography in the book of Enoch is a mirror of the divine world. The two 'edges' of the Cube are east and west and they become two halves of the same reality, except one side is darkness and death and the other light and life. The West is the place of the dead in many ancient Near Eastern traditions, and great fires and pollution are rampant; in contrast, the East has water and fruit trees that emanate beautiful fragrances with the sunrise. For some reason, this is how the author of Enoch decides to depict the fall and restoration in contrast to Genesis. It fills in more of the details surrounding the Tree of Life and the Garden of Eden that remain hidden from us, covered in foreign languages, mistranslations, and deliberate misinterpretations to ensure this teaching would not find ears willing to hear. The Messianic Kingdom is something that is always here with us now, but because no one taught us about this great spiritual antiquity, we lost it.

Enoch sees the 'beginning' of human time and how angels impervious to this time, continue to control human emotions and thoughts. Eternity is like a great tree that bears life-giving fruit. This is in contrast to the Genesis narrative that describes the negative aspects of the Tree of Knowledge that led to Adam and Eve's degeneration. They ate and learned both 'good' and 'evil,' and this event broke the symmetry of their unity. Suddenly, this world of innocence is shattered in pieces of bits we call time. The mysterious author of this book deliberately re-worked the theme to portray a tree with life-giving properties we must eat in order to engender eternal life. Bautch states,

Grelot, Milik, and Stock-Hesketh demonstrate that the description of Eden in Genesis 2 and 3 lies behind the location of the garden of Righteousness in 1 Enoch 32. Grelot, Charles, and Black think that 1 Enoch 25 may refer to the tree of life from Genesis 2-3. (206)

Let us look at some of this chapter and decide for ourselves.

Then Michael answered me, one of the holy angels who were with me and as their leader, and he said to me, 'Enoch, why do you inquire and why do you marvel about the fragrance of this tree, and why do you wish to learn the truth?' Then I answered him – I, Enoch – and said, 'Concerning all things I wish to know, but especially concerning this tree' (Nickelsburg 1 Enoch 1 312).

The tree he inquires about leads the way back to the 'garden of righteousness' in Genesis. How it does this is what no one ever explained to us. Apparently, a 'high mountain' with a peak symbolizes the Throne Chariot where the Divine Presence resides in the earth. The Tabernacle, Merkavah, and Temple all represent three developments of the same concept. The description of this great tree is similar to 'Jacob's Ladder.' The Tower of Babel structure imitates the true 'tree of life' and still covers it with coats of many colors and languages of the nations.

Where is the Beginning?

The geography of the map shows us that 'In the Beginning' is a 'place' beyond the 'fall'; when the Tree of Knowledge opens our eyes to mortal nakedness, civilization emerges as a necessary garment since our previous garment of 'immortality' has been lost. When he eats from the tree, he regains his vision. The first thing Enoch sees after eating from the tree is the residual fallout from an ancient angelic battle that occurred during the first angelic wars. Then he sees the place where the fallen angels are bound and how the spirits of many deceived souls were there with them, imprisoned by their own beliefs.

In the next quarter, he sees a beautiful land with trees and mountains.

I saw seven glorious mountains, all differing each from the other, whose stones were precious in beauty, and all the (mountains were precious and glorious and beautiful in appearance- three to the east were firmly set one on the other, and three to the south, one on the other (Nickelsberg I Enoch 24:2-3 312).

This is the place of the Tree of Lives, hidden in the midst of a forest of trees between seven mountains. The tree forbidden to us since the 'beginning' is not available until a particular time,

And (as for) this fragrant tree, no flesh has the right to touch it until the great judgment (I Enoch 25:4 312).

A beautiful heavenly fragrance captures Enoch's senses and lures him to the tree. In contrast, the next quarter reeks of all kinds of pollution, the smell of garbage, and desert land take over the once beautiful land of plenty, but beyond this, in the last quarter are the same seven mountains, except now the garden of righteousness is accessible. Even though Enoch seems to be on a geographical tour of the Universe, he is really traveling through time and peers into the future when humans will pollute and burn the earth; after this, the garden is open to new humanity once again. Bautch's research is indispensable for seeing the significance of this event. The following summarizes the Genesis/Enoch connection according to Stock-Hesketh:

He suggests that 1 Enoch 24-25 is an enantiomorph, a mirror image posited in the opposite direction of Genesis 2-3. In the biblical account, God is afraid that Adam, having the knowledge of good and evil, will take from the Tree of Life and live forever. (208)

445

Research in this field reveals the author of Enoch means to contrast the view of the Tree of Knowledge according to the theme in Genesis by explaining how humanity will one day be able to eat of the Tree of Life and live, reversing the effect of the original fall. Enoch's journey through time and geography serves to place historical events and ancient angelic sites in perspective in terms of our own perception of life.

The place of the fallen angels described as dark hollow pits, with great depths that have no measure might be referring to what we call a black hole. Of course, the ancients did not know this scientific concept. Nevertheless, the astronomical sections of Enoch seem inspired by actual cosmic events, and scientific analysis is present in the description of the stars rising and the sun's journey through the various degrees of the great gates of time of the universal circuit of Galilee. Like Sefer Yetzirah, this text also presents scientific data characteristic of various types of knowledge lost to us now.

Enoch's journey reflects the fall of divine energy into matter and how it divides, grows, and matures in a series of stages after a cataclysmic poisoning of the water and land that leads to the eventual purification and reconstruction of the earth and the Garden of Eden. There is definitely some event destined to happen due to the result of interference and manipulation by an outside source. The Apocalypse of John explains the events and details that lead up to the cosmological events.

Perhaps it is possible to learn about the 'Omega' from the 'Alpha,' for according to this story, humanity has only experienced the 'death' of the Garden that symbolically represents the 'end.' In the 'world to come' Olam Ha-Bah, or the eighth day, which is at the 'end' of the journey or week of seven days, humanity will once again wear the eight garments of light that give life. The Gnostics taught that 'freedom' and Kingdom are contained in the 'eighth sphere,' and to taste this is to free our consciousness from the powers of the 'archons' that rule over the darkness of our own fears and desires.

The darkness of our own consciousness blinds us to the true reality of the divine light and love that governs the Universe. The Heavenly Father/Mother Adam and Eve prepared a way to enter our consciousness; the only work we must do is find a way to eat the Tree of Life and live.

END OF TIMES

After weeks of extensive research and soul searching, Joel feels both excited and sad at the things he discovers. He cannot even remember the old voice that urged him to find a way to change Timka and win her back from the strange force that entered her life. Now, his determination to discover the secret of the eight days is all he can focus on. Joel begins to write down his thoughts now as he thinks about the 'End of Time.' At first, Joel did not take any of these ideas seriously; he, like many others, did not really understand the real nature of time. The end of times may actually begin whenever a person experiences the reality that our lives are images on the big screen full of drama and uncertainty, and the projector is a world of physical images and human suffering. He did not know anything about some far-off mystical place, nor did he realize an internal world of Thoughts dwells inside us all, enabling us to experience 'existence.'

Many people today have experienced altered states of consciousness due to various methods; some use meditation, others long for a mystical sensation of leaving the earth plane while meditating in their own homes and some were hurt through drugs and hallucinogens. There is another way; you do have time to find it now today, if you open your mind. Joel knows now for sure that the uniqueness of Hebrew prophets and Moses resides in the ability to experience all of time; this is something that seems paradoxical and impossible to us, even though there are hundreds of films in the theatre that describe the benefits and consequences of time travel. If time is a created thing, it too will dissolve with the 'rest' of the elements. We mentally separate events into sections of the past, present, and future, and this gives order to our perception of daily life events. As we live, move, and have our being in seven creative days, we exist in the illusion that we are moving forward through time, but this is really only human psychological reasoning. Stephen Hawking examined the relationship between matter in space and matter in time in A Brief History of Time, where he explains that matter moves through time as the Universe expands. However, he also says that if the Universe can contract, then matter can travel back in time. Joel once only believed in this common 'cosmological' explanation of time among many different scientists. Quantum Mechanics physicists study the spin time of sub-atomic particles and have determined there are three dimensions of time just as there are three dimensions of space. The latest research tells us the appearance of going forward in time is an illusion because the atoms that form our existence are spinning in three different time dimensions. Atomic time is based on the time it takes an electron to complete one revolution; it will continue to do this as long as the energy sustains its motion. Humans live in the 'dynamic' time of daily life as we go through the situations that become events leading to a conclusion. Then there is the time of the wandering 'planets' that revolve around the circuit of the Sun like a chain of objects bound by an invisible force we call gravity. This best represents the time of 'archons' fated to rule over and, to an extent, determine and influence the development of our unconsciousness.

Science knows through mathematical evidence that the spin motion of sub-atomic particles in 3D space is actually the cause of motion in 3D time. This illustration demonstrates how time is like a cone with three points. Instead of one steady stream of time moving from past to future, time actually consists of three dimensions that travel as one.

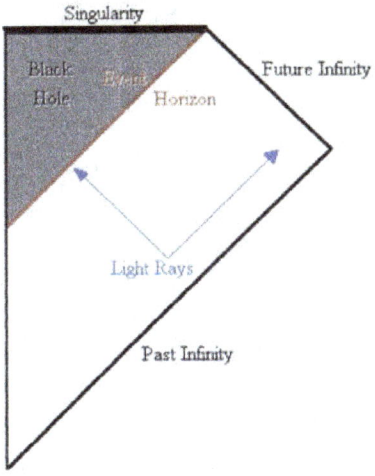

Figure 51 Penrose Design of Time

Our past is 45 degrees away from the future and our present intersects both at the bottom of the center, which is its singularity point. All three of the times continue to move forward, each in its respective degree and angle. Except, in 'dynamic time', we experience a circular time, and somehow, our present just never seems to catch up with the past unless we go back in time. This is because we perceive time in three distinct sections, but in apocalyptic times, this distinction does not exist. Joel's life will never be the same after experiencing these realities himself. He has grown stronger and wiser.

Eternal Time in the Kingdom

Time is a symbol of the measureless Day of Eternity. Eternity symbolizes the infinite possibilities of what is, but when the Angel of Time rests from the work of measuring the six days, the Kingdom suddenly awakens as the light rests on the seventh day. Adam Qadmon reflects the image of the Universe back unto us through teachings concerning the Sephiroth. Time will serve a different purpose in the New Age.

449

Carlos Suarez discovered the true mystery of the number 26 at the 'end' of time. This is what he says,

We must grasp what the Sepher Yetzirah says about the Sephirot (I,7): their end is in the beginning, and their beginning is in their end. This "end" is laid down in verse I,26 of Genesis, by the number 26, which makes us aware that the completion of YHWH is present from the beginning of human evolution, although it was not apparent at the beginning, nor is it even now, alas, the present condition of humanity. (49)

Joel learned that humanity has to tune in to the wave of creation to complete the sequence. Genesis, known for the seven "Let there be" commands that bring about the creation contains seven commands that undulate like the steps of a wave cycle that rest in a seventh movement that activates the eighth and the beginning of a new wave. Like the Atom, Adam has seven shells that only become stable after the eighth commandment. Gen. 1:26, "Let us make Adam in our Image," is the eighth commandment that 'speaks' humanity into existence. He is so amazed that this verse is evidence of a relationship between the number 26 and Adam, who reflects the image of Elohim. Each 'let there be' command is a step in the creation process, but Adam is stable only after the spirit of Eloah has rested on the seventh day. The eighth day signifies a return to the beginning of the week, or the original Day of Eternity, when the divine presence dwells with us. The World of Olam Atziluth, the World of Emanation that generates Eternity, consists of three realms that parallel the Kaddishim:

1st Holy	Highest Crown	Point	Iota
2nd Holy	Root of the Tree	Circumference	Alpha

3rd Holy	Attached and unified in all	Expansion	Omega

Moses, the author of Genesis, says Elohim created the earth on the very first day in a condensed state known as the realm of Eternity. Moses wrote,

These are the generations of the heavens and of the earth when they were created on the **Day** that Yahweh Elohim made the earth and the heavens. (Gen. 2:4)

Joel had no idea that the creation of Heaven and Earth takes place in 'one day,' contrary to popular opinion, which teaches a six-day creative process. He discovers, to his surprise that one of the primary arguments of scientists is that the earth is much older than the account described in Genesis, but this is a moot point when we realize that the six days do not describe 'dynamic' time. This 'one-day' motif demonstrates that the seven days evolve from within a single day or point in time. Eternity extracts itself from the confines of time to break into our physical world and release its oneness into our multiplicity!

After this creation, Elohim establishes an 'Aeon' of creations that are afterward gradually situated in a sphere divided into elements of time. The primordial time now is subsequently broken up into hours and days. At the redemption, this (primordial time) or, as Enoch says, the great 'Aeon of Light' will once again become the indivisible age called 'Time of the End' or the eighth day that starts a new beginning of a new world not measured by time. Unfortunately, many see the 'Time of the End' as a great destructive cataclysmic event, and some try to fulfill this destiny even at the expense of truth; others see the end of everything and wonder what the meaning of this temporary life filled with sorrow and suffering is. Like so many other concepts that we have looked at, this phrase does not necessarily mean the physical destruction of Earth. It is a process of transformation set in motion before the beginning of space and time. There are destined events that have to occur in historical time before the divine creation will be complete. Is there scientific evidence of two kinds of time?

Time and Time Again

Quantum Mechanics theorists now believe that sub-atomic particles operate under a different kind of time. Einstein's Relativity Theory illustrates how events in time occur in ordered sequential processes with very little room for deviation. Events produce actions that appear as motion that occur in time and nothing can happen without a cause and effect. In our world of 'dynamic' time, everything seems regulated and fixed to an extent. Even though Einstein understood the categories of past, present, and future have become obsolete in describing space-time, he still antagonized the early pioneers of Quantum physics who believed time behaved differently than he proposed. There are two sets of time in quantum mechanics and how human consciousness can alter our awareness of time is the latest area of research. In Quantum Mechanics, sub-atomic elements change from a particle into a wave with very little effort, and particles can be in many places all at the same time. This is a spiritual phenomenon exhibited during the resurrection when the Son of Man appeared among many different people. The sub-atomic particles eventually find a stable level, but until then, they spread out, so to speak, across many different potential 'homes.'

This parallels the human condition; our minds spread out among the various doctrines and belief systems of the world, and we try many different ideas to find our 'place' in this world. When we put on the eight garments of spiritual power, we find the stability we need to go past our own thresholds into the realm of 'freedom'. Karl-Josef Kuschel, author of Born Before

All Time, presents compelling research on the designated sections of time according to apocalyptic and ancient Near Eastern literature. Kuschel developed his outline of time during research on Karl Barth's work. Kuschel's research is very important to understanding the phases of time according to the operation of the Son of Man. Kuschel says the Creator that continually exists in all times has not really existed in this world until humans contain that aspect of the Creator that can actually be attained (111).

Kuschel's outline of four dimensions of time:

A	Given Time"	Human life in 3 modes: past, present, and future
B	Allotted Time"	Limitation of Human life
C	"Beginning Time"	Human Origins (Protology)
D	"Ending Time"	Human Destiny (Eschatology)

Kuschel describes Barth's view of how the Messiah transforms time in the eschaton,

At this last and highest stage, the pre-existence of the man Jesus coincides with his eternal predestination and election, which includes the election of Israel, of the church, and of every individual member of his body. (114)

Barth further demonstrates that Eternity rests in time through the resurrection of the Son of Man. When Enoch sees the Son of Man, he is enthralled and transformed by the 'Glory,' but when he learns the identity of the 'Glory,' he becomes the Son of Man. Enoch typifies the pre-existence of the human Son of Man, who gives life to all things through divine light and love. Until then, the mortal men that create civilizations continue to perceive time as an abstract idea forged from the Greek concept of Chronos; Barth says the Son of Man conquered the 'god of time' and thereby changed false time into "real-time" (114).

Kuschel's explanation of different "Times" presents a more consistent way of how human history and divine history intertwine at intervals. Until the Kingdom has become operative through "Ending Time," the apportionment of minutes, hours, days, and years is still necessary for human conception. Kuschel summarizes Barth's concept of eschatological time and our place in it. Barth says our time is,

The 'time and history of the sinful creature' to which the time of revelation also belongs – 'is included in a divine 'before all time.' (114)

Thus, our own time is included in the 'time before time,' but humanity is not able to distinguish the overlap. We can detect the overlap by examining the way authorities measure time since the destruction of the Temple in 70 A.D. Only the Son of Man, who represents the 'pre-existent man of time,' could overcome the measurer 'god' of this Kosmos known as Chronos. Kuschel writes,

In other words, the god Chronos can really be cast down only by one who was 'before all time' and, as a result, is the decisive determination of all time. Here, 'before all time' is not to be understood once again as a temporal definition to which the Son would be subject. (114-115)

Time will not cease to be; it will finally not become. Our daily reality takes place in a different time called 'this world' or the Olam Ha-Zeh; the Messianic Kingdom is not of 'this world' but from the time of Eternity. Heaven comes to earth and rests in human history through a literary mystery only revealed in the 'world to come' Olam Ha-Bah when Messiah sits down on the Throne of your Mind in the cloud of consciousness.

When Myth Becomes Reality

Kuschel gives us the key to open the sealed mystery when he says, "By being 'chosen and hidden' by God before the creation of the world, the Son of Man also becomes more real." Joel begins to piece together earlier research with his new findings and sees a distinct portrait of the figure of Enoch in apocalyptic literature. Suddenly, he understands he is also a type and shadow of the historical person born in Nazareth, projecting the future victory and glorification of the pre-existent Son of Man. At first, this story appears to be a mere myth to us, until the human Son of Man re-enacts it consciously and willfully, giving his life as a seed to be placed in the ground, waiting to become the living tree in the restored Garden.

The image of a tree is a common symbol of a spirit-filled human and the relationship of how all exist in the branches of our Universe. The Son of Man re-enacts the events of salvation in each of us when we see the divine image in ourselves. Myth becomes a reality for each of us when we realize the divine identity. There is every reason to believe that Yahoshua/Jesus had access to the books of Enoch and many other documents of that and previous ages. In an eighteenth-century critical review of apocalyptic literature entitled Books Which Influenced Our Lord and His Apostles, John E.H. Thomson describes how some mysterious person leads the Messiah down a long corridor to a room with old scrolls and documents. According to Thomson's work, he had finally come of age to access this material. His remarks on this awe-inspiring moment,

Where, in a cranium of two, the scanty but precious library of the house is kept. The swinging lamp is lit, and there He sits and reads far into the night of the strange visions recorded in the Books of Enoch, or of Baruch, about the Son of Man who was to sit on the throne of His glory, and before whom all shall appear, and of the blessings of the days of the Messiah. (16)

He read about his own previous life, forgotten now but remembered later. As he reads the texts, images of events evoke memories as the voices of cherubim whisper in virgin ears, seraphim burn his eyes with a panoramic vision of the 'beginning' and 'end'. He realizes he is the figure written about in this great book of antiquity and is transformed; this is the experience the Son of Man set in motion in the Tree of Life from the 'beginning.' The most important thing we can do is remember one of Thomson's suggestions,

Hence, to understand the time when Christ was in the world and the influences then at work, we must master the apocalyptic books. They, above all, are full of hope for Messianic times and the glories of the Messianic king, but to understand them, we must realize the background they had. (17)

Even though the background of this text remains ambiguous after years of research, and many have mixed emotions about its authenticity due to their own inability to decode the Semitic terms, it was very important to the earlier 1st-century community. Thomson believes the historical development of the literature and the political and social changes we subject it to all play a role in how an audience will perceive the material. Thomson's earlier research confirms the main obstacles that prevent this literature from regaining its place in the Canon.

Kuschel says there are two kinds of 'existence': one is an 'archetype' reality of heavenly existence, and one is a 'copy' of an earthly image of reality; they commingle at the end of the age. He says,

It is obvious that Apocalyptic, in particular, was able to 'use' this archetype-copy scheme. It expected all salvation solely from heaven; all the mysteries and benefits of salvation have existed from primal times – especially the heavenly Zion and paradise – and will appear on earth in the end-time. (216)

Salvation is in the 'beginning' and always has been, but the way to find it remains hidden since the beginning of the ages or the days of creation. Paul says the great mystery hidden from the foundation of the world is destined to come in its own time. The heavenly Kingdom is similar to a city that suddenly appears yet hidden from our perception. It is our destiny as the human race to learn how to see and perceive the reality of apocalyptic concepts in order to become free of the darkness, for this is when time becomes 'real-time,' and prophecy becomes history. Only then does the Way open the Truth that leads to Life. Consciousness of the heavenly reality is a channel opened in our minds and hearts that allows us to enter the other dimensions of reality. How does time become 'real time'? When the Son of Man awakens from sleep (ignorance), or when the individual is able to realize who the Son of Man is. It is a reciprocal relationship, and one relies on the impetus of the other to affect any change and create motion. Are we merely humans imagining we are angels? Are we angels clothed in garments of material flesh to cover our nakedness? Discovering the authentic identity of the Son of Man is tantamount to discovering the origin and destiny of our own human/angelic life.

Sleeper Awake!

Australian author Majella Franzmann describes the figure of the Son of Man as a 'revealer' in the Nag Hammadi literature. Franzmann comments on a section from a text:

The revealer appears as an eagle on the Tree of Knowledge so as to teach Adam/the copy of Adamas and the woman/the copy of Epinoia and to awaken them out of the depth of sleep. (23:26-31)

This 'revealer' descends into the underworld to waken anyone who can hear from their deep sleep. The 'deep sleep' of forgetfulness causes us to lose sight of our origin and destiny. How can we enter into 'real-time' after waking from the 'deep sleep'? Adam was put to sleep in order to have Eve removed from his 'side' or 'tselem'. Humanity remains in this 'deep sleep' until it receives the 'side' or image of the divine presence. We live in a cloned existence of ourselves known as the 'copy' in the above text. Perhaps 'real-time' is the final phase of the unfolding waves of electromagnetic energy when measuring time is not necessary. Real-time will mean the sun and moon are no longer necessary, for the physical Universe will wrap itself up as a scroll and fade away to give place to the realities of the sun and moon instead of the symbols. Isaiah speaks from the ancient view,

And all the hosts of heaven shall be dissolved, and the heavens shall be rolled together as a scroll: and all their host shall fall down, as the leaf falleth off from the vine and as a falling [fig] from the fig tree.(Isaiah 34:4)

The heavens and earth described as a scroll unfolded from within echoes the biblical allusion of the Word (Scroll) that dwells in the beginning upon the face of waters as in the seven days creation sequence of Genesis. Lift up your eyes to the heavens, and look upon the earth beneath: for the heavens shall vanish away like smoke, and the earth shall wax old like a garment, and they that dwell therein shall die in like manner: but my salvation shall be forever, and my righteousness shall not be abolished (Isaiah 51:6)

The scroll that contains the heavens and earth will not last forever; only the hidden salvation that leads to eternal life can give us immortality. More recently, John on the isle of Patmos saw how,

The heaven departed as a scroll when it is rolled together, and every mountain and island were moved out of their places. (Revelation 6:14)

What are the mountains and islands that move out of their places as the scroll rolls up, and how does a door to a different dimension open? Could it really be true that hades is our own self-image? According to the Gnostics, our soul imprisoned by 'archons' still feeds on our desires and fears. Franzmann comments on the Nag Hammadi perspective,

This final descent of the revealer into the Underworld in a three-part process is, in actual fact, a descent into the human person: 'I went that I might enter into the middle of the darkness and the inside of Hades. And I entered into the middle of their prison, which is the prison of the body. The revealer wakes the one who hears from his deep sleep- raises him up, and seals him with the light of water. (Franzmann Jesus in the Nag Hammadi Writings 101)

Franzmann further states that there is a reference to a 'copy' or clone of the Son of Man, one that is heavenly and one that is earthly, "as Havelaar points out, the Son of Man may be the equivalent of a figure in 82.15-17, i.e., the intellectual Pleroma of the Saviour" (97). This means the earthly Son of Man helps one to see the heavenly Son of Man, who represents a kind of heavenly hierarchy of Gnosis, in apocalyptic terms, the Tree of Life. One who knows the heavenly Son of Man can go to the place of the "Eighth," according to Franzmann,

This is also the case in Soph. Jes. Chr. Where the one who knows the Son of Man in knowledge and love must bring a sign of the Son of Man so that he can go to the dwelling places with those in the Eighth. (97)

When Joel experiences the Messianic Kingdom, secretly called the seventh day in mystic circles, his mortal intellect empties into the eighth day an Activated Intellect or Metatron, the world to come. Joel's thoughts transform as he enters a timelessness of peace and wisdom unknown by mortal man, and at first, he becomes terrified. As Thomas says, if you have overcome the Lion and seen the all, you will be amazed and then rule over the lower consciousness bound by time. The eighth day arrives when we recognize ourselves in the Son of Man and thereby realize how we are also part of the 'primordial Adam.' It opens a reality that measures divine justice in proportion to the act or thought we take to heart. Life becomes more real as we constantly realize the finiteness of earthly life and the infinity of an eternal consciousness.

The whole process serves the purpose of restoring the lost 'Alpha-Aleph' to Adam (spirit) and Eve (flesh) when we realize the 'end things' eschatology is realized in earthly history and heaven and earth become one. The 'End' represents judgment day, but it involves discernment, not punishment, and it stands between the Messianic Kingdom [Phase I] and the 'World to Come' [Phase II]. The seventh day awakens in the Messianic age as the children of light emerge from the conflict of the six days of creation.

The author of II Enoch outlines the apocalyptic timeline that only mystics can decipher, but at the 'End,' books start to break manmade seals as they usher in the future world of the eighth day. In this immediate age, the city begins to appear, but in the future world of the eighth day the heavenly city becomes the Eternal age to come. The eighth is the first appointed day of the new week of the 'world to come'. Previous aeons have already elapsed. Kreitzer sees a connection between II Enoch 32.1-33.2 and 65.6-10. He says,

A special relationship between the eighth day of creation and the first day in such a way that a periodization of history into a week of 1,000 years aeons results (Kreitzer Jesus and God in Paul's Eschatology 43).

Bereshith mystics believe the Beginning meets the Ending on the eighth day, which represents the 'Great Age.' All will have 'eternal places' within the heavenly mansions. The years do not represent an actual physical account of historical time, but it does signify things that happen in the realm of eternity. This is what Joel figures out as he unwittingly finds himself in the fifth dimension, where death and life are like night and day, and every morning is an adventure in the chaos of time. His heart beats so fast in his chest that his brain feels like it will explode as he thinks about all the things that he can see now that he did not believe before. He is very excited to tell some of it to Timka, but he knows he can never tell anyone about how to find the eighth day, for each one has to wake up to it in his or her own time. He reads a passage from II Enoch that he finds very interesting,

All time will perish, and afterward, there will be neither years nor months nor days nor hours. They will be dissipated, and after that, they will not be reckoned. But they will constitute a single age. And all the righteous, who escape from the great judgment, will be collected together into the great age (II Enoch 65:7-9).

This 'great age' revolves around the point of the seventh day in a wheel of timeless motion that will begin to emerge as the eighth day becomes the future world. The author of the epistle of Barnabas reworks II Enoch's 'eighth-day' motif.

Further, He says to them, "Your new moons and your Sabbath I cannot endure." Ye perceive how He speaks: Your present Sabbaths are not acceptable to Me, but that is which I have made, [namely this,] when, giving rest to all things, I shall make a beginning of the eighth day, that is, a beginning of another world. Wherefore, also, we keep the eighth day with joyfulness, the day also on which Jesus rose again from the dead. And when He had manifested Himself, He ascended into the heavens (Epistle of Barnabas Ch. 15).

461

The eighth day breaks into the midst of warring factions in every category of human existence. There are mental, emotional, spiritual, physical, and supernatural conflicts that seem to chase us down a dark, winding tunnel of uncertainty regarding our futures. The only way out of the catch-22 is to escape the confines of material consciousness and go back to the peace and understanding lost to us in the Garden of Eden. Humanity will either become scattered or divided against others; some individuals will overcome and eat the Tree of Life!

Figure 52 Broken Shards of Light

Aeon of Light

The 'Time of the End' or the eschaton represents the completion of the work of six days mystically called 'Bereshit' and known in Sefer Yetzirah as the 'edges of a Cube.' According to Enoch's vision, the righteous unite with this Aeon of Light, and it unites itself with them. They absorb each other, and as the heavenly and earthly natures commingle, they form a 'new man.'

The 'new man' can see a future already written in the past and realize how new things happen in the present. The story of Enoch is proof that the Son of Man did enter heaven and fight with fallen angels and powers on behalf of our lives, just as he saw it happen before in angelic history. To realize who the Son of Man is is to realize the future already is. According to Scholem, the participants actually:

Are having a part in the future Aeon or becoming worthy of it? It is rather a matter of an eschatological identity with the Aeon of creation to which everything returns. (Scholem Origins 74)

Our identities awaken our heavenly image above that dwells in heaven; it then comes down to connect with its earthly counterpart. Scholem explains how these 'new people' have already transcended the time barrier and traveled to the hidden Kingdom in the center of the Temple. Joel begins to dream aloud, and he hears his voice talking without making any sounds, "Within the seven veils of the palace of Truth, four kingdoms pulsate in shells of confusion, waiting for the order of harmony and balance to arrive. The moment life becomes alive in life unfolding from inside the abyss of unknown truths. Sacred truths seem to contradict reality, for things are not what they appear to be; to decode the labyrinth of illusions is the beginning step in the world of emanation. When we perceive truth as it really is and actually exists, it is the first movement of life in the lower world of our soul. This is the beginning stage of the new world, where reality is divided into fantasy and fallen angel myths. This is how something is made from nothing, as stated in Genesis. Once something emerges from nothing a divine chariot or Merkavah forms and takes us inside our own consciousness back into the Garden of Eden. There are four natures: Eagle, Lion, Ox, and Human find equilibrium once again. That is to say, man's spirit, nature, soul, and body are one with one common purpose: to find out where we came from, where we are going, and why we are here now.

Once truth rules over reason instead of emotions and instinct, the spirit can free our soul and body from its carnal nature. There are four kingdoms warring within all of us, and only when the fifth kingdom awakens from within will the battle cease.

Much of the terminology used by superstring theorists sounds mystical; some even say it is not really science at all but a new philosophy. The new string philosophers prove through five different mathematical equations how the dimensions exist in Witten's revolutionary 'M-Theory.' M- Theorists predict the Unification of the four forces will allow them to understand how the creation existed before Time. It may even produce evidence of a fifth force that science will eventually confirm. Similarly, none can really see the 'strings' yet, but the logic of math proves they are there. No mortal eyes can see the hidden Kingdom right now, but the logic of apocalyptic signs and an understanding of its eschatological relevance indicate its nearness. Susskind explains how particles have internal structures that can stretch, contract, and wiggle. Each string constitutes one of ten dimensions, and each is a large membrane that expands and stretches big enough to contain a galaxy. Quantum mechanics actually demonstrates the proof that can exonerate the Genesis narrative. Ironically, one of the main terms in Genesis is the 'firmament' that derives from the Hebrew word 'Rakia' which signifies to stretch, expand, and make broad. Ezekiel used the term 'Rakia' to describe how the firmament expands upon the Earth." Joel did not expect any of the changes that started happening in his life that began to occur at the same time he learned the secret of the eighth day. He knew he could not explain it to Timka or Alexa, yet it would take him more time, the time he felt he was running out of; world events continue to follow a trend towards violence, decadence, and oppression. The chaos of the 'Abomination of Desolation" is why Joel now understands and thinks, "No wonder we need to stand in the Holy Place!" At first, we cannot see any relevance to some things, but eventually, they grow more tangible. For cosmologists, it is the eleventh dimension that allows strings to stretch into a membrane.

Branes can change and grow in size as a mysterious six-dimensional shape at the core determines how and what form matter will assume. Peter Hayman argues the Universe is actually a six-sided cubic construct. Perhaps the 'Rakia' is the eleventh dimension that covers the earth like a veil dividing between the heavens and earth. The 11th phantom dimension seems to bring imbalance to the Harmonious arrangement of the 10. The decade is the perfect manifestation of the Monad or Unity, expressed in multiplicity or infinity. We cannot comprehend the reality we live in with our limited senses; the Kingdom is right there in front of us upon the earth, and it is inside us; it is real, yet we cannot see it. However, with the latest theories of quantum mechanics, we begin to realize how all things contain the possibilities of every event.

The spiritual world envisioned by apocalyptic mystics is such a 'place,' and Paul the Apostle says he, too, has been there. He said he traveled to the 'third heaven' where he saw and heard amazing things he could tell no man, yet beatings, sickness, and affliction characterize his life on earth; who could imagine that he might have envisioned the vast center of the Universe? What has happened is that all these different systems have confused a very simple concept: Adam once bore a 'Body of Glory', but it was not that full Glory to come; it foreshadowed the true Glory that only the 2nd Adam would restore to humanity. Each of the nations assigned their own characteristics to this Body; this is where the confusion of whether the Creator has a Body or not comes into play. I can see why not many people have been able to unravel the puzzle.

Timka says, "Simply put, this 'Glory' gives humanity the ability to walk through the 'darkness' that now occupies human consciousness. This is how we can walk right out of death into the understanding and knowledge of what truly is – Yahveh, the only Existing One, that no man has seen is clearly being manifested through the 2nd Adam, a life-giving Spirit."

Timka agrees with Segal, who finds very important parallels between the Son of Man theme and the figure on the Throne. It indicates a particular way Paul's doctrine developed; he states, "The enthronement helps us understand some of the traditions that later appear in Jewish mysticism and may have informed Paul's ecstatic ascent" (102). Furthermore, Segal says the transformation that takes place in the 'Son of Man' in 1 Enoch 71:1,

"It is an extraordinarily important event, as it underlines the importance of mystic transformation between the adept and the angelic vice-regent" (103). See below: "1 And it came to pass after this that my spirit was translated and it ascended into the heavens: and I saw the holy sons of God. They were stepping on flames of fire: Their garments were white [and their raiment], and their faces shone like snow." (Charles Pseudepigrapha I Enoch 71:1)

Although modern researchers continue to discover and unravel these obscure secret aspects of Jewish mysticism, "Paul himself remains the earliest author explicitly expressing transformation in Judaism" (104); for instance, Paul's idea of the 2nd Adam is reminiscent of the 'man of light 'motif found in Judaic, Hermetic, and Gnostic texts. Timka knows the teaching is very ancient, and is now assimilated into various cultures and belief systems, where each group adds or detracts from its original form. However, what is most important to us now is how Paul's development of the 'man of light' motif is altogether distinct from all these other views!" Timka is in her element now; she cannot believe that others are standing with her in the 3rd Heaven on Earth.

She thinks to herself, "It is not a myth; dreamers awake! It is really happening, and others can see and hear the Father's Voice!" She feels a warm tingling vibration go through her entire body she is held and comforted. It is as if she were floating on a cloud, with light, airy whisperings in her ears but no thoughts of this physical world, her soul translated into the invisible world beyond time and space.

Alexa learns to appreciate science more. She learns that "Brian Greene explained it well when he describes our reality as a "slice of bread in one big loaf of bread" demonstrating how we are trapped on a tiny slice among the slices or 'edges' of the cube. Our own consciousness keeps us bound inside the six days of conflict; piercing the veil of time is the only way to escape and reach the eighth sphere. The 'Rakia' or firmament that Moses saw in his vision symbolizes a division between earth and heaven; this membrane veils our dimension from the other dimensions. Veils were in the Tabernacle to divide the Holy Place from the other sections. Veils cover holy things-Divine Holiness is itself a kind of covering.

Aryeh Kaplan provides an interesting idea of how Eternity encircles the earth. He says the term 'Olam,' which means [universe & eternity], is derived from Elam, which means [concealment]; thus, the Universe 'conceals' the Creator so that the true image is not seen directly but is reflected in all that has been created. There were two veils, one at the entrance of the Holy Place and one in front of the Most Holy Place. Eternity is a veil that covers heaven, and time is the veil that surrounds earth or the Holy Place. The outer court represents Hades, the underworld or life outside the district of holiness. Elohim contains the Heavens-Firmament and Earth as the tabernacle is the house of the three rooms. They all understand what Paul explains in Romans 1:20 that the things created typify the invisible realities of the Universe," For since the creation of the world His invisible attributes are clearly seen, being understood by the things that are made, even his eternal power.

Joel says he is interested in learning more about "III Enoch, which describes the mysterious ethereal worlds of Metatron-Shekinah-Avir. Avir is a spiritual world with a mysterious circumference that exists everywhere but is found nowhere. It is beyond space and time. Elements behave very mysteriously at the sub-atomic level; they can become everything at once and then be nothing at all. Leo Schaya, author of Universal Meaning of the Kabbalah, says the 'supreme firmament' hangs over creation like a veil. The veil is like a plane of reflection that acts like a mirror. Divine consciousness projects light upon the sparks of the mirror emitting light to our thoughts that emanate the spirit to us. The sparks come into existence as the Son of Man measures them with form or with the six sephiroth. The measurer or Unique Cherub, the one who demonstrates the appearances of YHVH, is the former of 'all that is.' Ezekiel saw the "celestial/archetype man" on the Throne Chariot through Avir, the 'shining stone' that acts like a mirror. The vision was a mirror image of the word/sign imprinted in his mind. Schaya believes the spiritual world of the Kingdom dwells in the center of Avir. In Ezekiel 1:26-28 the English term 'appearance' really is 'Avir' in Hebrew, and the term 'likeness' represents Metatron. The Avir is a mysterious circle around the Shekinah that enspheres to our spiritual world or 3rd Heaven. Maybe it is the circle string of our own image. The 'Rakia' is a veil (firmament) that separates the waters above from the waters below.

Zhenya Senyak, in the Hebrew Book of the Dead, mentions the distinction between the Latin and Hebrew use of the term:

While a firmament, deriving from the Latin firmamentum, or supporting post, suggests a solid mass, the Hebrews looked at the raki'a differently 'And over the heads of the living creatures, there was the likeness of a raki'a, like the color of the terrible ice, stretched forth over their heads above. (18)

Timka also begins to speak; they are together now on the same page, speaking together as flames of fire above their heads shimmer and glow. She says, "Oddly enough, 'branes' is a short form of the term 'membranes', which also stretch and expand.

Therefore, you see our consciousness is like the Rakia; it can expand to receive more 'manna' and the sweet waters that still the fire of wrath. Senyak describes how the 'Rakia' is perceived in the book of Daniel the prophet, who first said it is capable of expansion,

Daniel (12:23) refers to the 'brightness of the raki'a.' A cold, bright, stretched-out membrane is much like the sky might look to the Ancient Hebrews (18).

Many ancient sources describe a world that evolves from a center surrounded by various firmaments. We took it for granted that their childlike perception of the Universe was meaningless compared to modern cosmology. Scientists now predict that membranes may contain parallel universes and that two branes may drift into each other, resulting in more Big Bangs.

Are 'big bangs' the 'beginning' of all new worlds? Well, now, with the recent research into the Toroidal Universe, this might prove to be true. The Torus is made of aether and produces aether; as the two tori intercommute, new stars, galaxies, and superclusters continue to emerge from the Ayin, and the Universe continues to expand.

Figure of Torus with Tori – Black Hole and Active Galactic Universe

Wormholes, Time & Tree of Life

The vast universe was much smaller, and it began to expand and get bigger as the Torus continued to stretch the fabric of space, but now the mathematical formulas that once supported the Big Bang theory fall apart when they try to explain point singularity. The Superstring theory provides real evidence of how space and time emerge from (Ayin) nothingness into (Yesh) some thingness. Gershom Scholem mentions an ancient reference in Note 43 of Origins and its parallel to the Sefer Yetzirah 2:6,

He formed substance out of chaos and made non-existence into existence. He carved great pillars from the air that cannot be grasped.

The air is another euphemism for Aether, which has seven levels of manifestation. Does this ancient text refer to the strings as pillars? If so, it describes the formation of branes from solar air, which, as we have discovered, is the Aether of Pythagoras. Joel is continually drawn to the one Name or equation. Einstein's world of General Relativity explains the physical Universe, but it takes Quantum Mechanics to explain how this world runs parallel to the Worlds to Come. The 'Glory' may actually come from the radiation or background noise found in the Universe as it branches out into four forces that surround the Garden of Eden. All their voices ring together as the Voice of Messiah, and just men made perfect come with 10,000 messages of salvation and hope. Joel begins to speak louder now. He feels as if a strong wind is moving him around the room, but he is standing still, and he can see little sparkles of gold lights flittering in the center of the room. He yells out to Timka and Alexa, "Do you see this? What is happening? I feel like there is a windstorm in the room – why is it so dark? Can anyone hear me?" Alexa and Timka also describe a similar situation; they, too, have to hold on to something, and they cannot see anything but the gold sparkles in the center of the room. Joel seems to be the only one who could speak now, "The Wisdom of the 32 paths of Sefer Yetzirah represent various spiritual paths of consciousness that surge within the Tree of Life that Enoch describes as 'fragrances'. Each branch of the tree contains ten sefirah; only now can humanity begin to understand how the reality of a multidimensional world is possible.

Scientific research into the mysterious properties of light continues to demonstrate the potent energy that gives us life. Habakkuk 3:4 says the "glow will be like light, [He has rays from His hand, and his hidden force is there]." Does this Hidden force disperse into the electromagnetic spectrum of waves? Waves all have frequencies and now we know that strings also operate through various frequencies. Are we riding on the wave of frequencies? How is this happening to all of us?

They heard tales when only one person could experience the Merkavah alone, but here, something different happens; all three of them have their own unique experience together, yet separately.

Alexa is able to speak after the momentary event of wind and darkness has passed. "All revolves around the Throne chariot of Pleiades the center of the constellations. From the biggest galaxy or the smallest particle or string to the trunk of a tree, there are circles that connect all life into one large unity of being. The structure of the tree just might have more in common with the Universe than we can ever imagine. Tree branches are similar to wormholes that branch off through the curvatures of space. See the diagram below to envision what a living multidimensional Universe might look like:

Kabbalists have found many different forms to express this Tree.

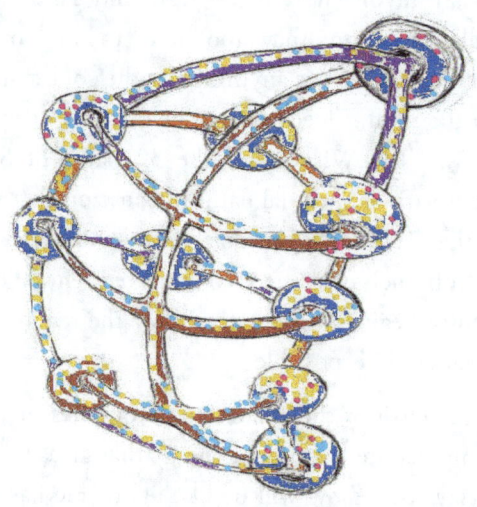

Visualizing a moving and dimensional Tree may help the seeker meditate on the cosmic motion of God's passage through the Worlds.

Figure 53 Senyak Hebrew Book of the Dead, Living Tree of Life (225)

Our universe may actually be only one of the 'sefiroth' in the great tree of life. This hidden light, once again activated during the eschaton in accordance with all the ancient prophecies, transforms the whole Kosmos into a new reality.

As the 'righteous ones' are filled with the 'true light,' they are also united with the 'age of light' and begin to reflect 'thought-filled light' into the new world. As they envision the 'Body' of the Universe, they transform into mirrors that refract the 'thoughtless light' back unto YHVH Elohim. Their 'good thoughts' fill the voided chapters of emptiness with the light of Eternity while it simultaneously shapes and forms their higher spiritual nature in the image of Elohim. Through their understanding and application of symbolic concepts, they now reflect the invisible reality of the Universe to the consciousness of all humanity. All those with ears to hear and eyes to see will stand in the Kingdom. Psalms 119 contains an important key that Joel discovers about how to escape the conflict of the six days. Aryeh Kaplan explains how this ancient Hebrew poem contains a secret code of the alphabet that has eight verses for each letter. He says,

"One significant feature of this Psalm is the fact that each letter is repeated eight times. This becomes very important when one realizes the meaning of the number eight (Kaplan, Aryeh Meditation and the Bible 140).

The number eight is a step above the physical world, according to ancient mystics. Kaplan says the Maharal of Prague, Rabbi Judah Low (1525-1609), taught that the number seven,

Refers to the seven days of creation, and hence, this number always denotes the perfection of the physical world. The number eight is the next step, and therefore, eight denotes one step above the physical. Whenever we find the number eight used, it is in reference to something that brings one into the spiritual realm (140).

Tamim is a Hebrew term that signifies the completion of the seven days, which, if attained, allows one to 'attain the eighth level' (141), a level above the seven days of creation. This stage of attainment meant one had imbibed all the lower forces of nature and transformed them into vessels of gold. The Gnostics also believed the body was a prison house of warring factions that bind our 'pneuma' to the influence of 'archons' that create our fates.

Kurt Rudolph's comprehensive work, Gnosis, outlines and defines the various aspects of Gnostic myths. Gnostics have a view of the destiny and fate of Adam that is similar to those of apocalyptic mystics, but it is less hopeful and one's life is subject to powers that rule over this earth. Rudolph says,

The goal of liberation can be attained only gradually with the aid of divine messengers and redeemers and lies either in death (of the body) or at the end of the world itself (109).

Gnostics see our life on earth as a great trial and prison that we can only escape through actual death. As in the first Adam all die so in the second Adam all will be born again, is what Paul taught the Gnostics that countered his gospel with debates from prevailing circles. Rudolph says many Mandaean hymns contain formulas for uniting the upper soul with the lower soul, "The body of Adam is the body of the world, and the soul of Adam is the totality of the souls" (109). Therefore, the souls of us all are subject to the same 'fates' controlled by the eight spheres or realms that surround the Kosmos. The Kingdom of the Six Days is a tyrannical prison house ruled over by demons and archons who rule with no love, mercy, or compassion. The 'fate' of those on earth, besieged by these 'archons' teachings, determines the amount of powers and authority they can administer and execute worldly justice. The 'archons' supposedly dwell in the eighth sphere in some Gnostic Ophite doctrines, but according to Rudolph, other doctrines teach a different aspect of the eighth sphere. Rudolph comments on two views of the eighth sphere,

The realm of the twelve signs of the zodiac (dodeka), which belongs to the same category as the tyrannical planets, or this sphere is an intermediate kingdom that already provides a transition to the real kingdom of light [in this capacity also it can be the dwelling place of the creator of the world; some systems see in the 'eighth' already the beginning of 'freedom' from the lower spheres] (Rudolph Gnosis 68-69).

He explains how Gnostics see the whole life experience as one big prison we must escape from, and in their days of violence and wars, it probably did seem that way. Many of us can relate to this feeling now, but this is not exactly what Barnabas taught. For the early assemblies, this earth is a proving ground where we gather 'garments' of faith, beauty, mercy, justice, strength, and victory so that we can stand in the kingdom whole and complete. Adam lived to be 930 his life was short of 70 years from being an eternal day of 1000. The spiritual nature attains the 1000 years, not the physical body. The seven days of creation are the 70 days Adam is missing; it represents our chance to walk once again with Elohim in the garden if we can eat from the Tree of Life and regain our 7 lost garments.

The attributes or sephiroth are the revealed seven days of creation that shape and form us for the new world of spiritual freedom. These hidden attributes, intelligence, wisdom, and understanding, represent the three ages that combine with human time, completing the week of 1000 years. This is why science will never be able to prove or disprove the existence of a Creator by using biblical time or human clocks and carbon 14 dating techniques." Timka held her thoughts for a long time within herself concerning the reconciliation she experienced. Now that Joel and Alexa stood by Timka together, they actually overcame all the sorrows and irritations that tried to block their entrance to the Kingdom; she felt whole and stronger than ever before. She said to them, "When we overcome the world's view on religion and science and learn to join the two together with Wisdom, we are restored. I am becoming everyone! I can see everyone has thought patterns, and I realize how energy is blocked, and this weakens the connection to inner attributes. However, when we look through thoughts contained in the Hebrew alphabet from Aleph to Tav – everything emanates from the meaning of the Hebrew letters."

"Each letter has two reflections, one positive and one negative. The Aleph-Tav created the Sephiroth to interact with us, and this is how we are all connected within through the letters. The Wedding Garment the Bridegroom expects to see is the Wisdom! When you can see the Unity, you are back in the original Vision Moses saw! Eternal time is beyond the realm of the seven days that we think is reality; it is beyond our understanding in our limited state. Life on the eighth day begins here in the midst of a great battle, but it is destined to take some of us into the time when there is no more time. As we begin to use our 'eyes of spirit' these 'spirit eyes' become mirrors that eternally reflect the image of יהוה back into the projected eyes of Adam Kadmon. Once the cycle is complete and the light is once again contained in the unity of equilibrium, the new aeon pours into Zion, the Kingdom of Messiah becomes a reality, and the entire creation returns to the 'Beginning.' Everyone will be able to see through the reflective circles of divine light waves that project the invisible Universe through the Wisdom of light. It begins today with each one of us. "What Joel discovers ultimately is that there appears to be a conflict between reason and faith because we each must learn how to transcend ambiguous meanings associated with spiritual terminology and scientific empirical data. Words often have various connotations and meanings depending on the age we live in. Words can be confused to manipulate situations and people, and the same is true of our modern religious concepts. Sometimes we must simply consult the ancient ones for a fresh look at today. When our double-sided personality and individuality are finally balanced, then will the Cherub with the Flaming Sword remove the barrier to the Tree of Life? Hidden inside the mysteries and riddles of ancient texts, buried beneath complicated symbols of scientific theories and mystical doctrines, is a living truth. In order to escape the dark confines of error and receive the light of symbols, we must find a way to connect with them.

Timka realizes that not everyone has to become a Merkavah mystic or practice the Kabbalah to understand the symbols. However, they must know the Son of Man and learn from his identity that alone can conquer 'time death,' a temporary veil that prevents us from entering Heaven. The terms described in the Sefer Yetzirah are like tools of construction that can provide a means to experience the 'thoughts of Yahweh.' Alexa says, "We must learn to see beyond our comfort zone and embrace other knowledge besides just religious or scientific fields; all knowledge is part of everything. This is how we learn to confront our blind spots and see clearly to embrace reality. As Emerson says, the true "Poets" he foresaw in the future would learn to live with symbols. Our reasoning continues to be a grave we cannot escape because the more we try to reason and figure out the "WHY" of Life, the more confused and desperate we become until, at last, we only understand our own mental reasoning, which is by nature biased and limited. This is the reality of human life in the confines of time. George Nickelsburg sums up the true value of the Enoch books,

Specifically, in a world that people perceive as the locus of alienation, oppression, and injustice, the seer presents evidence of salvation by transmitting a revelation about the future or the remote places in the cosmos where the reality and promise of salvation lie hidden.

"All we have to do is search for it as a pearl that has more value than anything on earth; then, it will reveal its mysterious face to us in all the splendor of the vast Universe." Timka says, "Is everything random and based on probabilities? No, the loss of destiny and purpose leaves the meaning of human life in a sea of despair. When we are absent from the center position of the Universe, our purpose becomes distorted, and materialistic scientific anarchy becomes the world's false panacea. Alexa interrupts and says, "Well, yes, until the revolution of strings and M-Theory jolted us back to our senses. Timka, do not forget that we all have an opinion and right to see things the way we do." Joel says, "Biblical critics of the gospels have an easy target to attack when theologians are so useless in defending the spiritual domain of the scriptures. Different tools of interpretation or hermeneutics can be a refreshing device and is essential to combat the problem of religious factions that seek to justify aggression with quotes from texts. Everything is relative, but relativity is not everything. If the Universe has no center, there would be no balance and without balance, the four forces that keep the world in orbit would not exist. There would be no atoms orbiting an axis and no strings vibrating waves. These are the realities behind the appearance of this material world. The center of all things is the reality of the reflected object."

The ideas found in Hebrew scripture are universal, not the center, but the place of distribution. All world religions are systems of belief and document the experience and mysteriousness of life. What our spiritual ancestors left us seems disjointed and confused when compared to each other. The spiritual experience (eternity) enters the human experience (time) whenever systems are recognized as merely scaffolds for faith. True faith is something experienced and known from within. It cannot come from without. Alexa begins to experience strange feelings as she listens to Joel; she feels compelled to disagree with him, even though there is no reason to. Instead, she says," Faith and religion are two different things.

Everyone has some kind of faith. It is a feeling of assurance that the car will start, the kids will come home from school, and we may go on vacation next month. Most people have faith, but is it the faith of the Son of Man? Is it more important to have faith in the Son of Man or faith like him? How can we ever combine the historical figure with the mythological images found in many traditional interpretations of the gospels? The authors of these mysterious relics from an ancient angelic civilization may help us survive our darkest hour if these discarded texts are once again accepted. The author of II Enoch wants the reader to know that this book serves as a guidepost that leads us to the Father and Son, but only if it is allowed to provide its own voice and ethos. Historical criticism seeks to discover the truth in order to classify and label events for its own sake, not for national or personal interest, but it tends to overlook the fluid concepts found in mystical doctrines." Timka cuts in and explains, "Selflessness is the substance, and selfishness is the shadow that casts a dark light on understanding the nature of reality. We must learn to embrace the reflection before we can absorb the reality. Our world of 'dynamic' time is that reflection, the one mirror we have at our disposal to view the heavens and enter the Timeless Kingdom of Eternity. Spiritual truths long ignored and cast aside by the most salient scientific theories of today can shed light on the sub-atomic invisible world of angelic physics.

The multilevel reality of things points to a definite pattern that is stamped into the very fabric of the Universe. Everything in the 'beginning' is first in a potential state until time and temperature provide form and shape. Particles transform into other particles and move into other dimensions we cannot see, and yet we find it so hard to believe in a resurrection."

Alexa adds, "Our Universe demonstrates a life constantly bound and then freed, which parallels the biblical view. The Universe itself is subject to this same reality, and when we begin to tamper with the amount of antimatter that exists in the Universe, then we begin to tip the scale of temperature above its normal range or stasis. Perhaps science will introduce the agent of change that causes the Universe to transform back to its original state of the (void and nothing). Genesis described the generations of time on the physical earth when it was void and chaos was King. As it was in the 'beginning,' so will it be in the 'end.' The first shall be last, and the last shall be first as we come to face the Face we really are. People of faith must also operate under a method. Spiritual beliefs and concepts should be re-examined in the light of new observations and facts, but this does not always happen on a large scale. Most of us are guilty of putting a 'hedge' or fence around the scriptures. We are afraid to question its authors or its edits, or we each decide what and how to apply scriptural doctrines. Many of us do not allow them to speak from their native culture, and often our personal interpretations take the place of objective biblical exegesis."

Then Joel finally says, "The 'hidden books' remain 'mysterious' only to those that refuse to read them. We should try to discover, sort, and recombine common spiritual and scientific motifs found in the ancient Near Eastern documents. Maybe then, we can begin to imagine how religion and science both lead to the same place (Makom), Beginning (Bereshith/big bang), and conclusion (Tau/multiple universes). How we can escape the conflict while we still have time is the real issue, not the rabbit trail controversy between science and religion."

Science keeps searching for answers to satisfy the human longing for reality, and through its inquisitive imagination and needs to know; it continues to discover how the Universe operates and why it came to be. Mystics experience how the Universe operates, and they know how it came to be and where it will go. Both worlds can only help us to expand our horizons if the bridge for communication between them is open. Analogous illustrations are the essence of the Messianic parables and are the only way to 'see' invisible things as we learn of the higher worlds through the lower world we live in.

These are tools used to shape, form and make ourselves in the image of Elohim so that we are not conformed to this world. As the Apostle Paul says in I Corinthians, beware of the 'wisdom' in the world. It is a deception, "Let no man deceive himself. If any man among you seems to be wise in this age, let him become a fool, that he may be wise. For the wisdom of this world is foolishness with Yahweh". Paul warns us to be careful of what we hear and believe from the legion of conspiracy teachings and controversies that come upon the earth like a flood of waters. We must always try to hold the beloved Crown of peace, love, and soul power and let no one rob us of it. The Crown is the knowledge of how the only Teacher of Righteousness really lives and exists in a Kingdom hidden from mortality.

In the beginning, Timka, Alexa, and Joel did not seem to agree on very much, but they now agree that the mysterious author or authors of Enoch describe an ancient prophet that describes the Son of Man as an intellectual Pleroma or Tree of Life that transforms humans into angelic beings. It is a lifelong journey into the dimensions of never-ending time, wherein they discover their true being and identity. We truly have yet to be born.

CONCLUSION

Perhaps, now you can perceive that Moses wrote about a living, dynamic Reality he refers to as Elohim; Moses first saw the Spirit of YHVH impressing the divine attributes upon his conscious imagination, thereby activating his visionary apparatus. The vision and revelation caused an effect of vibrating aethereal energy of the Word to engage his imagination. This spiritual influx over-rules his five senses, long enough to make him realize the importance of perceiving our human reality and true situation through a pattern he saw on the Mount, not through human reasoning. The Greeks refer to the same process as LOGOS - but they see it through the eyes of Greek Platonic concepts, without the innate understanding of a divine pattern. This may explain why spiritually advanced Philosopher-Kabbalists teach us that only the Primordial Archetype itself can emerge from the dust of elemental, organic mass through a process of self-limitation and disclosure, assimilating our atomic structure in order to convey a three-dimensional perception of life to our brain. Elohim caused Moses to experience an emanation of conscious life beyond the Fourth Dimension. Moses was imprinted with a three-dimensional copy of the Tabernacle; the image of Elohim was implanted in the Garden of his mind. The Voice of the Malakh YHVH, the Angel of the Berith (Covenant), was the only Voice Moses could follow. Behold, I send an Angel before you; walk in the Way of his path. When we are inspired, it feels like our thoughts are on fire and have a life of their own. This is a quickening of the Spirit from within, proof that there is an inner change in consciousness. Our soul responds to it through our body, even if our intellect still denies the Spirit.

The spiritual resurrection activates an internal transformation when the Son of Man can rise up in our spiritual consciousness by His own purpose and plan. He has declared the End right from the Beginning. Nobody can stop His purpose and plan, for no flesh can resist the Sephiroth of Intelligence, Wisdom, and Knowledge from operating in the Kingdom that is come.

Works Cited

Barbour, Ian G. When Science Meets Religion: Enemies, Strangers, or Partners?

Barclay, William. New Testament Words. Philadelphia: Westminster P. 1974. (68-70).

Barker, Margaret. The Great Angel: A Study of Israel's Second God.

Louisville: Westminster: John Knox P. 1992. (3, 10).

—-The Risen Lord: The Jesus Of History As The Christ Of Faith. Valley Forge: Trinity Press International. 1997.

—- The Revelation Of Jesus Christ. Edinburgh: T&T Clark. 2000.

—-The Secret Tradition. The Journal Of Higher Criticism. Vol. 2 #1.Spring 1995: (31-36).

Bautch, Kelley Coblentz. A Study of the Geography of I Enoch 17-19: 'No One Has Seen What I Have Seen'. Boston: Brill 2003. (51,152-154, 170-180, 199, 206-209).

Boring, M. Eugene. The Language Of Universal Salvation In Paul. JBL

105/2. 1986. (269-292).

Borsch, Frederick. The Son of Man in Myth and History. London: SCM Press. 1967.

Brennan, Richard P. Dictionary Of Scientific Literacy. New York: John Wiley & Sons. 1992.

Brownlee, William Hugh. The Meaning Of The Qumran Scrolls For The Bible. New York: Oxford University P. 1964. 289-291.

Capes, David B. Old Testament Yahweh Texts In Paul's Christology.

J.C.B. Mohr: Tubingen. 1992.(31, 32, 64, 65).

Chrapowicki, Maryla De. Spectro-Biology. Mokelumne Hill: Health Research 1965 reprint of 1938 edition. Diagram P 59.

Cohen, Martin. The Shi'ur Qomah: Liturgy And Theurgy In Pre- Kabbalistic Jewish Mysticism. Lanham: University Press of America. 1983.(77, 99).

Collins, John J. "A Throne In The Heavens: Apotheosis In Pre-Christian Judaism".

Death, Ecstasy, And Other Worldly Journeys. Ed. John J. Collins and Michael Fish-Bane. Albany: State University of New York Press. 1995. (95-105).

Dan, Joseph. The Ancient Jewish Mysticism. Tel Aviv: MOD Books, Naidat Press Ltd. 1993.

—- The Heart And The Fountain: An Anthology Of Jewish Mystical Experience. New York: Oxford University P. 2002.

. "The Religious Experience Of The Merkavah". Jewish Spirituality: From The Bible Through The Middle Ages. World Spirituality An Encyclopedic History Of The Religious Quest. V. 13. Ed. Arthur Green. New York: Crossroad P. 1996. (289-312).

—-The Unique Cherub Circle: A School Of Mystics and Esoterics in Medieval Germany. Texts And Studies in Medieval and Early Modern Judaism 15. Tubingen: Mohr Siebeck. 1999.

Davies, Paul. About Time: Einstein's Unfinished Revolution. New York: Simon & Schuster. 1996

Davis, Carl Judson. The Name And Way Of The Lord: Old Testament Themes, New Testament Christology. Journal For The Study Of The New Testament Supplement Series 129. Sheffield: Sheffield Academic Press. 1996.

DeConick, April D. Voices Of The Mystics: Early Christian Discourse In The Gospels of John and Thomas and Other Ancient Christian Literature. Journal for the Study of the New Testament Supplement Series 157. Sheffield: Sheffield Academic Press. 2001.

Delamarter, Steve. A Scripture Index to Charlesworth's The Old Testament Pseudepigrapha. New York: Sheffield Academic Press. 2002.

Dictionary Of Paul And His Letters. Eds. Gerald F. Hawthorne and Ralph P. Martin. Downers Grove: Intervarsity P. 1993. (501- 524).

Ehrman, Bart D. The Orthodox Corruption Of Scripture: The Effect Of Early Christological Controversies On The Text Of The N.T. New York: Oxford University P. 1993. (94, 95, 161).

Ellis, Earl E. Prophecy And Hermeneutic In Early Christianity. Grand Rapids: W.B. Eerdmans P.1978.(34).

Encyclopedic Dictionary Of The Bible. Trans. Louis F. Hartman. New York: McGraw Hill. 1963. (375-376).

Ethiopic Apocalypse of Enoch 1. Trans. E. Isaac. The Old Testament Pseudepigrapha.

Ed. James H. Charlesworth. (Vol. 1) Garden City: Doubleday. 1984 Filoramo, Giovanni. "The Transformation Of The Inner Self In Gnostic And Hermetic Texts". Transformations Of The Inner Self In Ancient Religions. Ed. Jan Assmann and Gedaliahu A.G. Stroumsa. Leiden: E.J. Brill. 1999. (138-147). Franzmann, Majella. Jesus In The Nag Hammadi Writings. Edinburgh:T&T Clark. 1996.

Freeman, Ira M. All About The Atom. New York: Random House.1955.

Freud, Sigmund. Moses And Monotheism.

Georgi, Dieter. The Opponents Of Paul In Second Corinthians.

John Riches. Edinburgh: T&T Clark. 1987.

HaLevi, Z'ev Shimon. Kabbalah: Tradition of Hidden Knowledge. London: Thames and Hudson: 1979.

Hall, Manly P. The Secret Teachings of All Ages: An Encyclopedic Outline of Masonic, Hermetic, Qabbalistic and Rosicrucian Symbolical Philosophy. The Philosophical Research Society, Inc. Los Angeles: 1977.

Harper's Bible Dictionary. Ed. Paul J. Achtemeier. San Francisco: Harper Collins P. 1985. (168-169).

Harper Collins Study Bible. Ed.Wayne A. Meeks. New York: Harper Collins P. 1993.

Hayman, Peter. "The Temple At The Center Of The Universe: Some Observations On Sefer Yetzirah" JJS 35. 1984: (164-84).

—- "Was God A Magician? Sefer Yesira And Jewish Magic. JJS 37, 1986: (176-182).

Hayutman, Dr. Yitzhak I. World, Adam And Adamah. http:// members.tripod.com/~The HOPE/olamadam.htm. 1-11.

Hebrew original 1988.

Hoeller, Stephan A. Jung And The Lost Gospels: Insights Into The Dead Sea Scrolls and the Nag

Hammadi Library. London: Quest Books Theosophical Publishing House. 1989.

Idel, Moshe. Kabbalah: New Perspectives. New Haven:Yale UP.

1988.(118,120-125).

Kaplan, Aryeh. Inner Space: Introduction To Kabbalah, Meditation And Prophecy. Brooklyn:

Moznaim Publishing Co., 1990. 29,137.

— Meditation and The Bible. York Beach: Samuel Weiser, Inc. 1981

— Sefer Yetzirah: The Book Of Creation In Theory And Practice. New York: Weiser Books. 1997

Koester, Craig, The Dwelling Of God: The Tabernacle In The Old Testament, Intertestamental Jewish Literature, And The New Testament. Washington: Catholic Biblical Association Of America. 1953.(37, 59, 61).

Kreitzer, Joseph L. Jesus and God in Paul's Eschatology. Journal for the Study of the New Testament. Edited by David Hill. Sheffield: JSOT Press. 1987

Kuschel, Karl-Josef. Born Before All Time? The Dispute over Christ's Origin. New York: Crossroad Publishing. 1992.

Leet, Leonora. The Secret Doctrine of the Kabbalah: Recovering the Key to Hebraic Sacred Science. Inner Traditions. Rochester 1999.

Lesses, Rebecca Macy. Ritual Practices To Gain Power: Angels, Incantations, And Revelation In Early Jewish Mysticism. Harvard Theological Studies. Harrisburg: Trinity P. 1998.

Levin, Saul. Divine Patronymic: Father of Joshua/Jesus. Suny Press. 1978.

Maimonides, Moses. The Guide For The Perplexed. Translated by M. Friedlander. New York: Dover Publications. 1956.

Marshall, Molly T. "The Fullness Of Incarnation: God's New Humanity In The Body Of Christ". Review and Expositor 93/2. (187- 201).

Moeller, Henry R. The Legacy Of Zion: Intertestamental Texts Related To The New Testament. Grand Rapids: Baker Book House. 1977.

Morray-Jones, Christopher R.A. "Transformational Mysticism In The Apocalyptic-Merkavah Tradition". JJS 43 (1992): (1-31).

Nickelsburg, George. 1 Enoch: A Commentary on the Book of Enoch.

Minneapolis: Augsburg Fortress Press. 2001.O'Collins, Gerald. S.J. Christology: A Biblical, Historical, And Systematic Study of Jesus. New York: Oxford University Press. 1995.

Ouaknin, Marc-Alain. Mysteries Of The Kabbalah. Translated from French Josephine Bacon. New York: Abbeville Press P. 2000.

Otto, Rudolph. The Idea Of The Holy. New York: Oxford UP. 1958. 64,190.

Otto, Rudolph. The Kingdom Of God And The Son Of Man: A Study In The History Of Religion. Trans. Floyd V. Filson and Bertram Lee-Woolf. Boston: Starr King Press. 1957. (207,212,214,215).

——. "The Resurrection As A Spiritual Experience". The Idea Of The Holy. Trans. John W. Harvey. New York: Oxford UP. 1958. 222-228.

Oxford Annotated Apocrypha Of The Old Testament. Ed. Bruce Metzger. New York: Oxford UP. 1977. XIII.

Pancoast, S. M.D. The Kabbala Or True Science Of Light: An Introduction to the Philosophy and Theosophy of the Ancient Sages Together with a Chapter on Light in the Vegetable Kingdom. Montana: Kessinger Publishing Co. (No publication date)

Pate, Dr. Marvin C. Adam Christology As The Exegetical And Theological Substructure Of 2 Corinthians 4:7-5:21. New York: University P of America. 1991.(37).

Pember, G.H. Earth's Earliest Ages. Westwood: Fleming H. Revell Co. (No publication date)

Reuchlin, Johann. On The Art Of The Kabbalah. Trans. Martin and Sarah Goodman. New York: Abaris Books. 1983. (97,101- 111,197, 251-253,287,325).

Rosenberg, Joel. "Biblical Traditions: Literature And Spirit In Ancient Israel". Jewish Spirituality: From The Bible Through The Middle Ages. World Spirituality: An Encyclopedic History of the Religious Quest. V. 13. Ed. Arthur Green. New York: Crossroad P. 1996. (86).

Rudolph, Kurt. Gnosis: The Nature and History of Gnosticism. San Francisco: Harper and Row. 1983.

Sacchi, Paolo. Jewish Apocalyptic and its History. Journal For The Study Of The Pseudepigrapha Supplement Series 20. Translated by William J. Short. Sheffield: Sheffield Academic Press. 1990.

Schaya, Leo. The Universal Meaning Of The Kabbalah. Trans. Nancy Pearson. Baltimore: Penguin Books. 1974. (76,120-122).

Schiffman, Lawrence H. Reclaiming The Dead Sea Scrolls: The History Of Judaism, The Background Of Christianity, The Lost Library OF Qumran. Philadelphia: Jewish P. 1994.

Scholem, Gershom. Origins Of The Kabbalah. Translated by Allan Arkush. Berlin: Walter de Gruyter & Co. 1987.

Scholem, Gershom. On The Mystical Shape of the Godhead: Basic Concepts in the Kabbalah. Schocken Books: New York 1991. (45, 84-87).

Schweitzer, Albert. The Mysticism Of Paul The Apostle. Trans. William Montgomery. John Hopkins UP. 1998. (76).

Scroggs, Robin. The Last Adam: A Study In Pauline Anthropology.Philadelphia: Fortress P.1966. (85-90).

Segal, Alan F. "Paul And The Beginning Of Jewish Mysticism". Death, Ecstasy, And Other Worldly Journeys. Ed. John J. Collins and Michael Fishbane. Albany: New York Press. 1995. (95-122).

Stanley, Christopher D. Paul And The Language Of Scripture: Citation Technique In The Pauline Epistles And Contemporary Literature. New York: Cambridge UP. 1992.

Stewart, Alec T. Perpetual Motion. (Marygrove Holdings) Stone, Michael. "On Reading An Apocalypse." Mysteries And Revelations Apocalyptic Studies Since The Uppsala Colloquium. Ed. John J. Collins and James. Charlesworth. JSP Series 9. England: Sheffield Academic P, 1991.(73).

Stroumsa, Gedaliahu G. "Form (s) Of God: Some Notes On Metatron And Christ". HTR 76:3.(1983).

Stuckenbruck, Loren T. Angel Veneration and Christology: A Study in Early Judaism and in The Christology of the Apocalypse of John. Tubingen: J.C.B. Mohr. 1995.

Suares, Carlo. The Sepher Yetsira. Boulder & London: Shambhala.1976

Sutcliffe, G.E. The New Astronomy And Cosmic Physiology. London: Rider & Co., Paternoster Row. (Early 1900's) No date given

Thiering, Barbara E. Redating The Teacher Of Righteousness. Australian and New Zealand Studies in Theology and Religion. Sydney: Theological Explorations. 1979.

Thiering, Barbara E. "The Date and Unity of the Gospel of Phillip". The Journal Of Higher Criticism. Vol. 2/1 Sp 1995. (102-111). Thomson, John E.H. Books Which Influenced

Our Lord And His Apostles: Being a Critical Review Of Apocalyptic Jewish Literature. Edinburgh: T&T Clark. 1891.

Tresmontant, Claude. Saint Paul And They Mystery Of Christ. Trans. Donald Attwater. New York: Harper & Brothers. 1957. (51, 54).

Wald, Stephen G. The Doctrine Of The Divine Name: An Introduction to Classical Kabbalistic Theology. Brown Judaic Studies 149. Atlanta: Scholars Press. 1988.

Young, Arthur M. The Reflexive Universe: Evolution Of Consciousness. San Francisco: Delacorte Press. 1995.

Zohar, Danah, Through The Time Barrier: A Study in Precognition and Modern Physics. London: Paladin Books. 1983.   http://archive.ncsa.uiuc.edu/Cyberia/Cosmos/InThe Beginning. html—In the Beginning-The Big Bang . Expo/Science & Industry/Cosmos in a Computer. Board of Trustees. University of Illinois. 1995.

http://www/damtp.Cambridge

—- Cosmology Phase Transitions In The Early Universe

—- Cambridge Relativity Quantum Gravity – M Theory

http://www.physics.rutgers.edu/~motl/universe/

Greene, Brian. "The Elegant Universe" PBS NOVA Video production. 2003.

gopher://ccat.sas.upenn.edu/00journals/kraftpub/Christia nity/ Joshua Kraft, Robert A. Was There A 'Messiah-Joshua' Tradition At The Turn Of The Era? Manchester: IOUDAIOS. 1992.

http://www.levity.com/alchemy/luria.html

McClean, Adam. Kabbalistic Cosmology and its parallels in the 'Big Bang' of Modern Physics.

http://bb.marygrove.edu/courses/1/IS326Fa0301/content/ _12779_ 1/5_in Pursuit.htm

Overbye, Dennis. "Other Dimensions: She's In Pursuit".
New York Times.

—-. "Paul's Soma Pneumatikon". Jesus Conference
Abstract. 1998. 1-2.

http://www.St-andrews.ac.uk/~www_sd/jconf_segal.html

www.ingramcontent.com/pod-product-compliance
Lightning Source LLC
Chambersburg PA
CBHW071658120626
46550CB00001B/26